West's Criminal Justice Series

Probation and Parole in the Criminal Justice System
Second Edition

Paul F. Cromwell, Jr.
Florida State University

George G. Killinger
Vice Chairman
Texas Board of Pardons & Parole

Hazel B. Kerper
Late Professor of Criminology
Sam Houston State University

Charls Walker, J.D.
Austin, Texas

WEST PUBLISHING COMPANY
St. Paul New York Los Angeles San Francisco

Library of Congress Cataloging in Publication Data

Main entry under title:
Probation and parole in the criminal justice system.

   Rev. ed. of: Probation and parole in the criminal
justice system / George G. Killinger. 1976.
   Includes index.
   1. Probation—United States. 2. Parole—United States.
3. Pardon—United States. I. Cromwell, Paul F.
II. Killinger, George Glenn, 1908–   . Probation and
parole in the criminal justice system.
KF9750.P77   1985   345.73'077   84–29190
ISBN 0–314–85256–5   347.30577

1st Reprint—1987

To Grace for her untiring support
— GGK

Contents

Preface to the Second Edition

In 1976 we wrote in the preface to the first edition of this book: "These two community-oriented processes [probation and parole] are the hope for positive change—the vehicle by which the entire system can be corrected and renewed." In the intervening years much has occurred that has given us pause to reflect upon that prophecy. Parole has come under great scrutiny by the public and by corrections professionals as well. Since the publication of the first edition, nine states have abolished their parole boards and others have seriously diminished the discretionary powers of their parole release decision makers. Yet parole remains, in 1985, the predominant means by which prisoners are released from incarceration. In its relatively short history, parole has come under attack on numerous occasions. In each instance it has emerged intact, modified perhaps, but nonetheless has continued as a viable aspect of the correctional process.

Probation, on the other hand, has grown continuously in acceptance, utilization, and sophistication since its official inception in Massachusetts in 1878. This system, which began as a legal measure for ameliorating the harshness of punishment and diverting the less sophisticated offender from the prison system, grew far beyond anything envisaged by its founders.[1]

In this second edition we have discussed changes in the legal and philosophical aspects of probation and parole since their inception over one hundred years ago. We have discussed the abolition-of-parole movement, the movement toward sentencing and parole guidelines, and the emergence of the "justice" or "just desserts" model of corrections.

This second edition has an added dimension—the use of supplemental readings after each chapter. These readings broaden the scope of the book and enlarge its viewpoint. In some cases the reading will complement the text, and

---

1. U.S. Department of Justice, *Attorney General's Survey of Release Procedures,* vol. 2, *Probation,* Washington, D.C., 1939.

in others the supplement provides a thoughtful counterpoint to the text. We include a *caveat* that the student should not attempt to reconcile the supplemental reading with its attendant chapter, and should instead recognize that the reading is presented to provoke thought and discussion, and to present points of view other than those of the authors.

Another new aspect of the second edition is the emphasis placed upon loss and restoration of rights upon conviction. Where we formerly discussed pardon and amnesty, we have included in Part III a detailed discussion of direct and collateral consequences of conviction, loss of civil rights, and restoration of rights through the various means available to the defendant and the probation/ parole officer. Part III is a comprehensive treatment of this often overlooked but vastly important aspect of the criminal justice system.

As in any such endeavor, we accept for ourselves the responsibility of the contents. Where we have erred, we alone are responsible; however, we must also acknowledge our debt and gratitude for the scholarship of others and for the advice and assistance of many persons without whom we could not have completed this text.

Paul F. Cromwell, Jr.
George G. Killinger
Charls Walker

January 1985
Tallahassee, Florida

Probation and Parole in the Criminal Justice System
Second Edition

I

PROBATION

History and Legal Foundations of Probation

INTRODUCTION

Early Criminal Law

The early criminal law as it developed in England was dominated by the objectives of retribution and punishment and characterized by rigid and severe penalties imposed upor the offender. The usual punishments were corporal—branding, flogging, mutilation, and execution. Capital punishment was common and was inflicted upon children and animals as well as men and women. At the time of Henry VIII, for instance, there were over 200 offenses punishable by death, many of them relatively minor offenses against property. Other widely used but less severe punishments included banishment, outlawry, and transportation.

Methods used to determine guilt—what today we would call criminal procedure—also put the accused in danger of life or limb. Trial might be by combat, or a person's innocence determined based on whether the accused sank when bound and thrown into a deep pond. The theory was that the pure water would reject wrongdoers. Thus, the choice was to drown as an innocent person or survive the drowning only to be otherwise executed. Sometimes the offender could elect to be tried "by God," which meant undergoing some painful and frequently life-threatening ordeal, or "by country," which was a form of trial by jury for which the accused first had to pay an "amercement" to the king.

The accepted premise was that the purpose of the criminal law was not to deter or rehabilitate, but to bring about justice for a past act deemed harmful to the society.

Early Efforts to Mitigate Punishment

In the early part of the Middle Ages, there were efforts to mitigate the severity of punishment. Royal pardons, usually paid for by the accused, were granted. Judges interpreted statutes narrowly or failed to apply them. Juries placed lesser value upon stolen property so as to bring the value below that which required the imposition of capital punishment. Prosecutors dismissed charges or charged offenders with lesser offenses. Devices such as "benefit of clergy" and "judicial reprieve" benefited some defendants, while sanctuary and abjuration enabled some criminals to gain immunity from punishment. Courts began to release certain offenders on good behavior for a temporary period, which allowed them time to seek a pardon or commutation of sentence. Gradually, an "inherent" power of certain courts to suspend sentence was recognized, although the existence and limits on that power were almost at once the subject of controversy.

Benefit of Clergy

Benefit of clergy was a privilege given to ordained clerics, monks, and nuns to be delivered to the church for punishment. Since clerical punishments were less severe, benefit of clergy had the effect of reducing the harsher punishments. Benefit of clergy was later extended to anyone who could read and the list of offenses for which it could be claimed was expanded. However, the procedure became so technical and legalistic that it was almost unworkable. It was finally abolished in 1827. *Sanctuary* referred to a place (usually a church or vestry) where the king's soldiers were not permitted entry for the purpose of taking the accused into custody. Offenders were hidden, if possible, until arrangements could be made to smuggle them onto a boat and out of the country. Offenders were required to "abjure the kingdom" under pain of immediate punishment if they returned to England without the king's permission. *Judicial reprieve* (from *reprendre,* to take back) amounted to withdrawing of sentence for an interval of time, similar to what is today called suspension of execution of sentence. During the period of judicial reprieve the offender was at liberty and imposition of other criminal sanctions postponed.

Early American Law

Although many early cases recognized the doctrine of benefit of clergy, the practice was never widespread in the American colonies. Instead, distinct American practices developed, such as security for good behavior and a practice known in Massachusetts as "filing."[1] *Security for good behavior,* also known as "good abearance," would be accepted in certain cases either before or after conviction. *Filing* was a procedure under which the indictment was "laid on file" in cases where justice did not require an immediate sentence; however, the court could impose certain conditions on the defendant. The effect was that the case was laid at rest without either dismissal or final judgment, and without the necessity of asking for final continuances. Massachusetts judges also often granted a *motion to quash* after judgment, using any minor technicality or the

---

1. Commonwealth v. Chase, Thacher's Criminal Cases, 267 (1831); recorded in vol. 11 of the Records of the Old Municipal Court of Boston, p. 199.

slightest error in the proceedings to free the defendant in cases where they thought the statutory penalties to be inhumane. *Suspension of imposition of sentence,* which freed a woman who had pleaded guilty without sentence being pronounced, occurred as early as 1830 in a Massachusetts court in the case of *Commonwealth v. Chase.*[2] This case is often cited as example of the early use of *release on recognizance* (from *recognocere,* to call to mind), as the court recited that the defendant was permitted, "upon her recognizance for her appearance in this court whenever she should be called for, to go at large."[3]

Some early forms of *bail* had the effect of suspending final action on a case, although the chief use of bail then as now was for the purpose of insuring appearance for trial. Since the sureties "went bail" and became responsible for the action of the defendant, they undertook supervision over the defendant at least to the extent of keeping track of the defendant's whereabouts, with the continuous availability of the defendant for further action by the court as one of the conditions of liberty.

All of these methods had the common objective of mitigating punishment by relieving selected offenders from the full effects of the legally prescribed penalties that substantial segments of the community, including many of the judges, viewed as excessive and inappropriate to the offense committed.

Imprisonment as Punishment

Although today imprisonment is an accepted and frequently used criminal sanction, this form of penalty developed late in the history of criminal law. Not until the latter part of the eighteenth and the beginning of the nineteenth century did incarceration replace capital and other forms of corporal punishment as the "preferred" method of dealing with offenders. Imprisonment also increased in use when other widely used sanctions such as banishment became less available. This occurred with the independence of the American colonies, which prevented their use from 1776 onward as a place of banishment for transgressors against the English crown. The use of other colonies for banishment such as Australia and New Zealand ended in the early nineteenth century.

Release from Imprisonment

Imprisonment as a penal sanction came about as part of a reform movement led by humanitarians such as John Howard and various Quaker groups. The underlying concept—that prisons should be used for reformation of the offender instead of for retribution and punishment—had received great impetus at the time of the French Revolution. The next step—using release from imprisonment as a rehabilitative device—was recommended by a Frenchman, Bonneville de Marsangy, public prosecutor of Versailles, as early as 1847. In that year, de Marsangy published a book in which he discussed the pardoning power, conditional liberation, police supervision of discharged convicts, aid upon discharge, and rehabilitation. Credit for laying the foundations of conditional liberation in its modern form is given to: two European administrators, one a Spaniard and the other a German; to Alexander Maconochie, who was in charge

---

2. *Id.*

3. *Id.*

of the English penal colony at Norfolk Island in New South Wales; and to an Irishman, Sir Walter Crofton. The *ticket-of-leave* system under which a convict was freed with a grant of land dates from 1790 in New South Wales. At about the same time, Sir Walter Crofton, the Irishman, employed *prisoners on public works* and permitted them to live an almost normal life in the community. The first experiments of this kind in the United States took place with juvenile delinquents from the New York House of Refuge, who were released from the institution and placed in the employment of private citizens.

Origins of Modern Release Procedures

From these early beginnings have developed suspension of sentence, and probation and parole as we know them today. "Nonjudicial probation" in use in some jurisdictions today and the "unofficial probation" in juvenile courts are similar to the early filing procedures in Massachusetts. Modern pretrial diversion procedures are likewise related to the Massachusetts filing practice. Work release, halfway houses, and various programs referred to collectively as "community-based treatment" also have their origin in the experiments of the early prison reformers and the changing philosophy of the objectives of punishment.

Bail and release on recognizance (particularly when viewed as correctional tools) are kin to security for good behavior. The ticket-of-leave that freed the offender to work his land in New South Wales has its modern counterpart in work release and a variety of community-based treatment programs. Sanctuary and diversion have points in common, as do benefit of clergy and modern sentencing provisions that require or permit specialized sentencing for certain classes of offenders or set up separate tribunals and unique dispositional alternatives for juveniles.

Executive pardon and other forms of executive clemency trace their origins to the royal pardon, it being logical that a "crime" that was seen as an offense against the king could be forgiven by the king. Early controversy about the nature of a suspended sentence and the extent to which a court had authority to withhold or delay the punishment of an offender gave great impetus to probation legislation and established legal precedents that today may determine whether a probationer is entitled to appointed counsel on probation revocation. The needs of the released prisoner for supervision and assistance were officially recognized in 1846 when Massachusetts appointed an agent to assist released prisoners; his function was to secure employment, tools, clothing, and transportation. These same functions are now among the responsibilities of the parole officer, who is paid by the state and expected to assist the parolee in exactly the same areas of concern.

The correctional system of the mid-1980s presents almost no programs that have not existed under one name or another at an earlier time in history. The indeterminate sentence controversy of the 1980s differs little from the same issue discussed at the first meeting of the American Prison Conference in Cincinnati in 1870.

The question of the rightful purpose of corrections did not spring full-blown upon the discipline in 1970; rather, it has been at the very heart of the criminal justice system since the Quakers introduced "reformation" to the colonial justice system—replacing, at least for a while, the cruelty of the Puritans and the harshness of the English criminal law and practices.

After three hundred years of experience, experimentation, trial, and error, we still must agree with Norman Carlson, director of the Federal Bureau of Prisons, who recently stated that "the only thing we can say with certainty is that we know comparatively little about how to deal effectively with offenders."

Even the question of the purpose of imprisonment has not been answered. Is the criminal justice system an instrument of retribution and punishment or an institution of reformation? The questions of the colonial Quakers, of William Penn and Benjamin Rush, have yet to be answered. The pendulum of public opinion and professional practice swings interminably from retribution to reformation, and as each is found wanting the pendulum swings back, leaving in its wake an endless path of failure. The lesson of history is that we have learned little from history.

Perhaps the most successful developments in criminal justice have been the release procedures of probation and parole—programs of supervised living in the community for offenders whose crimes and past history indicate that they pose minimal threat to society. This book addresses these issues, controversial though they may be, as the only real hope for the institution of corrections.

HISTORY AND LEGAL FOUNDATIONS OF PROBATION

Suspended Sentence

A suspended sentence is defined as an order of court that is entered after a verdict, finding, or plea of guilty, and which suspends or postpones the imposition or execution of sentence during the good behavior of the offender. While suspension of sentence is, in a few jurisdictions, a form of disposition of the criminal offender that is separate from and in addition to probation,[4] we will consider it here chiefly in its close historical and legal relationship to probation.

Where suspension of sentence exists independent of probation, it is distinguished from probation in that the offender is released without supervision. The only condition is the implicit, or sometimes explicit, imperative that the withholding or postponement of sentence that characterizes suspension of sentence will be revoked or terminated if the offender commits a new crime. As a disposition, suspension of sentence also differs from probation in that no term is specified. It is generally held, however, that the period of suspension of sentence is limited by the maximum period of commitment permitted by statute for the offense.

Two Kinds of Suspended Sentence

There are two kinds of suspended sentence—suspension of *imposition* of sentence and suspension of *execution* of sentence. In the case of suspension of imposition

---

4. Sol Rubin advocates a greater use of suspended sentence without probation, arguing that this would provide an additional sentencing alternative of particular value in a situation where apprehension and conviction have so thorough a corrective impact on the offender that supervision by probation is unnecessary. Sol Rubin, *The Law of Criminal Correction,* 2d ed. (St. Paul: West Publishing Company, 1973), 197–200.

of sentence, there may be a verdict or plea and a judgment, but no sentence is pronounced. In the case of suspension of execution of sentence, the sentence is pronounced, but its execution is suspended, which is to say the defendant is not committed to a correctional institution or otherwise taken into custody. As we shall see, the form of the suspension, whether of imposition or only of execution of sentence, leads to different legal consequences and directly impacts whether suspension of sentence is considered as a separate disposition of the offender, or as the basis for or equivalent to probation. The distinction may turn on such later issues as to whether the offender has been "convicted"; what civil rights he has forfeited; the term for which he may be committed upon resentence after revocation of the suspension; whether probation is a part of the criminal prosecution; whether the probationer on revocation of probation is entitled to counsel under the holding in *Mempa v. Rhay*,[5], or whether the revocation is governed by the right to counsel rules announced in *Morrissey v. Brewer*[6] and *Gagnon v. Scarpelli.*[7]

The Power to Suspend Sentence

Several variables must be considered when discussing the power to suspend sentence. For instance, it makes a difference whether 1) we are talking about the power to withhold or delay sentencing indefinitely or for only a temporary period or specific purpose; 2) we are referring to an inherent power in the courts to suspend sentence or such power granted to the courts by a legislative act; 3) we mean power to suspend imposition of sentence, power to suspend execution of sentence, or both; 4) suspended sentence amounts to a separate disposition or sentencing alternative or is connected with probation; 5) probation depends upon the existence of the power to suspend sentence or does not have the suspended sentence aspect; and 6) probation is actually deemed to be a sentence.

It is generally conceded that at common law the English courts had the power to suspend sentence for a limited period or for a specified purpose. This power was used, for example, in judicial reprieve, where there was a temporary suspension of imposition or execution of sentence and in which the defendant, who had neither the right of appeal nor the right to a new trial, could apply to the crown for an absolute or conditional pardon.[8]

Whether the common law recognized the inherent right of the courts to suspend sentence indefinitely is a matter of considerable dispute. Certain practices in both England and the colonies support the view that such a right was recognized.[9] Recognizance, used as early as 1830 in Massachusetts, permitted one Jerusha Chase, "upon her own recognizance for her appearance in this

---

5. Mempa v. Rhay, 389 U.S. 128, 88 S.Ct. 254, 19 L.Ed.2d 336 (1967).

6. Morrissey v. Brewer, 408 U.S. 471, 92 S.Ct. 2593, 33 L.Ed.2d 484 (1972).

7. Gagnon v. Scarpelli, 411 U.S. 778, 93 S.Ct. 1756, 36 L.Ed.2d 656 (1973).

8. A state-by-state survey of probation legislation can be found in the *Attorney General's Survey of Release Procedures*, vol. I, *Digest of Federal and State Laws on Release Procedures*, Washington, D.C., 1939 (hereinafter referred to as *Att'y Gen. Survey*, vol. I, *Digest*).

9. *Id.*

court whenever she was called for, to go at large."[10] Judicial reprieve was also cited as proof of the recognition of an inherent right in a court to suspend sentence indefinitely, particularly since in some cases the temporary suspension became indefinite when the court refused or failed to again proceed with the case.

As far as the United States was concerned, the matter was resolved in the so-called *Killetts* case, decided in 1916, in which the Supreme Court of the United States held that the federal courts had no power to suspend indefinitely the imposition or execution of a sentence.[11] The Court recognized that the temporary suspension of imposition or execution of sentence was frequently resorted to in both England and the colonies since errors occurring in the trial or miscarriage of justice could not under the then existing system be corrected by granting a new trial or by appeal. These temporary suspensions often became indefinite because of a court's failure to proceed further in a criminal case. The Supreme Court pointed out, however, that " * * * neither of these conditions serve to convert the mere exercise of a judicial discretion to temporarily suspend for the accomplishment of a purpose contemplated by law into the existence of an arbitrary judicial power to permanently refuse to enforce the law."[12] The Court went on to hold that the practice was inconsistent with the Constitution since "its exercise in the very nature of things amounts to a refusal by the judicial power to perform the duty resting on it, and, as a consequence thereof, to an interference with both the legislative and executive authority as fixed by the Constitution."[13]

Suspended Sentence and Probation

The Supreme Court indicated, somewhat inconsistently, that Congress had adequate power to authorize both temporary and indefinite suspension by statute.[14] An earlier New York court had, indeed, upheld the power of a court to suspend sentences indefinitely where this right had been conferred upon the court by statute.[15] The aspect of *Killetts* that recognized the right of the legislative authority to grant the power of indefinite suspension to the courts was to make probation as now defined and practiced in the United States largely a creature of statute.

The early controversy about the authority of the court to suspend sentence has also resulted in differing ideas as to the relationship between probation and suspended sentence. Depending upon the jurisdiction, there are four views that are commonly held: probation may be granted on suspension of imposition of sentence; probation may be granted on suspension of imposition or of execution of sentence; suspended sentence *is* probation; or probation does not have the

---

10. Commonwealth v. Chase, Thacher's Criminal Cases, 267 (1831); recorded in Vol. 1 of the Records of the Old Municipal Court of Boston, p. 199.

11. *Ex parte* United States, 242 U.S. 27, 37 S.Ct. 72, 61 L.Ed. 129 (1916).

12. *Ex parte* United States, 242 U.S. 27, 37 S.Ct. 72, 61 L.Ed. 129 (1916).

13. *Id.*

14. *Id.* The Supreme Court of Idaho has held recently that the legislature may not deprive a court of its power to suspend sentence. State v. McCoy, 94 Idaho 236, 486 P.2d 247 (1971).

15. People *ex rel.* Forsyth v. Court of Sessions, 141 N.Y. 288, 36 N.E. 386 (1894).

suspended sentence aspect.   The American Bar Association Standards Relating
to Probation has adopted this latter view, and suggests that probation should not
involve or require suspension of any other sentence.[16]   The matter is also
complicated by the problem of whether probation itself is or is not a sentence,
and by the varying definitions of "conviction."

Suspended Sentence as "Conviction"
There are two definitions of conviction.   The "narrow" definition, which
follows popular usage, applies the term conviction to a plea, finding, or verdict
of guilt.   The "broad" definition holds that conviction is a plea, finding, or
verdict of guilty, followed by a final judgment of conviction and sentence.
Conviction in the narrow sense is followed by the imposition of criminal
sanctions, but the determination of guilt is not accompanied by loss of civil
rights and privileges.   Conviction in the broad sense is followed by the
imposition of criminal sanctions *and* loss of civil rights and privileges.

Whether there is a conviction if sentence is suspended often turns on the
question of what is suspended.   A conviction is more likely reached if the
suspension has been of the execution, as contrasted with the imposition, of
sentence, although this is by no means always true.

Early Probation
The increasing awareness that prisons were not accomplishing their stated
purpose of reforming the offender and that suspension of sentence without
supervision was not providing a satisfactory alternative brought about the
development of probation as we know it today.   In 1841, John Augustus, a
bootmaker living in Boston, and Mathew Davenport Hill, an English lawyer
then holding the position as the Recorder of Birmingham, introduced the
practice of suspending sentence and releasing the offender under supervision.
John Augustus was the first to apply the term "probation" to his new method,
and thus became the first probation officer.   For this reason he is referred to as
the "father of probation," and probation is said to be of American origin.[17]

In light of his subsequent experience, John Augustus in his first case picked a
most unpromising candidate for probation—a common drunkard.   In his journal,
which appeared in 1852, he observed that:

> Great care was observed, of course, to ascertain whether the prisoners were promising
> subjects for probation, and to this end it was necessary to take into consideration the
> previous character of the person, his age, and the influences by which he would in
> future be likely to be surrounded.[18]

---

16. ABA Standards, Probation, § 1.1(b) reads: "In this report, the term 'probation' means a
sentence not involving confinement which imposes conditions and retains authority in the sentencing court to modify the conditions of the sentence or to resentence the offender if he violates the
conditions. *Such a sentence should not involve or require suspension of the imposition or the execution of any other
sentence."* [Emphasis added.]

17. *See* John Augustus, *A Report of the Labors of John Augustus, for the Last Ten Years, in Aid of the
Unfortunate,* (Boston: Wright & Hasty, 1852); reprinted as *John Augustus, First Probation Officer,* (New
York: National Probation Association, 1939).   *See also,* Supplemental Reading #1, *infra,* "John
Augustus: The First Probation Officer."

18. *Id.* at 34.

It is evident that he viewed probation as a selective process, although his first probationer was selected on his behavior, his manner of speech, and his protestation of a "firm resolve to quit liquor."

John Augustus continued his work in the Boston courts for eighteen years, during which he received some financial aid from other citizens of the community interested in the offender. His journal reports that of the first 1,100 probationers on whom he kept records, only one forfeited bond. As to reformation, he stated that if "only one-half of this number have become reformed, I have ample cause to be satisfied." [19]

As is true today, probation was not universally accepted. John Augustus repeated over and over that "the object of the law is to reform criminals and to prevent crime, and not to punish maliciously or from a spirit of revenge," and he did not hesitate to castigate the police, the judges, and others who did not share his views.[20] As a result, the newspaper of the time referred to him as a "fellow who is called John Augustus," who "seems to have a great itching for notoriety, and dollars," who "hangs and loafs about the Police and Municipal Courts, almost every day, and takes more airs upon himself than all the judges and officers."[21] The newspaper continued:

> We know something about this Peter Funk philanthropist, and peanut reformer, and unless he conducts himself henceforth with a great deal more propriety, we shall take it upon ourself to teach him decency.[22]

John Augustus and his immediate successors were not officials of the court and hence lacked official status, although in 1689 Massachusetts passed a law authorizing an agent of the state board of charities to investigate cases of children tried before the criminal courts. In 1878, almost twenty years after the death of John Augustus, adult probation in Massachusetts was sanctified by statute. A law authorizing the mayor of Boston to appoint a paid probation officer as a member of the police force was passed. The officer's jurisdiction was in the Boston criminal courts. For the first time, the probation officer was recognized as an official agent of the court. The statute included a provision that probation was to be available to "such persons as may reasonably be expected to be reformed without punishment." No other restrictions were inserted. Probation was thus made available in the city of Boston to men and women, felons and misdemeanants, and juveniles and adults, regardless of the nature of the offense or the amount or kind of punishment assessed.

Statewide probation was enacted in Massachusetts in 1890 with a provision that appears in many modern statutes, that the probation officer should not be an active member of the regular police force. This early legislation, while providing for probation officers, did not specifically grant to the courts the power to grant probation. Missouri in 1897 and Vermont in 1898 remedies this omission, although in Missouri the statute was labeled "An Act relating to the

---

19. *Id.* at 96.

20. *Id.* at 23.

21. *Id.* at 78–79.

22. *Id.*

parole of prisoners" and used the words "probation" and "parole" interchangeably.[23]

Several other states passed probation laws in the latter part of the nineteenth and early years of the twentieth century. The statutes varied in their provisions. Illinois and Minnesota provided for juvenile probation only; Rhode Island placed restrictions on eligibility and excluded persons guilty of certain offenses. Some states provided for statewide probation, while others followed the example set by Vermont and adopted the county plan.[24]

By 1925 probation was authorized by statutes in all forty-eight states; it is now so authorized in all fifty states and in the federal system.[25] The American Bar Association Standards Relating to Probation set forth the basic reasons why probation is a desirable disposition in appropriate cases:

• It maximizes the liberty of the individual and at the same time vindicates the authority of the law and effectively protects the public from further violations of law;

• It affirmatively promotes the rehabilitation of the offender by encouraging continued normal community contacts;

• It avoids the negative and frequently stultifying effects of confinement that often severely and unnecessarily complicate the reintegration of the offender in the community;

• It greatly reduces the financial costs to the public treasury of an effective correctional system;

• It minimizes the impact of the conviction upon innocent dependents of the offender.[26]

Early Probation—Federal

As we have noted, the Supreme Court in 1916 held that the federal courts had no inherent power to suspend indefinitely the imposition or execution of a sentence.[27] The Court ruled that the existing practice in some jurisdictions with respect to suspended sentence was inconsistent with the Constitution because its exercise amounted to a refusal by the judicial power to perform a duty resting on it. The Court indicated, however, that the power to suspend sentence could be given to the courts by statute.[28]

Between 1916 and 1925, several attempts were made to secure the passage of a law authorizing federal judges to grant probation. In the closing days of the session in 1925, the Congress enacted the National Probation Act. This act

---

23. In 1939, "probation" was still called "parole" in Missouri. The term "bench parole" is also used. "Bench parole" cannot be granted after the prisoner is delivered to the penitentiary. Penitentiary prisoners are released by pardon, commutation by the governor, merit commutation, good time allowances, or conditional pardon. *Att'y Gen. Survey,* vol. I, *Digest,* 615.

24. *Att'y Gen. Survey,* vol. I, *Digest.*

25. The National Probation Act which authorized federal judges to grant probation was enacted in 1925.

26. ABA Standards, Probation, § 1, 2.

27. *Att'y Gen. Survey,* vol. I, *Digest,* 1–35.

28. *Ex parte* United States, 242 U.S. 27, 37 S.Ct. 72, 61 L.Ed. 129 (1916).

authorized the federal district courts, except in the District of Columbia, to appoint not more than one salaried probation officer. In 1930 judges were empowered to appoint without reference to the civil service list and the limitation of one officer to each district was removed. The attorney general was charged with the duty of coordinating the probation system and probation officers were given certain duties with respect to parolees. The objectives of the probation law were stated by Chief Justice Taft as follows:

> The great desideratum was the giving to young and new violators of law a chance to reform and to escape the contaminating influence of association with hardened or veteran criminals in the beginning of imprisonment * * * The avoidance of imprisonment at the time of sentence was therefore the period to which the advocates of a Probation Act directed their urgency. Probation was not sought to shorten the term. Probation is the attempted saving of a man who has taken one wrong step and whom the judge thinks to be a brand who can be plucked from the burning at the time .of imposition of sentence.[29]

In the federal system, the courts have, by virtue of the statute, the power to suspend the imposition or execution of sentence. Only district courts may grant probation, since the statute confers the power only on courts having original criminal jurisdiction, as distinguished from appellate jurisdiction, which is the power to review a case previously heard by a lower court.

Depending upon the terms of the original probation, the order revoking probation could revoke either (1) the suspension of imposition of sentence, or (2) the suspension of execution of sentence. Where imposition of sentence was originally suspended and probation granted, and where the probation and suspension were later revoked, imposition of sentence is necessary before the offender can be imprisoned. Since the case reverts to its status at the time probation was granted, the court is free to impose any sentence that might originally have been imposed.[30] Where the court imposed sentence but suspended the execution thereof, the original sentence becomes operative when the suspension of execution is revoked.[31] It has been held, however, that when suspension of execution of sentence is revoked, the court may modify the original sentence so as to *decrease* the term of imprisonment,[32] but it cannot *increase* the punishment.[33]

Early Probation—California [34]

California courts have no inherent power at common law to suspend either the imposition or execution of sentence. The first statute that authorized the criminal courts summarily to hear "circumstances" which may be properly taken

---

29. United States v. Murray, 275 U.S. 347, 48 S.Ct. 146, 72 L.Ed. 309 (1928).

30. 18 U.S.C.A. § 725 (1934).

31. 36 Opinions Att'y Gen. 186 (1930). *Also* Crowder v. Aderhold, 46 F.2d 357 (5th Cir.1931).

32. United States v. Antinori, 59 F.2d 171 (5th Cir.1932).

33. United States v. Akerman, 61 F.2d 570 (5th Cir.1932).

34. Cal.Penal Code § 1203, Haymond and Burch (West 1874).

into view either in aggravation or mitigation of the punishment" was passed in 1872. The first general probation statute, passed in 1903, authorized the courts to suspend the imposition of sentence in the case of any person over sixteen if it appeared that there were circumstances in mitigation "or that the ends of justice will be subserved thereby." The period of suspension was restricted to the maximum term. Probation officers could arrest without a warrant, "if the interest of justice so requires, and if the court, in its judgment, shall have reason to believe * * * that conditions are violated or that the defendant is engaging in criminal practices, or has become abandoned to improper associates or a vicious life." The judges could appoint an officer of a charity organization or any citizen to serve without compensation as a probation officer.

The 1905 law allowed release only after investigation and written report by the probation officer and stated that the time of suspension could not count as any part of any term of imprisonment. Probation officers were selected by a probation committee consisting of "seven discreet citizens of good moral character" who were appointed by the judges of the superior courts.[35] In the 1911 act, probation was extended to all persons over eighteen and the court was allowed to suspend either imposition or execution of sentence in all cases.[36] Various changes in the law occurred in 1913 and 1917. The office of adult probation officer was created in counties of the second and third class in 1919, and in all counties in 1921. The juvenile court officers were designated as ex-officio adult probation officers except in certain counties.

A major amendment to the law was passed in 1923.[37] Probation was allowed to be granted after conviction by verdict or plea of guilty. The offenses of murder, robbery, burglary, rape by force, and violence where a deadly weapon was used or great bodily injury was inflicted were excepted from the application of the probation statute, and persons who had previously been found guilty of embezzlement or extortion could not be released on probation. Amendments in 1927 and 1929 made changes regarding the eligibility for probation, and the 1931 law reverted back to the 1923 provisions and eliminated certain major crimes from the operation of the law. For instance, it made persons armed with a deadly weapon at the time of commission of a crime or at the time of arrest ineligible for probation.[38] In 1935, the former provision, in which a jail term was allowed to be credited upon a sentence as a condition of probation, was stricken from the law. It was made the duty of probation officers to file reports as required with the state prison where the probationer was committed.[39]

Probation in California is administered on a county basis, although the Youth Authority offers certain counseling and advisory services.

---

35. 1905 Cal.Stat. at 162.

36. 1911 Cal.Stat. at 689.

37. 1923 Cal.Stat. at 291.

38. 1931 Cal.Stat. at 1633.

39. 1935 Cal.Stat. at 1706.

Early Probation—Illinois [40]

Illinois courts have no inherent power to suspend imposition of sentence indefinitely or for an unreasonable time; however, suspension of execution of sentence for an unreasonable time is allowed. There is no statutory authority for suspension of sentence. In 1911 the circuit and city courts were authorized to appoint probation officers and place adult defendants on probation. The number of officers was limited to twenty in a county; cities of 50,000 population or over that had a city or municipal court could appoint an additional officer. Under the 1911 act, probation could be granted only to first offenders convicted of certain enumerated minor crimes. In 1915 this was changed to permit probation in all cases except for certain enumerated major offenses. Manslaughter cases were made eligible to probation in 1935.[41]

Early probation in Illinois was under the control of local circuit and city courts, as was the authority to appoint probation officers. A state probation officer was created in 1923 and began to function in 1929, but was abolished in 1933. Probation officers were placed under the supervision of a chief probation officer for the county. The early law gave complete discretion to the court to grant or deny probation. Where probation was granted, the court entered an order to continue the case until the end of the probation period.

An investigation was mandatory before probation could be granted, but no investigation was required where the decision of the court was to refuse the application. The investigation was required to be accurate, complete, and prompt, and to provide information concerning the personal life and dependents of the defendant and other such facts that could aid the court in determining the propriety of probation, as in setting the conditions for the probationary period.

Certain probation conditions were mandatory, including provisions against violation of the criminal law; leaving the state without consent of the court; reporting once a month or as often as the court directed concerning whereabouts, conduct, and employment; appearing when called; and giving a bond with or without surety. Discretionary conditions were permitted that covered restitution or reparation, contributions from earnings for support, and the payment of fine or costs. According to the 1936 statute, the term of probation could not exceed two years, unless extended at the end of the period for an additional year.[42]

Early Probation—Texas [43]

The trial courts of Texas had no inherent power at common law to suspend indefinitely the sentence of a person convicted of a crime; this was true whether the suspension was of imposition or execution of sentence. In 1911, a statute that provided for suspension of sentence was enacted, but was immediately held unconstitutional as an interference with the governor's power to grant pardons, reprieves, and commutations. A new statute, enacted in 1913, was drafted to

40. *Att'y Gen. Survey,* vol. I, *Digest,* 298–332.

41. 1911 Ill. Laws at 277.

42. Ill.Ann.Stat. §§ 37–774, 47–775 (Jones 1936).

43. *Att'y Gen. Survey,* vol. I, *Digest,* 1061–1082.

meet the constitutional objections to the 1911 act. The 1913 act provided for suspension of sentence by the jury; in imposing sentence, the court was required to follow the recommendations of the jury. Since the court in so doing exercised no powers of clemency, this act was held constitutional as within the power of the legislature to define offenses and fix the punishment to be inflicted upon the offender. Under the terms of the Suspended Sentence Law enacted in 1931, the judgment of the court was that "conviction shall be suspended during the good behavior of the defendant." "Good behavior" meant that the defendant would not be convicted of any felony or any character or grade of offenses of theft, embezzlement, swindling, conversion, theft by bailee, or any other fraudulent acquisition of personal property. Thus, the convicted person was free to come and go at will without any supervision or restraint unless and until indicted, tried, and convicted of another crime.

In 1935 the power to suspend the imposition or execution of sentence and to place the defendant on probation was given to the courts of original criminal jurisdiction by constitutional amendment.[44]

In 1947 the Adult Probation Law was enacted, which permitted the judge (not the jury) to grant probation and suspend the imposition or execution of sentence of individuals convicted for certain felonies. Succeeding statutes deleted the provisions as to suspension of execution of sentence.[45]

The Suspended Sentence Law was replaced in its entirety in 1965.[46] Since that time, probation accompanied by suspension of imposition of sentence is the method of release for felony offenders for whom commitment to a penitentiary is not ordered. If the penalty assessed by judge or jury is over ten years, a felony offender is not eligible for probation.

In 1975, the statute was amended to allow an offender to be placed on probation prior to any adjudication of guilt having been entered. Variously referred to as conditional discharge or deferred adjudication, this type of release is otherwise governed by the standard terms of probation. Another variation was added in 1977 when the legislature created shock probation, a procedure by which an individual who actually had been sentenced and committed to prison could be brought back before the court and placed on probation, thus suspending further execution of sentence.[47]

Early Probation—New York [48]

New York courts could suspend imposition of sentence at common law; the weight of authority was against the authority to suspend execution of sentence. Later statutes gave the courts the power to suspend both imposition and execution of sentence as to all offenses defined by the penal law.[49]

Probation began in 1901 under a law that empowered all justices of courts that had original jurisdiction in all cities to appoint officers to investigate and

44. *Ex parte* Minor, 167 Tex.Crim. 170, 319 S.W.2d 114 (1959).

45. Texas Code Crim.Proc.Ann. art. 42.12 (Vernon).

46. *Id. See* W.A. Morrison, "Interpretive Commentary," 473.

47. Texas Code Crim.Proc.Ann. art. 42.12 (Vernon 1975 and 1977 revisions.)

48. *Att'y Gen. Survey,* vol. I, *Digest,* 766–818.

49. N.Y. Penal Law § 2188 (McKinney) as amended, 1933 N.Y.Laws 193 and 517: N.Y.Code Crim.Proc. § 470a.

report cases that the courts thought might deserve mitigation of punishment by way of probation. All classes of crimes were included where there were "circumstances of mitigation."[50]

In 1918 the courts were forbidden to place on probation those persons convicted of crimes punishable by death or life imprisonment, and in 1928 fourth offenders and those convicted of a felony committed while armed with a weapon were taken out of the scope of probation.[51] In 1928 the district attorney was given the right to be heard in felony cases before probation could be granted.[52] In 1930 suspension of sentence alone was forbidden without prior investigation and report.

The first independent commission for the supervision of probation was established in New York in 1907. The statute allowing county probation departments was passed in 1936.[53] This set up a probation system made up of probation officers appointed by the local courts and paid by the local governments but under state supervision. One of the four major divisions of the state department of corrections was the division of probation.[54] The department was under the statewide supervision of the director of probation. The Westchester County probation department was created in 1930 and its director was appointed by the judge of the children's court, the county judge, and the senior trial justice of the supreme court. In 1936, all counties with populations less than 600,000 and outside of New York City were authorized to adopt a similar organization. In New York City the court of general sessions had a chief probation officer, two deputies and additional officers appointed by that court; inferior courts of New York City had chief probation officers and deputy chiefs appointed and removed by the chief city magistrate.[55]

In 1939 any court, judge, or magistrate authorized to impose sentence could suspend either the imposition or execution of sentence and in its discretion place the defendant on probation. However, that power could not be exercised after imprisonment had been entered upon nor could the power be exercised in any case where the defendant was convicted (a) of a crime punishable by death or life imprisonment, (b) as a fourth offender, or (c) of a felony committed while armed with a weapon. No one could be placed on probation nor in felony cases receive a suspended sentence until the probation officer filed a report showing the circumstances of the offense, the criminal record, social history, and results of any physical and psychiatric examinations made.

The period of probation could not be longer than the maximum sentence for the offense in felony cases, nor longer than three years in other cases, except that the time during which a probationer hides out could be added to the period of probation.[56]

---

50. 1901 N.Y.Laws, 372, § 1.

51. 1920 N.Y.Laws 568.

52. 1928 N.Y.Laws 841.

53. N.Y. Code Crim.Proc. § 938b, added by 1936 N.Y.Laws 95.

54. N.Y. Correction Law § 7 (McKinney).

55. *Att'y Gen. Survey,* vol. I, *Digest,* 771.

56. N.Y. Penal Law § 2188 (McKinney) as amended, 1933 N.Y. Laws 107 and 513, N.Y. Code Crim.Proc. § 470a.

Early Probation—Juvenile

There is a tendency to think of juvenile probation only in connection with a juvenile court. Since the first juvenile court and apparently the use of the term "juvenile delinquency" began in Illinois in 1899, some writers trace the development of juvenile probation from that date. The truth is, however, that many of the principles, characteristics, and procedures that today we equate with juvenile courts were used long before any separate tribunals for the handling of juveniles came into existence.

As early as 1630, a guidebook that sanctioned special treatment of juveniles was prepared in England for the use of justices of the peace.

> And yet if an infant shall commit larceny, and shall be found guilty thereof before the Justice of the Peace, it shall not be amiss for them to respite the judgment and so hath it often beene [sic] done by the Judges.[57]

A report of criminal trials from the Old Bailey Sessions in London, 1686–93, contains an account of the trial of Chollis Searl, "a little youth, aged about twelve years," who was acquitted of picking pockets in a proceeding that would be familiar in today's juvenile courts.[58] One of the justices of the peace for the county of Warwick, writing between 1820 and 1827, proposed the appointment of legal guardians to children without supervision, to supply the place of their own relatives.

Between 1866 and 1871, a boy's "beadle" or "persuader" was employed as an unofficial probation officer by the Reformatory and Refuge Union in London. In 1881 an article on the "Massachusetts Method of Dealing With Juvenile Offenders," which advocated placing them on probation, was given wide publicity by the Howard Association of London.

Although the need for separate treatment of juveniles was recognized in the early nineteenth century, the development of special children's institutions proceeded more rapidly than did the development of special procedures and separate courts. Unfortunately, many of the special institutions came to be nothing more than children's prisons, and a system of contracting the labor of the children to private employers led to extremely harsh treatment and the outright exploitation of children's labor. To protect children from this exploitation, the New York Children's Aid Society shipped Manhattan street urchins to western farmers in wholesale lots to keep them from being committed to the House of Refuge. In 1890 the Children's Aid Society of Pennsylvania offered to place in foster homes delinquents who would otherwise be sent to reform school. Known as "placing out," this practice was an early form of juvenile probation.[59] The system of apprenticeship was also an early form of probation of children, used chiefly to detach poor children from their parents and attach them to new masters who were to teach them a trade.

---

57. Frederic L. Faust and Paul J. Brantingham, *Juvenile Justice Philosophy* (St. Paul: West Publishing Company, 1974), 44.

58. *Id.* at 45.

59. *Id.* at 62.

The Illinois Juvenile Court Act of 1899 combined the Massachusetts and New York systems of probation with several New York laws to provide delinquents with special court sessions and separate detention facilities.[60] In an article appearing in the *Harvard Law Review* in 1909, Julian W. Mack declared that juvenile court legislation

> * * * has assumed two aspects. In Great Britain and in New York, and in a few other jurisdictions, the protection [of children] is accomplished by suspending sentence and releasing the child under probation, or, in case of removal from the home, sending it to school instead of to a jail or penitentiary. * * * But in Illinois, and following the lead of Illinois, in most jurisdictions, the form of proceeding is totally different * * * * [P]roceedings are brought to have a guardian or representative of the state appointed to look after the child, to have the state intervene between the natural parent and child because the child needs it, as evidenced by some of its acts, and because the parent is either unwilling or unable to train the child properly.[61]

Mack continued with an analysis of the main principles involved in juvenile court legislation. The first principle was that children offenders ought to be kept separate from the adult criminals and should receive at the hands of the law a treatment differentiated to suit their special needs. The courts should be agencies for the rescue as well as the punishment of children. The second principle was that the parents of offenders must be made to feel more responsible for the wrongdoing of their children. The third principle was that no matter what the offense committed, the commitment of children in the common jails is an unsuitable penalty to be imposed. The fourth principle stated that taking children away from parents and sending them even to an industrial school was as far as possible to be avoided, and

> * * * that when it is allowed to return home it should be under probation, subject to the guidance and friendly interest of the probation officer, the representative of the court. To raise the age of criminal responsibility from seven or ten to sixteen or eighteen, without providing for an efficient system of probation, would indeed be disastrous. *Probation is, in fact, the keynote of juvenile court legislation.* [Emphasis added.][62]

Mack further related: "Whenever juvenile courts have been established, a system of probation has been provided for, and even where as yet the juvenile court system has not been fully developed, some steps have been taken to substitute probation for imprisonment of the juvenile offender. What they need, more than anything else, is kindly assistance; and the aim of the court, in appointing a probation officer for the child, is to have the child and the parents feel, not so much the power, as the friendly interest of the state; to show them that the object of the court is to help them to train the child right, and therefore the probation officers must be men and women fitted for these tasks.[63]

---

60. *Id.* at 63.

61. Julian W. Mack, *The Juvenile Court,* 23 Harvard Law Review 102 (1909), as quoted in Faust and Brantingham, *supra* note 54, at 159–69.

62. *Id.* at 162.

63. *Id.* at 163.

John Augustus:
The First Probation Officer*

The first probation law anywhere in the world was passed in Massachusetts in 1878. This law, Chapter 198, Acts of 1878, authorized the mayor of Boston to appoint from the police force or from the city at large a person to attend the criminal courts in Suffolk county, to investigate the cases of those charged with or convicted of crimes, and to recommend to the courts the placing on probation of those who might be reformed without punishment. The act provided for the compensation of the first statutory probation officer from public funds.

It is important to remember that the Act of 1878 did not create probation or initiate the probation movement. It created no new judicial power but provided only for the appointment and payment of a special officer in order that the courts might exercise more fully and broadly what had become a well-established, well-recognized and approved usage.

Defendants had been placed on probation in Boston as early as 1830. By judicial experiment and the use of volunteer probation officers, the probation movement came into being. The General Court, in enacting the Act of 1878, reflected the public opinion in favor of placing defendants on probation which had been forming for nearly fifty years.

The probation movement as it developed before legislation is the story of devoted men and women of Massachusetts, many of them volunteers, who saw in probation an opportunity for the rehabilitation of men and women, of boys and girls. Of these John Augustus made the first great contribution.

When on an August day in 1841 John Augustus appeared in the police court of Boston and the court bailed into his custody a poor inebriate who would otherwise have been committed to jail, probation was ready for its development. The courts were prepared; there was no lack of the human beings with whom probation is concerned; and John Augustus was imbued with the

---

* Excerpted from a paper read to the 35th Annual Conference of the National Probation Association, Boston, Mass., May 29, 1941, by John Moreland.

vision and the consecration necessary to make probation a really living movement.

Probation was not the discovery of John Augustus,—that came from the enlightened legal thought of Boston judges in the decade before him. But there could be no real development of probation until in addition to the legal thought and practice which made it possible, there was a demonstration which would show its possibilities and value as a treatment process, which would gain the interest, understanding and respect of the courts and of the public, and which would attract other workers to the field. Such a demonstration John Augustus, the bootmaker of Boston, made from 1841 until his death in 1859.

It was Augustus' practice to bail, after his conviction, an offender in whom there was hope of reformation. The man would be ordered to appear before the court at a stated time at the expiration of which Augustus would accompany him to the courtroom. If the judge was satisfied with Augustus' account of his stewardship, the offender, instead of being committed to the House of Correction, would be fined one cent and costs. The one cent and costs, which amounted generally to from three to four dollars, Augustus paid.

Who was John Augustus? What was it that took him from his boot factory to the police court in 1841? How did he do his work? Who financed it? How was he received by the personnel of the courts, by the press, and by the people of Boston? What were his accomplishments?

John Augustus was born in Burlington, Massachusetts (then part of Woburn) in 1785. About 1806 he moved to Lexington and carried on a shoe manufactory in part of his home. He apparently prospered as he owned a large tract of land on both sides of Bedford street. His old home, now renovated and restored at 1 Harrington Road, and known as the Jonathan Harrington house, faces the Lexington Common.

Although John Augustus was in business in Boston as early as 1820, he continued to maintain his Lexington home and possibly his Lexington business until 1829, when the Boston Directory lists him as living in Boston on Chambers street. It was in his shop at 5 Franklin avenue near the police court, now only an alley, that Augustus received from 1841, according to his own account of his work, frequent calls from those who sought his help. It was his business there that suffered owing to the time he was required to spend away from its bailing people in the courts or attending to their needs elsewhere.

All of Augustus' residences from 1841 on are of particular interest, because as soon as he began his work in the courts his home became the refuge of people he had bailed until more permanent plans could be made for them. From 1845 until his death in 1859 Augustus lived at 65 Chambers street, in the West End of Boston. Nothing remains today of this old house.

There can be no doubt it was the Washingtonian temperance reform movement which led Augustus to the police court and later to the municipal court in Boston. It was the conviction of all Washingtonians that the drunkard could be saved through understanding, kindness and moral suasion, rather than through commitment to prison.

The movement resulted in Boston in the formation of the Washingtonian Total Abstinence Society on April 25, 1841. Its members were pledged not only not to use intoxicating liquors themselves, but to reclaim and to restore to temperance those who were addicted to drunkenness.

The members were soon in the police court about the work to which they were pledged; and some of them were there before Augustus, as the first quarterly report of the society's auditor, published in July 1841, indicates:

I take this opportunity, in the name, and in behalf of this Society, of tendering to the Justices and Clerks of the Police Court, my hearty thanks for their kindness in affording (as far as consistent with duty) every facility to our members in their attempts to rescue and bring back to the paths of temperance, the *poor, forsaken, heartbroken* Drunkard, who came under their cognizance. Many, very many, have been taken from this Court and restored to their families and friends, who do not appear in the Reports from the Houses of Correction and Industry. Thus it will be seen that a heavy expense has been saved to the city, and many a person has been brought back to usefulness, unknown to the public.

THE FIRST PROBATIONER

Let Augustus describe in his own words the moving story of his first probationer:

In the month of August, 1841, I was in court one morning, when the door communicating with the lock-room was opened and an officer entered, followed by a ragged and wretched looking man, who took his seat upon the bench allotted to prisoners. I imagined from the man's appearance that his offence was that of yielding to his appetite for intoxicating drinks, and in a few moments I found that my suspicions were correct, for the clerk read the complaint, in which the man was charged with being a common drunkard. The case was clearly made out, but before sentence had been passed, I conversed with him a few moments, and found that he was not yet past all hope of reformation, although his appearance and his looks precluded a belief in the minds of others that he would ever become a *man* again. He told me that if he could be saved from the House of Correction, he never again would taste intoxicating liquors; there was such an earnestness in that tone, and a look expressive of firm resolve, that I determined to aid him; I bailed him, by permission of the Court. He

was ordered to appear for sentence in three weeks from that time. He signed the pledge and became a sober man; at the expiration of this period of probation, I accompanied him into the court room; his whole appearance was changed and no one, not even the scrutinizing officers, could have believed that he was the same person who less than a month before, had stood trembling on the prisoner's stand. The Judge expressed himself much pleased with the account we gave of the man, and instead of the usual penalty,—imprisonment in the House of Correction,—he fined him *one cent and costs,* amounting in all to $3.76, which was immediately paid. The man continued industrious and sober, and without doubt has been by this treatment, saved from a drunkard's grave.[1]

With this encouragement Augustus continued to appear in court to receive on probation alcoholics who appeared likely prospects for reformation, to rehabilitate them, and then to return with them to court for a report on their progress. By January 1842 he had bailed seventeen other alcoholics.

His real consecration to this work occurred in August 1842, when he could say.

I had labored about a year when it became evident that much, much good had been and might be performed, by laboring in the field in which I had commenced operations, and to promote this object, several kind and philanthropic individuals placed in my hands donations of various sums, which enabled me to accomplish a much greater amount of good than I could have done from my own limited means alone.

From this time on, Augustus' record is one of dedication to a cause, understood by some and misunderstood by others, to which he devoted the remainder of his life, much of his own financial resources, as well as the money contributed by Boston people. John Augustus set the general pattern to be followed by succeeding voluntary and official probation officers.

1. *John Augustus, First Probation Officer* (reprint of *Report of John Augustus* Boston, 1852) National Probation Association, 1939, p. 4.

During the first year, Augustus bailed only men, but thereafter, year by year until 1859, his probationers were men and women, boys and girls whose offenses represented every bailable crime.

When in December 1851 John Augustus consulted his records preparatory to publishing an account of his labors in behalf of unfortunates during the preceding ten years, he found he had bailed in the police or municipal courts 1102 persons, 674 males and 428 females. He had become bail for them to the amount of $19,464, and he had paid $2417.65 for fines and costs.

Although this alone may be considered an impressive record, it is to be remembered that he continued such work in the courts for about seven and one-half years more; and in addition he responded to calls for assistance from many in need of social services who were not court offenders. Up to 1858 we know that he had bailed 1946 persons, 1152 males and 794 women and girls.

OPPOSITIONS TO OVERCOME

In the conduct of his work inside and outside the court, John Augustus had to face opposition, misunderstanding, and even physical abuse. Charges were made that he was profiting financially from those whom he bailed even though many of them were so poor they were unable to pay the fine and costs. Much of the opposition and misunderstanding he gradually overcame. Some if it remained, and Augustus expressed it in words which have been used in reference to probation from time to time up to this day:

There is, however, much opposition to the plan of bailing on probation. Those who are opposed to this method tell us that it is rather an incentive to crime and, therefore, instead of proving salutary, it is detrimental to the interest of society, and so far from having a tendency to reform the person bailed, it rather presents inducements for them to continue a career of crime; the law is robbed of its terrors, and its punishments, and there is nothing, therefore, to deter them from repeating the offense with which they were previously charged.

To such thinking Augustus replied:

The premises upon which such reasoning is based is incorrect. Individuals and communities generally are but too prone to infer evil of a class, if they but occasionally observe it in individuals; if a person who has been bailed, or received the leniency of the court, proves false to his promises of amendment, people are ever ready to predict that all others will conduct in a similar manner; and this they persist in believing, although instances are very frequent, even three to one, where such persons have become good citizens, and regain their former station and relation in society. I shall leave the matter for others to discuss and decide, but I am content, feeling as I do, that by such humane means hundreds of the fallen have been raised even by my humble instrumentality.

Augustus varied his answers to his critics. To some he said that for each person bailed to him a commitment to a house of correction was prevented. To those who understood social progress and justice only in terms of a dollar saved, he pointed out that the public was saved the greater expense of caring for the person in jail. When he was charged with cheating the jails of their rightful tenants, he replied that his form of treatment was more effective; that it saved the offender for his family and for society and did not disgrace him forever as a commitment would. How modern is the sound of some of these charges that Augustus had to answer!

It was the court officers, the clerk, the turnkeys, and the process servers who were the first to oppose Augustus and who remained strongest in their opposition. Since their financial security was threatened in every case for which Augustus became bail, they lost no time or opportunity to show their displeasure over his work. For every person bailed by Augustus the officer lost the fee of either seventy-five cents or sixty-two cents payable on the taking of the offender to jail; the clerk lost twenty-five cents, and the turnkey was out forty cents. But Augustus was not deterred.

Although the opposition of the court officers was discouraging, the judges and the press were friendly, and influential people in the community gave him both moral and financial support.

SECURING FUNDS

There is no evidence that Augustus was anything more than a man of limited means. To accomplish the work he felt called to do more money was necessary than he could provide alone. Much if it had to come from others. It did not come, as was charged, from his probationers. In December 1851 Augustus wrote:

. . . The first two years 1841–42, I received nothing from any one except what I earned by my daily labor; in 1843, I received from various persons in aid of my work, seven hundred and fifty-eight dollars; in 1844–45–46, I received twelve hundred and thirteen dollars each year. I then gave up business at my shop, and for the last five years, my receipts have averaged, yearly, seventeen hundred and seventy-six dollars, all of which I have expended, and have

not a dollar of this sum. The money which I have thus received came from kind friends to the cause in which I was engaged.

The busy life of the first career man in the field of probation came to a close on June 21, 1859. The morning after his death the *Boston Herald* summed up the meaning of his life and work in these words:

DEATH OF A WELL KNOWN CITIZEN. Mr. John Augustus died at his residence in Chambers Street, this city, last evening after a somewhat protracted and lingering illness, superinduced by old age and a general prostration of the system from overtaxation of its powers. The deceased was well known in this community in connection with his benevolent exertions in behalf of poor criminals, the latter years of his life being almost entirely spent in ameliorating their condition by becoming bondsman for their good behavior, and providing means and opportunities that would tend to a reformation . . . .. Possessed of a living income from means accumulated in business pursuits, the deceased was in a position to carry out the dictates of a generous heart, and those who knew him best, give him credit for sincerity of purpose, although there are many who saw nothing in his conduct toward criminals that was not the offspring of selfish motives. Undoubtedly, Mr. Augustus was the means of doing much good in his daily walks through our courts and penal institutions, and a charitable community will not be backward in revering his memory with this fact in remembrance . . . .

2

Sentencing:
The Decision
to Grant Probation

Generally

The granting of probation to an individual offender involves many factors such as:

- availability of probation as a disposition
- power of the sentencing tribunal to grant probation
- eligibility of the individual offender for probation as fixed by statute
- criteria for granting or withholding probation as fixed by statute
- conditions of probation as fixed by statute
- availability and quality of probation services
- availability and quality of other sentencing dispositions
- methods of developing sentencing information
- whether probation is an appropriate disposition of the particular offender
- the right to probation
- the acceptance of probation

Availability of Probation as a Disposition

Since probation is a creature of statute, the first requirement for the granting of probation is that the state statutes provide for probation. All of the state and federal governments now provide for the probation of juveniles and extend probation to some, but not all, felony offenders.[1] Many of the states have

---

1. The definition of a felony varies from state to state; in some cases the definition relates to place of confinement; in others, to length of confinement. Typical definitions are:

Any offense punishable by death or imprisonment for a term exceeding one year is a felony. 18 U.S.C.A. § 1.

A felony is a crime which is punishable with death or by imprisonment in a state prison. Cal.Penal Code § 17(a) (West).

misdemeanor probation as well. It is not unusual to find that juvenile probation predated adult probation in a given jurisdiction, or that the first probation statute and the first juvenile court act were passed in the same year. As we have already noted, probation historically is closely related to suspended sentence. Depending upon the jurisdiction, probation can include suspension of imposition of sentence or suspension of imposition and of execution of sentence; probation may be equivalent to suspended sentence; the enactment of a probation statute may do away with suspended sentence; or probation may not involve a suspended sentence. The question of whether probation is a sentence is one that we will consider in greater detail hereafter.

Power of Sentencing Tribunal to Grant Probation

The power to grant probation is typically given to juvenile courts and to courts of general jurisdiction trying adult felony offenders. Lower courts may have jurisdiction to grant probation to a misdemeanant. The decision to grant probation is usually made by the judge who has the power to sentence. However, the state statutes may provide for jury sentencing. In such case, the jury may be given the power to place the defendant on probation, or the jury may be given the power to recommend probation with the judge bound to follow the jury's recommendation if certain conditions exist. In such states the judge may or may not have the power to place a defendant on probation, either under different conditions or notwithstanding the recommendation of the jury.[2]

In the federal system, any court having jurisdiction to try offenses against the United States has authority to grant probation.[3]

The power to modify the conditions of probation and to revoke probation commonly belongs to the tribunal authorized to grant probation.

Eligibility for Probation

Basic eligibility for probation is fixed by statute. Typically, there are few or no restrictions on eligibility for probation in the juvenile court. As to felony probation, restrictions on eligibility tend to be in the nature of declaring ineligible defendants convicted of certain specified offenses, usually crimes of violence, defendants upon whom a term longer than a specified number of years is assessed, and those defendants with a prior felony conviction.

Conditions of Probation
as Fixed by Statute

The conditions of probation as fixed by statute must also be taken into consideration in the probation-granting decision. This is not quite the same

---

2. In Texas, if the penalty assessed does not exceed ten years and the defendant has no prior felony convictions, the jury may recommend probation and the court is bound to follow the recommendation.

3. 18 U.S.C. § 3651.

problem as fixing the conditions for the particular defendant, it being assumed that it is possible, and even probable, that the defendant will fulfill the conditions. If the presentence information about the defendant shows that he or she cannot meet the statutory conditions that must be imposed, then it is useless to grant probation. The example that readily comes to mind is that of the chronic alcoholic whose past history indicates an inability to abstain from the use of intoxicating beverages. Yet, the nature of crime may be such that the statute requires that a condition of probation be that complete abstinence from the use of alcohol be achieved.

Such a situation imposes both a legal and practical dilemma upon the court. Has the court the right to assume out-of-hand that this time the defendant "won't make it" simply because on previous occasions the defendant has been unable to abstain? Conversely, can the court ignore the intractable nature of alcoholism, the lack of treatment facilities, and the discouraging statistics about "cures." In such a situation, the court's duty is probably to take all the factors into consideration in making the decision whether to grant probation, and to put such weight upon each factor as in its best judgment the situation seems to require, and to grant or withhold probation accordingly.

To avoid confronting the court with dilemmas of this sort, many authorities recommend that statutes refrain from making specific conditions for probation, leaving the matter open for the judge to exercise judgment based upon the most up-to-date information as can be obtained by competent presentence investigations about the defendant and about the treatment facilities and programs available.

Criteria for Granting or Withholding Probation

Criteria for granting or withholding probation are closely related to eligibility for probation. Indeed, it is sometimes difficult to differentiate between the two and statutes relating to eligibility for probation may be labeled "criteria for probation" and vice versa. However, a distinction between the two statutory enactments must be made and must be based on the premise that either a) the ordinary and expected form of disposition of the offender is commitment to an institution and the problem is to meet criteria for *granting* probation, b) or probation is deemed to be the preferred and expected disposition of the offender and the problem is to meet criteria for *denying* probation. With reference to the adult offender, the first kind of sentencing statute is more frequently found. However, model statutes and developing standards for probation emphasize the second type of statute and recommend that sentencing statutes provide that probation is the preferred form of criminal sanction, with incarceration to be ordered only when the welfare of the offender or the safety of the society clearly demonstrate the need for withholding probation and sentencing imprisonment.[4] Statutes relating to juvenile probation have always tended to be of the second type. The objective in the juvenile court is to avoid institutional commitment of the juvenile if possible. Thus, probation, suspension of judgment, or specialized placement are the most frequent court dispositions.

---

4. See Model Penal Code; *also* ABA Standards Relating to Probation.

The criteria for probation are often stated in general terms. The California statute, for example, provides that "If the court shall determine that there are circumstances in mitigation of punishment prescribed by law, or that the ends of justice would be subserved by granting probation to the defendant, the court shall have the power in its discretion to place the defendant on probation as hereinafter provided. * * * "[5]

The Texas statute gives authority to the court to grant probation to an eligible offender * * * "when it shall appear to the satisfaction of the court that the ends of justice and the best interests of the public as well as of the defendant will be subserved thereby."[6] New York follows its general statement with more specific criteria. Probation is allowed if the court is of the opinion that institutional confinement of the defendant is not necessary for the protection of the public; the defendant is in need of guidance, training or other assistance which, in the defendant's case, can be effectively administered through probation; and such disposition is not inconsistent with the ends of justice.[7]

The Model Penal Code, consistent with its position that the preferred sentence is either suspension of imposition of sentence or probation, requires an affirmative finding before imprisonment is allowed that imprisonment is necessary for the protection of the public, and lists quite detailed criteria that are to be accorded weight in favor of withholding sentence of imprisonment.[8]

---

5. Cal.Penal Code, § 1203 (West).

6. Tex.Code Crim.Proc.Ann. art. 42.12B, § 3. (Vernon).

7. N.Y.Penal Law § 65.00–1 (McKinney). The court may not, however, impose a sentence of probation in any case where it sentences a defendant for more than one crime, and imposes a sentence of imprisonment for any one of the crimes, or where the defendant is subject to an undischarged indeterminate or reformatory sentence of imprisonment which was imposed at a previous time by a court of the state and has more than one year to run. *Id.*

Where the court imposes a sentence of conditional discharge for a felony, the court must set forth in the record the reasons for its action. *Id.* § 65.05–1(b).

8. Model Penal Code § 7.01 Criteria for withholding sentence of imprisonment and for placing defendant on probation.

(1) The court shall deal with a person who has been convicted of a crime without imposing sentence of imprisonment unless, having regard to the nature and circumstances of the crime and the history, character and condition of the defendant, it is of the opinion that his imprisonment is necessary for protection of the public because:

(a) there is undue risk that during the period of a suspended sentence or probation the defendant will commit another crime; or

(b) the defendant is in need of correctional treatment that can be provided most effectively by his commitment to an institution; or

(c) a lesser sentence will depreciate the seriousness of the defendant's crime.

(2) The following grounds, while not controlling the direction of the court, shall be accorded weight in favor of withholding sentence of imprisonment:

(a) the defendant's criminal conduct neither caused nor threatened serious harm;

(b) the defendant did not contemplate that his criminal conduct would cause or threaten serious harm;

(c) the defendant acted under a strong provocation;

(d) there were substantial grounds tending to excuse or justify the defendant's criminal conduct, though failing to establish a defense;

(e) the victim of the defendant's criminal conduct induced or facilitated its commission;

The American Bar Association Standards Relating to Probation also proceed from the premise that a sentence not involving total confinement is to be preferred in the absence of affirmative reasons to the contrary.[9] The *Standards* emphasize that probation should not turn upon generalizations about types of offenses or the existence of a prior criminal record, but should be rooted in the facts and circumstances of each case. The court should consider the nature and circumstances of the crime, the history and character of the offender, and available institutional and community resources. Probation should be the sentence unless: the sentencing court finds that confinement is necessary to protect the public from further criminal activity by the offender; the offender is in need of correctional treatment that can be most effectively provided if the offender is confined; or it would unduly depreciate the seriousness of the offense if a sentence of probation were imposed. Whether the defendant pleads guilty, pleads not guilty, or intends to appeal is not relevant to the issue of whether probation is an appropriate sentence.[10]

The National Advisory Commission establishes suggested criteria for sentencing the nondangerous offender that give preference to probation over commitment.[11] The pattern is to list the permissible disposition on an ascending scale, the least serious disposition being mentioned first. The court would be required to impose the first of the alternatives that would reasonably protect the

---

(f) the defendant has compensated or will compensate the victim of his criminal conduct for the damage or injury that he sustained;

(g) the defendant has no history of prior delinquency or criminal activity or has led a law-abiding life for a substantial period of time before the commission of the present crime;

(h) the defendant's criminal conduct was the result of circumstances unlikely to recur;

(i) the character and attitudes of the defendant indicate that he is unlikely to commit another crime;

(j) the defendant is particularly likely to respond affirmatively to probationary treatment;

(k) the imprisonment of the defendant would entail excessive hardship to himself or his dependents.

(3) When a person has been convicted of a crime and is not sentenced to imprisonment, the Court shall place him on probation if he is in need of the supervision, guidance, assistance or direction that the probation service can provide.

9. ABA Standards Sentencing Alternatives and Procedures, § 2.5(c). Examples of legitimate reasons for selection of total confinement in a given case are: (i) Confinement is necessary in order to protect the public from further criminal activity by the defendant; or (ii) The defendant is in need of correctional treatment which can most effectively be provided if he is placed in total confinement; or (iii) It would unduly depreciate the seriousness of the offense to impose a sentence other than total confinement. Id.

10. ABA Standards, Probation, § 1.3.

11. Nat'l Advisory Comm'n Standards, Corrections Standard 5.2—Sentencing the Nondangerous Offender.

State penal code revisions should include a provision that the maximum sentence for any offender not specifically found to represent a substantial danger to others should not exceed five years for felonies other than murder. No minimum sentence should be authorized by the legislature.

The sentencing court should be authorized to impose maximum sentence less than that provided by statute.

The National Advisory Commission Standards are similar in most regards to those of the Model Penal Code. *Also see* the American Correctional Association Standards in the appendix.

public safety. The record of the court must show affirmative justification for confinement.

Availability and Quality of Probation Services

The decision to grant probation is affected by the availability and quality of probation services. A judge may consider it useless to grant probation if there is no organized adult probation office in the locality, if the probation department gives no supervision whatever to the misdemeanant placed on probation, or if the case load of existing probation officers is so great that no meaningful and consistent supervision is possible. On the other hand, efficient and effective probation services may be overused. At a time when the Miami juvenile probation department was widely acclaimed for its successes, parents became overeager to use its services. One officer was heard to remark ruefully: "The parents call us now if Junior refuses to take the garbage out in the morning."

The organizational structure of probation services and the training and ability of the probation officers also affect the availability and quality of probation services.[12] In some states, probation is a part of the judicial branch of government, while in others it is part of the executive branch. Probation may be administered on a local or statewide basis and may or may not be combined with parole services. Juvenile and adult probation may be under a single administration or there may be separate juvenile and adult probation departments. The trend seems to be toward the establishment of statewide probation departments in the executive branch of government.[13] This does not, however, remove the probation-granting decision from the courts.

The National Advisory Commission views the probation officer primarily as a community resource manager for probationers, a function that differs substantially from the traditional concept that probation is a form of social casework. The commission stated that, "Although [assigning a probationer to an individual probation officer] helps staff keep track of probationers, it does little to influence conditions in offenders' lives that make the difference between success and failure * * *. The probation officer's role should shift from that of primarily counseling surveillance to that of managing community resources."[14]

Quality of probation service is also determined by the qualifications of probation officers. These vary widely from place to place even when minimum qualifications for probation officers are set out in the probation statute. One state has very stringent qualification requirements and will certify only those persons who have successfully completed education in an accredited college or university and can demonstrate two years full-time paid employment with juveniles or adults in responsible probation or correctional work or other appropriate social welfare work.[15] The same state for a long time had no

---

12. For more detailed discussion of this subject, see Chapter 6, *infra*, Administration of Probation.

13. Nat'l Advisory Comm'n Standards, Corrections Standard 10.1—Organization of Probation.

14. Nat'l Advisory Comm'n Standards, Corrections Standard 10.2—Services of Probationers.

15. Tex.Code Crim.Proc.Ann. art. 42.12, § 10 (Vernon.) One year of appropriate graduate study may be substituted for the required year of experience.

minimum statutory qualifications for juvenile probation officers, except that they be persons of good character. The American Bar Association Standards Relating to Probation suggest that a minimum qualification should include possession of a bachelor's degree, supplemented by a year of graduate study in social work, corrections, counseling, law, criminology, psychology, sociology, or related fields; [or a year of full-time casework, counseling with community, correctional or juvenile agencies and dealing with offenders or disadvantaged persons.] A significant number of probation officers in a department should have a graduate degree in one of the subjects enumerated. These qualifications do not preclude the use of citizen or lay volunteers to assist qualified probation officers.[16]

Unfortunately, neither statutory requirements nor recommended qualification standards for probation officers assure that adequate probation services will be available to the sentencing court. In many areas, no probation department exists. Under such circumstances it is not uncommon for the judge to act as his own probation officer by setting up conditions and by requiring that defendants report to the court at regular intervals. Police and prosecution officials are sometimes pressed into service as unofficial probation officers, although placing a released person in custody of police or prosecution officials should be considered an unsound and unwise practice.[17] In some cases, probation reverts to the days of John Augustus when supervision over the conditionally released offender was by a concerned citizen, often a member of the clergy.

The use of probation varies widely throughout the country and even within a single state.[18] This is so partially because of the unavailability of probation services, and also because of differing sentencing philosophies and different degrees of community acceptance and involvement in probation.

A study of the district courts in the United States showed the percentage of defendants placed on probation varied from 78.3 percent in the western district of Michigan to 13.9 percent in the northern district of West Virginia. Northeastern districts tended to have high percentage rates of defendants placed on probation and were characterized as districts most favorable to defendants. Low probation rates characterized the central United States. A block of districts in the mountain and northern plains regions, including Colorado, Utah, and North Dakota, used probation relatively heavily.[19] The authors of the study quote a distinguished legal journal to the effect that "what counts against the offender is not only *what* he does but *where* he does it."[20]

---

16. ABA Standards, Probation, § 6.5.

17. ABA Standards, Probation, § 6.1(b) states for example that it is appropriate for probation services to be administered at either state or local levels, but in no event should control be vested in an agency having prosecutorial functions.

18. Rubin, *supra,* at 248 reports the result of a national survey that showed that 31.6 percent of the offenders in twenty-five states studied were placed on probation or given a suspended sentence, but the percentage varied from 64.6 percent placed on probation in Rhode Island to 15.7 percent placed on probation in North Dakota. By 1984 the incidence of probation as a disposition ranges from 40 percent to 80 percent, depending upon the offense and jurisdiction.

19. Keith D. Harries and Russel P. Lura, *The Geography of Justice: Sentencing Variations in U.S. Judicial Districts.* Judicature, vol. 57, no. 9 (April 1974), 392–401.

20. *The Geography of Sentence,* 43 J.Crim.L. 363 (1952) as quoted. Id.

Similar research in California disclosed that the use of probation in California's superior courts varied from 12.5 percent in one county to 61.5 percent in two counties. The use of probation by judges varied for some judges from 12 percent or less of their cases to 61.5 percent of the cases of other judges.[21] This and subsequent studies that reached similar results brought about the establishment in 1966 of California's Probation Subsidy Program, under which the state offered financial inducements to counties that reduced their commitment rate to state institutions by placing more offenders on probation.

Changes in statutory sentencing structures, which mandate the use of probation except for in the most serious offenses, will, of course, require a rapid increase in the availability of probation services. Such changes are being recommended.[22]

Availability and Quality of Other Sentencing Dispositions

Granting probation also depends upon the availability and quality of other sentencing dispositions. If suspension of sentence or conditional release without supervision are available dispositions, one of these may better serve the needs of the particular offender than would probation. Probation plus a fine may be equitable in certain cases, or probation accompanied by a jail sentence may seem to the sentencing court to be a preferred disposition over "straight" probation without a jail sentence.

New dispositions, called periodic imprisonment or intermittent imprisonment, are coming into use.[23] Periodic imprisonment is a sentence of imprisonment served on certain days or during a certain period of days, or both, to permit a defendant to work, seek work, conduct a business, attend to family needs, attend an educational institution, or obtain medical or psychological treatment. Some offenders may be entitled to unconditional discharge, which is a disposition commonly available in juvenile courts but not often available to the adult offender who has been convicted of a felony. The court may also be influenced toward granting probation by its knowledge of deplorable conditions in the adult prison system or of lack of treatment in youth institutions, or by the fact that no specialized facilities such as are needed for sex offenders or narcotic addicts are available in the community or in the state institutions.

The deplorable conditions in some penal institutions have been brought to public attention by recent court decisions that have declared entire prison systems to be in violation of the Eighth Amendment prohibition against cruel

---

21. Second Interim Report of Special Study Commission on Correctional Facilities and Services: Probation, Jails and Parole. Sacramento (Jan. 16, 1957).

22. California Youth Authority, *California's Probation Subsidy Program: A Progress Report to the Legislature, 1966–1973.* Sacramento. Department of Youth Authority (January 1974).

The legislature should authorize the sentencing court in every case to impose a sentence of probation or a similar sentence not involving confinement. It may be appropriate to provide for limited exception to this principle but only for the most serious offenses such as murder or treason. ABA Standards Sentencing Alternatives and Procedures, § 2.3(a).

23. Tex.Rev.Civ.Stat.Ann. art. 5118b (Vernon), and Tex.Code Crim.Proc.Ann. art. 42.03 (Vernon).

and unusual punishment.[24] Similarly, sweeping "clean them up or close them up" decisions directed toward jails in both urban and rural communities have encouraged the enactment of misdemeanant probation statutes and increased the use of misdemeanor probation.[25] Juvenile dispositions are also influenced by the programs being offered in the juvenile institutions and even more by the lack of juvenile probation services in some areas. The rate of commitment to state juvenile institutions is routinely higher from counties where commitment is the only viable dispositional alternative.

The American Bar Association Standards Relating to Sentencing Alternatives and Procedures take a strong stand in favor of increasing the dispositional alternatives available to the sentencing judge. "The sentencing court should be provided in all cases with a wide range of alternatives, with gradations of supervisory, supportive and custodial facilities at its disposal so as to permit a sentence appropriate for each individual case," says the standard relating to statutory sentencing structure.[26] The necessity of developing on a statewide

---

24. Holt v. Sarver, 309 F.Supp. 362 (E.D.Ark.1970), *aff'd*, 442 F.2d 304 (8th Cir.1971); Landman v. Royster, 333 F.Supp. 621 (E.D.Va.1971).

25. Jails in all sections of the country have been affected. Sinclair v. Henderson, 331 F.Supp. 1123 (E.D.La.1971) [New Orleans Jail]; Taylor v. Sterrett, 344 F.Supp. 411 (N.D.Tex.1972) [Dallas County Jail]; Wayne County Jail Inmates, et al v. Wayne Co. Board of Commissioners, No. 73217 [1 Prison Law Reporter 5, 51, 186], Cir. Court Wayne Co.Mich. [Wayne Co. Jail]; Brenneman v. Madigan, 343 F.Supp. 128 (N.D.Cal.1972) [Alameda County Jail]; Jones v. Wittenberg, 323 F.Supp. 93, 330 F.Supp. 707 (N.D.Ohio 1971), *aff'd* Jones v. Metzger, 456 F.2d 854 (6th Cir.1972) [Lucas County Jail]; Hodge v. Dodd, No. 16171 [1 Prison Law Reporter 263] N.D. Georgia, May 2, 1972 [Gwinett Co. Jail]; Rhem v. McGrath, 326 F.Supp. 681 (D.C.N.Y.1971) [The Tombs, N.Y.]; Brown v. Pitches, No. C–24464, Los Angeles Co., Cal.Sup.Court, May 18, 1972 [Los Angeles Co. Jail]; Cruz v. Hauck, 404 U.S. 59, 92 S.Ct. 313, 30 L.Ed.2d 217 (1971); 475 F.2d 475 (5th Cir.1972) [Bexar County, Texas, Jail]; Jansson v. Grysen, No. 9–130–71 C.A. [1 Prison Law Reporter 256] W.D. Michigan, June 5, 1972 [Ottawa County Jail]; Garrison v. Hickman, No. 2280 [1 Prison Law Reporter 257] (Consent Order) W.D.Mo., June 7, 1972 [Jasper County Jail]; Reyes v. Hauck, 339 F.Supp. 195 (W.D.Texas, 1972) [Bexar County Jail]; Collins v. Schoonfield, 344 F.Supp. 257 (D.Md.1972) [Baltimore City Jail]; Jones v. Wittenberg, 323 F.Supp. 93 (N.D.Ohio, 1971) [Lucas County Jail]; United States v. Wyandotte County, Kansas, 343 F.Supp. 1189 (1972) [Wyandotte County Jail]; Hamilton v. Schiro, 338 F.Supp. 1016 (E.D.La.1971) [Orleans Parish Prison]; Brown v. United States, 342 F.Supp. 987 (E.D.Ark.1972) [Pulaski County Jail]; Inmates of Suffolk County Jail v. Eisenstadt, No. 71–162–G [2 Prison Law Reporter 389] D.Mass., June 20, 1973 [Suffolk County Jail]; Obadele v. McAdory, No. 725–103(N) [Prison Law Reporter 413] S.D.Miss., June 19, 1973 [Hines County Mississippi Jail].

26. ABA Standards, Sentencing Alternatives and Procedures, § 2.1(b).

Examples of types of dispositions which might be authorized are set out in Standard 2.4(a) as follows: Attention should be directed to the development of a range of sentencing alternatives which provide an intermediate sanction between supervised probation on the one hand and commitment to a total custody institution on the other and which permit the development of an individualized treatment program for each offender. Examples of the types of dispositions which might be authorized are: (i) confinement for selected periods to a local facility designed to provide educational or other rehabilitative services; (ii) commitment to a local facility which permits the offender to hold a regular job while subject to supervision or confinement on nights and weekends; (iii) commitment to an institution for a short, fixed term, followed by automatic release under supervision.

Special facilities are said to be desirable, as set out in Standard 2.6(a): It is desirable, both on a local and on a statewide, areawide or nationwide basis, that facilities be developed to provide special treatment for certain types of offenders, particularly the young, and that the court be authorized as a sentencing alternative to employ such facilities in appropriate cases. *Id.*, § 2.1(b).

basis facilities to provide for special treatment of certain types of offenders, particularly for the young, is also emphasized.[27]

An increased use of diversion strategies will tend to reduce the use of "straight" probation, but may not reduce the need for probation services since many diversion programs involve probation-type supervision of the offender. An increase in halfway houses, day-care centers, and specialized institutions for the care of alcoholics and drug addicts will provide the sentencing authority with additional dispositional alternatives that may tend to reduce the use of probation. On the other hand, making probation the usual and preferred disposition will place new burdens on probation services. It is evident that the relationship of probation or other sentencing dispositions is changing as sentencing philosophy and the availability of other dispositional alternatives for the care and custody of the offender also change.[28]

Methods of Developing
Sentencing Information

The information required to enable a judge to impose an appropriate sentence is developed in a postplea hearing, in a presentence investigation, or in some states, in a presentence conference. In jury sentencing, a sentencing hearing is held at which the jury is furnished with information about the defendant's general reputation and character.

If probation is one of the dispositions being considered, the need for accurate and complete information is particularly evident. Not all offenders will benefit from probation. Some offenders must be incarcerated, either for the public good or because the offender needs specialized treatment that is not available in connection with probation. In some cases, the nature and circumstances of the crime dictate incarceration of the offender, especially if the public's ideas of fairness and justice in the criminal process are to be upheld and vindicated. Granting probation thus demands an investigative process that will inform the

---

27. *Id.*, § 2.6.

28. *See, for example,* Nat'l Advisory Comm'n. Standards, Corrections, which recommend adding sufficient probation staff to handle expanded Release on Recognizance (ROR) programs. Standard 10.05—Probation in Release on Recognizance Programs.

Each probation office serving a community or metropolitan area of more than 100,000 persons that does not already have an effective release on recognizance program should immediately develop, in cooperation with the court, additional staff and procedures to investigate arrested adult defendants for possible release on recognizance while awaiting trial, to avoid unnecessary use of detention in jail.

1. The staff used in the ROR investigations should not be probation officers but persons trained in interviewing, investigation techniques, and report preparation.

2. The staff should collect information relating to defendant's residence, past and present; employment status; financial condition; prior record if any; and family, relatives, or others, particularly those living in the immediate area who may assist him in attending court at the proper time.

3. Where appropriate, staff making the investigation should recommend to the court any conditions that should be imposed on the defendant if released on recognizance.

4. The probation agency should provide pretrial intervention services to persons released on recognizance.

sentencing authority of the circumstances of the offense and the nature of the offender.

Of the three methods of obtaining sentencing information, the one most closely identified with the granting of probation is the presentence investigation.[29] In fact, the origins of the presentence investigation can be traced to the use of probation as a disposition. In many states, the only time a presentence investigation is required by law is when the offender is to be placed on probation.[30] In such cases the statutory authority and statutory requirements for the presentence investigation and report are contained in the probation statutes. In juvenile court, the judge is routinely furnished with a social history report prior to the dispositional hearing.

Presentence reports are seldom required or used in misdemeanor probation. In some instances, this is because there is no provision made for misdemeanor probation. When a presentence report is prepared in a misdemeanor case, it will be shorter and more summary in nature. In practice, the judge who sentences for a misdemeanor relies upon the police officer for information about the defendant's previous criminal history and the circumstances of the offense. The defendant is usually given a right to speak to the question of sentencing and the judge may question the defendant about the defendant's family and circumstances.

New York law has codified the common law right of allocution, which is the right of the defendant to speak to the sentence.[31] The defendant is also given the right to submit a written memorandum that sets forth any information that may be pertinent to the question of sentence.[32] One or more presentence conferences may be held to resolve conflicts and discrepancies in sentencing information received by the court and to assist the court in its consideration of the sentence.[33]

---

29. See Chapter 3, *infra*, Preparation and Use of the Presentence Report.

30. Though no person is to be placed on probation and execution of sentence is not to be suspended without probation report, a sentence may be imposed without a report in discretion of the court. People v. Barrett, 33 A.D.2d 633, 305 N.Y.S.2d 111 (1969).

31. McKinney Consol.Laws CPL § 380.50.

32. *Id.,* § 390.40.

33. The method of conducting the presentence conference is set out:

Presentence conference. 1. Authorization and purpose. Before pronouncing sentence, the court, in its discretion, may hold one or more presentence conferences in open court or in chambers to (a) resolve any discrepancies between the presentence report, or other information the court has received, and the defendant's presentence memorandum submitted pursuant to § 390.40 or (b) assist the court in its consideration of any matter relevant to the sentence to be pronounced.

2. Attendance. Such conference may be held with defense counsel in absence of the defendant, or the court may direct the defendant attend. The court may also direct that any person who has furnished or who can furnish information to the court concerning sentence attend. Reasonable notice of the conference must be given to the prosecutor, who must be afforded an opportunity to participate therein.

3. Procedure at conference. The court may advise the persons present at the conference of the factual contents of any report or memorandum it has received and afford any of the participants an opportunity to controvert or to comment upon any fact. The court may also conduct a summary hearing at the conference on any matter relevant to sentence and may take testimony under oath. In the discretion of the court, all or any part of the proceedings at the conference may be recorded by a court stenographer and the transcript made part of the presentence report. *Id.,* § 400.10.

The American Bar Association Standards Relating to Sentencing Alternatives and Procedures recommend a presentence conference [34] and the development of a broad range of services and facilities from which the court can obtain more complete information about the defendant's mental, emotional, and physical condition.[35] The National Advisory Commission Standards *Corrections* set up a sentencing hearing specifying the duties of defense counsel to become familiar with sentencing alternatives to be followed with a recommended sentence that "most accurately meets the needs of his client and enhances his liberty." [36]

Probation as an Appropriate Disposition

Once it has been established that probation is available as a sentencing alternative, that the sentencing tribunal has authority to grant probation, that the offender before the court is eligible for probation, that probation services are available, and that other sentencing dispositions are not mandated or more desirable, there then remains the most important consideration to be evaluated in the decision to grant or withhold probation—namely, the appropriateness of probation to the particular offender. Individualized justice, that noble ideal of the criminal justice system, demands that the penalty fit not only the crime but the criminal. When one of the available alternatives in the sentencing process is probation, the conditions that accompany it must be affirmatively determined to be an appropriate disposition of the particular offender, and the equally important objectives of protection of society and the maintenance of social order must be carefully weighed. Does this mean that the eligible offender has a *right* to probation? A related question is: Does the offender have the right to refuse probation?

Right to Probation

The general rule is that eligibility for probation does not infer a right to probation. Probation is awarded and withheld at the discretion of the sentencing court. To phrase it differently, the decision to grant or withhold probation is a discretionary act of the trial court and there is neither a constitutional or statutory right to probation. However, the statutes provide for probation and the eligible offender has a right to be *considered* for probation. When the statute provides for a class of offenders to be considered for probation, the defendant is entitled to fair treatment and is not to be made the victim of whim or caprice. Thus, it has been declared that a judge was in error for considering probation only for defendants who pleaded guilty and for refusing to consider probation for a defendant who pleaded not guilty and stood trial. The court in the one case carefully pointed out that there was nothing to bar the judge who entertains an application to probation from considering [*among other things*] whether the

---

34. ABA Standards, Sentencing Alternatives and Procedures, § 4.5.

35. *Id.,* § 4.6.

36. National Advisory Commission Standards, Corrections Standard 5.18—Sentencing Hearing: Role of Counsel

Sentencing courts should immediately develop and implement guidelines as to the role of defense counsel and prosecution in achieving sentencing objectives.

defendant pleaded guilty or stood trial when the defendant had only a frivolous defense. The error occurred when the judge refused to consider as a class all defendants who had stood trial.[37] A judge who announced that he could "never grant probation to a drug pusher," committed a similar error.[38]

In a few recent cases the appellate courts have ordered a trial court to place a defendant on probation even when the language of the statute was permissive.[39] The general rule has long been that review of a trial court's refusal to place a defendant on probation is limited to the extent of ascertaining whether the trial court did, in fact, exercise discretion or whether it acted in an arbitrary manner. The New Jersey reviewing court that in effect ordered the trial court to grant probation, said that the "sentencing judges should direct the punishments they impose to the goal of reformation," and directed probation for a first offender who was charged with possession of a small amount of marijuana.[40]

Acceptance of Probation

The general rule is that probation cannot be imposed upon a defendant without the defendant's consent. If conditions are imposed without the consent of the defendant, and then violated, there is a question of whether or not the violation can be used to revoke probation. The laws of several states thus provide that individuals being granted probation must be furnished with a written statement of the terms of their probation and that they must accept the conditions of probation before being given their liberty.

Appeal from an
Order Granting Probation

The question of whether a probationer is entitled to appeal from an order granting probation and thus from the conditions imposed in that order presents some difficulties. The difficulties arise from the legal uncertainty as to whether an order granting probation is a "final order" from which an appeal may lie, and from the fact that in some states probation is seen as an act of clemency.[41] Generally, defendants may appeal from any final order or decree adverse to them. A conviction followed by a fine or sentence of imprisonment has quite uniformly been held to be a final order from which an appeal may lie, but there has been less agreement when the question regards the right to appeal from a conviction that is followed by probation or a suspended sentence.

---

37. United States v. Wiley, 267 F.2d 453 (7th Cir.1959), *on remand* 184 F.Supp. 679 (N.D.Ill.E.D. 1960).

38. *See also* Burns v. United States, 287 U.S. 216, 53 S.Ct. 154, 77 L.Ed. 266 (1932).

39. People v. Harpole, 97 Ill.App.2d 28, 239 N.E.2d 471 (1968); People v. Seaman, 40 A.D.2d 944, 339 N.Y.S.2d 245 (1972); People v. McAndrew, 96 Ill.App.2d 441, 239 N.E.2d 314 (1968); State of New Jersey v. Ward, 57 N.J. 75, 270 A.2d 1 (1970).

40. State of New Jersey v. Ward, 57 N.J. 75, 270 A.2d 1 (1970).

41. There is language in some California cases to the effect that probation is an act of clemency. People v. Bagley, 218 Cal.App.2d 809, 32 Cal.Rptr. 663 (1963); People v. Fernandez, 222 Cal.App.2d 760, 35 Cal.Rptr. 370 (1963).

The trend of the law is to eliminate the obstacles to appeal by a defendant placed on probation. Recommended standards on probation suggest that probation statutes should provide for the right to appeal.[42]

Collateral Attack upon Conditions of Probation

The usual method of changing or modifying the terms and conditions of probation as originally imposed is by motion or application filed in the sentencing court. As to any changes or modifications not sought by the probationer, the probationer should have prior notice of the request for change and an opportunity to be heard. If the proposed change would lead to a longer term on probation or to confinement, the procedures for notification and hearing should be generally equivalent to those set up for revocation of probation. If the modifications are sought by the probationer, easy access to the court for the purposes of clarification or modification should be provided.[43] When the probationer objects to terms and conditions as set forth in the original order granting probation, but cannot secure the desired change or modification from the sentencing court, the probationer's recourse may be an appeal from the order granting probation, if such appeal is provided for in the probationer's jurisdiction. However, an appellate court seldom modifies the terms or conditions of probation set by a sentencing court unless the terms and conditions are illegal or incapable of being performed. Also, the need for change and modification in the term or conditions for probation may arise after the period for appeal from the order granting probation has expired. In such a situation, the probationer must resort to the legal remedy that permits a collateral attack upon the order granting probation. By collateral attack, we mean an attempt to avoid, defeat, or evade a conviction order of the court by using an incidental proceeding that is not part of the appeal process. The legal remedies most widely used for this purpose are the common law writ of habeas corpus and special postconviction procedures set up by statute.[44]

Habeas corpus and postconviction procedures will be discussed more fully in the chapter on the legal rights of probationers.[45] We should note here, however, that the use of the writ of habeas corpus for the purpose of changing or modifying conditions of probation or parole has always presented particular problems, arising out of the fact that habeas corpus is historically "the great writ of liberty," the remedy of deliverance from illegal custody. Since the probationer whose probation has not been revoked is not under physical restraint, many courts refuse to extend the use of the writ where the remedy sought is merely a

---

42. ABA Standards, Probation, § 1.1(e) provides that a sentence to probation should be treated as a final judgment for purposes of appeal and similar procedural purposes.

43. *See for example,* ABA Standards, Probation, § 3.3.

44. A remedy is collateral if it does not seek to challenge the verity of the trial itself (as does appeal). Petition for habeas corpus and post-conviction motions are generally considered to be a separate civil proceeding as distinguished from the original criminal case. Heflin v. United States, 358 U.S. 415, 79 S.Ct. 451, 3 L.Ed.2d 407 (1959).

45. *See also,* Kerper and Kerper, Convicted, pp. 207–210, 219–244, 258–276, 321–325.

change in the conditions of liberty.[46]   Other jurisdictions have moved away from the "total release" requirement of the ancient writ of habeas corpus and permit the use of the writ to challenge the conditions of probation and parole.[47]

Special postconviction procedures set up by statute frequently recognize the rights of persons not in custody to use habeas corpus to test existing restraints upon their liberty such as those associated with probation and parole.   The American Bar Association Standards Relating to Post Conviction Remedies recommend the waiving of the custody requirement, declaring that postconviction relief should not be dependent upon the applicant's attacking a sentence of imprisonment then being served or another present restraint, "Even though the challenged sentence did not commit the applicant to prison, but was rather a fine, probation, or suspended sentence." [48]

The probationer or parolee, who seeks to test the terms and conditions imposed after the time for appeal is passed, will need legal assistance to identify the remedy available and the extent of the relief afforded.   Since habeas corpus and other postconviction remedies are seen as civil actions, the probationer or parolee is not generally entitled to counsel at state expense.

---

46. Parker v. Ellis, 362 U.S. 574, 80 S.Ct. 909, 4 L.Ed.2d 963 (1960).

47. Jones v. Cunningham, 371 U.S. 236, 83 S.Ct. 373, 9 L.Ed.2d 285 (1962) (parole). California extends the writ to probationers, In re Hernandez, 64 Cal.2d 850, 51 Cal.Rptr. 915, 415 P.2d 803 (1966); and parolees, *Ex parte* Collie, 38 Cal.2d 396, 240 P.2d 275 (1952), *cert. den.* 345 U.S. 1000, 73 S.Ct. 1145, 97 L.Ed. 1406 (1953).

In Texas, the writ is applicable in all cases of confinement and restraint where there is no lawful right in the person exercising the power, or where, though the power in fact exists, it is exercised in a manner or degree not sanctioned by law.   Tex.Code Crim.Proc.Ann. art. 11.23 (Vernon).

48. ABA Standards, Post-Conviction Remedies, § 2.3. *See also* Second Revised Uniform Post-Conviction Procedure Act, § 1(a)(5).

Sentencing and Corrections*

The Sentencing of Criminal Offenders is a Reflection of Multiple and Often Conflicting Social Objectives

These objectives are—

• **Rehabilitation**—removing or remediating presumed causes of crime by providing economic, psychological, or socialization assistance to offenders to reduce the likelihood of continuing in crime

• **Deterrence**—sanctioning convicted offenders to reduce crime by making the public and the offender aware of the certainty and severity of punishment for criminal behavior

• **Incapacitation**—separating offenders from the community to reduce the opportunity for further commission of crime

• **Retribution**—punishing offenders to express societal disapproval of criminal behavior without specific regard to prevention of crime by the offender or among the general public.

Attitudes About Sentencing Reflect Multiple Objectives and Other Factors

Hogarth's research on judicial sentencing attitudes and practices has shown that judges vary greatly in their commitment to one or more of these objectives when imposing sentences. Public opinion, as well, shows considerable divergence about the objectives to be served in sentencing. Like judges and the general public, legislators and the criminal penalties they fashion tend to mirror this lack of consensus.

Further complicating sentencing laws is the need for such penalties to be grounded in concerns for—

• **Fairness**—the severity of the punishment should be commensurate with the crime

• **Equity**—like crimes should be treated alike

• **Social debt**—the severity of punishment should take into account prior criminal behavior.

---

* Reprinted from U.S. Department of Justice, *Report to the Nation on Crime and Justice,* (Washington: Bureau of Justice Statistics, Oct. 1983).

Judges are Usually Given a Wide Range of Discretion in Sentencing Offenders

Maximum sentences are generally set by law, but judges can sometimes impose—

• Alternatives to imprisonment such as probation, fines, restitution to victims, or community service (such as cleaning up a public park),

• Combined sentences of a short period in a local jail (or prison in some States) followed by probation in the community, or

• Sentences to prison with a minimum time to be served in confinement or they can leave the sentence duration indeterminate (to be set by paroling authorities).

Disparity and Uncertainty Resulted from the Lack of Consensus Over Sentencing Goals

By the early 1970's, researchers and critics of the justice system began to reveal that the mixed goals of the justice system and the discretionary opportunities for judges to fashion sanctions had—

• Reduced the *certainty* of sanctions, thereby presumably eroding the deterrent effect of corrections,

• Resulted in disparity in the *severity* of punishment with differences in the length and duration of sentences, and

• Been based on assumptions that could not be validated about the ability of various programs to change offender behavior or predict future criminality.

Sentencing Reforms of the 1970's Took Two Approaches—Administrative and Statutory

The administrative approach called on judges and parole boards to accept and apply voluntary guidelines for the kind and duration of punishment to be imposed on offenders for each type of crime and to regularize the sentencing adjustments made for such factors as the seriousness of the offense and the offender's criminal record.

The statutory approach called for laws that specify mandatory prison terms for specific crimes and fixed terms of imprisonment for certain classes of crimes.

Reforms of the 1970's sought to—

• Clarify the aims of sentencing
• Reduce disparity and discretion
• Channel limited resources into a more predictable penalty system
• Provide sanctions consistent with the "just deserts" concept.

Between 1975 and 1982—

• 10 States, beginning with Maine, abolished their parole boards

• Several States established administrative guidelines for determining parole release to minimize disparities in the length of prison stay

• More than 35 States enacted laws that require minimum sentences to incarceration for specified crimes

• Many States began to experiment with new forms of sentencing guidelines designed by the judiciary or by appointed sentencing commissions.

How many people are under some form of correctional supervision?

More than 1% of the U.S. population is under some form of correctional sanction.

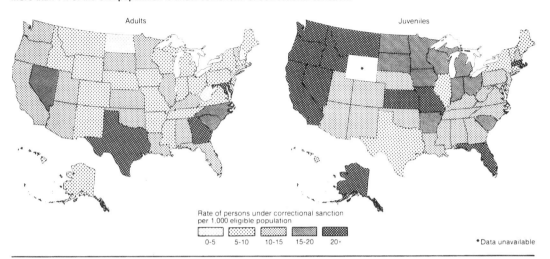

Adults   Juveniles

Rate of persons under correctional sanction
per 1,000 eligible population

0-5   5-10   10-15   15-20   20+   *Data unavailable

Sources: "Prisoners in 1981," BJS bulletin, May 1982 "Census of jails and survey of jail inmates: Preliminary report," NPS bulletin SD-NPS-J-6P, February 1979. *Children in custody, 1979*, U.S. Bureau of the Census, forthcoming. "Probation and parole," BJS bulletin, August 1982. *State and local probation and parole systems*, February 1978.

Resident population—U.S. Bureau of the Census Supplementary Report P-25, number 913. Data on 1979 eligible juvenile population provided by U.S. Bureau of the Census, August 1982.

More than 2.4 million persons are estimated to be under some form of correctional care, custody or supervision

- 1.2% of all adults over age 18
- 1 in 45 adult males
- 1 in 441 adult females
- 1.5% of all eligible juveniles (age 10-17)

Adults (total)	1,973,000
Prison	369,000
Jail	158,000
Parole/other	224,000
Probation	1,222,000
Juveniles (total)	455,000
Detention*	74,000
Parole/aftercare	53,000
Probation	328,000

* In public and private facilities

Sources: *Prisoners in State and Federal institutions 1981*. *Survey of jail inmates 1978*. *Parole in the United States 1979*. *Probation in the United States 1979*. *Juveniles in custody 1979*. *State and local probation and parole systems, 1978*.

Three out of four persons under correctional sanction are being supervised in the community.

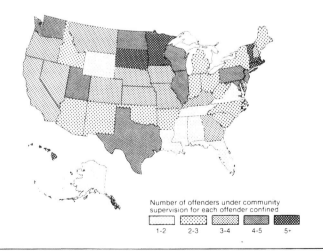

Number of offenders under community
supervision for each offender confined

1-2   2-3   3-4   4-5   5+

Sources: "Prisoners in 1981," BJS bulletin, May 1982. "Census of jails and survey of jail inmates: Preliminary report," NPS bulletin SD-NPS-J-6P, February 1979. Children in custody, 1979. Office of

Juvenile Justice and Delinquency Prevention. "Probation and parole," BJS bulletin, August 1982. *State and local probation and parole systems*, February 1978.

Current Sentencing Alternatives Reflect Multiple Objectives

What Types of Sentences Are Usually Given to Offenders?

Death penalty—In some States for certain crimes such as murder, the courts may sentence an offender to death by eletrocution, exposure to lethal gas, hanging, lethal injection, or other method specified by State law.

- As of 1982, 36 States had death penalty provisions in law.
- Most death penalty sentences have been for murder.
- As of year end 1982, six persons had been executed since 1977; and 1,050 inmates in 31 States were under a sentence of death.

Incarceration—The confinement of a convicted criminal in a Federal or State prison or a local jail to serve a court-imposed sentence. Custody is usually within a jail, administered locally, or a prison, operated by the State or the Federal government. In many States, offenders sentenced to less than 1 year are held in a jail; those sentenced to longer terms are committed to the State prison.

- More than 4,300 correctional facilities are maintained by Federal, State, or local governments including 43 Federal facilities, 791 State-operated adult confinement and community-based correctional facilities, and 3,500 local jails which are usually county-operated.
- On a given day in 1982, approximately 412,000 persons were confined in State and Federal prisons and approximately 210,000 persons were confined in local jails.

Probation—The sentencing of an offender to community supervision by a probation agency, often as a result of suspending a sentence to confinement. Such supervision normally entails the provision of specific rules of conduct while in the community. If violated, a sentencing judge may impose a sentence to confinement. It is the most widely used correctional disposition in the United States.

- State or local governments operate more than 2,000 probation agencies. These agencies supervise nearly 1.6 million adults and juveniles on probation.

Split sentences and shock probation—A penalty that explicitly requires the convicted person to serve a period of confinement in a local, State or Federal facility (the "shock") followed by a period of probation. This penalty attempts to combine the use of community supervision with a short incarceration experience.

- 1977 and 1978 California data reveal that by far the most common disposition in felony cases was a combined sentence of jail and probation.

Restitution—The requirement that the offender provide financial remuneration for the losses incurred by the victim.

- By 1979, nearly all States had statutory provisions for the collection and disbursement of restitution funds. In late 1982, a restitution law was enacted at the Federal level.

Community service—The requirement that the offender provide a specified number of hours of public service work, such as collecting trash in parks or other public facilities.

- By 1979, nearly a third of the States authorized community service work orders. Community service is often imposed as a specific condition of probation.

Fines—An economic penalty that requires the offender to pay a specific sum of money within the limit set by law. Fines are often imposed in addition to probation or as an alternative to incarceration.

• Many laws that govern the imposition of fines are undergoing revision. These revisions often provide for more flexible means of ensuring equality in the imposition of fines, flexible fine schedules, "day fines" geared to the offender's daily wage, installment payment of fines, and a restriction of confinement to situations that amount to intentional refusal to pay.

Changes in Sentencing Have Resulted in Changes in Correctional Practices

Many of the sentencing reforms have led to changes in the way correctional systems operate.

• The growth of determinate and mandatory sentences over the past decade and dissatisfaction with the uncertainties of indeterminate sentences (particularly the concept of linking sentence duration to rehabilitative progress or predictions of future behavior by paroling authorities) have led, perhaps most important, to modifications of the parole decision. Many States are experimenting with parole guidelines systems and amendments to good-time and other incentives for controlling behavior during confinement and determining a release date.

• New administrative requirements have also been attached to such traditional correctional practices as collecting victim restitution funds; imposing fees for probation supervision, room and board, and services provided; and operating community-service punishments.

• The various sentencing reforms have led to small changes in the correctional clientele, such as lowering the age of juvenile court jurisdiction in some States; enactment of guilty but mentally ill provisions in a few States; and, in a small number of jurisdictions, the recent advent of laws providing for life sentences without parole.

States Primarily Use Three Strategies for Sentencing

• **Indeterminate sentences** usually provide a minimum and a maximum term, either of which may be reduced by "good time" (time credits gained by inmates for good conduct or special achievement) or by a decision of the paroling authorities. The maximum sentence may be set as a range (for example, 5 to 10 years) rather than a specific number of years.

• **Determinate sentences** usually provide a fixed term that may be reduced by good time or parole. Judicial discretion may be available to grant probation or suspend the sentence. Sentencing laws generally provide a maximum (or a range) for sentence duration. Determinate systems are usually based on a definite length for a sentence that can be increased or decreased for aggravating or mitigating factors or on guidelines that define sentence lengths, deviations from which must be justified by sentencing judges.

• **Mandatory prison sentences** are defined by law and must be given upon conviction; the judge is not permitted to grant probation or to suspend the sentence.

Most States Apply a Combination of Sentencing Strategies

Many States may have a predominant orientation toward one strategy (for example, indeterminate) and require another strategy (for example, mandatory sentences) for specific offenses. The strategies utilized by States are constantly evolving, thus complicating overall classification. As of September 1981, for example, some States that required mandatory prison sentences for certain offenses used a predominantly indeterminate strategy while others used a determinate strategy.

Most States Have Some Mandatory Sentencing Provisions

	Type of sentencing	Mandatory sentencing	Mandatory offenses
Alabama	Determinate	Yes	Repeat felony
Alaska	Determinate, presumptive	Yes	Murder, kidnaping, firearms, repeat felony
Arizona	Determinate, presumptive	Yes	Firearms, prior felony convictions
Arkansas	Determinate	Yes	Robbery, deadly weapons
California	Determinate, presumptive	No	
Colorado	Determinate, presumptive	No	
Connecticut	Determinate	Yes	Sex assault with firearm, burglary, repeat felony, assault on elderly
Delaware	Determinate	Yes	Murder, kidnaping, prison assault, robbery, narcotics, deadly weapon, habitual criminal, obscenity, others
Florida	Indeterminate	Yes	Drug
Georgia	Determinate	Yes	Armed robbery, burglary, drugs
Hawaii	Indeterminate	No	
Idaho	Determinate	Yes	Firearm, repeat extortion, kidnap or rape with bodily injury
Illinois	Determinate	Yes	Major offenses, specified felonies and offenses, repeaters, weapons
Indiana	Determinate, presumptive	Yes	Repeat felony, violent crime, deadly weapons
Iowa	Indeterminate	Yes	Forcible felonies, firearms, habitual offenders, drugs
Kansas	Indeterminate	Yes	Sex offense, firearms
Kentucky	Indeterminate	No	
Louisiana	Indeterminate	Yes	Drugs, violent crime
Maine	Determinate	No	

Maryland	Determinate, guidelines	Yes	Repeat violent offenders, handgun
Massachusetts	Indeterminate	Yes	Firearm, auto theft, drug trafficking
Michigan	Indeterminate	Yes	Murder, armed robbery, treason, firearms
Minnesota	Guidelines	No	
Mississippi	Determinate	Yes	Armed robbery, repeat felony
Missouri	Determinate	Yes	Dangerous weapon, repeat felony
Montana	Indeterminate	Yes	Firearms
Nebraska	Indeterminate	No	
Nevada	Determinate	Yes	2nd degree murder, 1st degree kidnaping, sexual assault, firearm, repeat felony
New Hampshire	Indeterminate	Yes	Firearms
New Jersey	Determinate, presumptive	Yes	Sexual assault, firearms
New Mexico	Determinate, presumptive	Yes	Firearms
New York	Indeterminate	Yes	Specified violent and nonviolent felonies
North Carolina	Determinate, presumptive	Yes	Armed robbery, 1st degree burglary, repeat with firearm
North Dakota	Determinate	Yes	Firearm
Ohio	Indeterminate	Yes	Rape, drug trafficking
Oklahoma	Determinate	Yes	Repeat felony
Oregon	Guidelines, indeterminate	Yes	Drugs
Pennsylvania *	Guidelines, indeterminate	Yes	Selected felonies with firearms, within 7 years prior convictions, in or near public transportation
Rhode Island	Indeterminate	No	
South Carolina	Determinate	Yes	Armed robbery, drugs, bomb threat
South Dakota	Indeterminate	No	
Tennessee	Determinate, indeterminate	Yes	Specified felonies, firearms, repeat felony
Texas	Determinate	Yes	Repeat felony, violent offenses
Utah	Indeterminate	No	
Vermont	Indeterminate	Yes	Drugs, violent crime
Virginia	Indeterminate	No	
Washington	Indeterminate	Yes	Firearms, rape, repeat felony

West Virginia	Indeterminate	Yes	Firearms in felony
Wisconsin	Indeterminate	No	
Wyoming	Indeterminate	No	

* Pennsylvania updated as of December 1982.

Sources: *A survey of mandatory sentencing in the U.S.,* Richard S. Morelli, Craig Edelman, Roy Willoughby, Pennsylvania Commission on Crime and Delinquency, *September 1981. Judicial and executive discretion in the sentencing process: Analysis of felony State code provisions,* Criminal Courts Technical Assistance Project (Washington: American University, January 1982). *A national survey of parole-related legislation.* Michael Kanvensohn, (San Francisco: Uniform Parole Reports, December 1979).

In All States, a Majority of Offenders Are Under Community Supervision Rather than Confinement

	Confined		Under supervision			Confined		Under supervision	
	Adults *	Juveniles *	Adults *	Juveniles *		Adults *	Juveniles *	Adults *	Juveniles *
Alabama	12,468	770	15,382	5,476	New Mexico	2,279	572	4,624	1,655
Alaska	1,062	373	1,454	892	New York	36,510	4,716	88,551	11,963
Arizona	7,695	1,218	15,608	3,944	North Carolina	18,557	1,201	45,247	7,244
Arkansas	4,560	901	6,718	4,546	North Dakota	425	193	1,227	1,403
California	57,453 *	14,859	166,677	57,225	Ohio	20,345	3,734	36,471	21,669
Colorado	4,430	1,191	13,871	3,868	Oklahoma	6,924	1,265	17,400	4,197
Connecticut	4,647	614	26,962	2,296	Oregon	5,137	1,239	15,943	7,317
Delaware	1,716	206	4,517	800	Pennsylvania	15,763	3,272	63,361	16,975
Florida	33,501	2,740	51,582	16,372	Rhode Island	962	207	5,959	2,194
Georgia	22,299	1,419	66,202	10,259	South Carolina	10,855	767	22,476	7,136
Hawaii	1,202	145	5,465	1,245	South Dakota	946	382	5,259	1,359
Idaho	1,492	307	2,462	2,531	Tennessee	12,375	1,546	13,510	7,672
Illinois	19,257	1,691	74,196	10,376	Texas	42,433	3,118	173,473	15,728
Indiana	10,355	2,048	24,255	11,662	Utah	1,815	438	8,119	1,683
Iowa	3,367	814	10,635	5,387	Vermont	534	142	3,671	332
Kansas	3,746	1,425	14,162	5,152	Virginia	13,465	1,613	18,316	8,215
Kentucky	6,082	925	22,300	5,085	Washington	7,773	1,631	29,050	9,557
Louisiana	14,622	1,424	17,793	5,672	West Virginia	2,356	286	3,335	9,103
Maine	1,185	466	3,182	976	Wisconsin	6,242	1,273	22,920	
Maryland	12,888	1,547	54,200	7,019	Wyoming	802		1,335	
Massachusetts	6,096	804	30,618	15,222	Federal	28,133		65,293	
Michigan	20,700	2,714	32,135	18,701					
Minnesota	3,528	1,450	33,633	8,179	U.S. total	526,408	71,792	1,445,798	381,194
Mississippi	6,983	442	8,402	3,991					
Missouri	8,983	1,516	22,140	12,383					
Montana	1,102	291	3,011	2,097					
Nebraska	2,271	745	8,025	2,227					
Nevada	3,037	452	6,843	3,464					
New Hampshire	746	400	2,337	1,196					
New Jersey	10,831	1,815	45,032	12,045					

* Includes estimated 2,093 adult inmates under the jurisdiction of the California Youth Authority.

** Juvenile data from Wyoming excluded to protect confidentiality guarantees.

Sources: *Prisoners in 1981,* BJS bulletin, May 1982. *Census of jails and survey of jail inmates: Preliminary report,* NPS bulletin SD–NPS–J–6P (Washington D.C. Department of Justice, February 1979). *Children in custody 1979* (Washington: U.S. Bureau of the Census, forthcoming). *Probation and parole,* BJS bulletin, August 1982. *State and local probation and parole systems,* February 1978.

3

The Presentence Investigation

Functions and Objectives

The device of the presentence investigation report is one of the major contributions of probation to the administration of criminal justice. As early as 1931, one writer stated, "No court should ever undertake the disposition of an offender without being fully advised through an investigation concerning his antecedents, environment, and personality, including his physical and mental condition. Only when these facts are correctly presented can the court act intelligently and constructively." [1]

The recent American Bar Association Standards Relating to Probation states: [2]

(a) All courts trying criminal cases should be supplied with the resources and supporting staff to permit a presentence investigation and a written report of its results in every case.

(b) The court should explicitly be authorized by statute to call for such an investigation and report in every case. The statute should also provide that such an investigation and report should be made in every case where incarceration of one year or more is a possible disposition, where the defendant is less than twenty-one years old, or where the defendant is a first offender, unless the court specifically orders to the contrary in a particular case.

The American Bar Association also recognizes that although the primary purpose of the presentence report is to provide the sentencing court with succinct and precise information upon which to base a rational sentencing decision, potential use of the report by other agencies should be a factor in determining the content and length of the report.

---

1. Smyth, *Organizing a County Probation Department,* Yearbook, National Probation Association (1931), 91 et seq.

2. ABA Standards, Probation, Standard 2.1.

The American Correctional Association Standards for Adult Probation and Parole Field Services states:

> The primary purpose of the presentence report shall be to provide the sentencing court with timely, relevant and accurate data to identify the most appropriate sentencing alternative and correctional disposition. The secondary purpose of the presentence report shall be to serve the needs of any correctional institution or field agency which may receive the offender.[3]

The original function of presentence reports was to assist the court in resolving the issue of whether to employ probation. Over the years, however, many new and important uses for the information gathered by the report have been found. The total use to which presentence reports are now put encompasses the entire range of correctional programs.

The Presentence Investigation Report,[4] a monograph prepared to guide U.S. probation officers in preparing presentence reports, delineates five functions of the report:

(1) to aid the Court in determining the appropriate sentence;

(2) to assist the Bureau of Prisons institutions in their classification, institutional programs and also in their release planning;

(3) to furnish the U.S. Parole Commission with information pertinent to its consideration of parole;

(4) to aid the probation officer in his supervision efforts during probation and parole, and;

(5) to serve as a source of information for research.[5]

Contents of the Presentence Report

What are the essentials of a good presentence report? One of the earliest references, in 1910, held that the purpose of the presentence report was "to learn the character and ability of the person under consideration, the influences that surround him and those that may be brought to bear in the event of probation."[6]

One author held that, "What the investigation seeks is a full understanding of the offender from the point of view of his possible *reintegration* into society as a self-sufficient and permanently useful member."[7]

---

3. American Correctional Association Standards for Adult Probation and Parole Field Services, 1981, p. 196.

4. Administrative Office of the U.S. Courts, *The Presentence Investigation Report,* Publication No. 105 (Washington: GPO, 1978).

5. The Administrative Office of the U.S. Courts first published "The Presentence Investigation Report" in 1965. In that year among the five functions of the report delineated were terms such as *treatment programs;* changed to *institutional programs* in the 1978 version and *to aid the probation officer in his rehabilitation efforts* . . .; changed to *supervision efforts* in the 1978 version. [italics ours] This subtle change in wording reflects the movement of correctional philosophy from a *treatment* to a *just deserts* or *justice* model orientation.

6. Bolster, *Adult Probation, Parole and Suspended Sentence* 1 J.Crim.L. 444 (1910).

7. Ferris, "The Case History in Probation Service," *in* Glueck, Probation and Criminology (1933).

The *Presentence Investigation Report* monograph of 1965 stated that a satisfactory report "describes the defendant's character and personality, evaluates his or her problems and needs, helps the reader understand the world in which the defendant lives, reveals the nature of his or her relationships with people, and discloses those factors which underlie the defendant's specific offense and conduct in general. It suggests alternatives for sentencing and the supervision process." [8]

And, in 1982, the presentence report was described as delineating "the major internal and external factors which made the person become an offender, which of these forces are still operational and what are the expected effects of the various alternatives in sentencing." [9]

The model presentence report developed for U.S. probation officers utilizes a "core" concept. Certain information, identified as the core, is essential to every report, while other information is defined as only "pertinent" or supplementary. The amount of information that is *essential* and the amount that is *pertinent* determines the length and content of the report. The U.S. Probation Service specifies that reports should be factual, germane, precise, and succinct.

Each report is prepared only after a thorough investigation has been conducted into the defendant's background. The probation officer evaluates the facts and reports only the information that will help the court understand the individual and the circumstances of the offense. A concise report, fully read, is considered more effective than a lengthy one that is not considered or used. [10]

The effectiveness of a presentence report is directly related to the success with which the findings are communicated and the extent to which it is utilized.

The length and content of the report also depend upon the seriousness of the offense. The greater the consequences of a judgment, the more likely it is the court or subsequent decision-making body will need a greater range and variety of information. Where an individual has committed a violent or potentially violent offense, consideration of release on probation, prison classification committee decisions, and parole release decisions will all require more knowledge of the individual than if the individual were a situational, nonviolent first offender.

The U.S. Probation Service presentence report consists of the following core categories and subsections:

1. Offense (core)
   Official version
   Defendant's version
   Codefendant information
   Statements of witnesses, complainants,
      and victims

2. Prior Record (core)
   Juvenile adjudication
   Adult arrests
   Adult conviction

---

8. *The Presentence Investigation Report,* Monograph No. 103 (1965).

9. Yona Cohn, *On the Presentence Report,* Federal Probation (Sept. 1982).

10. *The Presentence Investigation Report, supra,* at 6.

3. Personal and Family Data (core)
> Defendant
> Parents and siblings
> Marital
> Education
> Employment
> Health
>> Physical
>> Mental and emotional
> Military service
> Financial condition
>> Assets
>> Liabilities

4. Evaluation (core)
> Alternative plans
> Sentencing data

5. Recommendation (core)

Writing the evaluative summary is perhaps the most difficult and painstaking task in the entire presentence report. It has a significant bearing on the future course of the defendant's life. It is in writing the evaluative summary that probation officers call into play their analytical ability, their diagnostic skills, and their understanding of human behavior. It is there that they bring into focus the kind of person that is before the court, the basic factors that brought the person into trouble, and what special helps the defendant needs to resolve those difficulties.

The opening paragraph of the evaluative summary should concisely restate the pertinent highlights that are in the body of the report. There should follow in separate paragraphs those factors that contributed in some measure to the defendant's difficulties and an evaluation of the defendant's personality. (Note: A fuller description of the defendant's personality should appear under Health— Mental and Emotional).

A word of warning is in order, since the presentence reports used in state courts are seldom as complete as those prepared by the United States probation officer, according to the outline that was just discussed. Courts without probation staffs lack the necessary personnel to prepare exhaustive reports, or indeed, any reports at all. Also, many judges refuse to read lengthy presentence reports and require instead that they be furnished with only short, succinct summaries.

Presentence reports are seldom used in misdemeanor cases. When a presentence report is prepared in a misdemeanor case, it will be shorter and more summary in nature. In practice, the judge who sentences for a misdemeanor relies upon the police officer for information about the defendant's previous criminal history and the circumstances of the offense. The defendant is usually given a right to speak to the question of sentencing and the judge may question the defendant about family and circumstances.

Legal Problems Concerning the Presentence Report

It is beyond the scope of this work to consider all of the legal questions surrounding the preparation and use of the presentence investigation report. Two problem areas will be discussed—when the presentence report should be made and whether the defendant is entitled to see the report.

The preferred practice is to conduct the presentence investigation and prepare the presentence report after adjudication of guilt. The commentary appended to ARTICLE 4.2 of the American Bar Association's Standards Relating to Sentencing Alternatives and Procedures gives four reasons why the presentence investigation should not be undertaken until after the finding of guilt: (1) The investigation represents an invasion of the defendant's privacy if the defendant is later acquitted. The defendant's friends, employers, and relatives must be questioned and embarrassing questions asked; (2) certain information is sought from the defendant in preparing the report. This places the defendant in an awkward position if it is expected that the defendant talk to the probation officer before trial; (3) the material in the presentence report is not admissible at the trial on the question of guilt, and there is a chance that it may come to the attention of the court before guilt is determined; [11] and (4) there are economic arguments against compilation of a report that may never be used.

Exceptions to this rule are allowed when the defendant's attorney consents that the preparation of the report may begin before conviction and plea. This recognizes the fact that under certain circumstances the prompt preparation of the report is of advantage to the defendant.

A question much more difficult than when the presentence report is to be made has to do with whether the defendant should be permitted to see the presentence report and have the opportunity to refute any statements contained therein. Compulsory disclosure has generally been opposed by judges and probation officers. [12] The main argument against disclosure is that persons

---

11. Calland v. United States, 371 F.2d 295 (7th Cir.1966).

12. *See* Additional Views of Judge Stanley with Respect to the Compulsory Disclosure of Pre-Sentence Reports. American Bar Association Standards Relating to Sentencing Alternatives and Procedures.

Because the issue is so fundamental, and the evidence against non-disclosure is so overwhelming, I feel compelled to register my views with respect to the portion of this report which favors compulsory disclosure of presentence reports.

The problem has recently received the attention of the Judicial Conference of the United States and the United States Supreme Court. After a study extending over a period of some three years, the Judicial Conference and the Supreme Court, acting upon the recommendations of the Advisory and Standing Committees on Rules of Practice and Procedure, approved Rule 32(c)(2) of the Federal Rules of Criminal Procedure, which makes disclosure of presentence reports discretionary. During the course of its study, the Advisory Committee obtained the views of circuit judges, district judges and federal probation officers. The survey disclosed the following:

Circuit Judges
    40 opposed compulsory disclosure,
     7 were in favor of compulsory disclosure,
     4 expressed no opinion;

Footnote 12 continued.

District Judges
    250 opposed compulsory disclosure,
     18 were in favor of compulsory disclosure,
      2 expressed no opinion;

Federal Probation Officers
    340 opposed compulsory disclosure,
     20 were in favor of compulsory disclosure,
      8 expressed no opinion.

It has been repeatedly held that there is no denial of due process of law for a court to consider the report of a presentence investigation without disclosing its content to the defendant, or giving him an opportunity to rebut it. Williams v. Oklahoma, 358 U.S. 576, 79 S.Ct. 421, 3 L.Ed.2d 516 (1950); Williams v. New York, 337 U.S. 241, 69 S.Ct. 1079 (1949).

A majority of the Committee not only recommends compulsory disclosure to counsel for prosecution and defense, but also recommends that provision be made for any part of the report to be controverted by the production of evidence. In the recent case of Specht v. Patterson, decided April 11, 1967, the United States Supreme Court reaffirmed its decision in Williams v. New York, supra, which recognized that probation workers "have not been trained to prosecute, but to aid offenders;" that most of the information "relied upon by judges to guide them in the intelligent imposition of sentences would be unavailable if information were restricted to that given in open court by witnesses subject to cross-examination;" and that the type and extent of information gathered by probation officers "make totally impractical if not impossible open court testimony with cross-examination," since such a procedure could "endlessly delay criminal administration in a retrial of collateral issues."

For other convincing arguments opposing compulsory disclosure, see Judicial Conference Committee on Administration of the Probation System, Judicial Opinion on Proposed Change in Rule 32(c) of the Federal Rules of Criminal Procedure—A Survey (1964); Keve, The Probation Officer Investigates 6–15 (1960); Parsons, "The Presentence Investigation Report Must be Preserved as a Confidential Document," Fed.Prob., March, 1964, p. 3; Barnett and Gronewold, "Confidentiality of the Presentence Report," Fed.Prob., March, 1962, p. 26; Wilson, "A New Arena is Emerging to Test the Confidentiality of Presentence Reports," Fed.Prob., Dec., 1961, p. 6; "Federal Judge's Views on Probation Practices," Fed.Prob., March, 1960, p. 10; Sharp, "The Confidential Nature of Presentence Reports," 5 Catholic U.L.Rev. 127 (1955).

Perhaps the overriding issue involved is that most of the valuable information contained in presentence reports would no longer be available if disclosure should be made mandatory. Certainly, former employers and members of a defendant's family would hesitate to give information if the report is to be read by the defendant or his counsel, and such persons are subject to being brought into court to establish the accuracy of the information given. Further, experience teaches that a disclosure of information given by members of the defendant's family would often result in a complete breakdown of family relationships. It is no answer to the problem to say that sources of confidential information can be withheld, because anyone experienced in the field knows that more often than not the information itself discloses the source.

It is the considered judgment of most experts in the field that compulsory disclosure would result in a pre-sentence report containing nothing more than information related by the defendant himself, and that obtained from public records and documents. In my judgment, this would work to the detriment of defendants, since it would require judges to sentence on the basis of guesswork and inadequate information. It has always been my practice, and the practice of most judges with whom the matter has been discussed, to voluntarily disclose derogatory information, not testified to by witnesses, that affects the length of the sentence. Such practice should be encouraged, but is a matter that should be left to the enlightened judgment and sound discretion of the trial judge.

Since the evidence against compulsory disclosure is so overwhelming, and the Supreme Court has repeatedly held that no constitutional issue is involved, I simply see no basis for embarking upon a course that "would undermine modern penological procedural policies that have been cautiously adopted throughout the nation after careful consideration and experimentation." Williams v. New York, supra. Edwin M. Stanley, Member of Advisory Committee on Sentencing and Review.

having knowledge about the offender will refuse to disclose the information if they know that they can be called into court and subjected to cross-examination, or even if they know that the defendant will be able to find out the names of persons who give information about the defendant. The argument here is that disclosure of the presentence report to the defendant will dry up the sources of information. It is also contended that to permit the defendant to challenge the presentence report would interminably delay the proceedings. The fear is that the defendant will challenge everything in the report and transform the sentencing procedure into a new trial of facts. A third argument is that it would be harmful to the defendant to have some of the information in the report—as for example, the evaluation of a psychiatrist or even of the probation officer who is to be the defendant's probation supervisor. It is also stated that after conviction a case ceases to be an action at law and becomes a social problem. Those who adhere to this position maintain that there should be no compulsory disclosure of the presentence report. Some maintain that the report should be a completely private document; others would permit disclosure at the discretion of the trial judge.

The opposing views that advocate disclosure of the presentence report are that in simple fairness, convicted persons should have access to the information upon which their sentence is to be based so that they can correct inaccuracies and controvert falsehoods. It is pointed out that in jurisdictions where the accused has access to the reports, the sources of information have not dried up, nor has the sentencing hearing turned into a prolonged adversary proceeding. Supporters of this position argue that attorneys for the defendant cannot properly perform their constitutional duty to assure the accuracy of the information used in sentencing without having access to the information upon which the judge is expected to act.

The United States Supreme Court has held that there is no denial of due process of law for a court to consider the report of a presentence investigation without disclosing its contents to the defendant or giving the defendant an opportunity to rebut it.[13] However, in the case of *Kent v. United States,* which involved the certification of a juvenile for trial in an adult criminal court, a somewhat different result was reached.[14] The court's waiver of jurisdiction was based upon a social history report that was given to the judge, but access to the

---

13. Williams v. Oklahoma, 358 U.S. 576, 79 S.Ct. 421, 3 L.Ed.2d 516 (1959).

Williams v. New York, 337 U.S. 241, 69 S.Ct. 1079, 93 L.Ed. 1337 (1949).

In *Williams v. New York,* the jury recommended life imprisonment. Their recommendation was not binding upon the court. After receipt of the presentence report which showed according to the judge that the defendant had confessed to thirty burglaries in the area where the murder occurred, that appellant possessed "a marked sexuality" and was a "menace to society," the court sentenced the defendant to death. The sentence of death was upheld upon appeal. The Supreme Court pointed out that strict evidentiary procedures "hedge" the guilt finding process, but the sources of evidence for sentencing purposes have historically been much wider. "Undoubtedly the New York statutes (providing for presentence reports) emphasize a modern philosophy of penology that the punishment should fit the offender and not merely the crime."

14. * * * [The Juvenile Judge] * * * may not for purposes of a decision on waiver, receive and rely upon secret information, whether emanating from its staff or otherwise. * * * Kent v. United States, 383 U.S. 541, 86 S.Ct. 1045, 16 L.Ed.2d 84 (1966).

report was denied to the attorney for the juvenile. The Supreme Court stated that the report should have been made available to the defense attorney.

A New Jersey decision went even further. In *State v. Kunz*,[15] the presentence report contained a statement that a stolen vehicle ring, specializing in Cadillacs, was being operated by an individual "whose contact in New Jersey" was the defendant, and that the defendant had been involved in several purchases of stolen automobiles in New Jersey. This information was given to the defense counsel, who claimed that the report was wholly false. However, the defense counsel was unable to obtain a copy of the report, nor was the defendant given the opportunity to controvert the charges. Upon appeal, the Court remanded the defendant to the trial court for resentencing, stating in its opinion:

> Furthermore, we take this occasion to announce that in all future sentencing proceedings, defendants will be entitled to disclosure of the presentence report with fair opportunity to be heard on any adverse matters relevant to the sentencing. Although persuasive constitutional arguments have been advanced * * * this step is not being taken as a matter of constitutional compulsion for the Supreme Court holdings to date do not indicate it * * * and we are not now prepared to find that it is of constitutional dimension under our State Constitution. It is being taken as a matter of rudimentary fairness and though it may entail some administrative difficulties they can readily be minimized by proper handling. Thus the presentence report may first be examined by the trial judge so that matters which will actually play no part in the sentencing process may be excluded. In this fashion irrelevances may be eliminated, confidential sources may be protected, and disclosure may be avoided of diagnostic matters which would be harmful to the defendant's rehabilitation if he were told about them. The report, as thus edited and furnished to the defendant, must of course contain *in toto* the presentence material which will have any bearing whatever on the sentencing and the trial judge must so recognize in his deliberation and determination.

There is a trend toward what might be called a "middle position", on the question of disclosure of the presentence report. While the entire report, which contains the names of the informants, is not disclosed to the defendant, it may be shown to the defendant's attorney. Or, the defendant and the defendant's attorney may be informed as to the nature of any adverse information in the report and given the opportunity to controvert such information.

After an exhaustive consideration of the reasons for and against disclosure of the presentence report to the defendant, the American Bar Association Standards Relating to Sentencing Alternatives and Procedures adopted a position in favor of disclosure.[16] The Model Penal Code would require that the court advise the defendant or the defendant's counsel of the factual contents and the conclusions of any presentence investigation or psychiatric examination and afford fair opportunity, if the defendant so requests, to controvert them. The sources of confidential information need not, however, be disclosed.[17]

---

15. State v. Kunz, 55 N.J. 128, 259 A.2d 895 (1969).

16. American Bar Association Standards Relating to Sentencing Alternatives and Procedures, §§ 4.3 and 4.4.

17. Model Penal Code, § 7.07(5).

Effective August 1, 1975, the Federal Rules of Criminal Procedure were amended with reference to disclosure of the presentence report. Rule 32(c)(3) reads:

(A) Before imposing sentence the court shall upon request permit the defendant, or his counsel if he is so represented, to read the report of the presentence investigation exclusive of any recommendation as to sentence, unless in the opinion of the court the report contains diagnostic opinion which might seriously disrupt a program of rehabilitation, sources of information obtained upon a promise of confidentiality, or any other information which, if disclosed, might result in harm, physical or otherwise, to the defendant or other persons; and the court shall afford the defendant or his counsel an opportunity to comment thereon.

(B) If the court is of the view that there is information in the presentence report which should not be disclosed under subdivision (c)(3)(A) of this rule, the court in lieu of making the report or part thereof available shall state orally or in writing a summary of the factual information contained therein to be relied on in determining sentence, and shall give the defendant or his counsel an opportunity to comment thereon. The statement may be made to the parties in camera.

(C) Any material disclosed to the defendant or his counsel shall also be disclosed to the attorney for the government.

(D) Any copies of the presentence investigation report made available to the defendant or his counsel and the attorney for the government shall be returned to the probation officer immediately following the imposition of sentence or the granting of probation. Copies of the presentence investigation report shall not be made by the defendant, his counsel, or the attorney for the government.

(E) The reports of studies and recommendations contained therein made by the Director of the Bureau of Prisons or the Youth Correction Division of the Board of Parole pursuant to 18 U.S.C.A. § 4208(b), 4252, 5010(e), or 5034 shall be considered a presentence investigation within the meaning of subdivision (c)(3) of this rule.

The federal rule as now promulgated appears to draw an intermediate line between complete disclosure and complete secrecy.

In those states and federal districts practicing disclosure, the release of the presentence report has not resulted in the problems that have been anticipated by the opponents of the practice. Rather, it has apparently led the probation services to develop skills that more objectively analyze the offense and the offender. With greater objectivity has come greater reliance by the courts on the reports, and a resultant increase in the number of reports requested and persons granted probation.[18] Analytical rather that judgmental aspects of the reports makes them not only of greater value to the courts, but also more acceptable to the offender, for in them the offender may see that perhaps someone understands or at least attempts to understand the offender's problems. This latter effect frequently results in a closer relationship between the offender and the probation officer. Further, disclosure is a requirement for fairness to the

_____

18. From interviews by the authors of probation officers and judges in courts practicing disclosure.

defendant. Thus, the presentence investigation report is an integral part of the correctional system and should be made available to the defendant or the defendant's counsel.

Availability of Presentence Reports under the Freedom of Information Act of 1974

Since the passage of amendments to the Freedom of Information Act (FOIA) and the Privacy Act of 1974, state and federal courts have experienced numerous demands from prison inmates for copies of the presentence report. The purpose of the amendments to the Freedom of Information Act include making government records more available for examination and copying by individuals. The Privacy Act of 1974 was designed to protect certain government records on individuals and to prevent their indiscriminate use. The acts prescribe procedures to permit access to the records and to otherwise safeguard their integrity. SECTION 3 of P.L. 93–503 (Freedom of Information Act) amends 5 U.S.C.A. § 552 by adding a new subsection (e) more clearly defining "agency." The Privacy Act incorporates by reference this same subsection and its definition.[19]

Furthermore, the U.S. Court of Appeals for the Tenth Circuit has previously held that a presentence report is *not* an agency report, and, therefore, would not be available to the public under 5 U.S.C.A. § 552, since the courts of the United States are exempt from the Freedom of Information Act.[20] [Emphasis added.] This case appears to remain good authority.

While it is true that U.S. probation officers perform various duties as requested by the U.S. Parole Commission and are thus "agents" of the Commission for some purposes, such as parole and postrelease planning, the preparation of presentence reports is *not* one of those duties.[21] [Emphasis added.] Presentence reports are used by the U.S. Bureau of Prisons and the Parole Commission because the courts have permitted such use. The reports are not converted, however, by such use into documents of "agencies" subject to the prescription of the FOIA. Access to such reports at the parole release hearings, when available to the Parole Commission, were given to inmates by the Parole Commission and Reorganization Act.[22] Nothing in the act, however, alters the fact that the presentence report is a court document that is not within the purview of the FOIA. It cannot be obtained under the FOIA by an inmate or parolee from the Parole Commission.[23]

Conclusions

The ultimate merit of probation as a correctional tool is dependent to a very great extent upon the nature and quality of the presentence report. Probation is

---

19. Freedom of Information Act Amendment, 5 U.S.C.A. § 522, 88 Stat. 1516, P.L. 93–502 (Nov. 2, 1974) and Privacy Act of 1974, 5 U.S.C.A. § 522a, 88 Stat. 1897, P.L. 93–579 (Dec. 31, 1974). The basic definition of "agency" for the title is still found in 5 U.S.C.A. § 551(1).

20. 18 U.S.C. § 3655, as amended by P.L. 94–233, sec. 14 (Mar. 15, 1976); 18 U.S.C. § 4203(a)(4) (Mar. 15, 1976).

21. 18 U.S.C. §§ 4207, 4208 (Mar. 15, 1976).

22. See text of act in Appendix, *infra.*

23. Cook v. Willingham, 400 F.2d 885 (10th Cir.1968).

in essence a method of individualization and is predicated upon the proper selection of offenders to be accorded this community-based correctional treatment. Although the primary purpose of a presentence investigation report is to examine and expose the factors that will mitigate for or against successful community adjustment in lieu of incarceration, use of the report should not be limited to the courts, but should be made available to prison authorities for classification and treatment purposes, and to the parole board to aid in the determination of parole grants and future aftercare needs of the offender.

On the Presentence Investigation*

THE PRESENTENCE SOCIAL INQUIRY REPORT

The content of the presentence report submitted to the court is expected to assist the court in its deliberations on the disposition of a given case. The reasons behind this are due to the fact that the adjudication did not provide the court with adequate information about the offender needed for a good disposition. It simply presented to the court a picture of the person to be punished for his indictable delinquency and a list of previous convictions submitted by the prosecution informing the court of the offender's history as a criminal person, leaving many important backgrounds unknown to the court, such as what kind of son, husband, father, worker, supporter, etc. the offender is—backgrounds considered by either the court or the legislator as of importance for the proper selection of disposition.

The history of criminal prosecution and punishment goes back for many thousands of years and is tightly connected with organized society. But in just less than 100 years has the probation officer become an integral member of the criminal justice system. With increased concern of society about the welfare of man in many fields of life, the criminal should also be looked upon as a person and not just an offender. One outcome of this approach is the consideration that the punishment affects the person more than just in his role of an offender. Other functions are affected as well. The punishment, and especially imprisonment, hits the person thoroughly. Many such punishments have after-effects long after the offender has completed serving his sentence and returned to normal society. Thus the presentence report is intended to meet this target.

What aspects of the offender's life should be investigated? There are legislations which spell them out, while others leave it to the discretion of the probation officer. The following areas are usually included:

1. An assessment of the parental family of the offender as a supporter of physical, moral, and educational needs.

* Yona Cohn, *Federal Probation,* (Washington D.C.: Administrative Offices of the U.S. Courts, Sept. 1982). Reprinted with permission.

2. The offender's level of performance in adjustment to various settings, such as school, job, and recreational institutions, since inadequate performance in these settings is often used by the probation officer to explain a social and antisocial behavior.

3. His criminal background in an attempt to interpret this behavior psychologically and culturally—an approach significantly different from the one experienced by the offender while being interrogated by the prosecution.

There is no doubt that with this information the judge is provided with a broader and a more personal picture of the person to be adjudicated by him. Nor is there doubt as to the difficulties the judge is facing in translating this information into a specific punishment. Whether the criminal is to be sent to prison, or should be kept within the community with a probation officer; or, in case he is to be imprisoned, for what period, are questions which are hard to answer according to the data submitted in the report. In practice, the judge uses a yardstick based on general sentencing practice on a given crime. He will use the data included in the report to find out whether this person shows unique features which would suggest using more individual criteria for the disposition. Judges differ as to the level of uniqueness of the offender required to give way to a more individual decision.

The introduction of an investigation report was also facilitated by the development of behavioral sciences. Thus the report may be wasted should it be used only to give a lively picture of the offender, however important it may be.[1] Research findings could help the probation officer address himself to more specific questions relevant to the disposition of the case, with a reasonable degree of reliability and confidence.

These are some of the questions:

1. The major internal and external factors which made the person become an offender (the historical and situational forces involved).

2. Which of these forces are still operational after the crime has been committed?

3. What are the expected effects of the various alternatives in sentencing?

THE PRESENTENCE INVESTIGATION

Collecting the data needed to make a well-founded recommendation could be viewed as a rational process. First, the data is collected; secondly, this data is scrutinized as to its reliability and its relevance; thirdly, the data is integrated into a comprehensive picture of the offender as a person; fourthly, inferences are drawn for an individual recommendation.

In reality, however, these stages are not logically separated. The probation officer reaches a tentative recommendation at an early stage of his investigation. Once some pieces of information are at his disposal, such as the offenses, the criminal background, adjustment to socializing institutions (family, school, job), the recommendation is already more or less fixed in his mind. A vast amount of contradicting data would be required to modify it. Changing the tentative recommendation is especially hard as the perception of the data is done selectively. Data contradicting the first conclusion is often preconsciously ignored. The probation officer who feels relatively independent of the court as to the acceptance of his recommendation is more likely to be open to including it in the report not supportive to his recommendation than his colleague who feels more dependent on the

---

1. Edward E. Peoples (ed.): *Readings in Correctional Casework and Counselling,* Goodyear, 1975, p. 45.

court,[2] that is, sharing the doubts with the court.

In order to put the many pieces of information into a comprehensive whole, the probation officer uses certain causation theories. He does not have to have them formulated as such, but looking at a number of such reports, the reader may recognize some of them used as organizing principles by the probation officer (pet theories). Here are just a few examples: the crime committed is a symbol and expression of the adolescent's fight for autonomy; the commitment of the crime is a result of waning parental authority; the crime is a part of the fight between deprived subculture and the depriving establishment; the crime reflects the confusion of the youngster emerging from a traditional subculture into a permissive society (the former restraints are ineffective while new ones have not been established). Other probation officers, using more psychological frameworks may explain the crime either as a result of a faulty superego or a deficient ego. Others may refer to the reinforcement the offender receives from his delinquent environment in committing a crime.

These theories might be helpful if used critically, but would distort the picture if indiscriminately applied, forcing the data to fit the theory.

CONDUCTING THE INVESTIGATION

There are three major sources for the data: interview(s) with the offender, interviews with other significant persons, relevant documents from other sources such as psychological or psychiatric reports as well as statements from social workers or teachers.

The interviewing of the offender is the most important part of the inquiry and is most used in preparation of the report.[3] These interviews are normally conducted in the probation office. The offender generally meets the probation officer with suspicion, because the meeting often takes place immediately after the police interrogation so that much of that emotional experience is carried over, especially by first offenders. The defendant wishes to use the interview to promote what he considers the best interests. His reporting is therefore defensively selective and often deliberately distorted. Some of his defenses are preconscious, and can be neutralized by the probation officer either by penetrating them by relating to his underlying motives for hiding them, or by the gradual establishment of a positive transference, which would reduce anxiety, so that the defenses may lose their purpose and so wither away. The difference between approaches reflects the difference of the offender, but it is often the personality of the investigator which explains the difference in approach as well.[4] Generally the more aggressive probation officer who uses the direct approach, the "no nonsense" man when relating to his probationer, is more identified with the court system than his colleague who considers himself primarily as a helper, and is identified with one of the helping professions. In contrast to the "penetrator," the anxiety reducer may rely more upon carefully formulating the questions by avoiding emotionally "loaded"

---

2. I.H. Lowe and I.D. Steiner: "Some Effects of the Reversibility and Consequences of Decisions on Post-Decision Information Preferences," *Journal of Personality and Social Psychology*, 1968/8, pp. 172–179.

3. Charles L. Newman: "Concepts of Treatment in Probation and Parole Supervision," in *Readings in Corrections and Counselling*, (ed.) Edward E. Peoples, Goodyear Publishing Co., Inc., Santa Monica, 1975, pp. 61–72.

4. Yona Cohn: *The Court and the Probation Officer*, Ministry of Social Welfare, Department of Research, Jerusalem, 1974.

words. He would also be aware of the need for careful timing of delicate subjects and would introduce a delicate question in order to probe the level of anxiety, leave the topic when anxiety blocks the offender, move gently to another topic, and return to it at a later stage of the interview when some trust has been established. This more dynamic approach yields not only more of the required information, but also makes it more reliable, and promotes a deeper understanding of the dynamics of the offender's personality.

In such an interview, as well as in all interviews, we have a "body-talk" in addition to a "mouth-talk," and that refers to both the probation officer and the offender. The probation officer has to listen with his ears and look with his eyes. Facial expressions, body posture, gesticulation of the offender confirm the verbal utterances or contradict them. The defendant may control primarily his verbal and facial expression, leaving the trunk and the hands to "tell" the true story to the probation officer, who is tuned to receive hidden messages and to decipher them correctly. All this goes for the probation officer as well as the offender himself, who is often a careful listener and observer, to the surprise of the probation officer. This is the case as the outcome of his contacts with probation officers and other officials may affect him in various significant areas of his life.

One point quite often overlooked is the "message" sent to the interviewee by the layout of the room in which the interview is conducted; does it look more like an office or a treatment room?

We have already stated that messages are sent by the probation officer as well—messages of which he is scarcely aware. These messages often reflect his part in the directing of the interchange. He sends facial and verbal cues of what he wants his defendant to say. The professional probation officer needs the help of a supervisor to sift objective data (which the offender wants to offer) from reflective data (what the probation officer wants him to say) produced by the offender.[5]

Most attention is given by the probation officer to the verbal output of the offender. This can be used as it is, or may need some rephrasing to include it in the report to the court. A sudden jerky movement of the knee, clenching of the fingers, or a sudden backward movement of the upper part of the body as if to move away from the probation officer may be more authentic than the uttered word, as it is done unintentionally, but this needs interpretation to be of use in the report. The court may be prepared to have verbal quotations in the report to substantiate a statement of the probation officer. However, the descriptions of the various body movements, even with attached interpretations, would seem to the court rather odd. This does not mean that the various physical expressions, and the context in which they emerged, should be ignored. They may become useful to the sensitive probation officer to verify or contradict verbal utterances, and may convey content on their own.

Here is just a short example that we see in action:

When a youngster appears with his parents before the probation officer he sees the family operating: Who sits closest to the boy? Who is the recognized spokesman? Or when someone tries to talk, is he interrupted by someone else? Does the boy try to give his version, in spite of other members of the family who try to keep him silent? This situation may be further structured by placing just one chair in front of the probation officer, with two others pushed back a little, before the family enter the room. Who "grabs" the chair close to

5. Yona Cohn: "Job Related Inservice Training in Corrections," *Federal Probation*, 44/2 (June 1980), pp. 48–56.

the desk, and who takes care that the others also get seated? The probation officer who uses such structured observation may use home visits to verify it. He may initiate some systematic research in this field to increase the use of structured and unstructured observations in the investigation.

MAKING THE RECOMMENDATION

In making a recommendation the probation officer has to decide whether he should recommend that the offender is to remain in the community, and if so, under what conditions; or if he recommends his committal, where to and for how long.

As in many decisions, this matter is also based on objective considerations consciously arrived at, as well as on subjective considerations operating in the decisionmaker's unconscious. Many are clear-cut cases; that is, other probation officers would reach identical conclusions. Others are more in-between cases, and here subjective considerations play their part. We identify countertransference symptoms: The offender is either sympathetic or antipathetic to the probation officer—feelings related to his own life experience of which he is hardly aware.

Another factor operating in the mind of the probation officer is the importance he attaches to having his recommendation accepted by the court. The rejection of his recommendation is often felt as a personal rejection especially by the inexperienced worker or the one whose only professional identification is with the court.

The presentence report, which is a direct outcome of the investigation, is an instrument for the promotion of individualized sentencing by the court. In addition, it may serve the probation officer as a channel for the input of relevant scientific findings with regard to sentencing into the criminal justice system, if and when he has such findings to offer the court.

4

Terms and Conditions of Probation

Conditions of Probation Fixed by Statute

In the proper administration of probation, the term and conditions of probation are tailored to the needs of the particular offender. To accomplish this objective, probation statutes give the court considerable latitude in determining what conditions are to be imposed upon the defendant as part of the probation. The defendant is, of course, subject to the jurisdiction of the court during the period of probation.

Discretion to fix conditions of probation is derived from the power of a court to determine the nature and extent of the criminal penalties to be imposed upon the defendant, and its inherent or legislatively-granted power to suspend the imposition or execution of sentence and to grant probation. Probation statutes state the power in general terms. For example, the federal probation statute provides that the court "when satisfied that the ends of justice and the best interests of the defendant will be served thereby may suspend the imposition or execution of sentence and place the defendant on probation for such periods and upon terms and conditions as the court deems best."[1]

It is usual, however, for this broad grant of power to be accompanied by legislative provisions that either mandate certain required or minimum conditions of probation or that enumerate specific conditions that the court may in its discretion impose.[2] The discretionary conditions set out tend to be general in

---

1. 18 U.S.C.A. § 3651ff.

2. The California statute reads: If the court shall determine that there are circumstances in mitigation of punishment prescribed by law, or that the ends of justice would be subserved by granting probation to the defendant, the court shall have power in its discretion to place the defendant on probation as hereinafter provided * * *. Cal.Penal Code § 1203 (West).

nature and include requirements that the probationer shall obey all laws of the United States, the state, and the municipality; that the offender support any dependents; that the offender avoid associating with criminals and other persons of ill repute; that the offender remain within the jurisdiction; and that the offender report regularly to the assigned probation officer.

Conditions of probation are at the discretion of the court having jurisdiction over the case. However, Texas law suggests the following stipulations for probationers: [3]

1. Commit no offense against the laws;

2. Avoid persons or places of disreputable or harmful characters;

3. Avoid injurious or vicious habits;

4. Report to the probation officer as directed;

5. Permit the probation officer to visit him at his home or elsewhere;

6. Work faithfully at suitable employment as far as possible;

7. Remain within a specified place;

8. Pay his fine, if one be assessed, and all court costs whether a fine be assessed or not, and make restitution or reparation in any sum that the court shall determine;

9. Support his dependents;

10. Participate in any community-based program;

11. Reimburse the county in which the prosecution was instituted for compensation paid to appointed counsel for defending him;

12. Remain under custodial supervision in a community-based facility, obey all rules and regulations of such facility and pay a percentage of his income to the facility for room and board;

13. Pay a percentage of his income to his dependents for their support while under custodial supervision in a community-based facility; and

14. Pay a percentage of his income to the victim of the offense, if any to compensate for any property damage or medical expenses sustained by the victim as a direct result of the commission of the offense.

Illegal Conditions

Although the trial court has broad discretion in imposing the terms and conditions of probation, the powers are not boundless. Conditions imposed must be reasonable and relevant to the offense for which probation is being granted. Accordingly, it has been held: a condition of probation that (1) has no relationship to the crime of which the offender was convicted; that (2) relates to conduct that is not of itself criminal; and that (3) requires or forbids conduct that is not reasonably related to future criminality, does not serve the statutory ends of probation and is invalid.[4]

---

3. Tex.Code Crim.Proc.Ann. art. 42.12 (Vernon).

4. People v. Dominguez, 256 Cal.App.2d 623, 64 Cal.Rptr. 290 (1967).

A court cannot impose conditions in granting probation that cannot be fulfilled within the period fixed by the court as term of probation.[5] Banishment as a condition of probation is void.[6] A condition that a defendant not become pregnant without being married was held void as not related to robbery, for which she was convicted, and her future pregnancy had no reasonable relationship to future criminality.[7] In a significant case, a defendant was placed on probation for five years on condition that he refrain from the use of alcoholic beverages of any kind. His probation was revoked because he violated the condition. He appealed, alleging that a psychiatric examination would have shown that he was a chronic alcoholic and that he was not responsible at the time of the act. The appellate court remanded the case on the ground that the district court may have imposed an impossible condition, particularly if psychiatric testimony established that his alcoholism had destroyed his power of volition and prevented his compliance with the condition.[8] In *Morgan v. Wofford,* the court refused to strike down a Georgia statute that permitted an order of restitution to the victim be a condition of probation, but held that the amount of restitution could not be determined solely by the probation officer without giving the probationer an opportunity to be heard.[9]

An order of a juvenile court requiring regular attendance at Sunday school and church was held to be unconstitutional, as "no civil authority has the right to require anyone to accept or reject any religious belief or to contribute any support thereto."[10] Banishment from the state for five years was declared to be illegal in Michigan,[11] as was a requirement that a defendant move from a neighborhood.[12] Sentencing a minor offender to a fine after he failed to satisfy the court with his effort to write an essay on why the citizenry should respect the police, was rejected by the appellate court,[13] as was a requirement that a defendant donate blood to the Red Cross.[14]

Conditions Upheld

A requirement that a 23-year-old defendant afflicted with syphilis, who had pleaded guilty to rape of a 13-year-old girl, submit to vasectomy was upheld.[15] A requirement that a 9-year-old child live apart from her family until she was 18 was upheld,[16] as were conditions that a probationer remain within a specified

---

5. *Ex parte* Acosta, 65 Cal.App.2d 63, 149 P.2d 757 (1944).

6. People v. Dominguez, 256 Cal.App.2d 623, 64 Cal.Rptr. 290 (1967).

7. People v. Dominguez, 256 Cal.App.2d 623, 64 Cal.Rptr. 290 (1967).

8. Sweeney v. United States, 353 F.2d 10 (7th Cir.1965).

9. Morgan v. Wofford, 472 F.2d 822 (5th Cir.1973).

10. Jones v. Commonwealth, 185 Va. 335, 38 S.E.2d 444 (1946).

11. People v. Baum, 251 Mich. 187, 231 N.W. 95 (1930).

12. People v. Smith, 252 Mich. 4, 232 N.W. 397 (1930).

13. Butler v. District of Columbia, 120 U.S.App.D.C. 317, 346 F.2d 798 (1965).

14. Springer v. United States, 148 F.2d 411 (9th Cir.1945).

15. People v. Blankenship, 16 Cal.App.2d 606, 61 P.2d 352 (1936).

16. *Ex parte* Walters, 92 Okl.Crim. 1, 221 P.2d 659 (1950).

place,[17] that a probationer not violate any law of the state or of the United States,[18] that a probationer who was guilty of crimes growing out of a demonstration against the war not participate in demonstrations,[19] that a defendant who was convicted of selling LSD submit himself and his property to search and seizure at any time by law enforcement officers;[20] that a defendant who had been convicted of bookmaking activities carried on by telephone not have a telephone in his home or upon any property under his control;[21] and that a defendant avoid use of alcohol in any form.[22] A Texas court has stated that generally a probationer's liability is conditioned upon conduct above that which is required of the ordinary citizen.[23]

Conditions of probation that require a defendant to pay costs or make restitution are generally upheld, provided that the amounts ordered to be paid are not excessive in view of the financial condition of the defendant. A wealthy defendant convicted of arson was required to pay $139,000 in reparations, which was the amount paid by the insurers for fire loss. This was upheld.[24] A person who presented false claims to the welfare department was required to pay $544.[25] Fines may also be imposed according to the provisions of some statutes. When this is permitted, the fine imposed as a condition of probation cannot exceed the maximum fine allowed by statute. Thus, where maximum fine was $200, a $1,000 fine as a condition of probation was excessive.[26] In California, jail detention may be ordered as a condition of probation, and when so ordered it is not regarded as punishment but as part and parcel of supervised effort toward rehabilitation.[27]

The statutes generally provide that the probationer must be given copies of the conditions of probation. Oral, unrecorded conditions are invalid.[28] The conditions must be stated with sufficient clarity to apprise the probationer of what is expected.[29]

Conditions of Probation as Recommended

The suggested standards for the administration of probation take into consideration the case law concerning legal and illegal conditions. Most such standards

---

17. Miller v. State, 168 Tex.Crim. 570, 330 S.W.2d 466 (1959).

18. Guinn v. State, 163 Tex.Crim. 181, 289 S.W.2d 583 (1956).

19. People v. King, 267 Cal.App.2d 814, 73 Cal.Rptr. 440 (1968), cert. den. 396 U.S. 1028, 90 S.Ct. 576, 24 L.Ed.2d 524 (1970).

20. People v. Kern, 264 Cal.App.2d 962, 71 Cal.Rptr. 105 (1968).

21. People v. Stanley, 162 Cal.App.2d 416, 327 P.2d 973 (1958).

22. Perkins v. State, 103b S.W.2d 286 (1965); *Ex parte* Walters, 92 Okl.Crim. 1, 221 P.2d 659 (1950); Sweeney v. United States, 353 F.2d 10 (7th Cir.1965).

23. Jackson v. State, 165 Tex.Crim. 380, 307 S.W.2d 809 (1957).

24. People v. Alexander, 182 Cal.App.2d 281, 6 Cal.Rptr. 153 (1960).

25. People v. Marin, 147 Cal.App.2d 625, 305 P.2d 659 (1957).

26. People v. Labarbera, 89 Cal.App.2d 639, 201 P.2d 584 (1949).

27. Petersen v. Dunbar, 355 F.2d 800 (9th Cir.1966).

28. People v. George, 318 Mich. 329, 28 N.W.2d 86 (1947); Cox v. Fogle, 84 Ohio App. 179, 82 N.E.2d 875 (1948); N.Y.Civ.Prac.Law § 410.10 (McKinney).

29. People *ex rel.* Benacquista v. Blanchard, 267 App.Div. 663, 48 N.Y.S.2d 22 (1944).

follow the pattern in the Model Penal Code set out below.[30] The American Bar Association Standards Relating to Probation recommend that the only condition required by statute be that " * * * the probationer lead a law-abiding life during the period of probation. Conditions imposed by the court should be designed to assist the probationer in leading a law-abiding life, and be reasonably related to his rehabilitation and not unduly restrictive of his liberty or incompatible with his freedom of religion. They should not be so vague or ambiguous as to give no real guidance."[31] The list of conditions deemed appropriate to be imposed by the court include cooperating with a program of supervision; meeting family responsibilities; maintaining steady employment, or engaging or refraining from engaging in a specific employment or occupation; pursuing prescribed educational or vocational training; undergoing available medical or psychiatric treatment; maintaining residence in a prescribed area or in a special facility established for or available to persons on probation; refraining from consorting with certain types of people or frequenting certain types of places; and making restitution of the fruits of the crime or reparation for loss or damage caused thereby. The American Bar Association Standards suggest that conditions requiring payment of fines, restitution, reparation, or, provision of family support should not go beyond the probationer's ability to pay, that the

---

30. Conditions of Suspension or Probation.

(1) When the court suspends the imposition of sentence on a person who has been convicted of a crime or sentences him to be placed on probation, it shall attach such reasonable conditions, authorized by this section, as it deems necessary to insure that he will lead a law-abiding life or likely to assist him to do so.

(2) The court, as a condition of its order, may require the defendant: (a) to meet his family responsibilities; (b) to devote himself to a specific employment or occupation; (c) to undergo available medical or psychiatric treatment and to enter and remain in a specified institution when required for that purpose; (d) to pursue a prescribed secular course of study or vocational training; (e) to attend or reside in a facility established for the instruction, recreation or residence of persons on probation; (f) to refrain from frequenting unlawful or disreputable places or consorting with disreputable persons; (g) to have in his possession no firearm or other dangerous weapon unless granted written permission; (h) to make restitution of the fruits of his crime or to make reparation, in an amount he can afford to pay, for the loss or damage caused thereby; (i) to remain within the jurisdiction of the court and to notify the court or the probation officer of any change in his address or his employment; (j) to report as directed to the probation officer and to permit the officer to visit his home; (k) to post a bond, with or without surety, conditioned on the performance of any of the foregoing obligations; (l) to satisfy any other conditions reasonably related to the rehabilitation of the defendant and not unduly restrictive of his liberty or incompatible with his freedom of conscience.

(3) When the court sentences a person who has been convicted of a felony or misdemeanor to be placed on probation, it may require him to serve a term of imprisonment not exceeding thirty days as an additional condition of its order. The term of imprisonment imposed hereunder shall be treated as part of the term of probation, and in the event of a sentence of imprisonment upon the revocation of probation, the term of imprisonment served hereunder shall not be credited toward service of such subsequent sentence.]

(4) The defendant shall be given a copy of this article and written notice of any requirements imposed pursuant to this section, stated with sufficient specificity to enable him to guide himself accordingly. Model Penal Code, § 301.1.

31. ABA Standards, Probation, § 3.2.

performance bond required in some jurisdictions should not be employed, and that probationers should not be required to pay the costs of probation.[32]

The National Advisory Commission would authorize but not require the imposition of a range of specified conditions; would require that any condition imposed in an individual case be reasonably related to the correction program of the defendant and not unduly restrictive of the defendant's liberty or incompatible with the defendant's constitutional rights; and would direct that conditions be fashioned on the basis of factors relating to the individual offender rather than to the offense committed.[33]

Jail as a Condition of Probation

In some jurisdictions, the court may order a term in jail as a condition of probation. The federal probation statute states that the court, when satisfied that the ends of justice and the best interests of the public and the defendant will be served, thereby "may impose a sentence in excess of six months and provide that the defendant be confined in a jail-type institution for a period not exceeding six months and that the execution of the remainder of the sentence be suspended and the defendant placed on probation for such period and, upon such terms and conditions as the court deems best."[34]

The practice of combining a jail sentence with probation, in effect making a jail sentence a condition of probation, has been widely followed in California.[35] Studies from that state showed that during 1965–72, straight probation accounted for 35.9 percent of sentencing dispositions, while probation and jail accounted for 35.3 percent.[36] Thus, for those years, almost half of the probated sentences in California included a jail term.

The arguments in favor of using a jail sentence in connection with probation are set out in a study of Ohio's practice of "shock probation." Shock probation is seen as a treatment tool that is a compromise between the advantages of incarceration and those of probation. The proponents of this program claim that short-term incarceration, coupled with the supervision of probation, is not only relatively effective but humanitarian as well, and that the recidivism rate is

---

32. *Id.*

33. Nat'l Advisory Comm'n Standards, § 16.11.

34. 18 U.S.C.A. § 3651ff.

35. The statute recites: The court, or judge thereof, in the order granting probation and as a condition thereof may imprison the defendant in the county jail for a period not exceeding the maximum period fixed by law in the instant case * * * or may in connection with granting probation, impose either imprisonment in the county jail or fine, or both, or neither * * *. Cal.Penal Code § 1203.1 (West).

The statute has been upheld against challenges. In one case the court stated that jail detention may be ordered as a condition of probation and when so ordered is not regarded as punishment but as part and parcel of supervised effort toward rehabilitation. Petersen v. Dunbar, 355 F.2d 800 (9th Cir.1966).

The period of commitment to county jail as a condition of misdemeanor probation is limited to one year. Cal.Penal Code § 19a (West). *Ex parte* Hays, 120 Cal.App.2d 308, 260 P.2d 1030 (1953).

36. California Youth Authority. Commitments and Sentences of Felony Defendants Convicted in California Criminal Courts 1965, 1972, by Type of Sentence. California's Probation Subsidy Programs, Table 9, p. 29.

significantly lower than the national average of recidivism for offenders not granted shock probation (shock probation figures showed a success rate of 85 percent). The benefits of shock probation are particularly evident with reference to offenders who are married and have dependents and other outside attachments, and with persons who have had some previous altercation with the law but have not yet become a part of the serious criminal element.

The Model Penal Code also permits a thirty-day period of imprisonment in connection with a probated term for a person convicted of a felony or misdemeanor.[37]

The American Bar Association Standards Relating to Sentencing Alternatives and Procedures include among the range of sentencing alternatives "commitment to an institution for a short, fixed period followed by automatic release under supervision,"[38] although the commentary on this section recognizes widespread opposition to combining jail with probation.

A few states specifically prohibit the use of a term of imprisonment as a condition of probation. The National Advisory Commission, which also recommends against the practice, states the reasons as follows:

> The goal [of probation] should be to maintain in the community all persons who, with support, can perform there acceptably and to select for some type of confinement only those who, on the basis of evidence, cannot complete probation successfully, even with optimal support.
>
> With this goal in mind, the practice of commitment to an institution for the initial period of probation (variously known as shock probation, split sentence, etc.) as the Federal and some State statutes permit, should be discontinued. This type of sentence defeats the purpose of probation, which is the earliest possible reintegration of the offender into the community. Short-term commitment subjects the probationer to the destructive effects of institutionalization, disrupts his life in the community, and stigmatizes him for having been in jail. Further, it may add to his confusion as to his status.[39]

Obviously, different jurisdictions have arrived at different conclusions as to the effectiveness of combining a jail term with a probated one. Probation "purists" see the practice as a negation of the basic meaning and objective of probation. Others believe that an initial period of incarceration makes the offender more receptive to probation supervision and significantly improves the person's chances of making successful community adjustment. In many cases, outcome may depend not so much upon the method used as upon the care with which offenders are selected when there is an option to include or not include incarceration as a condition of probation.

Fine as a Condition of Probation

In many states, a sentence to pay a fine accompanies probation. New York, for example, has many possible dispositions of a convicted defendant. Among

---

California law also authorizes placement of the defendant in a diagnostic facility for observation and treatment for a period not to exceed 90 days. Cal.Penal Code § 1203.03 (West).

37. Model Penal Code § 301.1(3).

38. ABA Standards, Sentencing Alternatives and Procedures, § 2.4(a)iii.

39. Nat'l Advisory Comm'n Standards, Corrections, p. 321.

these are a conditional discharge, a fine, conditional discharge plus a fine, probation, and a fine plus probation.[40] The disposition of probation alone is sometimes referred to as "straight probation." Similar nomenclature is used in states where jail is a condition of probation, the one disposition being referred to as "straight probation," the others as "probation and jail," "split sentence," or, as in Ohio or Texas, "shock probation." The wording of the statute makes it clear in some cases that the payment of the fine when so ordered is a condition of probation; in other cases the fine plus probation is treated as a separate disposition from straight probation.

Participation in Special Programs as a Condition of Probation

There is an increasing tendency to couple the grant of probation with the requirement that the defendant participate in specialized programs, as for example, programs for the treatment of drug addiction and alcoholism. The probation also may be accompanied by such provisions as intermittent or periodic imprisonment, or residence in a halfway house. The question of custody and the duties of the probation officer in such cases may be difficult. A few statutes attempt to clarify these points.

In Texas a probationer may be required to "participate in a community-based program" and/or "remain under custodial supervision in a community-based facility." In such cases, the probationer can be required to participate in, or even live in, a narcotics or alcohol rehabilitation program or facility. The Texas court can require the probationer to serve a term in a restitution center or secure employment and make specified restitution to the victim of the probationer's crime. In such cases, the employer of a probationer participating in a residential restitution program is required to "deliver" the probationer's salary to the restitution center director who will then deduct the cost of the probationer's food, housing, supervision, travel to and from work, support of the probationer's dependents, and restitution to the victims of the offense committed by the probationer. The remainder is given to the probationer upon release.[41]

Conditions of Juvenile Probation

Juvenile court statutes typically provide for a wide range of dispositional alternatives for both the adjudicated delinquent and the child in need of supervision.[42] Suspended judgment, placement in both public and private institutions and programs, and various forms of informal supervision are available. Participation in special addiction treatment programs is frequently a condition of juvenile probation. Sometimes the conditions imposed in juvenile

---

40. A fine must be distinguished from a civil penalty (damages); forfeiture (of goods, property or rights); costs (imposed in connection with expenses of the trial or hearing); and restitution or reparation (in that a fine is payable to the state or other unit of government while reparation or restitution is made to the victim).

41. Tex.Code Crim.Proc.Ann. art. 42.12 § 6 (Vernon).

42. Sometimes called "Persons in Need of Supervision (PINS), or Minors in Need of Supervision (MINS)."

probation take the form of obligations upon the parent or guardian as well as, or in lieu of, conditions upon the juvenile. In some states, a list of permissible conditions appears as rules of court instead of statutory enactments, although the statute may specifically state that permissible terms and conditions shall be defined in rules of court.

The New York Family Court Act, for example, provides that rules of court shall define permissible terms and conditions of probation, and places a two-year limit on probation for the adjudicated delinquent and one year for the adjudicated person in need of supervision. An additional year of probation may be required by the court under exceptional circumstances.[43] The applicable rule of court sets out permissible terms and conditions of probation under which the child may be required to obey the lawful commands of parents or other persons legally responsible for the child's care. These provisions require the child to:

- keep all appointments with the probation officer;
- attend school regularly or be suitably employed;
- be home at night by the hour set by parents or other persons legally responsible for the child's care;
- notify the probation officer immediately of any change in residence, school, or employment;
- remain within the county of residence and obtain permission from the probation service of the court for any absence from the county in excess of two weeks;
- answer all reasonable inquiries of the probation officer;
- avoid known criminals and persons of known disreputable or harmful character;
- cooperate with the auxiliary services of the court, including the probation service, in seeking and accepting medical and/or psychiatric diagnosis and treatment, including family casework or child guidance;
- submit records and reports of earnings and expenses; and
- contribute to his or her own support when financially able to do so.

The juvenile may also be required to:

- spend part of the probation period, not to exceed two years, in a facility provided by the Division of Youth;
- attend a nonresidential program of youth rehabilitation approved by the court;
- take clinic or similar treatment for narcotic addictions;
- refrain from driving a motor vehicle; and
- abstain from intoxicating liquors.

A recent revision of the Texas Family Code prescribes conditions of probation in general terms only. At the dispositional hearing of the adjudicated delinquent, the court may "place the child on probation on such reasonable and

---

43. N.Y.Fam.Ct. Act § 757 (McKinney).

lawful terms as the court may determine for a period not to exceed one year, subject to extensions not to exceed one year each." [44]

In California, any person under the age of eighteen years who is a ward of the juvenile court may be placed under the supervision of a probation officer. When such ward is placed under the supervision of the probation officer or committed to the officer's care, custody, and control, the court may make any and all reasonable orders for the conduct of such ward, including the requirement to work and earn money for the support of any dependents or to effect reparation and, in either case, to keep an account of any earnings and report the same to the probation officer and apply such earnings as directed by the court. The court may impose and require any and all reasonable conditions that it may determine fitting and proper to the end that justice may be done and the reformation and rehabilitation of the ward enhanced. [45]

Individualized Probation Conditions

As the National Advisory Commission has pointed out, the conditions imposed are a critical factor in probation:

> In too many cases, courts mechanically adopt standard conditions for all probationers. Conditions should be tailored to fit the needs of the offenders and society, and no condition should be imposed unless necessary for these purposes. Statutes should give the court great latitude in imposing sentence, particularly where juveniles are concerned. [46]

The Commission notes that for most teenagers, jails are too severe and fines are usually paid by parents. Other forms of retribution have much more meaning, such as washing school buses, cleaning up parks, or serving in hospital emergency rooms. "Conditions that are unrelated to any useful purpose serve mainly to provoke the probationer and make unnecessary work for the probation officer." [47]

The position of the Advisory Commission is well taken. The practical problems of tailoring the conditions to the individual offender, whether the offender be adult or juvenile, felon or misdemeanant, remain. As in all sentencing, accurate and precise information about the offender is essential. However, the sources of that information are often few and difficult to contact. Verifying information is a special problem, particularly if the offender challenges the accuracy of the presentence report or social history. Even after adequate verified information is at hand, just how to *use* that information in the sentencing and disposition—as for example, in fixing conditions of probation—is a complicated matter.

Some things are self-evident. It does no good, for example, to require that the probationer obtain treatment for drug addiction if no treatment programs are available in that locality. It is self-defeating to direct that the probationer seek

---

44. Tex.Fam.Code Ann. tit. 3, § 54.04(d)(1) (Vernon).

45. Cal.Welf. & Inst.Code § 730 (West).

46. Nat'l Advisory Comm'n Standards, Corrections Standard 5.4—Commentary, pp. 159–160.

47. *Id.*

such treatment in a neighboring city if one of the conditions of probation is to not drive an automobile. A probation condition that the alcoholic refrain from using alcoholic beverages is little more than an expression of pious hope on the part of the sentencing court or of the legislature if including the condition is required by statute. A stipulation that the probationer support any dependents is meaningless if the offender has no job skills or the job skills are related to a licensed occupation for which the license will be denied. The major shifts in the concepts of probation recommended by the National Commission—that probation be the disposition of choice and preferred disposition, and that probation supervision change from its casework orientation to a goal-oriented service delivery system—depend upon identifying needs of the probationer and educating probation officers as community resource managers. These in turn depend upon the development of a wide range of community services not yet in existence and upon greatly expanded involvement of the community in the welfare of the offender.

Because of the fact that in many states the requirement for a presentence report is tied to the use or contemplated use of probation as the disposition, a change in sentencing philosophy that mandates probation as the usual and preferred form of disposition, with committees.

Term of Probation

The power to fix the term (i.e., length) of probation is usually given to the sentencing authority, although maximum and sometimes minimum limits may be set by statute. These limits are often closely related to the maximum term fixed by statute for the offense had the offender been committed to a penal institution instead of being placed on probation. This came about at least in part to correct what was recognized as a glaring weakness in suspended sentence procedures—it was difficult to determine when the offender was free of the sentence. With no limit fixed, the offender could live out life in a kind of legal limbo, subject at any time to being called back and sentenced for the offense, and uncertain as to whether he or she had been "convicted." Thus, neither the offender nor persons dealing with the offender could determine whether the offender was suffering from the penalties and disabilities that are the collateral consequence of a conviction.

Legislative fixing of maximum terms of probation and court imposition of a stated term of probation avoided these abuses in the suspended sentence system. The modern trend, however, has been to specify limits for probation that are less than the limits for commitment. Similar term limitations are also specified for conditional discharge, that first cousin of probation that seems to have all of the attributes of probation except supervision. In some states, the court is empowered to extend the length of probation during the original term. In many states, the court is given authority to terminate probation at any time within the probation period or after a certain portion of the probation period has been served. Early termination statutes may or may not include provisions for setting aside the conviction and restoring civil rights lost by the offender.

Modern standards for probation share the common characteristic of recommending fixed, relatively short probation terms, with authority given to the court to terminate the probation at any time during the probated period. The Model Penal Code suggests a probation of five years upon conviction of a felony or two years upon conviction of a misdemeanor or petty misdemeanor.[48] The American Bar Association Standards Relating to Probation contain a provision that neither supervision nor the power to revoke should be permitted to extend beyond a legislatively fixed time, which should in no event exceed two years for a misdemeanor or five years for a felony.[49] The National Advisory Commission states that a sentence of probation should be for a specific term not to exceed the maximum sentence authorized by law, except that probation for misdemeanants may be for a period not exceeding one year.[50]

As has been noted, the court is sometimes given authority to extend a term of probation or to terminate probation prior to the expiration of the time limits imposed. The procedures that should be required for such action are discussed elsewhere in connection with modification of probation conditions.

Term of Juvenile Probation

In some jurisdictions, the maximum term of probation of the adjudicated juvenile is coextensive with that of juvenile court jurisdiction. Thus, if the juvenile court has jurisdiction over the person until twenty-one years of age, probation supervision may extend until the twenty-first birthday. A shorter term may be fixed for a program of informal probation. However, modern juvenile court legislation usually fixes shorter terms. The term of probation under the new Texas juvenile court act is one year, with successive one-year extensions allowed.[51]

Imposing Term and Conditions of Probation

It is of great importance that the offender have a clear understanding of the term and conditions of probation. The length of probation should be stated in the order granting probation. The probation conditions should be in writing, should be clearly stated, and should be read and explained to the offender if there is any doubt of the offender's ability to read and comprehend the written instructions. While it has been held that an offender is presumed to know about statutory requirements concerning probation, such requirements should be included in the stated conditions if they place restraints upon behavior of the probationer. Oral and informal conditions and instructions, whether from the court or the probation officer, are not binding upon the defendant,[52] although it has been held that some generally stated conditions may be sufficient to adequately inform the defendant of the conditions of probation. A written copy

---

48. Model Penal Code, § 301.2.

49. ABA Standards Relating to Probation § 1.1(d); ABA Standards Relating to Sentencing Alternatives and Procedures, § 2.4.

50. Nat'l Advisory Comm'n Standards Correction Standard 5.4.1.

51. Tex.Fam.Code Ann. § 54.04(d)(1) (Vernon).

52. People v. George, 318 Mich. 329, 28 N.W.2d 86 (1947); People v. Sutton, 322 Mich. 104, 33 N.W.2d 681 (1948).

of the conditions of probation should be given to the probationer, and many probation statutes so provide.[53]

If the probation officer becomes a community resource manager instead of the supervisor of the probationer in a one-to-one relationship, the problems of communication between probationer and probation officer will exacerbate. Carefully drawn, written instructions as to behavior are relatively simple to explain to a probationer as compared to teaching the probationer how to make use of the services of a supervisor whose role is that of a community resource manager. The inability to "cope" is a characteristic common to a great number of offenders. This inability is particularly great when the offender needs help in unusual or emergency situations. The experience of United States Army personnel charged with investigating and possible return to duty of soldiers absent without leave shows that the precipitating cause of the unauthorized absence is apt to be a personal or family problem with which the soldier simply does not know how to deal, nor does the soldier know how or where to turn for the legal, medical, or counseling help needed. The success of the community resource manager concept in probation will be in no small part determined by the extent to which the probation officer can get the probationer to identify needs and to call upon the probation officer for help in sufficient time to enable them to jointly explore possible solutions.

The intangibles represented in community resource management for the probationer are going to be difficult to put into probation conditions and explain to the probationer. A probation condition that the probationer will call upon the probation officer for assistance in times of personal and family emergency hardly seems realistic, which means that the challenge to the probation officer is going to be one of establishing the kind of relationship that will make it normal and natural for the probationer in trouble to seek advice and assistance. It goes without saying that the burden of knowledge of community resources and of "ways and means" of problem solving placed upon the probation officer by such a concept are enormous.

Modification of Term and Conditions of Probation

With respect to the modification of the term and conditions of probation, two sets of circumstances must be differentiated: the situation where the modification will result in a shorter term or less restrictive conditions and the situation where modification will extend the term or impose additional restrictions. Authority to modify the term of probation by decreasing the term and discharging the offender prior to the completion of the term should be placed in the court.[54] The court should likewise have authority to modify the conditions of probation on application of the probationer, the probation officer, or upon its own motion. The probationer should have free access to the court for the

---

53. *See, for example,* Tex.Code Crim.Proc.Ann. art. 42.12, § 6 (Vernon).

54. The sentencing court should have the authority to terminate probation at any time. Authority should be exercised prior to the term fixed in the original sentence if it appears that the offender has made a good adjustment and that further supervision or enforced compliance with other conditions is no longer necessary. ABA Standards Relating to Probation, § 4.2., Probation.

purpose of clarification or explanation of the probation conditions. This power of modification preserves the flexibility of probation as a correctional tool, since it allows for changing conditions and for the gradual increase in the ability of the probationer to handle personal affairs, which is one of the major objectives of probation.

Giving the court the power to discharge the offender from probation supervision prior to the expiration of the stated probation term recognizes the fact that many probationers do not need probation services for the full time period originally set, and has the advantage of removing from the probation rolls offenders whose reintegration into the community is complete or at least is complete enough to make it probable that they can manage without further intervention by the probation officer. Maintaining a connection between probationer and probation officer for a period of time after formal discharge from probation during which the probationer can obtain assistance if needed would have much to recommend it. This practice, of providing a "lifeline" after formal discharge, is often used by psychiatrists and counselors as a means of providing emotional support for the former patient or client. It would be particularly appropriate to the community manager concept of the probation officer who would thus be available for general short-term advice or assistance after the formal probation relationship had terminated.

Probation statutes grant power to the court to enlarge as well as decrease term and conditions of probation. Generally speaking, this power when granted must be exercised within the time limits of the original probated term, although disappearance of the probationer may "toll" or interrupt the running of the term of probation. The court loses the power to modify conditions after the offender is committed to an institution or after probation has been terminated by court action or by the passage of time.

The recommended standards on probation include provision that the court retain the power to modify the term and conditions of probation. The Model Penal Code states that during the period of suspension or probation, the court, on application of a probation officer or of the defendant, may modify the requirements imposed on the defendant or add further requirements authorized by the section setting forth permissible conditions. The court shall eliminate any requirements that impose an unreasonable burden on the defendant.[55] The American Bar Association Standards Relating to Probation recite that conditions should be subject to modification or termination by the court.[56] The National Advisory Commission standard recommends that the court should be authorized to impose such conditions as are necessary to provide a benefit to the offender and protection to the public. The court also should be authorized to modify or enlarge the conditions of probation at any time prior to expiration or termination of sentence.[57]

The desirability of giving the court authority to modify the term and conditions of probation is generally accepted. The issues that give rise to controversy are technical issues that involve a determination of when a proba-

---

55. Model Penal Code § 301.2.

56. ABA Standards Relating to Probation, § 3.3.

57. Nat'l Advisory Comm'n Standards, Corrections Standard 5.4.

tion period has ended and the policy issues of what procedures should be required before the court can exercise its authority to modify the original term and conditions of probation, particularly if the modification is in the direction of extending the term or imposing more restrictive conditions.

Tolling of Probation Term

To "toll" the running of a sentence or a period of time limitation means to interrupt it, to "stop the clock." It is usual for probation statutes to provide that the term of probation is "tolled" if the defendant is charged with a violation of probation and flees the jurisdiction or cannot be found. The Illinois statute, for example, provides that when a petition is filed charging a violation of a condition of probation, the court may order a summons for the offender to appear or a warrant for the offender's arrest. "The issuance of such warrant or summons shall toll the sentence of probation or of conditional discharge until the final determination of the charge, and the term of probation or conditional discharge shall not run so long as the offender has not answered the summons or warrant." [58]

Procedures for Modifying
Term and Conditions of Probation

It can be argued, of course, that the procedures for modifying the term or conditions of probation should be the same or similar to those associated with the granting of probation in the first instance. However, a little reflection shows that to require an appearance of all parties before the court, complete with counsel, to change the reporting day from Friday to Wednesday, or to clarify the meaning of a condition upon application of the defendant, would be unnecessary and would in no way promote the objectives of probation. Changes that impose longer, harsher, or more restrictive conditions upon the offender would appear to demand more formal procedures than changes that lead to relaxed supervision or an early discharge of the defendant from probation.

A number of states authorize early termination without statutory guidelines as to when the power should be exercised. A significantly larger number permit early termination or discharge from further supervision upon the satisfaction of statutory criteria or the taking of certain procedural steps. The statutory requirements may be that the "ends of justice be served," that a hearing and a showing of good cause be made, or that the release be upon satisfactory fulfillment of conditions, where the best interests of the public and probationer will be served. The most frequent requirement is a showing that the probationer has satisfied the condition of probation. Presence of the probationer is a usual requirement if the modification will extend the term or impose more restrictive conditions.

When the early discharge procedures also have as their objective the prevention of a conviction with its serious consequences to the offender, or are part of

---

58. Ill. Unified Code of Corrections § 1005–6–5(2).

a process that seeks to "wipe out" the conviction and restore the offender to the enjoyment of his or her civil rights, considerable formality and careful record keeping in the court would benefit both the state and the defendant.

The American Bar Association committee working with sentencing and probation standards gave considerable thought to these procedural problems. One of the first considerations was to distinguish between modifications in probation conditions that may lead to confinement of the defendant and those that do not. The standards recommend, for example, that prior to revocation of probation there should be a review of conditions, followed by changes where necessary or desirable, and a formal or informal conference with the probationer to reemphasize the necessity of complying with the conditions.[59] The right of the probationer to apply to the court for a clarification of change of conditions was stated without recommendation as to a conference or hearing. A request for clarification provides an avenue for resolving disputes between probationer and probation officer about the meaning of a condition, it being assumed that generally such disputes would be worked out without court intervention.[60]

Where a modification in the terms and conditions of probation may lead to confinement, procedures should correspond to those required for revocation of probation.[61] Whether this would include the "on-site hearing" demanded by *Gagnon v. Scarpelli*[62] as well as the probation revocation hearing before the court is still an open question. If modifications suggested are so extensive as to raise this question, the matter should probably be identified as a revocation hearing. Instead of following procedures for modification of term or conditions, the revocation procedures would be followed.

The whole thrust of recent "due process" cases would suggest that if the modification would impose new or additional burdens on the probationer, there should be a hearing, preceded by notice, at which the defendant would be given an opportunity to object to the suggested modification and refute any misstatements as to the facts upon which the modification is based.[63] Appearance before the court insures that the matter will be decided by an impartial tribunal and the decision based on matters before the court. The probationer should be given a written copy of the modified conditions and care taken to assure the probationer understands the continuing requirements of the probation.

---

59. ABA Standards Relating to Probation, 5.1(b).

60. *Id.,* § 3.1(c).

61. *See generally* Revocation of Probation, *infra.*

62. Gagnon v. Scarpelli, 411 U.S. 778, 93 S.Ct. 1756, 36 L.Ed.2d 656 (1973).

63. Morrissey v. Brewer, 408 U.S. 471, 92 S.Ct. 2593, 33 L.Ed.2d 484 (1972).

Probation and Parole Conditions: Recent Decisions*

OWENS v. KELLEY

681 F.2d 1362 (11th Cir.1982)

The defendant was convicted of two felony charges regarding the possession of controlled substances and was placed on probation under various conditions. Among the conditions imposed were the requirements that the probationer participate in a specific rehabilitation program, that he submit to warrantless searches and seizures by probation authorities or police officials, and that he submit to periodic polygraph or psychological stress evaluations (PSE). The probationer brought a civil rights action under Section 1983 making the following claims: (1) the program entitled Emotional Maturity Instruction violated his First Amendment rights because it consisted of "religious" instruction; (2) the condition regarding the Fourth Amendment waiver was improper and overbroad; and (3) the polygraph/P.S.E. requirement violated his right to be free from self-incrimination. The dis-

trict court granted summary judgment in favor of the defendants and appeal was taken.

First, fourth and fifth amendment violations claimed by probationer. Court held conditions valid.

On appeal the court held first that summary judgment in relation to the probationer's religious claim was improper. Summary judgment is only appropriate where there are no material facts in dispute. While the actual program in the instant case may not have contained "religious" material, the probationer had testified that instruction within the program was often based on Biblical teachings. Finding it clear that a probation condition could not require the adoption or practice of a particular religion, and finding that material facts were in dispute in the instant case, the court held that

---

* Reported in *Probation and Parole Law Reports,* (Warrensburg, Missouri: Knchans-Miller Publications). Used with permission of the publisher.

summary judgment was improper. Stated the court:

> In searching for the proper teaching of an EMI course it is probably difficult to locate one who can teach morality without reference to religion, but that is the task which must be accomplished. We recognize that there is a fine line between rehabilitation efforts which encourage lawful conduct by an appeal to morality and the benefits of moral conduct to life of the probationer, and efforts which encourage lawfulness through adherence to religious belief. Nevertheless, this is the line that must not be overstepped. It will be the function of the District Court on remand to determine whether Owens has been placed in a program that does overstep this line.

Turning to the Fourth Amendment claims, the court found that while the claim was one of first impression in the 11th Circuit, other courts had addressed the issue with mixed results. In *United States v. Tonry,* 605 F.2d 144 (5th Cir.1979), the court fashioned a test for the propriety of probation conditions. That test follows:

> The conditions must be "reasonably related" to the purposes of the Act. Consideration of three factors is required to determine whether a reasonable relationship exists: (1) the purposes sought to be served by probation; (2) the extent to which constitutional rights enjoyed by law-abiding citizens should be accorded to probationers; and (3) the legitimate needs of law enforcement.

Noting that Georgia statutes did not specifically delineate the purposes of probation, the court found that Georgia case law established two essential purposes: the rehabilitation of the offender and the protection of the public. The court held that the condition in the instant case reasonably related to rehabilitation because it sought to dissuade the probationer from the illegal possession of controlled substances and it provided supervising officials with a mechanism to determine whether or not rehabilitation was

actually occurring. While the information obtained as a result of a search could be used as a basis for revocation, it could also be used to determine supervision and counseling levels. Furthermore, the condition advanced the purpose of protecting the public by deterring future illegal conduct and enhancing law enforcement ability to detect illegal conduct.

Turning to the second *Tonry* factor, the rights that should be accorded probationers, the court found that while Fourth Amendment protections applied to the probation setting, the state had a compelling interest in setting some limitations upon probationers. Furthermore, probationers have a diminished expectation of privacy because of their conviction. Because the state has an interest in rehabilitation and protection of the public and because probationers enjoy a diminished expectation of privacy, the court found the condition to be proper. The court went on to reject the propositions that probation searches must be based on probable cause or even the lesser standard of reasonable suspicion. Citing *Latta v. Fitzharris,* 521 F.2d 246 (9th Cir.1975) for the position that a probation or parole officer should know more about a probationer or parolee than anyone else, with the exception of perhaps his family, and noting language from *Latta* which indicated a probation search could be conducted on a mere "hunch," the court held that to impose a stricter standard would subvert the goals of rehabilitation and public protection. Acknowledging that probation searches must be "reasonable" and carried out in furtherance of the purposes of probation, the court held that a search that was intimidating or harassing and performed for reasons totally unrelated to the conviction or rehabilitation were improper. Concluded the court:

> Owens and amicus finally argue that if warrantless searches are to be permitted we should only allow such searches by probation supervisors and not by law enforcement officers. We are not con-

vinced, however, that such a distinction should be drawn. While the primary task of supervising Owens' probation rests with the state probation supervisors, law enforcement officers can lend legitimate assistance by conducting searches pursuant to the probation condition. As noted earlier such searches are lawful so long as they are in fact conducted for probationary purposes. They cannot be conducted as "a subterfuge for criminal investigations." *United States v. Consuelo-Gonzalez,* 521 F.2d at 267.

Regarding the probationer's Fifth Amendment claims, the court found the claim to be without merit. The probationer was not required to "answer" incriminating questions and he could assert his Fifth Amendment privilege against self-incrimination if he so desired. Furthermore, there was nothing in the condition which indicated that the results would be used as a basis for probation revocation. Indeed, the court found that such a practice was impermissible under *State v. Chambers,* 239 S.E.2d 324 (1977). The court went on to hold that such a condition was no more intrusive than a requirement that a probationer answer all reasonable inquires by his probation officer.

As a final matter, the court found that the trial judge imposing the condition was immune to liability under Section 1983 because the complaint had not demonstrated that the actions taken were outside the judge's capacity as a judge. However, the county could be held liable were the district court to find, on remand, that the rehabilitative program violated the appellant's First Amendment rights.

The order granting summary judgment was reversed and the matter was remanded for further proceedings.

STATE v. MORGAN

389 So.2d 364 (La.Sup.Ct.1980)

The appellant contested the condition of her probation which required her to stay out of the French Quarter in New Orleans during the time of her probation claiming that said conditions amounted to banishment. The defendant had been convicted of attempted prostitution and this was a second offense.

Probationer alleged condition amounted to banishment. Court found no merit to claim.

Reviewing the above issue the court stated as follows:

Other states have invalidated conditions requiring that a probationer leave a particular city, county or state. See, for example, *Hoggett v. State,* 101 Miss. 269, 57 So. 811 (1912); *People v. Baum,* 251 Mich. 187, 231 N.W. 95 (1930); *In re Scarborough,* 76 Cal.App.2d 648, 173 P.2d 825 (1946); and *Weigand v. Commonwealth,* 397 S.W.2d 780 (Ky., 1965). However, the French Quarter is a small geographical area; an historical district of New Orleans with carefully delineated boundaries. In addition to antiquity, it is noted for night life, drinking, and prostitution. A restriction against entering a relatively small geographical area of one city can hardly be equated with loss of citizenship, or banishment from a city, county or state. Compare *State v. Chestnut,* 11 Utah 2d 142, 356 P.2d 36 (1960); *State v. Collett,* 232 Ga. 668, 208 S.E.2d 472 (Ga., 1974); and *Wilson v. State,* 151 Ga.App. 501, 260 S.E.2d 527 (Ga., 1979). Moreover, the condition of probation is reasonably related to Ms. Morgan's rehabilitation.

LSA–C.Cr.P. art. 895.A provides:

"A. When the court suspends the imposition or execution of sentence and places a defendant on probation, it shall require the defendant to refrain from criminal conduct and it may impose any specific conditions reasonably related to his rehabilitation, including any of the following:

"That the defendant shall:

*   *   *

"(8) Refrain from frequenting unlawful or disreputable places or consorting with disreputable persons; . . .". A trial judge has wide latitude in imposing conditions of probation. *State v. Credeur,* 328 So.2d 59 (La., 1976). The proviso that defendant remain out of the French Quarter is apparently based upon the theory that Ms. Morgan's rehabilitation would best be served by removing her from an environment in which offenses of prostitution are frequently committed. The condition is reasonable and within the trial judge's discretion.

Finding no merit to the defendant's claims, the court affirmed the conviction of sentence.

BROWN v. STATE
406 So.2d 1262 (Fla.Dist.Ct.App.1981)

It was not improper for the court to impose a condition that defendant "stay away from bars."

It was not improper for the trial court to impose as a condition of the defendant's probation that the defendant "stay away from bars". Stated the court:

> The record reflects that appellant has a lengthy history of varied involvement in crime, including association with drug dealers. During prior probationary periods he was often unemployed and was considered to be generally lazy by his probation officer. Apparently, the trial judge felt hanging around bars with the associations often found there was not conducive to appellant's rehabilitation and to the protection of the public from future criminal activity in which appellant might, as a result, become involved.

The judgment of the trial court was affirmed.

OYOGHOK v. MUNICIPALITY OF ANCHORAGE
641 P.2d 1267 (Alaska Ct.App.1982)

Condition that prohibited defendant from being within a certain area of the city was not improper.

The condition which prohibited the defendant from being within a certain area of the city was not improper. The defendant had been convicted of soliciting for prostitution and the condition was directed toward keeping her out of an area known for street prostitution. Such condition was related to the prevention of future criminality and rehabilitation and the revocation of the defendant's probation could be based on a violation of this special condition. Stated the court [footnotes omitted]:

> In assessing Oyoghok's claim, we must determine whether the challenged condition of probation was reasonably related to the goal of her rehabilitation and whether it was unduly restrictive of her liberty. *Sprague v. State,* 590 P.2d 410, 417 (Alaska 1979). *See also Roman v. State,* 570 P.2d 1235 (Alaska 1977). While we believe Oyoghok's arguments have a good deal of merit when viewed in the abstract, we do not think they are persuasive under the circumstances of this case. All of Oyoghok's violations occurred at night, in the virtual epicenter of the proscribed area. These incidents were unrelated to travel by Oyoghok through the area or to her use of stores, restaurants, or offices in the vicinity. At no point has Oyoghok contended that she was lawfully employed or seeking employment in this area, nor does it appear from the record that Oyoghok resided in the restricted area or had any legitimate need to visit or travel through it.

The revocation was affirmed.

PARKERSON v. STATE
274 S.E.2d 799 (Ga.Ct.App.1980)

The defendant was granted probation on the following condition: "Defendant is to remove himself and his wife immediately from the Waycross Judicial Circuit, particularly Charlton County and specifically from where he is now living. Defendant is further ordered to stay out of the Waycross Judicial Circuit during his entire probation period." The defendant appealed claiming that this condition was invalid.

Condition requiring defendant and his wife to leave town. Court held banishment was a reasonable condition against defendant but not against the wife.

Stated the court:

> Code Ann. § 27–2709 gives jurisdiction to the trial court to determine the question of probation of a defendant who has been found guilty of a criminal offense; Code Ann. § 27–2711 permits the court to determine the terms and conditions of probation, and lists 10 conditions of probation. It is well settled that the conditions enumerated in that section are not exclusive, but the trial court may impose other requirements not specifically listed therein. *Wood v. State,* 150 Ga.App. 582, 583, 258 S.E.2d 171 (1979); *Gay v. State,* 101 Ga.App. 225, 113 S.E.2d 223 (1960). Banishment of one convicted of a crime from a county or counties has been held to be a reasonable condition of probation. *State v. Collett,* 232 Ga. 668, 208 S.E.2d 472 (1974).

> We know of no statute or other authority, however, which grants jurisdiction to the trial court to banish a person *other than* the convicted criminal as a condition of his probation. Not only would such a condition unreasonably restrict an innocent party's freedom to travel, but it imposes a condition on the probationer over which he has no control. Such a condition, banishing appellant's wife from the Waycross Judicial Circuit is, therefore, invalid and unenforceable.

The judgment was affirmed with the exception of the condition as to the wife.

WILKINSON v. STATE
388 So.2d 1322 (Fla.Dist.Ct.App.1980)

A condition of probation is invalid if it: (1) has no relationship to the crime for which the defendant was convicted; (2) relates to conduct which is not in itself criminal, and (3) requires or forbids conduct which is not reasonably related to future criminality. In the instant case the defendant was convicted of carrying a concealed weapon. The court found the condition that the defendant not live with a female to whom he was not married or related to be improper.

STATE v. PARKER
286 S.E.2d 366 (N.C.Ct.App.1982)

Although there was nothing in the record indicating a relationship between the defendant's crime, cutting down a light pole to purposely injure the victim, and the condition that the defendant not possess a firearm or other dangerous weapon, the condition was proper. The court held that a relationship did not have to be established to validate the condition because the condition was one of the sixteen statutory conditions under G.S. § 15A–1343(b)(1–16).

Conditions must be reasonably related to defendant's crime.

Stated the court:

> We feel that the legislature intended the "reasonably related" language of G.S. 15A–1343(b)(17) to serve as a check on the discretion of judges in devising conditions of probation. Where, as here, the judge elects to impose one of the conditions enumerated by the statute, no such check is needed since our

legislature has deemed all of these conditions "appropriate" to the rehabilitation of criminals and their assimilation into law-abiding society.

The order of revocation was affirmed.

ORDONEZ v. STATE
408 So.2d 760 (Fla.Dist.Ct.App.1982)

It was improper to revoke appellant's probation for violation of a condition that required him to obtain a high school or a G.E.D. diploma, other factors being favorable.

It was improper to revoke the appellant's probation for his violation of a condition which required him to obtain a High School or General Equivalency diploma. While the court acknowledged that probation could have originally been revoked for the appellant's failure in this regard, in the instant case the probated conviction, breaking and entering, was approximately seven years old and the defendant had made attempts, albeit feeble, to comply. Stated the court:

> The fact is, however, that appellant's probation was not revoked at the hearing in 1976. Instead, the term of probation was extended another two years, during which appellant made little progress toward fulfilling the special condition. At his next hearing in 1978, the condition not having been fulfilled, another two year extension was negotiated.
>
> Finally, in 1980, after six years of probation, appellant attended the hearing which resulted in the ruling and the adjudication appealed here.
>
> Appellant stands before the court a young man of twenty-four, to be now convicted of a felony he committed seven years ago. He has not been arrested for a crime in the interim. He has steady employment and has recently been promoted to management level. His family and friends are apparently supportive of his transition to maturity

and honesty, although only his mother was called upon to testify. Others were present and we presume their testimony was to be favorable.

> The special condition of probation was intended to assist in appellant's rehabilitation. Its goal was to make appellant a useful, law-abiding citizen, a valuable member of society. It appears that this goal has been reached, nothing to the contrary appearing in the record. We are thus prompted to reflect on the question of what good it would do to punish appellant for failing to accept what was intended as guidance; how would it now benefit appellant or society?

The above considerations led the court to conclude that revocation would serve no purpose at this time. The revocation was reversed.

UNITED STATES v. STINE
675 F.2d 69 (3d Cir.1982)

In this case the defendant appealed claiming that the condition of probation requiring him to receive psychological counseling was an unconstitutional infringement on his right to privacy.

Trial court did not abuse its discretion by imposing a condition that defendant receive psychological counseling.

Disagreeing with the appellant, the court noted that the terms and conditions of probation were matters entrusted to the discretion of the trial court. The standard on appellate review is whether or not a trial court has abused its discretion when imposing conditions. Making this determination, the court noted that a probation condition could impinge on a constitutional freedom so long as the trial court weighed the purpose of probation, the extent to which the probationer should be accorded the rights enjoyed by other members of society, and the needs of law enforcement. Stated the court:

> The district court carefully considered these factors and determined that in view of Stine's courtroom behavior and criminal record, psychological counseling could both promote his rehabilitation and decrease the likelihood that his aberrant behavior would recur to the potential harm of society. We therefore agree with the district court that the condition was reasonably related to the purposes of probation and that the impact on Stine's rights was no greater than necessary to carry out these purposes. *Cf. Higdon v. United States*, 627 F.2d 893 (9th Cir.1980) (requirements that defendant perform charitable work and forfeit all assets were harsher than necessary to achieve rehabilitation or public protection).

Finding that the trial court adequately stated the findings upon which the counseling condition was based, the court affirmed the judgment imposing the special condition.

HEROLD v. STATE

449 A.2d 429 (Md.Ct.Spec.App.1982)

The defendant was placed on probation pursuant to his conviction for assault and battery and a fourth-degree sexual offense. As a condition of probation the defendant was required to attend a mental health program. He attended the program but was "unsatisfactorily" terminated. Because of this termination, the defendant's probation was revoked and the sentence of confinement was executed. The defendant appealed.

Defendant was required to attend a mental health program as condition of probation. He was terminated "unsatisfactorily." Probation revoked. Remanded for further proceedings.

On appeal the court noted that the presentence report contained substantial information regarding the defendant's mental instability and his potential for explosive behavior. However, the court also noted that a defendant placed on probation has a right to remain on probation so long as the conditions of probation are not violated. In the instant case probation was not revoked on the basis of the defendant's violation of the special condition because the defendant had in fact attended the program as required. Rather, revocation was based on the defendant's failure to improve his mental stability. Furthermore, the defendant had secured a private psychiatrist and was willing to undergo treatment with this psychiatrist. Under these circumstances, the court was unwilling to say that the order of the trial court was appropriate. Stated the court:

> In this case, the court demonstrated a proper concern for the interests of society and the potential risk to the public if appellant continued at large without improvement of his mental condition. However, appellant was willing to undergo therapy and had secured the services of a forensic psychologist toward the end. In effect, he would be changing from a public mental health program to a private one, which carried the proffered guarantee that: 1. he would be hospitalized if he became a danger to himself or others; 2. his refusal to commit himself voluntarily if so ordered by Dr. Shapiro would be a violation of probation; and 3. his failure to adhere to treatment plan set up by Dr. Shapiro or any resistance to his recommendations would be reported to the court. We think that this mental health program may well have been adequate to meet the trial judge's quite understandable concern. At all events, we think the proposal was worthy of careful consideration and would justify further proceedings at which Dr. Shapiro's testimony could be received. "[W]ithout attempting to fix blame, . . . the sole objective at this time should be to remedy the situation and to obtain the needed treatment for defendant." *People v. Welch*, 78 Ill.App.3d 184, 33 Ill.Dec. 761, 397

N.E.2d 94, 97 (1979). See *People v. Bowman,* 73 A.D.2d 921, 423 N.Y.S.2d 242 (1980). The cited cases demonstrate that those seeking psychiatric help do not always succeed initially in obtaining it. Nor do those who obtain it necessarily benefit from it initially. The very inability to benefit from counseling is a symptom of the condition that necessitates counseling. It should not also be a premise for punishment. Accordingly, we shall remand for further proceedings.

Without affirming or reversing the judgment of the trial court, the court remanded the matter for further proceedings.

PEOPLE v. TOWNSEND

414 N.E.2d 483 (Ill.App.Ct.1980)

Fine as a condition of probation held valid.

The $9,000 fine as a condition of probation was properly imposed upon the defendant who was convicted of possession of narcotics. The court inquired as to the defendant's ability to pay and properly relied on the defendant's intent to profit from his crime. Such intent is an aggravating factor and could have justified a more severe sentence.

The order of the trial court was affirmed.

UNITED STATES v. TURNER

628 F.2d 461 (5th Cir.1980)

Reimbursement of court appointed counsel fees is not permitted as a condition of probation.

Reimbursement of court appointed counsel fees is not permitted as a condition of probation. *United States v. Jiminez,* 600 F.2d 1172 (5th Cir.1979). 18 U.S.C. § 3651 allows for only three monetary conditions: fines, resti-

tution, and support payments to dependents. Disagreeing with the First Circuit, in *U.S. v. Santarpio,* 560 F.2d 448, *cert. denied,* 434 U.S. 984, 98 S.Ct. 609, 54 L.Ed.2d 478 (1977), the court found that payment for court appointed counsel could not be considered a "fine" within the meaning of the above section. Furthermore, such payments could not be considered restitution to "aggrieved parties". The conviction was affirmed, however, the condition of payment of counsel fees was deleted.

ABEL v. STATE

383 So.2d 325 (Fla.Dist.Ct.App.1980)

Where defendant adjudicated insolvent, probation could not be revoked for failure to pay supervision fees.

Where, as here, the defendant had been adjudicated insolvent and no evidence was presented as to the defendant's ability to pay the costs of supervision, it was improper to revoke probation for the defendant's failure to pay such costs. The revocation was affirmed as to the defendant's failure to work diligently, his failure to file monthly reports, and his change of his residence without permission.

RINTO v. STATE

628 S.W.2d 159 (Tex.Ct.App.1982)

Where defendant failed to establish inability to pay supervision fees, trial court did not abuse its discretion in revoking probation.

The court held that the defendant's probation could properly be revoked on the basis of the defendant's failure to pay certain fines.   The defendant had failed to establish by preponderance of the evidence that he was unable to make the required payments. Stated the court:

> Here appellant invoked this affirmative defense and took the stand in his own behalf, testifying that he had been employed and had earned from $100 a week to $950 a month at various times. He further testified that at the time he stopped making payments he was working at day labor jobs, making enough to pay for rent, food, and gasoline.   At no time did appellant make partial payments or contact anyone in Galveston to explain his situation.
>
> Appellate review of a revocation of probation is a limited inquiry.   The question is whether the trial judge abused his discretion in ordering the revocation.   It is, after all, the trial judge who determines "the credibility of witnesses and the weight to be given to their testimony."   *Ausborne v. State,* 499 S.W.2d 179, 180 (Tex.Crim.App.1973); *Ross v. State,* 523 S.W.2d 402, 403 (Tex. Crim.App.1975).   We must review the evidence "in a light most favorable to the verdict." *Jones v. State,* 589 S.W.2d 419, 421 (Tex.Crim.App.1979).
>
> In our opinion, appellant did not sustain his burden and prove, by a preponderance of the evidence, his inability to pay.

The revocation was affirmed.

ADAMSON v. STATE

383 So.2d 294 (Fla.Dist.Ct.App.1980)

Where, as here, the appellant had been adjudicated insolvent, it was improper to revoke probation for failure to pay supervision costs without specifically finding that the appellant was able to pay.   The finding of the probation violation for the appellant's failure to pay was stricken.   The revocation was affirmed on the basis of the appellant's change of residence without permission and the appellant's violation of the law.

DELUCA v. STATE

383 So.2d 751 (Fla.Dist.Ct.App.1980)

Failure to pay fees, costs generally.

While the revocation was affirmed as a result of the probationer's violation of the law, the court found insufficient evidence to sustain the finding that the probationer was able to pay the cost of extradition and supervision.   The court remanded the matter to the trial court with orders to strike the finding of violations based on defendant's failure to pay.

NORRIS v. STATE

383 So.2d 691 (Fla.Dist.Ct.App.1980)

Condition to "live honorably" invalid.

While the probationer's conduct in committing battery upon his wife was sufficient to sustain a violation of probation for violating the law, the condition requiring the defendant to "live honorably" was disapproved.

PEOPLE v. BROWN

403 N.E.2d 1324 (Ill.App.Ct.1980)

Pursuant to his conviction for unlawful delivery of less than 30 grams of heroin, the defendant was placed on probation on condition that he spend three months in jail, pay a $500 fine, pay $70 in restitution and pay court costs.   The defendant appealed claiming, inter alia, that he was entitled to $5 credit toward his fine for each day incarcerated prior to trial.

Defendant claimed $5 per day in jail credit toward his fine, credit was allowed.

The court held that, pursuant to ch. 38, § 110–14 of the Ill.Rev.Stat., 1977, the defendant was entitled to such credit. Further, his failure to make a timely request for such credit did not waive the issue as the record reflected no notice to the defendant that he was entitled to such credit.

UNITED STATES v. RESTOR

529 F.Supp. 579 (Dist.Pa.1982)

A condition of probation which required air traffic control union officials, convicted of contempt in relation to their participation in work stoppage, to perform eight hours of community service per week was not improper. Stated the court [footnotes omitted]:

> The court has been unable to find any case in the Third Circuit dealing with the question of the legality of community service work as a condition of probation. However, several courts in other circuits have approved the concept as a proper approach to rehabilitation in appropriate situations where the probation conditions in total are reasonably related to the rehabilitation of the offender and the protection of the public. *Higdon v. United States,* 627 F.2d 893 (9th Cir.1980); *United States v. Pastore,* 537 F.2d 675 (2d Cir.1976). The Fourth Circuit has commented that:
>
> We do not suggest that compelling charitable service is an appropriate condition of probation in every case, but we think it an acceptable one here. Certainly the rehabilitative potential of such service is greater than the rehabilitative program of most prisons. The donation of charitable services to the community is both a deterrent to other potential offenders and a symbolic form of restitution to the public for having breached the criminal laws. *United States v. Arthur,* 602 F.2d

660, 664 (4th Cir.), *cert. denied,* 444 U.S. 992, 100 S.Ct. 524, 62 L.Ed.2d 422 (1979).

Community service restitution allowed as condition of probation.

Dealing with the situation in the instant case, the court stated:

> We believe that in the instant cases community service is particularly appropriate. The defendants were officers of a labor organization consisting of individuals whose job it was to assist in air traffic control to promote the safety and efficiency of air commerce. They were employees of the government and hence paid by all taxpayers. When defendants became dissatisfied with the status of the contract negotiations through which they were seeking improved working conditions and higher wages, they attempted to force the government to accede to their demands by engaging in what was patently an illegal work stoppage. Not only was the strike a violation of their oath, their contract and the civil laws, but it was also in violation of the criminal code and a direct order of this court. Defendants were attempting through illegal means to extract from their fellow citizens employment benefits including wage increases, which defendants were unable to obtain through lawful collective bargaining.

The court went on to note that even though a probation condition may have incidental punitive effects, such circumstance did not render the condition illegal.

The request for a stay was denied.

BURCHELL v. STATE

419 So.2d 358 (Fla.Dist.Ct.App.1982)

Condition that defendant "not father any children during probation period" struck.

The per curiam opinion follows:

We strike from the conditions of defendant's probation condition # 12, which states that the defendant "[m]ust not father any children during probation period." See *Rodriguez v. State,* 378 So.2d 7 (Fla. 2d DCA 1979). Otherwise, we affirm the defendant's conviction and sentences.

GARDNER v. STATE

632 S.W.2d 851 (Tex.Ct.App.1982)

While a court may impose only those conditions of probation set forth in Section 6, because Section 6 was amended in August of 1978 to allow confinement as a condition of probation, a condition of 30 days confinement was properly imposed.

Incarceration for thirty days as a condition of probation was properly imposed. Restitution order was proper. *

As to the issue of restitution, the court stated:

> Finally, appellant complains of being required to make restitution to the Trust which has been discharged in bankruptcy. We find no merit in this ground of error. It may be possible for a trustee in bankruptcy, a creditor or other party to establish a right to the money in other proceedings. However, this does not provide appellant a basis for an attack against a condition of probation ordering him to make restitution to the entity from which it was taken. The condition of restitution was within the power of the trial judge to order, and the amount was supported by the evidence. Appellant's fourth ground of error is overruled and the conviction is affirmed.

STATE v. ROWTON

645 P.2d 551 (Or.Ct.App.1982)

Oregon court could impose condition of payment of trial counsel.

While ORS 135.055 authorizes a trial court to impose the payment of "trial" counsel as a condition of probation, that section does not empower a trial court to impose costs for appellate counsel.

UNITED STATES v. RESTOR

679 F.2d 338 (3d Cir.1982)

Community service restitution approved in federal court.

Regarding the condition of 8 hours of community service per week, imposed after a finding of contempt in relation to the defendant's failure to obey an order which enjoined a strike, the court stated:

> As defendants concede, community service may be a proper condition of probation. *See United States v. Arthur,* 602 F.2d 660, 664 (4th Cir.), *cert. denied,* 444 U.S. 992, 100 S.Ct. 524, 62 L.Ed.2d 422 (1979). The district court's exercise of discretion in imposing community service as a condition of probation will be within the power granted to it by 18 U.S.C. § 3651 (1976) "so long as it is reasonably related to rehabilitation of the probationer, . . . deterrence of future misconduct by the probationer or general deterrence of others, [or] deserved punishment." *United States v. Tonry,* 605 F.2d 144, 148 (5th Cir.1979).

* In *Villery v. Florida Parole and Probation Comm.,* 396 So.2d 1107 (Fla.Dist.Ct.App.1981) a probationer unsuccessfully argued that she should be eligible for parole while serving a prison term as a probation condition.

The district court found that defendants had engaged in antisocial conduct, and that community service work was necessary "to reinstate [them] in society, . . . [to] 'integrate [them] in a working environment, and inculcate in [them] a sense of social responsibility.'" In light of this finding, we do not believe that the district court would abuse its discretion if it were to reinstate the community service requirement.

The sentence was vacated on other grounds.

MEREDITH v. RAINES

640 P.2d 175 (Ariz.Sup.Ct.1982)

May parole be revoked on the basis of a special condition orally imposed by the probation officer?

Arizona court approved revocation of parole for violation of special condition orally imposed by probation officer. No violation of due process. *

Answering in the affirmative, the court noted that while probation conditions must be written as set forth by the court, the parole situation is a different matter. Stated the court:

> A parolee, however, is still considered to be in the custody of the State Department of Corrections, a part of the executive branch of government. The rules of procedure before the Board of Pardons and Paroles were promulgated under the authority of A.R.S. § 31–401, et seq. Even though we may require all conditions of probation to be in writing, it does not follow that the Board of Pardons and Paroles must do likewise so long as minimum standards of due process and equal protection are maintained. *Morrissey v. Brewer,* 408 U.S. 471, 92 S.Ct. 2593, 33 L.Ed.2d 484 (1972).

Defendant points to the United States Supreme Court which has held that due process requires a written record be made of prison disciplinary proceedings. *Wolff v. McDonnell,* 418 U.S. 539, 94 S.Ct. 2963, 41 L.Ed.2d 935 (1974). We believe that there are, however, substantial differences between due process requirements in a prison disciplinary hearing described in *Wolff,* supra, and the requirement of written conditions of parole. Although we might believe that difficulty could be avoided by requiring written conditions, where, as here, there is no question as to the conditions imposed, that Meredith had the right to refuse them, R5–4–202(d)(2), Arizona Administrative Rules and Regulations, and that he admittedly violated such conditions, there can be no prejudice to the parolee due to the fact the conditions were verbal rather than written.

The parole board has wide discretion in performing its duty to determine the worthiness of a particular parolee to continue in that status. The conditions of supervision provided for in R5–1–312, Arizona Administrative Rules and Regulations, are broad enough to allow the parole board a great deal of discretion in revocation decisions, and yet still provide a parolee with the minimum notice that his conduct is violative of those conditions. Written conditions would be preferable, but they are not required to insure adequate notice.

In the instant case the probation officer orally imposed a condition of non-association with a woman who had complained of harassment by the parolee. After information indicated that the condition had been violated, a hearing was held wherein the parolee admitted the violation. Though he did not specifically agree to the condition imposed, the court noted that he did remain at liberty after it was imposed. Under these circumstances, the court found no violation of due process.

---

* A 1979 Arizona case, State v. Salazar, 595 P.2d 196 (1979) also approved an oral order by a probation officer. A 1977 Florida case, 344 So.2d 913 (Fla.Dist.Ct.App.1977) held that the court had the sole authority to impose conditions.

IN RE BOLLEY
181 Cal.Rptr. 111 (Cal.Ct.App.1982)

It was improper for the trial court to grant probation on condition that the defendant waive the maximum statutory limit for a probationary period. Stated the court:

> Penal Code section 1203.1 provides, inter alia, that a court or judge may grant probation and suspend the imposition or execution of sentence for a period of time not exceeding the maximum possible term of such sentence, except when the maximum possible term is five years or less in which case the period of probation may continue for five years. The power of the court with regard to probation is strictly statutory, and the court cannot impose a condition of probation which extends beyond the maximum statutory term of probation. (*In re Acosta* (1944) 65 Cal.App.2d 63, 64, 149 P.2d 757.) A court cannot establish a period of probation longer than the maximum period of imprisonment for the offense involved. (*People v. Goldberg* (1975) 45 Cal.App.3d 601, 603, 119 Cal.Rptr. 616.) Any attempt to do so is null and void. (Id., at p. 604, 119 Cal.Rptr. 616; see also, *People v. Williams* (1956) 144 Cal. App.2d 144, 300 P.2d 734.)

It was improper for the trial court to grant probation on the condition that the defendant waive the maximum statutory limit for a probationary period.

The trial court in this case denied petitioner's application for probation solely because petitioner did not consent to a period of probation beyond the maximum term the court was empowered to grant or impose. That is not a proper ground upon which a court may deny an application for probation. Petitioner is entitled to have his application for probation considered without regard to his refusal to consent to an unauthorized period of probation.

The writ of habeas corpus was granted.

STATE v. DEAN
306 N.W.2d 286 (Wis.Ct.App.1981)

The defendant, Dr. Alice Dean, was convicted of mail fraud and false swearing. The trial court suspended the sentence and placed her on probation on the following conditions:

1. the defendant was to reside at the Holy Family Church in Karnataka State, India, for three years and provide nursing or pediatric service to poor children;

2. the defendant was to surrender her medical license;

3. the defendant was prohibited from practicing psychiatry during probation; and

4. the defendant was ordered to make restitution in the amount of $13,285 within 90 days by selling her assets.

Condition that defendant reside in India invalid. No authority to require a probationer to leave the state.

The defendant appealed claiming that the trial court had no authority to impose a condition of uncompensated medical service in India.

The court noted that while a trial judge has wide discretion in imposing conditions of probation, this discretion is limited by statute. The applicable limitation in the instant case was the fact that India was not a member of the Interstate Compact. Furthermore, there was no authority for the trial court to require a probationer to leave the state. Thus, the order was invalid in so far as it required the defendant to reside in India.

The matter was remanded for alternative conditions.

UNITED STATES v. FURUKAWA
596 F.2d 921 (9th Cir.Ct.App.1979)

Appellant's probation was revoked as a result of his "association" with individuals who were not "law-abiding." On appeal the appellant claimed that the probation officer was without authority to give instructions that were not within the specific limits of the conditions imposed. He further claimed that his contacts with these individuals could not be considered as "association" and further that since he was unaware of previous convictions of one individual, revocation on the basis of association with that individual was improper.

Appellant's probation revoked as result of association with individuals who were not "law abiding." Revocation upheld. *

As to the first claim the court held that since the probation officer had determined that one of the individuals appeared to be involved in "law-violating" activity, the instructions by the probation officer that appellant not associate with that individual were reasonable and proper. The court further found that such instruction by the probation officer was reasonably related to the appellant's rehabilitation and to protection of the public. As to the second contention, the court held testimony reflected that the appellant's association fell within the defi-

nition of "planned meetings and prolonged contact" and it was not error for the court to give more weight to this testimony than to that of the defendant. Regarding the third claim, the court held that while the defendant may not have been aware of past convictions, he was aware of past arrests and was aware of the individual's status as a gambler. This, according to the court, was sufficient to put appellant on notice that this individual was not "law-abiding."

SOROKA v. STATE
598 P.2d 69 (Alaska Sup.Ct.1979)

The court held firstly that since the warrantless search by the probation officer of the defendant's trailer was not made pursuant to the condition of probation requiring that defendant submit to searches of his person, the probation officer was required to establish probable cause for the search in order for that search to be held valid. The court went on to note that while there was insufficient probable cause to search, the initial entry by the probation officer into the trailer was a justifiable visit. Once inside, the discovery by probation officers of cocaine in "plain view" furnished the required probable cause to seize the contraband and to search other areas of the trailer.

Warrantless search by probation officer held valid. **

---

* Nonassociation conditions are frequently challenged on a number of grounds: Although usually upheld, they have been invalidated more often than most probation and parole conditions. A frequent and usually unsuccessful challenge is that the condition is so vague that it violates due process. *See generally* State v. Allen, 12 Or.Ct.App. 278, 506 P.2d 528 (1973) and United States v. Dane, 570 F2d 840 (9th Cir.1977) *cert. denied,* 436 U.S. 959 (1978).

** In some jurisdictions probationers and parolees are routinely given a condition requiring them to consent to various kinds of searches. This condition always embraces searches by probation and parole officers and sometimes also extends to searches by law enforcement personnel. It frequently covers searches of the offender's person, dwelling, auto, and property. People v. Natak, 77 Cal.App.3d 568, 143 Cal.Rptr. 629 (1978); United States v. Workman, 585 F.2d 1205 (5th Cir.1978); and U.S. v. Consuelo-Gonzalez, 521 F.2d 259, 266 (9th Cir.1975).

As to the issue of sentencing, the court noted that the trial judge stated that he was basing his sentence solely on the first offense and the probation violation. The court noted further that the sentencing judge did not discuss the nature of the original offense or the criteria to be considered in sentencing. *State v. Chaney,* 477 P.2d 441, Alaska 1970. As far as the court could ascertain from the record, the sentence was based only on the fact that probation was violated. Thus, the record was inadequate to determine whether the judge was clearly mistaken in imposing the sentence he did. Accordingly the case was remanded for resentencing.

BAKER v. STATE
428 So.2d 684 (Fla.Dist.Ct.App.1983)

Probation could be revoked for driving a motor vehicle when condition specified license to drive was suspended. *

Although the probation condition merely stated that the defendant's license to drive would be suspended, his probation could be revoked for driving a motor vehicle. The essence of the condition imposed was to keep the defendant from driving a motor vehicle.

BROCK v. STATE
299 S.E.2d 71 (Ga.Ct.App.1983)

The court found that the condition of probation suspending the defendant's driver's license was a proper condition.

Although the Department of Public Safety has the authority to cancel, suspend or revoke a driver's license under certain circumstances set forth in Code Ann.Ch. 68B–3 (now OCGA §§ 40–5–50 through 40–5–66), said statute does not purport to deprive a court of competent jurisdiction of the authority to suspend a driver's license as a condition of probation. In our view, suspension of a defendant's driver's license after his conviction of a traffic-related offense is a reasonable condition of probation.

The judgment of the trial court was affirmed.

---

* *See* also People v. Willi, 77 A.D.2d 711, 430 N.Y.S.2d 428 (Sup.Ct.1980) Probationer convicted of drunk driving cannot operate motor vehicle during five year probation term.

More restrictive approaches totally bar offenders from buying or driving a motor vehicle during all or part of their probation or parole period. The less restrictive view requires the permission of the probation or parole officer, or the court or board before the offender can buy or drive a vehicle or obtain a driver's license.

5

Organization and Administration of Probation Services

The Probation System

The operation of a probation system is best understood if at the outset we distinguish between probation as a disposition and probation as a process. As used in this chapter, *probation as a disposition means the aspects of probation that lead to the granting and revocation of probation. Probation as a process means the furnishing of probation services.* Obviously, the two functions are closely related and frequently overlap. As we shall see, different jurisdictions have different probation systems. However, there is significantly less diversity in probation as a disposition than in the manner of providing probation services.

Probation as a Disposition

Probation as a disposition is court related, which is to say that, within the statutory limits laid down by the legislature, the power to grant and revoke probation is in a court. The federal government permits all courts having jurisdiction of the offenses for which probation may be used to place defendants on probation.[1] This is generally true in state jurisdictions also. Thus, if the state provides only for felony probation, courts of general jurisdiction with power to try felony cases have the authority to grant and revoke probation. If misdemeanor probation is provided for, courts with misdemeanor jurisdiction may grant and revoke misdemeanor probation. In a few states, the power to grant probation is limited to courts of record.[2] Juvenile courts are given the power to grant probation by the legislative act that creates them.

---

1. 18 U.S.C.A. § 3651.

2. A court of record is a court the appeals from which are heard "on the record," that is, the case is not re-tried in the appellate court which instead makes its decision from the record of the proceedings taken in the lower court.

That the authority to grant probation resides with a court is not surprising, especially when considering that probation developed out of the court's power to sentence criminal offenders and (depending upon the point of view) from either its inherent or legislatively-granted power to suspend the imposition or execution of sentence. The power to revoke probation quite logically goes along with the power to grant it.

Today, although there are differences of opinion as to the exact nature of probation, which involve, for example, whether probation is a sentence, whether it is a conviction, whether it rests upon suspension of imposition of sentence or of execution of sentence, or both—there is almost unanimous agreement that granting and revoking probation as a disposition is a judicial act. Thus, administration of probation as a disposition is in a court.

As states enacted probation legislation, they did not do so uniformly. They followed the local organizational pattern of Vermont or the state organizational pattern of Rhode Island, combined adult and juvenile probation services, organized probation with parole services or kept them separate, developed joint or separate agencies for felony and misdemeanor probation services, placed probation services in the executive or judicial branch of government or adopted various combinations of the above.[3] By 1972, the National Advisory Commission on Corrections singled out Ohio as merely one of many examples of confused and overlapping probation organization.

In Ohio, juvenile probation is a local function in the judicial branch, but the state aid program is in the executive branch. Adult probation can be either a state or local function. A state agency in the executive branch can provide probation service to local courts, or they may establish their own. Where local probation exists, the control may be shared by both branches in an arrangement under which the county commissioners and judges of the court of common pleas must concur on appointments.[4]

Administration of Probation Services—Illustrative Patterns

The following patterns for delivery of probation services are illustrative of the varied forms of administering probation services:

• Probation services administered locally; parole services administered by statewide agency; juvenile and adult probation administered separately.

• Probation services administered locally; juvenile and adult probation administered together; parole administered by a separate statewide agency.

• Juvenile and adult probation and parole supervision combined.[5]

---

3. For a chart showing the organizational pattern for probation and parole services in the United States, *see* Final Report of the Joint Commission on Correctional Manpower and Training, a Time to Act 5 (1969).

4. Nat'l Advisory Comm'n Standards, Corrections, pp. 313–314.

5. This is the pattern in the federal system. A United States probation officer also supervises parolees.

• Adult probation administered by local agencies but subject to supervision by a state agency; parole administered by separate statewide agency.[6]

• Probation administered by local courts; parole administered by statewide parole agency; juvenile and adult probation combined.

• Probation in the executive branch except in certain large cities where probation is in judicial branch.

The functions of the police, district attorneys offices, and other correctional agencies are considered as functions performed by agencies and persons acting as representatives of the executive branch of government.[7]

As we have already noted, major arguments about delivery of probation services revolve around statewide versus local administration, executive versus judicial administration, separation of probation from parole, and separation of adult and juvenile probation services. The National Advisory Commission on Corrections sums up the pros and cons as follows:

> On balance, the arguments for placement of probation in the executive branch of government are more persuasive. Such placement would facilitate a more rational allocation of probation staff services, increase interaction and administrative coordination with corrections and allied human services, increase access to the budget process and establishment of priorities, and remove from the courts an inappropriate role. For these reasons, this report calls for inclusion of probation departments within unified State correctional systems.[8]

However, other recommendations of the commission are that staff performing services for the courts (as distinguished from services to pretrial releases and probationers) should be under the administrative control of the courts, and that juvenile intake services be under the supervision of the courts.[9]

Probation Services— State v. Local Administration

There are arguments pro and con for a statewide administration of probation services. The arguments in favor of a state-administered probation system include:

• A state-administered system is free of local political considerations and can recommend new programs without approval by local political bodies.

• A state-administered system provides greater assurance that goals and objectives can be met, and uniform policies and procedures developed; there is more efficiency in the disposition of resources.

• County probation agencies are small and lack resources for providing staff training, research programs, and services to probationers.[10]

---

6. This is the basic pattern in New York and Texas.

7. Paraphrased from Nat'l Advisory Comm'n Standards, Corrections, pp. 313–314.

8. *Id.* at 314.

9. *Id.*

10. Paraphrased from Nat'l Advisory Comm'n Standards, Corrections, pp. 315–316.

The arguments against a state-administered system stress the fact that:

• There is a need for local conditions and resources to be taken into account.

• The probationer remains in the local community and can be best supervised by a person thoroughly familiar with the local community.

• Local agencies are best equipped to experiment with new procedures and better methods because of their smaller size. Mistakes are not so costly and far-reaching.

• State policies are often rejected by local communities that then refuse to cooperate with the probation system that is dependent upon local acceptance for operational efficiency and success.[11]

Probation Services—
Recommended Administration

At the time the American Bar Association Standards Relating to Probation were published, adult probation services were administered in conjunction with parole services in thirty states. Some fourteen states retained local administration; in all but one of these the probation system was court administered. The remaining states had statewide administration of probation, but in an agency separate from the parole system. Aside from stressing the fact that probation services should not be under the same organizational structure as that which directs prosecution of offenses, the framers of the American Bar Association Standards did not take a position in favor of any particular formula for the allocation of administrative authority for probation services between local and state government. They agreed with the Model Penal Code [12] and the National Council on Crime and Delinquency [13] that adequate services can be developed through a multiplicity of approaches.[14] The National Advisory Commission on Corrections, however, opted for a state-administered system, or at the very least, a state administrative agency in the executive branch vested with a duty and authority to develop standards for local probation systems that provide for a minimum acceptable level of functioning. The state agency would also be responsible for establishing policies, defining statewide goals, providing staff training, assisting in fiscal planning and implementation, collecting statistics and other data to monitor the operations of local probation agencies, and enforcing changes when necessary.[15]

Probation Services—an Overview

Administration of probation services in the United States is characterized by differences both in philosophy and procedures.[16] In many cases, the differences

---

11. *Id.*

12. Model Penal Code § 401.12, comment at 147.

13. National Council on Crime and Delinquency, Standard Probation and Parole Act §§ 3.3, 7.7.

14. ABA Standards Relating to Probation, Commentary, pp. 75–76.

15. Nat'l Advisory Comm'n Standards, Corrections, pp. 315–316.

16. It is helpful to distinguish here between probation services rendered to a court and probation services provided to a probationer. There is overlap of course. For example, how should a

have arisen more by historical accident than otherwise. For example, of the states that passed early probation legislation, Massachusetts (in 1898) gave the power to appoint the probation officer to the mayor of the city of Boston, subject to confirmation by the board of aldermen, and placed the officer under the general control of the chief of police of the city, but paid the officer from the county treasury. Vermont, in the same year, adopted a county plan of organization. The county judge in each county had the power of appointment, the officer the power to serve all of the courts in the county:[17] Rhode Island the following year (1899) adopted a statewide and state-controlled probation system.[18]

Illinois provided for probation in the first juvenile court act (1899), but did not provide for adult probation until 1911 when the circuit and city courts of Illinois were authorized to appoint probation officers and place adult offenders on probation. A state probation office was created in 1923, but did not begin to function until 1929, and was abolished in 1933.[19]

California, the third state in the union to enact a probation statute, followed the Vermont pattern of county-based probation administration, and in 1903 provided for adult as well as juvenile probation.[20]

In New York, probation began in 1901 under a law that empowered all justices of courts having original criminal jurisdiction in all cities to appoint officers to investigate and report cases to the courts that might deserve mitigation of punishment by probation. The first independent commission for the supervision of probation was established in 1907. By 1939, the probation system was made up of probation officers appointed by the local courts and paid by local governments, but under state supervision. Later, the Division of Probation in the charge of a director of probation was located in the then Department of Correction. The most recent enactment established in New York is a state department of correctional services, which has as one of its divisions the Division of Probation.[21]

Changing Concepts of Probation— Their Impact on Administration

As we have noted previously, concepts of the nature and objectives of probation are undergoing considerable change. The shift is from probation based upon a medical model, which implies illness and treatment; to probation as a form of community resource management for the benefit of the probationer who needs help readjusting and reintegrating into the community as an independent individual. In the opinion of many authorities, there has been an overemphasis on social casework and too little development of appropriate service programs

---

presentence report be classified if it is used to inform the court prior to sentencing but is also used by the probation officer as a source of information and a diagnostic tool in working out the details of probation supervision?

17. Att'y Gen. Survey, Probation 22–23, n. 75.

18. *Id.* at 25.

19. Att'y. Gen. Survey, *Digest,* pp. 299–300.

20. *Id.* at 105–106.

21. N.Y.Correct.Law § 2 (McKinney).

and too little utilization by the probation system of services available to the probationer in service agencies located outside the system itself.[22] According to the National Advisory Commission on Corrections, to implement an effective system for delivering services to all probationers, it will be necessary to:

1. Develop a goal-oriented service delivery system.

2. Identify service needs of probationers systematically and periodically, and specify measurable objectives based upon priorities and needs assessment.

3. Differentiate between those services that the probation system can provide and those that should be provided by other resources.

4. Organize the system to deliver services, including purchase of services for probationers, and organize the staff around work loads.

5. Move probation staff from courthouses to residential areas and develop service centers for probationers.

6. Redefine the role of probation officer from caseworker to community resource manager.

7. Provide services to misdemeanants.[23]

The Commission also recommends placing a release on recognizance program in each probation office serving large communities.[24]

Obviously, such a major change in the conceptual nature of probation and the objectives of a probation system dictates changes in the organization and administration of the agency charged with delivering probation services. The role of the probation officer will be significantly altered, which requires different qualifications and training. Even less global changes in the concept of probation as for example, accepting probation as the disposition of first choice for the convicted offender—will require a much larger probation staff and redirect the sentencing information furnished the court. Instead of concentrating on the criteria for granting probation, the presentence report must set forth reasons for incarceration, particularly if incarceration is being considered as a dispositional alternative.[25]

The new concept is that "the probation system has a responsibility to assure that probationers receive whatever services they need."[26] If probation makes any such commitment to the probationer, it is obvious that the demand upon social services of all kinds will be greatly increased. It is argued that the savings in institutional costs will go a long way towards meeting the increased costs of probation.[27] It will not be seriously contended, however, that fewer correctional dollars will be required.

The new probation system would have to have resources to purchase services such as foster care, psychiatric treatment, marital counseling, alcohol and drug

---

22. *See, generally,* Nat'l Advisory Comm'n Standards, Corrections, ch. 10, pp. 311–330.

23. *Id.* at 320.

24. *Id.* at 339.

25. *See* Ch. 5, *infra.*

26. Nat'l Advisory Comm'n Standards, *supra* note 22.

27. It has been estimated that institutionalization costs ten times what putting a man on probation costs.

treatment, education, and training. Probationers would need remedial educa-tion, vocational training, employment opportunities, and specialized programs in schools, colleges, and universities. The probation department would have direct responsibilities in receiving and classifying probationers, and giving them direct services such as information, referral, follow-up and supervision, and in addition would have the responsibility of monitoring and evaluating the services fur-nished.[28] The conflicts that would develop between the probation system and other social service agencies and law enforcement agencies are not difficult to predict.

The Traditional Probation Officer—
How Selected

Depending upon the situs of probation services in the judicial or executive branch of government, the probation officer is selected by the court or courts authorized to grant probation, or by the director of the executive department or agency in which probation services are housed. If there is only one felony trial court in the county, the probation officer is selected by the judge trying felony cases. Where two or more probation officers are needed, the usual pattern is that the judge or judicial body appoints a chief probation officer who in turn selects assistants, subject to the approval of the advisory body. Salary scales are fixed and broad policy matters are determined by the judicial body given the power to select the chief probation officer.

In the federal system, for example, the judges of each federal district court appoint a chief probation officer, who is under the overall supervision of the administrative office of the United States courts. Collectively, the United States probation officers are called the United States Probation Service. The chief probation officer selects the subordinate probation officers.[29] Salary and mini-mum qualifications are fixed by statute or determined by the Administrative Office of the United States Courts. Since in the federal scheme, the United States probation officer also supervises parolees, parolees are assigned for supervision to the appropriate chief probation officer by the United States Parole Commis-sion, which is the federal agency in the Justice Department responsible for administering the federal parole system. The assignment is based primarily on geographic considerations. The individual officer who will supervise a particular parolee is selected by the chief probation officer who makes the assignment on the basis of the special needs of the probationer or parolee and the special skills of the probation officer, with due consideration as to case load, geographic location, and other matters. The courts also assign to the United States probation officers juveniles sentenced under the Federal Juvenile Delinquency Act.

The U.S. Parole Commission may request United States probation officers to perform such duties with respect to all persons on parole who have been sentenced under the Federal Youth Corrections Act as are necessary for main-

---

28. *Id.* at 322.

29. The selection is, however, subject to the approval of the Chief U.S. District Judge of the judicial district, who officially "appoints" all U.S. probation officers.

taining proper supervision of such persons.[30] A United States probation officer also supervises offenders at liberty under mandatory release,[31] military parole,[32] and pretrial release.

In a state where probation services are locally administered and parole services are statewide, there are usually two sets of supervisory officers. The appointment of the parole officers is made by an administrative department or by a board supervising the department. Power to appoint the chief probation officer is usually in the judiciary, although other methods of selection include appointment by the county governing body, the governor, a state board upon nomination by a judge, or the judiciary from a list supplied by a state agency.

Where juvenile and adult probation services are administered locally but separately, a chief probation officer for adult probationers may be chosen by the judge or judges of the criminal courts; the chief probation officer who adminis-ters the juvenile probation department may be chosen by the juvenile judge or a juvenile board. Sometimes the juvenile board has authority not only to select the chief juvenile probation officer but also to designate which court will be the juvenile court and handle the cases involving juveniles in the particular geo-graphic area.[33]

If juvenile and adult probation are administered locally, the juvenile proba-tion department may be assigned the responsibility for adult probation by statute, as in California.[34] Or the judge or judges, with the approval of the juvenile board (if there is one) of the county may authorize the chief probation officer or chief juvenile officer to establish a separate division of adult probation and appoint adult probation officers as required, as in Texas.[35] Actual supervi-sion of both adult and juvenile probationers may in some cases be by the same officer,[36] or the probation officer for juveniles may be restricted from serving as probation officer for adults and vice versa.[37]

Advisory Boards

The underlying reason for providing panels of judges, juvenile boards, state boards, county commissioners, or other statutory bodies is that some method of assisting the judiciary in screening potential appointees is desirable. Such bodies also act as advisors to the judiciary in setting broad general policy, salary scales, and the like.

Although the authority to select the chief probation officer may reside with the judge, the judge does not as a rule actually administer the probation

30. *See, generally,* 18 U.S.C.A. § 5010ff; and U.S.C.A. § 5031ff.

31. 18 U.S.C.A. § 4164.

32. In 1944 the federal probation service was asked by the U.S. Army to extend its facilities for the supervision of its parolees.

33. This is the situation in Texas. Tex.Fam.Code Ann. § 51.04 (Vernon).

34. Cal.Welf. & Inst.Code § 1760.7 (West), [except for two counties which have separate juvenile and adult probation departments].

35. Tex.Code Crim.Proc. art. 42.12, § 10 (Vernon).

36. The usual situation in California.

37. The Texas statute so provides.

department. That function is performed by the chief probation officer who is given the power to appoint assistants and handle the day-to-day work of the department.[38]

The American Bar Association Standards Relating to Probation set forth what they see as the best interrelationship between the judiciary, an advisory body, and the chief probation officer in a locally administered probation system:

a. Responsibility for appointing chief probation officers in local probation departments should reside solely in the chief judge of the court or an appropriate judicial body. Consideration should be given to the creation of an agency or committee to advise in recruiting and screening chief probation officers. Such a committee should consist of representatives of government, the judiciary, the bar, and the community.

b. Chief probation officers should make all appointments of probation personnel in accordance with a merit system. After a probationary period, tenure should be granted and removal permitted only after a hearing conducted with a civil service commission or other career service organization.[39]

The Traditional Probation Officer's Role

Let us first consider the probation officer's traditional role as a caseworker in one-to-one therapeutic relationships with probationers, and then in the role as a community resource manager or broker of services. In all probability, the casework concept will prove to have more durability in juvenile rather than adult probation, since casework more nearly approximates the parental relationship most juveniles need, and more accurately expresses in practical terms the doctrine of *parens patriae,* which characterizes the juvenile court. A "new model" juvenile probation officer would, of course, expand the referral role and otherwise provide the juvenile with specialized assistance from other community social and youth services.

Social Casework

Social casework has been defined as "a method by which a social worker, through a relationship which is largely one-to-one (worker and client), brings about mutual interaction between himself and client, hopefully to effect in the

---

38. *See, generally,* National Council on Crime and Delinquency Probation and Parole Directory.

39. ABA Standards Relating to Probation § 6.4.

The ABA Standards read in part as follows:

6.1 Legislative responsibility; administrative structure.

(a) Legislative bodies should appropriate sufficient funds so that all trial courts administering criminal justice will have adequate probation services and personnel in order to implement properly the standards developed in this report. (b) It is appropriate for probation services to be administered at either the state or local level, but in no event should control be vested in an agency having prosecutorial functions.

6.2 Establishing Minimum Standards. Minimum standards for probation services should be formulated and enforced by an appropriate state agency and should be applicable to all probation departments within the state * * *. [Here follows recommendations as to such minimum standards.]

client an adjustment to his social and psychological situation that will permit him to live more comfortably with himself and among others." [40]

"The nucleus of the casework event is that a *person* with a *problem* comes to a *place* where a *professional representative* helps him by a given *process.*" [41] Social group-work differs from social case-work in that in social group-work the relationship is largely one-to-group, between the worker and a set of individuals who conceive of themselves as a group. [42]

In applying the casework concepts to the correctional field, Dressler lists twelve basic canons:

1. The focal concern of probation and parole workers is in the social functioning of individuals.

2. All behavior is purposive.

3. One human being can help another.

4. People can and do change.

5. Although people can and do change, there is generally some resistance to change, particularly with respect to long-established habits of thought, feeling, and action.

6. People can be helped only if they want help.

7. The basic tool of casework is the interview.

8. Personality is precious.

9. The client must be accepted despite any faults or differences.

10. The caseworker is nonjudgmental.

11. Authority is a tool in casework.

12. Each social agency has its particular function and limits.

Canon number ten is explained by pointing out that the caseworker does not pass judgment on the client's *feelings,* and that when working with a juvenile who often lacks the judgment to know what is best, the probation officer may need to be quite directive. [43]

Since a great many of the early probation officers were social workers, particularly those in the juvenile court, the terms "diagnosis" and "treatment" became commonly used when defining the role of the probation officer in the correctional setting. These terms originated in the medical field and imply an illness to be "cured" by the probation practitioner much as the medical practitioner remedies an illness.

The criticism of this approach to the probationer is that it overlooks any connection between crime and such factors as poverty, unemployment, poor housing, poor health, and lack of education. The assignment of a certain number of cases to a probation officer implies that the probation officer has full responsibility for all the individuals concerned, and also assumes, incorrectly,

---

40. Dressler, *supra,* at 161.

41. *Id.* quoting Helen Harris Perlman, *Social Casework, a Problem-Solving Process.* (Chicago: University of Chicago Press, 1927), p. 4.

42. *Id.* at 162.

43. Dressler, *supra,* 166–171.

that the officer possesses all the skills needed to deal with the variety of human problems presented.[44]

Since a probation officer was supposed to know probationers on an individual level, a standard casework ratio of fifty probationers to one probation officer was accepted, although there was little research done to determine whether a smaller, or even larger, casework load would prove more effective.[45] Irrespective of the surface acceptance of the one to fifty ratio, the President's Crime Commission reported that 97 percent of all probationers were supervised by probation officers whose case load exceeded fifty persons.[46] A study made in San Francisco showed that probationers in a case load of 250 probationers performed about as well as those in the ideal case load of 50 probationers.[47]

Criticism of the social work approach to probation also came from another source—the legal profession. Lawyers and judges pointed out that, particularly in the juvenile courts, individuals, whether committed to an institution or placed on probation, were being denied their fundamental due process rights. In the landmark case of *In re Gault*, the Supreme Court of the United States declared that a juvenile, as well as an adult, cannot be deprived of liberty without due process of law, specifically, the right to notice of the charges, right to counsel, right to confrontation and cross-examination, and the privilege against self-incrimination.[48] As a result of this and subsequent decisions, the adjudicatory stage of a juvenile court proceeding closely resembles a criminal trial. This demands attitudes and skills from the probation officer that are not included in the traditional "diagnosis" and "treatment" model.

The Traditional Probation Officer—
Qualifications and Training

Qualifications for probation officers may be set out in the statute, or set by the administrative authority charged with the responsibility for operating the probation system. Sometimes only basic or minimum qualifications are set out in the statute with specific criteria determined by the administrative authority. Nationwide, the educational standards set by statute or administrative regulation range from high school graduation to advanced degrees plus prior experience.

There are great variations in the type of educational preparation deemed suitable for a probation officer. As is to be expected, jurisdictions wedded to the social casework model tend to require education in the social sciences and

---

44. Nat'l Advisory Comm'n Standards, Corrections, p. 317.

45. *Id.* The ABA Standards Relating to Probation speak of supervisory units, taking into consideration the other work of probation officer such as making presentence reports. The units were computed by rating one probationer under supervision as one unit and a pre-sentence investigation as five units. ABA Standards Relating to Probation, Commentary following section 6.1(a), fn.*

46. The President's Commission on Law Enforcement and Administration of Justice, The Challenge of Crime in a Free Society, pp. 168–169.

47. James Robison et al., The San Francisco Project, Research Report No. 14 (Berkeley: University of California School of Criminology, 1969), as quoted in Nat'l Advisory Comm'n Standards, Corrections, p. 319.

48. Application of Gault, 387 U.S. 1, 87 S.Ct. 1428, 18 L.Ed.2d 527 (1967).

the possession of the Master of Social Work (M.S.W.) degree. Other jurisdictions do not accept the view that conventional social work training is the best preparation for work in probation. They point out that persons trained in many different fields are just as likely to perform well as probation officers, and that a diversity of skills should be represented in any large probation office. Some feel that former offenders who have had training or experience in community organizations or in counseling with persons with special problems are particularly effective as part of the probation team, because they have a similar background to many of the individuals who make up a probation officer's work load.

Advocates of broader-based and nonacademic qualifications for probation officers stressed the importance of the ability to get along with and to motivate people—a skill not ordinarily developed in a classroom—and insisted that the possession of a college education or a specific degree not be made an essential requirement for the probation officer.

The framers of the American Bar Association Standards Relating to Probation considered the various points of view and came to the conclusion that while the core of the probation department should be professionally educated, two types of persons can be effectively used in most probation offices even though they do not meet normal educational standards. These two types of persons are former offenders and volunteers. Many studies were cited showing the successful use of the former addict in treatment programs for addicts, and of former offenders as data collectors in research programs, interviewers in probation departments, and as intermediaries and participants in group therapy efforts.[49] The successful use of volunteers in the Municipal Court of Royal Oak, Michigan, and the use of a small group of carefully selected women to help delinquent girls in Philadelphia were reported.[50]

Thus, the American Bar Association established standards relating to the qualifications for probation officers and other personnel in a probation office. These standards require probation officers to possess a bachelor's degree supplemented by a year of graduate study in social work, corrections, counseling, law, criminology, psychology, sociology, or related fields; or a year of full-time casework counseling and community or group-work experience in a recognized social, community, correctional, or juvenile agency that deals with offenders or disadvantaged persons, or its equivalent as determined by the hiring agency. Possession of graduate degrees in one of these fields was recommended for a significant number of probation officers in a department. However, the standards conclude:

> While the core of any probation department should be professionally educated and trained personnel, it is desirable that the staff include individuals who may lack such professional qualifications but have backgrounds similar to those of the probationers themselves. In addition, in appropriate cases, citizen volunteers should be used to assist probation officers.[51]

49. *See* ABA Standards Relating to Probation, Commentary, pp. 96–98.

50. *Id.*

51. ABA Standards Relating to Probation, p. 6.5.

The Role of Probation Officer as Community Resource Manager

Obviously, wherever the different concepts of probation are adopted, there will be a need for a different type of probation officer. Instead of being primarily a counselor dispensing "treatment," the major responsibility would be to identify the needs of the probationer, both felon and misdemeanant, to mesh those needs with the range of available services, and to supervise the delivery of these services.[52] While the probation officer would continue to provide services to the courts, the officer would also function in connection with court-related diversion programs such as release on recognizance (ROR).[53] The officer would have a great many responsibilities in connection with reorganizing the probation service system, such as community planning and development, purchasing services, developing new services, and monitoring and evaluating the services to which the probationer is referred. Since the probation system would directly provide certain services, the probation officer would need to differentiate between the services that the probation system should provide and those that should be provided by other resources. For example, if supervised release is a part of an ROR or other pretrial release program, the officer would perform the supervisory service or arrange for supervision.

The National Advisory Commission Standards are based upon this conceptual nature of probation and the objectives of a probation system, with the probation officer recognized as a community resource manager instead of a social caseworker. Probation would be placed organizationally in the executive branch of state government. The state correctional agency would be given responsibility for establishing statewide goals, policies, and priorities, and for program planning, staff development and training, planning for manpower needs and recruitment, collecting statistics, monitoring services, and conducting research and evaluation. During the period when probation is being placed under direct state operation—and presumably in those states where probation would continue to be locally administered—the state correctional agency would be given authority to supervise local probation. The state correctional agency would operate regional units, establish standards relating to personnel and services for courts and probationers, consult with local probation agencies, assist in developing uniform record and statistical reporting procedures, assist in evaluating the number and types of staff needed in each jurisdiction, and provide financial assistance through reimbursement or subsidy to the probation agencies meeting the standards.[54]

The commission further recommended the development of a goal-oriented service delivery system that would identify needs of probationers, allocate resources, and establish priorities. Services directly provided by the probation department would be limited to those defined as belonging distinctly to probationers; other services would be obtained from other agencies. The staff delivering services to probationers in urban areas would be separate and apart

---

52. Nat'l Advisory Comm'n Standards, Nat'l Corrections, p. 322.

53. *Id.,* Standard 10.5.

54. Nat'l Advisory Comm'n Standards, 10.1—Organization of Probation.

from the staff delivering services to the courts, although they would belong to the same agency. The probation system would deliver to probationers a range of services by a range of staff. Staff would be organized according to work loads or task groups, not case loads, and would include staff teams related to groups of probationers and differentiated programs based on offender typologies.[55]

To render more efficient services to the courts, the probation staff could streamline the presentence reports by providing only information relative and pertinent to sentencing disposition, making complete presentence reports before sentencing in only a limited number of cases. Other information would be added to the probationer's file as part of an on-going process of assessing the probationer's needs, identifying major problems, and determining priorities for service delivery.

The service broker probation officer would move from the courthouse to the part of the community where probationers reside; would provide services during evening hours and on weekends to accommodate probationers who are working; would include probated misdemeanants among other responsibilities; and would work in close relationship with all of the institutions and agencies capable of furnishing services for the probationer. No small part of the probation officer's task would be to redefine the role of probation officer from caseworker to community resource manager in the minds of the courts, the probationers, the community, and the probation officer.

The Probation Officer as Community
Resource Manager—Qualifications and Training

The community resource manager type of probation officer would not be a caseworker, a group worker, nor a social worker. The broker of services probation officer would be a person who places emphasis on classifying offenders according to their needs and providing appropriate services. The probation officer would have to be knowledgeable about available resources, able to assist the probationer in obtaining the services, and prepared to follow up on the case to ensure that the probationer would indeed obtain the needed services. Proper performance of this new role would demand organizational and administrative skills of a high order. The officer's education and qualifications, therefore would continue to include basic education in the social sciences such as psychology and sociology, and would expand to encompass public administration, personnel practices, operational analysis, program planning, implementation and evaluation, and research methods.

Under this system, educational qualification for probation officers would be graduation from an accredited four-year college. A comprehensive development and training program would recruit and train a full range of probation personnel, including volunteers, women, and ex-offenders. The program should range from entry level to top level positions. Provision would be made for effective utilization of a range of personnel on a full-time or part-time basis by using a systems approach to identify service objectives, and specifying job tasks

---

55. *Id.,* Standard 10.2.—Services to Probationers.

and range of personnel necessary to meet the objectives. Jobs would be reexamined periodically to ensure that organizational objectives were being met. In addition to the probation officer, there would be new career lines in probation, such as development of staff to care for the needs of misdemeanants and to organize and administer pretrial release programs such as release on recognizance. Advancement (salary and status) would be along two tracks: service delivery and administration.[56]

The Role of the Probation Officer in the "Justice" Model of the 1980s

The latest challenge to the existing approaches to probation springs from a growing commitment to a *justice* model, which advocates an escalated system of sanctions directly related to the social harm resulting from the offense and the culpability of the offender. The justice model repudiates the notion that probation is a sanction designed to rehabilitate offenders in the community, and presents the concept that a sentence of probation represents a proportionate punishment lawfully administered for certain prescribed crimes.[57]

The Justice Concept

In the justice model of probation, the probationary term is not viewed as an alternative to imprisonment, but rather as a valid sanction in itself. The popular view that probation is an alternative to incarceration leads to a logical conclusion that probation is an expression of leniency. For the offender, the opposite may be true. In lieu of incarceration, the offender may be deprived of certain liberties for an inordinate and often unspecified period of time. But the public often feels that the offender is "getting off." There is no question that justice and the welfare of the community are best served with the imprisonment of *some* offenders. But for the *majority* who can safely remain in the community the public must feel that an appropriate penalty is imposed. Probation should, therefore, be viewed as a separate and distinct sanction requiring just penalties that are graduated in severity and length of time, and which are proportionate with the seriousness of the crime.[58]

The Role of the Justice Model Probation Officer

The probation penalty should include the following two basic conditions or elements: (a) some degree of deprivation of personal liberty, and (b) reparation to the victim or to the community.[59] As we have already stated, research seems to indicate little difference in recidivism between probationers on large case loads as opposed to small case loads. The justice model holds that current

56. *Id.*, Standard 10.3—Misdemeanant Probation; Standard 10.4.—Probation Manpower; Standard 10.5—Probation in Release on Recognizance Programs.

57. Robert J. Gemignani, Rethinking Probation, Change, vol. 5, no. 4 (1983).

58. *Id.* at 2.

59. *Id.*

practices of counseling, surveillance, and reporting accomplish very little and have minimal impact on recidivism. On the other hand, probation that consists of monitoring court orders for victim restitution or community service and ensures that the imposed deprivation of liberty is carried out, represents a clear and achievable task.[60]

Justice model probation views the role of offender assistance as specifically geared to helping probationers comply with the conditions of their probation, and that the traditional rehabilitative function should be *voluntary* and brokered through social agencies within the community. As already noted, the primary responsibility of the probationer is to satisfactorily complete the conditions imposed by the court. Likewise, the primary task of the probation officer is to assist the probationer in the satisfactory completion of those conditions. The probation agency, however, should be prepared to assist those individuals who *voluntarily* request rehabilitative assistance.[61]

The Justice Model Officer— Qualifications and Training

Like the community resource manager, the justice model officer need not be a social worker, counselor, or caseworker. The justice model officer will have a broad range of training, including coursework in criminal justice, law, public administration, and management. The justice model officer would have a broad range of skills, capable of firmly enforcing the orders of the court, offering casework upon request, and having the knowledge of the community resources necessary to broker the services the probationer may need and voluntarily request.

Interstate Compacts on Probation

Before we complete our consideration of probation administration, we must mention the interstate compacts for supervision of probationers and parolees, both adult and juvenile.

At one time, no method was provided for supervising a probationer or parolee outside the state where the individual was convicted, in spite of the fact that transient offenders are often arrested and convicted far away from home where they have relatives and ties in the community. As a result, there was often no way to provide for supervision of the offender in the very place that would offer the best chance for success on probation or parole. Pursuant to the Crime Control Consent Act passed by Congress in 1936, a group of states entered into an agreement under which they undertook to supervise probationers and parolees for each other. The agreement, known as the Interstate Compact for the Supervision of Parolees and Probationers, was signed by all states by 1951. A similar agreement, known as the Interstate Compact on Juveniles, provides for return of runaways, escapees, and absconders, and for cooperative supervision of probationers and parolees. The compact on juveniles

60. *Id.* at 3.

61. *Id.*

has an amendment that provides for out-of-state confinement of juveniles. Each state enacts the compact as part of its state laws.[62]

The compacts identify a "sending state" and a "receiving state." The "sending state" is the state of conviction. The "receiving state" is the state that undertakes the supervision. The offender must meet certain residence requirements with reference to the receiving state. Ordinarily, the probationer or parolee must either be a resident of the receiving state, have relatives there, or have employment there. The receiving state agrees to accept the offender and provide the same supervision as is accorded a probationer or parolee in the receiving state. The offender who obtains the benefits of out-of-state supervision waives extradition. The sending state may enter the receiving state and take custody of the probationer or parolee who has violated the terms of release without going through extradition proceedings, and a supplementary agreement permits the violator to be incarcerated in the receiving state at the expense of the sending state if both states agree.

Parole boards usually designate one member of their number to be the "Interstate Compact Administrator." That person handles the details of arranging the supervision of parolees who are either sent out of the state for supervision or received into the state after conviction in another state. Where probation is locally administered, the compact does not work as smoothly for probation supervision as for parole supervision. However, some exchanges take place and probation supervision or detention and care of runaways and absconders is provided by the receiving state.

---

62. *See, for example,* Interstate Parole Reciprocal Agreement, Ill.Ann.Stat. ch. 38, §§ 123–5, 123–6 (Smith-Hurd).

California Interstate Compact on Juveniles, Cal.Welf. & Inst.Code §§ 1300–1308 (West).

The Five Faces of Probation*

In seeking to meet the challenge of crime and delinquency, the modern probation officer finds himself caught up in a peculiar double bind. He must serve the needs of his probationers, on one hand, and the needs of the community, on the other. This two-sided facet of the probation officer's function is a result of evolutionary changes in both the conception and scope of probation. It represents corrections' attempt to discover the most effective means of accomplishing humane but realistic treatment of offenders.

The law mandates that probationers should be "helped" to overcome or neutralize their antisocial behaviors. At the same time probation is aimed as "protecting" the community from those same overt behaviors. The dilemma which this poses is well known to probation officers who must put this dual task into some manageable perspective in their work. Too often, the training of correctional personnel shows features of choosing one goal over the other. Depending on whether one's orientation comes from psychology, sociology, crimi-nology, social work, counseling, etc., probation styles tend to treat the dual goals as somewhat mutually exclusive.

Out of this duality here emerges what may be termed the "five faces of probation." This is taken to mean that probation officers manifest certain strategies, approaches, or styles of "probationing" which reflect their degrees of concern for meeting the stated goals of help and protection. Each of these styles "shows its face" to the probationer and starts the interaction which leads to five differential outcomes in probation officer-probationer relationships.

This set of relationships can be examined and clarified where viewed in terms of a Probation Grid. The grid concept stems from Blake and Mouton's[1] well-known "Managerial Grid" used so successfully by them for training managerial personnel. Such a construct has been applied to other content areas like decisionmaking, change, and leadership. This article proposes to explicate a Probation Grid stemming directly from the probation objectives of helping individuals and protecting the community.

---

* From Louis Tomaino, *Federal Probation,* 39/4 (Dec. 1975), pp. 37–41.

1. Robert Blake and Jane Mouton, *The Managerial Grid* (Houston: Gulf Publishing Co., 1964).

These objectives will be expressed as the probation officer's concern for effective *control* over his client's illegal behaviors, and the probation officer's concern for satisfactory *rehabilitation* of his probationer. These concerns, for analytical purposes, are seen as being independent of each other, though in practice, probation officers may impose a relationship on them which manifests the five faces of probation. Therefore in the grid model, the two dimensions are oriented at right angles to each other. The horizontal axis of the Probation Grid represents the goal of control experienced by officers, and the vertical axis reflects his concern for rehabilitation of the probationer.

This article is interested in the degree to which a probation officer is concerned about the two grid dimensions. Therefore, as in the Blake-Mouton grid, each axis is scaled from 1 to 9 in order to reflect degree of concern. The value 1 denotes low or minimal "concern for" while 9 symbolizes high or maximal "concern for." By arranging the concerns at right angles to each

other and by providing a scalar arrangement the probation faces of probation officers can be assessed from the frame of reference which they bring to the relationship between the concerns. "Concern for" is not a static term rooted only in the officer's attitude. What is significant is how that officer is concerned about control, or about rehabilitation or about how these concerns fuse.

The Probation Grid is presented in figure 1. Three faces of probation in the grid assume that concerns for control and rehabilitation are in basic conflict with each other and are mutually exclusive. The officer who has this frame of reference finds himself choosing one concern over the other, but not both, as his probation focus. The probation faces which result from this forced choice, reading in grid fashion (right and up) are the 9/1, 1/9, and 1/1. Each of these faces will be evaluated according to its primary characteristics in probation counseling.

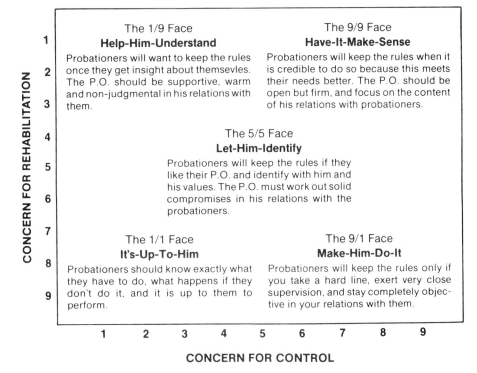

CONCERN FOR REHABILITATION

The 1/9 Face
Help-Him-Understand
Probationers will want to keep the rules once they get insight about themsevles. The P.O. should be supportive, warm and non-judgmental in his relations with them.

The 9/9 Face
Have-It-Make-Sense
Probationers will keep the rules when it is credible to do so because this meets their needs better. The P.O. should be open but firm, and focus on the content of his relations with probationers.

The 5/5 Face
Let-Him-Identify
Probationers will keep the rules if they like their P.O. and identify with him and his values. The P.O. must work out solid compromises in his relations with the probationers.

The 1/1 Face
It's-Up-To-Him
Probationers should know exactly what they have to do, what happens if they don't do it, and it is up to them to perform.

The 9/1 Face
Make-Him-Do-It
Probationers will keep the rules only if you take a hard line, exert very close supervision, and stay completely objective in your relations with them.

CONCERN FOR CONTROL

Control is defined as a condition in which the probationer is under close behavioral surveillance by his probation officer and is not violating probation rules. Rehabilitation is defined as a condition obtained when the probationer is not violating his probation rules, is not under close surveillance, and apparently has internalized some prosocial behaviors.

The lower right-hand corner of the grid represents a maximal concern for control and a minimal concern for rehabilitation. This frame of reference is based on the assumption that probations will respond only when they have to, under coercive surveillance with swift penalties when they do not conform. It is not suggested that probation officer's with a 9/1 face have no interest in their clients but rather this interest becomes manifested only under rigid control variables. The 9/1 officer sincerely believes that probationers need a strict leader who governs their otherwise hedonistic tendencies.

A 9/1 officer believes that control is rehabilitation and that his most crucial obligation is to protect community interests via strict limits placed on his clients. If the community is properly protected a kind of *fait accompli* effect is produced in the probationer whose illegal behaviors are blocked through control. Such a system of enforced cooperation induces clients to accept probationary conditions without having to internalize them. Interaction between probation officer and probationer tends to be formal, official, and largely a question of "one upsmanship" on the side of the probation officer.

This one-dimension probation face may be effective. It could also lead to false security that a client is under control when, in fact, his compliance is only superficial. Kelman[2] has demonstrated that conformity behavior which occurs under conditions of high power remains intact only so long as there is surveillance. Removal of close monitoring results in a decrease of conformity behavior and a return to more prepotent modes of acting which may well be antisocial. Combined with the hostility and resentment which a 9/1 probation face often produces in others, this approach represents an unstable form of behavior management.

The probation officer's 9/1 face says to the probationer, "I expect you to keep these probationary conditions. I'll do what I can to help you but you will have to 'toe the mark' and there is no room for error."

THE 1/9 FACE

The 1/9 is designated by the upper left hand grid position which indicates high probation officer concern for rehabilitating his probationer and small concern for controlling him. In this approach the probation officer's overriding motivation is based on the assumption that individuals are basically good and will seek appropriate, legal behaviors once they are helped to understand themselves. This self-knowledge will promote growth, foster prosocial attitudes, and terminate in satisfactory observance of probationary rules.

The 9/1 face is rejected as constituting an effort by the community to impose its own values of correct behavior on the probationer. This is seen as antithetical to the free choice condition needed if the client is to foster his own adaptation to the orders of the court. The face projected to the probationer in this framework is a warm, supportive, and nonjudgmental countenance. The probation officer tends to emerge primarily as a therapist who facilitates insight

---

2. Herbert C. Kelman, *Compliance, Identification, and Internalization: Three Processes of Attitude Change,* Journal of Conflict Resolution 2: (1958) 51–60.

on the client's part. He learns to form a close relationship with the probationer and refines a repertoire of clinical skills aimed at rehabilitation.

Unlike the 9/1, a 1/9 face produces probationary supervision under conditions of freedom, mutuality, and a high level of client decisionmaking. The psychodynamics of individual probationers emerge as more potent than the social determinants of crime or delinquency. This also poses a dilemma for probation officers. A 1/9 face lends itself to manipulation, a perception that it is permissive and there is some likelihood of being "conned."

The probation officer's 1/9 face says to the probationer, "I hope that you will understand the need for these probationary conditions. I will support you in every way I can and help you make your own decisions in a way that you will find contentment and not fell threatened by me."

THE 1/1 FACE

The lower-left grid location refers to probation officers who manifest minimal concerns for both control and rehabilitation. In this face, probationers are thought of as autogenous and, therefore, will change or fail to do so as a result of their own motivation. No conscious or systematic probation strategy will be effective because circumstances, spontaneous occurrences, and genetic chance are the important variables. If individual probationer tendencies for illegal behaviors are in conflict with external probationary attempts to alter them, the probation officer must set up a situation to evaluate what happens. His role is to appraise and advise his client about failure to conform, keep the court informed on the probationer's observance of the rules, and operate as an observer of progress rather than initiator of behavioral change.

Considerable energy is invested into the logistics of probation. Records are well-maintained, reports are current, and probationer contacts are regular. However, the limited affective involvement with clients, and a mechanical approach to probation leaves this officer with no dynamic probation face. It should be noted that such an outcome is not necessarily due to the officer's personality. A 1/1 probation program or administration might well promote status quo values which frustrate aggressive probation officers who then revert to "reporting" procedures as a way to fill the role assigned in their work.

The probation officer's 1/1 face says to his probationer, "I'm sure you understand these conditions of probation. It's up to you to stick to them. No one can do it for you. If you need me be sure to contact me."

In the grid center is found the 5/5 probation officer who proceeds on the assumption that both control and rehabilitation are necessary but that full concern cannot be given to both. This face demonstrates a belief that probationers need leadership; they have not benefited from sound identification figures in the past; in fact, their very alignment with deviant models probably induced their earliest extra-legal actions. Individuals have strong needs for positive affiliations with others and probation officers provide this opportunity for probationers.

The 5/5 face must have and display the personal, psychological, social, and culturally valued qualities which probationers can learn to assume. The probation officer works hard at gaining trust and respect by demonstrating a "regular guy" face which can be trusted to understand the "real" problems encountered by probationers.

A positive relationship between probation officer and client has always been central to good probation but not necessarily with the view of maintaining the personal charisma of the officer. In the 5/5 face this likeableness becomes crucial. If the probationer likes his probationer officer and attempts, therefore, to please him, then the likelihood of his breaking court orders is less. By implication, this helps to secure some control while also helping the individual probationer to alter some of his antisocial predispositions.

Some work completed in recent years by attraction theory psychologists suggests that a 5/5 face holds promising components for the probationer officer-probationer relationship. Aronson[3], for example, thinks that increasing rewards and punishments from a person have more impact on his attractiveness than constant, invariant rewards and punishments. For the probation officer who must so often "start from scratch" with his probationer, Aronson's minitheory seems to be significant for developing 5/5 attractiveness in his work.

The probation officer's 5/5 face suggests to probationers that "you and I will work together in keeping these probation rules. I know how you must be feeling and thinking and if you stick with me you can make it."

THE 9/9 FACE

By orienting the concern for control and the concern for rehabilitation at right angles to each other, it is possible to clarify probation faces reflected to individuals who are on probation. The countenances postulated so far indicate an orientation toward an incompatibility of the dual concerns. This dichotomization has bedeviled corrections for decades.

The 9/9 face seeks to integrate concerns for control and rehabilitation. The 9/9 probation officer brings full concern for both dimensions of the grid at the same time.

This means he creates conditions which help a probationer help himself but limited by the reality of probationary conditions. This means that he stresses goals rather than personality traits of his probationer. These traits are treated as important but not necessarily in cause and effect fashion. Instead, the probationer is helped to select from goals calculated to meet his needs more effectively within a legal framework. The 9/9 face organizes legitimate choices and through a collaborative relationship induces the client to act in accord with prosocial expectations.

Underlying a 9/9 face is the notion that probationers are more likely to exert control over themselves and become rehabilitated when they can internalize what is expected of them.

> Internalization can be said to occur when an individual accepts influence because the content of the induced behavior—the ideas and actions of which it is composed—is intrinsically rewarding.[4]

Put another way, it may be said that clients change when it makes sense to do so because there is some kind of "pay off." Their needs are met in better fashion. In the 9/1 face probationers tend to see resentment or fear; in a 1/9 face they are inclined to see chances to manipulate their probation officer; in a 1/1 face, probationers may read apathy; in a 5/5 profile a tenuous balance of charisma shows up. The 9/9 face projects credibility and says to the probationer "let's put our heads together, take a look at what needs to be done, how we may be able to go about doing it and determine the best way of finishing a realistic probation program."

It seems reasonable to assert that probation officers reflect all of these faces with various probationers under different circumstances. Each carries with it a different set of probable outcomes. This article suggests

---

3. Elliot Aronson, *Who Likes Whom and Why*, Psychology Today, (August 1970), 48–50, 74.

4. Kelman, *supra* at 54.

that a basic 9/9 face is more likely to give equitable attention to concerns for both control and rehabilitation. If true, we may hypothesize that this set of conditions is most likely to meet the needs of both probationers and community.

Social Services in Probation Under a "Justice as Fairness" Model*

Providing social services is not the responsibility of the justice system which, for both economic and policy reasons, must narrow its scope. Given the array of public, publicly funded, and private agencies, which are—or should be—better equipped than corrections to handle offenders' needs within the community, probation's traditional responsibility for providing social services should shift to determining how they can be obtained from other existing agencies. Under a justice-as-fairness approach to sentencing, counseling, or casework is not a legitimate role of probation.

Under a justice-as-fairness model, probation represents a proportionate penalty within a broader scale of penalties. Deprivation of liberty and reparation make up the probation sanction and when both are achieved, the offender's obligation to society is fulfilled. Although changing the offender's behavior may result from this sentencing approach, that is not its primary purpose. Its primary purpose is to mete out sanctions commensurate with the harm done. Conditions or probation aimed at alleviating the offender's perceived problems would be, in fact, out of place in a proportionate sentencing scheme since such a scheme is aimed at the offense, not the offender. Yet special needs of offender's come to the attention of probation officers—and this creates an opportunity if not an obligation to respond with some form of assistance.

VOLUNTARY AND BROKERED SERVICES

It must be stressed that, under this concept of probation, attending to the social service needs of offenders is an activity separate from and collateral to enforcing the sanction. Thus, the offender's need for services or involvement in a social service program should in no way determine the nature or length of probation. And since there is no coercion of the offender to take advantage of social services, there should be no penalty for failure to participate in any services or programs.

---

* Lynn Zeller Barclay, *Change: A Juvenile Justice Quarterly,* Sept. 1983. Reprinted with permission.

Shifting from coerced use of services to voluntary use would be welcomed presumably by not only the offender but by social service agencies as well. The *Corrections* report of the National Advisory Commission on Criminal Justice Standards and Goals points out that the casework/treatment model of corrections was originally borrowed from the social work profession but that the corrections approach . . . *has been warped . . . by a failure to absorb two of the most basic tenets of social work. The first of these is that, for casework to be effective, the individual must perceive that he has a problem and be motivated to seek help; this is the principle of voluntarism. The second is that the goals of the casework process must be established by the client; this is the principle of self-determination . . .*

In defining resource brokerage, *Promising Strategies in Probation and Parole* states that "a major function of probation and parole should be the identification of existing community resources and the development of strategies for assuring their ready availability to the probationer and parolee." Resource brokerage, then, means more than simply referring the probationer to social service agencies since "the problems of (offenders) needing services are interrelated, while the sources of help are fragmented among agencies and often within each agency" (Community Resources Management Team Training Materials). There may also be conflicting goals among agencies dealing with the same client. If resource brokerage is adopted by probation departments, the probation officer would have the important perhaps novel role of helping offenders sort through the bureaucratic maze to obtain the most appropriate available services. This would require a shift from the traditional, almost adversarial role ("You'd better go out and get a job or you're liable to get revoked") to an advocacy role ("I'd better help you figure out how you should go about getting a job since you say you really need one").

Structuring resource brokerage in major metropolitan areas is a formidable task requiring a great deal of thought, care and planning. Some type of categorizing of caseloads would be needed to allow probation as a whole and individual officers to budget whatever time is set aside for resource brokerage. A caseload breakdown in terms of level of offender need would be:

1. No/low needs: Most probationers will either not request services or will merely need a referral to another agency or agencies.

2. Medium needs: Some probationers will want help in locating the appropriate services but will be capable of obtaining them themselves.

3. High needs: Some probationers will have especially complex or multiple problems and may want the probation officer to assume an advocacy role.

During their probation term, probationers will undoubtedly change categories so that "high needs" would, we hope, be reduced to "medium" or "low needs" after a crisis period is weathered or desired services are arranged and used for a period with no problems. Nonetheless, if probation is serious about successfully brokering services, it needs to recognize the considerable amount of time this can entail. To have the most impact with limited resources, probation's efforts should focus mainly on the "high needs" cases—the group of probationers most needing and least able to obtain social services. These are the cases in which probation can possibly make the real difference between the offender getting or not getting desired services.

Resource brokerage can be achieved in varied ways: e.g., through informal, personal connections between probation officers and service providers; through interagency agreements; or through purchase of service arrangements. But the term "brokerage" itself implies a willingness on the part of social service agencies to collaborate in the delivery of needed services. In the absence of such willingness, probation may have to turn to advocacy to secure available services that are withheld or obscured. The advantages and disadvantages of three possible approaches to helping obtain services for offenders who want them—referral, brokerage, and advocacy—are as follows:

Referral. Probation collects and updates information on available services, including eligibility criteria, and gives relevant listings to the probationer who can make contact directly. This approach assumes the offender will be persistent. Its advantages are that time and money are saved; the offender is required to take responsibility for obtaining services; and services are obtained voluntarily. Its disadvantages are that it does not address the most needy offenders who cannot wade through bureaucracies to get services nor encourage service providers to give special consideration to probation-referred clients.

Brokerage. The probation officer works with the offender to identify priority needs and the best service agency. The probation officer fills out a referral form and lets the offender do the rest. This approach assumes that agencies want to help. Its advantages are that it requires less time than advocacy; the probation officer can better link the offender's needs with agencies' capability to respond; and it requires offenders to follow up if truly motivate. Its disadvantages are, again, that it may not adequately address the most needy offenders; it does not assure that the targeted agency actually provides the needed services for the offender; and it replaces more time and research than referral.

Advocacy. The probation officer works with the offender to identify priority needs, identifies possible referral agencies; arranges for receipt of referral and agreed-upon service to be provided; requests a report back from the provider; and is available to the offender and provider throughout the service period to help resolve any problems. This approach assumes the offender is unable to negotiate for him or herself and agencies are unwilling to go out of their way to respond. Its advantages are that probation can better link an offender's needs with agency capabilities; the offender has the best shot at getting the needed service; the probation officer can monitor the service provider's responsiveness; the offender and provider will likely be more satisfied with the experience; and the offender must still follow up if truly motivated. Its disadvantages are that it requires a great deal of time and special interpersonal skills to obtain agency cooperation.

Problems in Resource Brokerage

Probationers as "Undesirable" Clients. The probationer as client presents problems for many social service agencies. Agencies are concerned about "dangerousness," the possibility that participation is coerced by probation (which may violate their program policy), their "legal" responsibility (since the client is under obligation to the court), offenders' lack of motivation and the frustrations of dealing with "society's misfits." According to Martin Rein, agencies "tend to accept the type of client that will deliver all the rewards that professionals and agencies want and need. The good client is cooperative, motivated to use what is offered, capable of improvement, and eventually, able to express gratitude." Since probation is unlikely to refer very many offenders who meet any, let alone all, of these criteria, it needs to develop strategies to improve agency responsiveness.

Agencies accustomed to providing crisis or one-time services usually are willing to accept almost any referral, but special efforts are often required to get other agencies to provide suitable services. To obtain such services from unenthusiastic agencies, probation departments can:

• Assure the agency that it has no legal responsibility for assuring the probationer's attendance or compliance with program rules since participation is voluntary.

• Assure the agency that the probation officer is available and anxious to handle any questions or problems that arise.

• Inform the agency of the probationer's history so it knows what to expect thus reducing unwarranted fears (e.g., about dangerousness).

• Help the agency set realistic expectations for offenders so it will not fear failure.

Agency Reluctance to Provide Special Services. At times, probation officers will want an agency to tailor its services for a specific need or bend the rules to allow early acceptance or some other special arrangement for an offender. Aside from agency reluctance to deal with probationers, there may also be a general unwillingness to add to an already overloaded case-load provide free or reduced rate services for yet another category of clients, or make exceptions for anyone. To help improve agency responsiveness, probation can:

• Cultivate the agency by visiting staff, showing interest in learning about their services, and providing information on probation's role. If treated with special attention, with luck, the agency will feel obligated to respond in like ways.

• Substitute nagging for money. If the agency hears from probation often and loudly enough, it may start coming up with the desired arrangements.

• For special cases, explain the need for a special one-time arrangement and promise not to abuse the favor in the future.

• Avoid making frivolous or uninformed requests or promises that cannot be kept. Agencies do not want to be taken advantage of, and abusing their services even once

may reduce or eliminate their cooperation forever.

• Know the agency's eligibility requirements and refer only those who are eligible and really in need. ·

• Make clear that probation will only refer offenders who have asked for the service, but explain offender characteristics (e.g., lack of motivation or impulsiveness). That way, the agency will not be surprised or blame probation when offenders' "needs" change suddenly and they stop attending.

Need for Interpersonal Skills. Clearly, the probation officer doing resource brokerage has to "manage" not only probationers but also service providers. Interestingly, both service providers and offenders need the same things from probation—respect, attention, structure, limits, and praise. Resource brokerage therefore requries an ability to cooperate, resolve conflicts, negotiate, and advocate for client services.

In particular, there can be a tremendous amount of negotiation involved. There would be no need for resource brokerage in the first place if offenders could successfully negotiate their way through complex bureaucracies. Probation's role is thus to intervene to help offenders get services before anger and frustration overcome motivation. And if probationers are present during the negotiation with service providers, they will know that probation takes their needs seriously and will go to bat for them. If the offender "screws up" in the social service program, the agency needs to know that automatic expulsion is not always warranted, and that the probation officer may be right back there advocating for the offender again and again.

Negotiation is also required to persuade agencies to accept a new role under probation's resource brokerage model. While social service agencies are suffering from funding cutbacks, probation can promote its model as a more efficient and logical way to deal with dwindling resources.

Limiting Probation's Role

The American Probation and Parole Association's "Critical Issues, Strategies and Missions in Probation Project" recently prepared a working paper suggesting several strategies for limiting probation's role in resource brokerage. For example, probation could be the catalyst for forming a community council that would take primary responsibility for resource brokerage. Representatives from probation, social service agencies, the United Way, and community and business leaders would work together to identify existing resources; make arrangements for streamlining the referral process from probation; reduce duplication of services; and push for new services when needed. The United Way or other umbrella agency could be encouraged to take on a larger role in channeling referrals, especially if convinced that probation cannot properly or adequately function as a social service broker. In a large or diverse probation district, working with regional councils or neighborhood umbrella agencies would probably be most efficient.

Students, college programs, and professional and trade organizations could be recruited to take a lead role in coordinating referrals and obtaining desired services. Probation, a community council or other agency would have to sponsor or supervise these activities. Another suggestion calls for "probationers with needed skills to provide assistance to other probationers in exchange for time off the sentence or as a community service as a condition of probation."

Probation needs to reduce its financial burden as well. One option is to charge probationers seeking services a fee to cover the costs to probation of resource brokerage. This assumes, often incorrectly, that probationers have the resources to pay not only required restitution but also added fees. If probation chooses to prepare and regularly update a directory of services (or regional directories), local businesses or a United Way-type agency could be approached to cover publishing costs or take on the whole directory project as an annual public service.

Realistic Expectations

Given the current constraints on most probation departments in the United States, proposing a shift to resource brokerage may sound like adding insult to injury. But seen in the context of a justice-as-fairness model, this shift is not only practical but essential. It would save time for many probation departments by reducing the probation officer's casework tasks and transferring the service delivery role to non-justice system agencies. The shift is essential because the probation officer must refocus virtually all efforts on enforcing the sanction. Services are not sanctions and therefore would not be imposed by the court.

If we can convince the public and judges that probation *is* a sentence and that the sentence *will be* enforced, perhaps probation will again be taken seriously for an array of offenses and offenders who are now being committed to county jails and state prisons. Focusing on probation as a community sentence would help appease the public, which understandably is clamoring for offenders to be held accountable for their crimes. The public, however, has come to expect too much from the criminal justice system, and we must help bring those expectations back into the realm of reality.

We will never be able to make good on a promise to make long-term changes in offenders' behavior or lifestyles (rehabilitate), or to reduce crime. But we *can* deliver on a promise to be socially responsible toward offenders and to enforce fair sentences. If we thereby reduce the goals and expectations of probation to planning and overseeing an equitable sentence imposed by the court, we stand a much better chance of achieving success and, in turn, public support.

6

Revocation of Probation

In our discussion of revocation of probation, several distinct but overlapping and interrelated aspects of the process will be considered: the *decision* to revoke probation, which includes the decisions of the probation officer to recommend and of the court to order revocation; the *legal procedures* for revocation of probation, which are governed by several recent court decisions and involve technical legal matters that should be understood by the probation officer; the problems of sentencing or resentencing after revocation of probation; and appeals and other legal proceedings taken after revocation by the probationer as an attempt to set aside the revocation or the sentence.

The Decision to Revoke

As we have seen, release on probation is a conditional release, which is to say that the liberty of the probationer is not absolute, but is subject to conditions. Violation of the conditions can result in revocation of probation and the commitment of the offender. Needless to say, revocation of probation is a serious matter to the probationer.

Although a probationer's right to be at liberty in the community is subject to certain restrictions, imposed both by law and the court order granting probation, the probationer's status is in many fundamental ways equal to that enjoyed by persons who have not been charged or convicted of an offense. The probationer can continue to live free in the community, can work at suitable employment, can enjoy the association of family and friends, can participate in community activities, and can generally enjoy the benefits that a free society offers its members.

Revocation of probation is a serious matter to the probation officer as well. The traditional probation officer is very apt to view revocation of probation as a "failure."[1]

Before the relationship has deteriorated to the point where revocation of probation is being considered, the probation officer has invested considerable time and effort to rehabilitate the probationer. The probation officer has developed a genuine interest in the probationer and has become acquainted with the probationer's family. The officer may feel strongly that commitment will mitigate against rather than facilitate the ultimate adjustment of the probationer to society, and will be concerned about the impact of the commitment on the family. The *community resource manager* type of probation officer will see probation revocation in terms of an inability to locate and arrange for the probationer's needs, or as a failure of the community to provide the necessary resources. The *justice model* probation officer will view the revocation decision as a failure on the part of the probationer to live up to the terms of the contract or agreement with the court.

Despite conscientious efforts of the probation officer, a percentage of probationers will fail. These failures are not failures of the system, the community, or the probation officer, but rather are the failure of the probationer to put forth effort to succeed and adjust in free society.

Revocation of probation is also a serious matter to the community. Commitment of the offender will increase the cost to the community, since keeping an offender under probation supervision is much less expensive than paying for care and treatment in a correctional institution. Commitment of the breadwinner will mean that the family must go on relief or, to a greater extent than before, make demands upon the welfare resources of the community.

Revocation of probation thus is not treated lightly. Not every violation of the probation conditions will result in revocation. Sometimes the probation officer will permit a whole series of minor violations before taking the offender before the court; when there, the officer may recommend modifying the conditions imposed, with the hope that a change in the conditions will increase the chance of successful adjustment. The new standards being developed for probation stress the importance of giving the probationer easy access to the court if an explanation of the conditions is not being given by the probation supervisor, of if the probationer desires a change or modification of the conditions. Recent statutory enactments and court decisions have formalized the procedures necessary for revocation of probation and have set up remedies for the probationer who desires to appeal or otherwise obtain relief from an order revoking probation.

---

1. The traditional officer's attitude toward these revocational decisions reflects the rehabilitative rather than punitive focus of the probation/parole system. Revocation * * * is, if anything, commonly treated as a failure of supervision. While presumably it would be inappropriate for a field agent never to revoke, the whole thrust of the probation/parole movement is to keep [individuals] in the community, working with adjustment problems there, and using revocation only as a last resort where treatment has failed or is about to fail.

Quoted in Gagnon v. Scarpelli, 411 U.S. 778, 93 S.Ct. 1756, 36 L.Ed.2d 656 (1973).

Authority to Revoke Probation

It must be kept clearly in mind that although the probation officer or the probation department can recommend revocation of probation, only the court has authority to revoke probation. This authority remains with the court that granted the probation, for example, the sentencing court,[2] unless the case has been transferred to another court that is given the same powers as the sentencing court.[3] The federal probation statute and state statute provide for transfer of jurisdiction in appropriate cases to allow the probationer with the court's permission to change residence from one place to another and still remain under supervision. This change of residence may be from part of the state to another or, in the case of the federal offender, from one part of the country to another. The transfer of jurisdiction from one court to another is to be distinguished from the situation under the interstate compacts where supervision only becomes the responsibility of an out-of-state probation department. When transfer is under the interstate compact, authority to modify the conditions of probation, revoke probation, or terminate probation remains with the court in the sending state.

When Can Probation Be Revoked?

Ordinarily, probation can be revoked at any time within the probated term. Upon the revocation of the probation, the court loses jurisdiction over the defendant. Few problems are presented by this general rule if the acts that constitute violation of probation, the hearing on whether to revoke probation, and the order revoking probation all occur during the original probated term.

But different sets of facts present special problems. For example: What is the situation if the probation violation occurs during the probated term, but the probation officer or the court do not become aware of the violation until after the original term has expired? What if the violation occurs during the probated term, and the probation officer and the court become aware of the violation, but the probationer has absconded and cannot be found so that a hearing on revocation can be held before the expiration of the term? Should there be a different result if the attempted revocation takes place within the period for which the probationer could have been sentenced for the crime committed than if the revocation takes place after the maximum sentence time has expired? Does it make any difference that probation was based upon suspension of imposition of sentence, suspension of execution of sentence, or was granted in a state where probation is a sentence? Are the results arrived at in a particular case affected by whether or not the probationer is credited on his original sentence for the time successfully served on probation?[4] The answers given to

---

2. Authority to grant probation lies with having jurisdiction to try the offense. 18 U.S.C.A. § 3651. State statutes are similar.

3. *Id.* § 3653. The court to which transfer is made has all the power previously possessed by the court from which transfer is made, except that the period of probation cannot be changed without the consent of the sentencing court.

4. Time successfully completed on probation is not credited on the original sentence in Texas and California.

these questions depend upon the statutory and case law in the particular jurisdiction. A few states hold, for example, that revocation of probation may occur at any time during the period within which the defendant might have been imprisoned, even though that is longer than the term of probation.

Other states, such as New York, provide for a determination of delinquency (i.e., determination that a violation of probation conditions has taken place) that has the effect of tolling (i.e., interrupting) the running of the probated term. The court can make an order of delinquency whenever it has reasonable cause to believe that the defendant has violated a condition of the probation. This determination interrupts the period of the sentence as of the date of the delinquency.[5]

Both the American Bar Association Standards Relating to Probation and the National Advisory Commission Standards provide that revocation of probation based solely upon the commission of another crime should await the disposition of that charge,[6] except that the court should have the discretionary authority to detain the probationer without bail. "Disposition of the charge" probably would include a plea of guilty, or a finding of guilt and sentence, but would not extend to final disposition, which in some cases would wait for the action of the superior court upon an appeal.

Under certain circumstances, the effect of these provisions would permit a revocation after the original term of probation had expired. For example, if a probationer was arrested during the period of original probation for commission of a new crime, and either detained or let out on bail pending disposition of the new charges, the original period of probation could expire during this waiting interval without affecting the right of the court to revoke probation if the defendant was convicted of the new crime.

Grounds for Revocation

Probation may be revoked by the court if the probationer commits a new crime or violates a condition of probation.[7] To warrant revocation of probation, the probationer's offense need not be a felony or a misdemeanor involving moral

---

In the federal system, upon revocation of probation, the court may require that the defendant serve the sentence imposed, or any lesser sentence, and if imposition of sentence was suspended, it may impose any sentence that originally might have been imposed. 18 U.S.C.A. § 3653.

5. N.Y.Civ.Prac.Law § 410.30 (McKinney). Declaration of delinquency: If at any time during the period of probation or conditional discharge the court has reasonable cause to believe that the defendant has violated a condition of the sentence, it may declare the defendant delinquent and file a written declaration of delinquency. Upon such filing the court must promptly take reasonable and appropriate action to cause the defendant to appear before it for the purpose of enabling the court to make a final determination with respect to the alleged delinquency.

N.Y. Penal Law § 65.15(McKinney). When a person has violated the conditions of probation of conditional discharge and is declared delinquent by the court, the declaration of delinquency shall interrupt the period of the sentence as of the date of the delinquency and such interruption shall continue until a final determination as to the delinquency has been made by the court pursuant to a hearing held in accordance with the provisions of the criminal procedure law.

6. ABA Standards Relating to Probation, § 5.3; Nat'l Advisory Comm'n Standards § 5.4.5.

7. Jackson v. State, 165 Tex.Cr.R. 380, 307 S.W.2d 809 (1957).

turpitude.[8] A crime not yet prosecuted or not successfully prosecuted may be the basis for revocation.[9] But the arrest and filing of a complaint against the probationer would not alone authorize revocation,[10] nor would revocation be authorized when the probationer was arrested and charged with an offense but later acquitted.[11] There is no requirement that the conviction of the new crime become final before probation can be revoked.[12] A plea of guilty to another offense is sufficient to justify revocation.[13]

Violations other than commission of a new offense are called *technical violations*. The practice in many courts is to report a new offense as a technical violation unless the probationer is actually convicted of the new crime. Revocation on technical grounds has been upheld upon a mere showing that the probationer has engaged in illegal conduct. Thus, evidence that showed that before a burglary, the probationer had been in company with those who committed the burglary and shared in the fruits of the burglary, and that a pistol taken in the burglary was found in the probationer's possession justified revocation.[14] In another case, where the probationer was identified as having attempted to pass as true a stolen and forged check, the revocation was upheld.[15] Similarly, the probation granted a defendant was justifiably revoked when the defendant committed the act of pandering while free on bail and awaiting the pending appeal of the jail sentence that was imposed with the probation.[16] Where a defendant was shown to have been driving an automobile while intoxicated, probation could be revoked.[17]

Revocation of probation for other types of technical violations has been upheld under a large variety of circumstances. The following are representative: engaging in a scuffle with campus police during a demonstration which violated the condition that the probationer not participate in demonstrations;[18] nonpayment of a fine imposed as condition of probation;[19] failure to pay off civil judgments for fraud although probationer was able to pay;[20] failure to make child support payments;[21] failure to report;[22] and making false statements to

---

8. *Id.*

9. People v. Wilkins, 169 Cal.App.2d 27, 336 P.2d 540 (1959), *cert. den.* 359 U.S. 995, 79 S.Ct. 1130, 3 L.Ed.2d 983 (1959).

10. Flores v. State, 169 Tex.Crim. 2, 331 S.W.2d 217 (1959).

11. Jianole v. United States, 58 F.2d 115 (8th Cir.1932).

12. Swanson v. State, 170 Tex.Crim. 441, 342 S.W.2d 112 (1961).

13. People v. Schwartz, 80 Cal.App.2d 801, 183 P.2d 59 (1947).

14. Villarreal v. State, 166 Tex.Crim. 610, 217 S.W.2d 207 (1958).

15. Madeley v. State, 165 Tex.Crim. 83, 303 S.W.2d 798 (1957).

16. People v. Gish, 230 Cal.App.2d 544, 41 Cal.Rptr. 155 (1964).

17. Alexander v. State, 161 Tex.Crim. 66, 274 S.W.2d 831 (1955).

18. People v. King, 267 Cal.App.2d 814, 73 Cal.Rptr. 440 (1968), *cert. den.* 396 U.S. 1028, 90 S.Ct. 576, 24 L.Ed.2d 524 (1970).

19. *Ex parte* McVeity, 98 Cal.App. 723, 277 P. 745 (1929).

20. People v. McClean, 130 Cal.App.2d 439, 279 P.2d 87 (1955).

21. Olivas v. State, 168 Tex.Crim. 437, 328 S.W.2d 771 (1959).

22. House v. State, 166 Tex.Crim. 41, 310 S.W.2d 339 (1958).

secure probation.[23] Probation revocation was upheld where the defendant deserted his wife and children to live with a dissolute woman whom he was aiding and which violated the immigration laws of the United States.[24]

On the other hand, probation cannot be revoked where there has been no violation, nor can revocation be arbitrary or capricious.[25] There can be no revocation where the conditions of probation are so indefinite that the accused and authorities cannot know with certainty what the conditions are.[26] But revocation has been upheld where the court had reason to believe that the accused was associating with lawless or improper persons, or was engaged in criminal practices, although no express condition of probation had been violated.[27] In New York, failure to appear before the court upon notice is a violation for which probation can be revoked, although this condition does not specifically appear in the sentence.[28]

Notice and Hearing

The American Correctional Association Standards require: at least three days prior to the preliminary hearing, a probationer/parolee is notified in writing of the time and place of the hearing, and of the specific violation(s) charged. The probationer/parolee is also advised in writing of the right to:

- present evidence and favorable witnesses
- disclosure of evidence
- confront adverse witness(es) unless the witness(es) would be subjected thereby to a risk of harm.
- have counsel of choice present, or, in case of indigent persons who request assistance to adequately present their case, have counsel appointed.
- request postponement of the hearing for good cause.[29]

Although a few states have had statutes that explicitly allowed revocation without notice to the probationer,[30] and some statutes are silent on the matter, the majority of the states and the federal government require that there be a hearing after notice to the probationer of the intended revocation.

---

23. *Id. See also: In re* Bine, 47 Cal.2d 814, 306 P.2d 445 (1957).

24. People v. Mancha, 133 Cal.App.2d 685, 284 P.2d 931 (1955).

25. *In re* Solis, 274 Cal.App.2d 344, 78 Cal.Rptr. 919 (1969).

26. People v. Root, 192 Cal.App.2d 158, 13 Cal.Rptr. 209 (1961).

27. Glenn v. State, 168 Tex.Crim. 312, 327 S.W.2d 763 (1959).

28. N.Y.Civ.Prac.Law § 410.40(1) (McKinney).

29. American Correctional Association, Standard 2–3146 (1980).

30. A California case presents an extreme example. The defendant was convicted of attempted robbery in 1936 and imposition of sentence was suspended. He was placed on probation for ten years. In 1937, in his absence, a report of violation of probation for failure to report was filed; probation was revoked, and a bench warrant issued. No further action was taken for fifteen years, during which the defendant married and had children, and apparently led an exemplary life. In 1951 he was sentenced to state prison for the time provided by law. The revocation was upheld on the ground that after probation had been revoked there was no limit to the time within which sentence can be pronounced. People v. Brown, 11 Cal.App.2d 406, 244 P.2d 702 (1952).

In *Escoe v. Zerbst*,[31] decided in 1935, the Supreme Court of the United States rejected a claim that revocation of probation without notice or hearing was unconstitutional. The Court said:

> * * * we do not accept the petitioner's contention that the privilege (probation) has a basis in the Constitution, apart from any statute. Probation or suspension of sentence comes as an act of grace to one convicted of a crime, and may be coupled with such conditions in respect of its duration as Congress may impose.

But in 1957, in *Mempa v. Rhay*,[32] the court required not only notice and hearing but representation by counsel in a case where imposition of sentence had been deferred and sentencing took place after revocation of probation:

> In sum, we do not question the authority of the State of Washington to provide for a deferred sentencing procedure coupled with its probation provisions. Indeed, it appears to be an enlightened step forward. All we decide here is that a lawyer must be afforded at this proceeding whether it be labeled a revocation of probation or deferred sentencing.

Whether *Mempa v. Rhay* requires a hearing in cases where sentence was imposed and probation followed, suspension of execution instead of suspension of imposition of sentence has been answered differently by different courts. In *Skidgell v. State*,[33] the Supreme Judicial Court of Maine gave Mempa a narrow reading, stating, "We consider the holding in Mempha (sic) limited to requiring appointment of counsel for indigents in hearings on revocation of probation only in cases where sentence is to be imposed."

Other courts pointed to the general due process requirements of the fifth and fourteenth amendments. These courts found no significant differences between the rights of the probationer on revocation, whether imposition or merely execution of sentence had been suspended at the time of granting probation.[34]

Several important developments occurred in 1972. In a California case, *People v. Youngs*,[35] imposition of sentence was suspended and the defendant placed on probation. Three years later, probation was summarily revoked on allegations by the defendant's probation officer of a failure to comply with certain terms of his probation. When the defendant was arraigned for sentencing, his attorney raised the issue of actual violation of the terms of probation, but without

---

31. Escoe v. Zerbst, 295 U.S. 490, 55 S.Ct. 818, 79 L.Ed. 1566 (1935).

32. Mempa v. Rhay, 389 U.S. 128, 88 S.Ct. 254, 19 L.Ed.2d 336 (1967), applied retroactively in McConnel v. Rhay, 393 U.S. 2, 89 S.Ct. 32, 21 L.Ed.2d 2 (1968).
   Deferred sentencing had dictated a similar ruling in California. Although it was then generally held that the probation statute did not require notice and hearing on revocation, if the sentence was suspended without imposition of sentence, the defendant on revocation was entitled to be represented by counsel since it was an arraignment for sentence. *Ex parte* Levi, 39 Cal.2d 41, 244 P.2d 403 (1952).

33. Skidgell v. State, 264 A.2d 8 (Me.1970).

34. Lester v. Foster, 207 Ga. 596, 63 S.E.2d 402 (1951).

35. People v. Youngs, 23 Cal.App.3d 180, 99 Cal.Rptr. 901 (1972).

hearing witnesses on defendant's behalf the court revoked probation and imposed sentence. The court recognized that under the then prevailing law a probationer had no right to a hearing preceding a revocation of probation, but held that following such a revocation he was entitled to a hearing between the act of summary revocation and the act of imposing sentence, in order to challenge an erroneous or false allegation of violation. The court further held that he was entitled to representation by counsel, to be advised of the alleged violation, to be given an opportunity to deny or explain it, and if necessary, to present witnesses on his own behalf.

By far the most significant development was the decision by the United States Supreme Court in *Morrissey v. Brewer.*[36] In that case, which concerned a revocation of parole, the Court declared that before parole could be revoked, the parolee was entitled to minimum due process safeguards. At a parole revocation hearing these were stated to include: (a) written notice of the claimed violations of parole; (b) disclosure to the parolee of evidence against him or her; (3) opportunity to be heard in person and to present witnesses and documentary evidence; (d) the right to confront and cross-examine adverse witnesses (unless the hearing officer specifically finds good cause for not allowing confrontation); (e) a neutral and detached hearing body such as a traditional parole board, members of which need not be judicial officers or lawyers; and (f) a written statement of the fact finders as to the evidence relied on and reasons for revoking parole. The Court stated:

> We turn therefore to the question of whether the requirements of due process in general apply to parole revocations. As Mr. Justice Blackmun has written recently this Court now has rejected the concept that constitutional rights turn upon whether a governmental benefit is characterized as a right or as a privilege * * * Whether any procedural protections are due depends upon the extent to which an individual will be condemned to suffer grievous loss * * *. The question is not merely the "weight" of the individual's interest but whether the nature of the interest is one within the contemplation of the "liberty or property" language of the Fourteenth Amendment * * *[37]

With reference to parole revocations, the Court spelled out a two-step procedure that included an on-site hearing to determine probable cause, and a revocation hearing "which must lead to a final evaluation of any contested relevant facts and consideration of whether the facts as determined warrant revocation."[38]

California was the first state to consider a probation revocation in light of the decision of *Morrissey v. Brewer.* In *People v. Vickers,* the California Supreme court generally held that proceedings for revocation of probation granted after a conviction and imposition of sentence were bound by the United States Supreme Court's determination in *Morrissey* to the extent that the decision established minimal due process requirements on parole revocation since probation proceedings cannot be distinguished in principle insofar as demands of due process are

36. Morrissey v. Brewer, 408 U.S. 471, 92 S.Ct. 2593, 33 L.Ed.2d 484 (1972).

37. *Id.*

38. *Id.*

concerned. However, the California court decided that the proceedings for revocation of probation need not be identical to those established in *Morrissey* for parole revocation, provided they assure equivalent due process safeguards. Accordingly, the California court recognized the validity of a summary termination of probationer's status in case of an absconding probationer if that probationer were accorded a hearing that conforms to the *Morrissey* standards after being taken into custody. The court said:

> A different situation is presented, however, when a parolee's right to liberty is the subject of proceedings had before his arrest or actual deprivation of his conditional liberty. Such a situation commonly develops when a parolee unilaterally elects to escape the restraints imposed on his liberty and severs the lines of communication with those assigned to supervise him; in effect, he absconds. Should he remain at liberty without proceedings had against him he could conceivably complete his term and the Authority would lose jurisdiction in the matter * * * Due process does not require that the defendant profit by such wrongdoing and we read *Morrissey* as applicable only in those instances wherein an actual seizure of the individual has occurred. It is this loss of liberty which compels the procedures set forth in *Morrissey*. Accordingly, a summary termination of his status through revocation while the parolee remains at liberty and unavailable to the authorities does not fall within the prescription of *Morrissey*. Once taken into custody, however, due process requires that he be accorded both preliminary and formal hearings which conform to *Morrissey* standards. The purpose of the hearings would not be to revoke parole as such revocations would have already been summarily ordered, but rather to afford the defendant an opportunity to require the Authority to establish that the alleged violations did in fact occur and justify the revocation.
>
> For the same reasons we have held that *Morrissey* is applicable to probation, as well as parole revocation proceedings, we conclude that a summary termination of probationary status in the case of an absconding probationer comports with due process requirements if he is accorded a hearing which conforms to *Morrissey* standards after being taken into custody.[39]

On the question of right to counsel—a determination not made in *Morrissey* —the California court announced *as a judicially declared rule of criminal process* that a probationer is entitled to the representation of retained or appointed counsel at formal proceedings for the revocation of probation, or following such summary revocation in appropriate cases.[40] [Emphasis added.] However, the California court refused to apply *Morrissey*, or its decisions in *Youngs* and *Vickers*, retroactively.[41]

In May 1973, the Supreme Court extended to probationers the right to preliminary and final revocation hearings under the conditions specified in *Morrissey v. Brewer*. It further mandated a case-by-case determination of the need for counsel in the sound discretion of the state authority responsible for administering the probation and parole system. If the probationer's or parolee's version of a disputed issue can fairly be represented only by trained counsel, appointment of counsel for the indigent probationer or parolee should be made,

---

39. People v. Vickers, 25 Cal.App.3d 1080, 102 Cal.Rptr. 418 (1972).

40. *Id.*

41. People v. Nelson, 25 Cal.App.3d 1075, 102 Cal.Rptr. 416 (1972).

"although participation by counsel will probably be both undesirable and unnecessary in most revocation hearings." [42]

Sufficiency of Notice

In accordance with developing due process concepts, recent cases are demanding an increasing degree of specificity in notices of an intended revocation of probation. Allowing sufficient time for preparation of a defense is also being mandated. In a Texas case, for example, the defendant was served with a notice of a motion to revoke probation on the day of the hearing, and given oral information that one of the bases of the revocation would be theft by false pretext instead of felony theft as set out in the written notice. It was held that the defendant had been denied rudiments of due process by failure to give him adequate and prior notice to prepare his defense.[43] In another Texas case, the state's motion to revoke probation alleged that the defendant "violated paragraphs (a), (b), and (c) of his Conditions of Probation." Defendant claimed the pleadings were insufficient. The denial of his motion by the trial court was reversed on appeal. The appellate court stated that the state's pleadings were not sufficient to give the defendant fair notice of the conduct or acts for which the state intended to offer evidence to prove a violation of the conditions of probation.[44]

The right to representation by appointed counsel at a parole revocation hearing was not decided in *Morrissey v. Brewer*. However, by the mid-eighties, by statute or court decision, all jurisdictions provide counsel at a probation revocation hearing.[45]

Nature of Hearing

The requirements of minimum due process in a revocation hearing have not changed the basic character of the probation revocation hearing. The Court in *Morrissey v. Brewer* said, "We begin with the proposition that the revocation of parole is not part of a criminal prosecution and thus the full panoply of rights due a defendant does not apply to parole revocation." Thus, a hearing on probation revocation is still a hearing and not a trial. A hearing is not governed by the rules concerning formal criminal trials.[46] It is not necessary that all the technical provisions in criminal procedure be followed in a proceeding for

---

42. Gagnon v. Scarpelli, 411 U.S. 778, 93 S.Ct. 1756, 36 L.Ed.2d 656 (1973). *But see* Lane v. Attorney General, 477 F.2d 847 (5th Cir.1973), appointment of counsel required where statute permitted retained counsel on parole revocation. *See also* Cottle v. Wainwright, 477 F.2d 269 (5th Cir.1973).

In Pannell v. Jones, 2 Prison Law Reporter 347 (Erie County, N.Y.Sup.Ct., April 13, 1973) a hearing and representation by counsel were required to revoke aftercare status of a narcotics addict.

43. Kuenstler v. State, 486 S.W.2d 367 (Tex.1972).

44. Burkett v. State, 485 S.W.2d 578 (Tex.1972).

45. Tex.Code Crim.Proc.Ann. art 42.12, § 3b (Vernon).

People v. Price, 24 Ill.App.2d 364, 164 N.E.2d 528 (1960); People v. Vickers, 25 Cal.App.3d 1080, 102 Cal.Rptr. 418 (1972).

46. People v. Sweeden, 116 Cal.App.2d 891, 254 P.2d 899 (1953).

revocation of probation.[47]   Hearing on motion for revocation of probation is not required to be formal and may be held in vacation.[48]   A proceeding to revoke probation is not a "trial" as that term is used and contemplated by the Constitution in regard to criminal cases.[49]   The result of a probation hearing is not a conviction, but a finding upon which the trial court may exercise discretion by revoking or continuing probation.[50]   The defendant is not entitled to a jury trial on revocation of probation.[51]   Proof beyond a reasonable doubt is not required to show violation of the conditions of probation; a clear and satisfactory showing is sufficient.[52]

Early cases that held that the defendant need not be present for revocation of probation have probably not been overruled if the hearing at which the defendant is not present is a summary hearing to revoke the probation of an absconding defendant, and the defendant is given a proper due-process hearing after arrest and prior to commitment.   However, cases that announce a general rule that the defendant need not be present at a revocation hearing have been overruled.

The American Bar Association Standards

The American Bar Association Standards Relating to Probation suggest alternatives to probation revocation, including a review of the probation conditions and their modification where necessary, a formal or informal conference with the probationer to reemphasize the necessity of compliance with the conditions, and a formal or informal warning that further violations could result in revocation.[53] Formal arrests of probationers could be made only upon probable cause and by issuance of a warrant except where the probationer has been arrested without warrant for another crime.   Probation officers should not be authorized to arrest probationers.   Revocation of probation based solely upon commission of another crime would await the disposition of that charge, except that the court would have the discretionary authority to detain the probationer without bail.   The revocation proceeding would be in open court, following written notice.[54]   The probationer would be represented by retained or appointed counsel; the burden of proof of the violation would be by a preponderance of the evidence.[55]   The

---

47. People v. Cirullo, 40 Ill.App.2d 181, 189 N.E.2d 381 (1963).

48. Dunn v. State, 159 Tex.Crim. 520, 265 S.W.2d 589 (1954).

49. Lynch v. State, 159 Tex.Crim. 267, 263 S.W.2d 158 (1953).

50. Soliz v. State, 171 Tex.Crim. 376, 350 S.W.2d 566 (1961).

51. People v. Price, 24 Ill.App.2d 364, 164 N.E.2d 528 (1960).
People v. Larson, 17 Ill.App.2d 417, 150 N.E.2d 224 (1958).

52. People v. Vanella, 265 Cal.App.2d 463, 71 Cal.Rptr. 152 (1968); People v. Johns, 173 Cal.App.2d 38, 343 P.2d 92 (1959); Morrissey v. Brewer, 408 U.S. 471, 92 S.Ct. 2593, 33 L.Ed.2d 484 (1972).   Reasonable grounds of belief that parolee violated parole are required at the informal hearing.

53. American Bar Association Standards Relating to Probation, § 5.1.

54. *Id.* §§ 5.2, 5.3.

55. *Id.* § 5.4.

Model Penal Code provisions are similar except that they do not provide for appointed counsel.[56]

Proceedings Following Revocation

In cases where sentence has been imposed and its execution is suspended, the defendant whose probation has been revoked is committed to begin the service of sentence. In the event that imposition of sentence has been suspended, the statutes commonly give the court the authority to sentence the defendant as though no probation had been granted.[57]

The American Bar Association Standards Relating to Probation provide that, "Sentence should be imposed following a revocation according to the same procedures as are applicable to original sentencing proceedings." [58]

Special Problems
Under Interstate Compacts

Special problems arise after revocation of probation of a probationer who is under supervision in a state other than the state of conviction. The Interstate Compact for the Supervision of Parolees and Probationers provides that any state that has signed the compact will accept supervision of a parolee or probationer who meets the residence requirements set forth in the compact, and will supervise the probationer at the same level of supervision that it gives to its own cases. The sending state may retake a person being supervised in another state simply by (a) having its officer present appropriate credentials, and (b) proving the identity of the person to be retaken. The probationer, on requesting and accepting out of state supervision waives extradition prior to leaving the sending state, although formal extradition procedures may be resorted to if necessary.

It is well established that the sending state can retake a probation violator being supervised under the compact without resorting to formal extradition procedures. The receiving state is bound to surrender the probationer unless a criminal charge is then pending against the individual in the receiving state, in which case the probationer cannot be retaken without the consent of the receiving state until discharged from prosecution or from any imprisonment for such offense. The practical effect is that the sending state cannot retake the probationer into custody until all local charges are disposed of. Some states admit a probationer to bail pending disposition of charges for revocation of probation. Other states hold that the right to bail does not apply to persons who have been tried and convicted.

---

56. Model Penal Code, § 301.3.

57. Cal.Penal Code § 1203.2 (West).

Ill.Ann.Stat. ch. 38, § 117–3 (Smith-Hurd).

N.Y. Penal Law § 60.10 (McKinney).

In Texas, the punishment is adjudged prior to sentencing to probation. Upon revocation, the defendant is committed for the term of the punishment assessed. Tex.Code Crim.Proc.Ann. art. 42.12, § 8 (Vernon).

58. American Bar Association Standards Relating to Probation, § 5.4(1).

The validity of the waiver of extradition has been upheld against a challenge that it violated the constitutional rights, and was invalid because it would not become operative until some future date. It is also generally held that the sending state alone has authority to determine upon what basis a violator may be returned—the reasons for return are not reviewable by the receiving state.[59]

Alternatives to Revocation

There are available alternatives to revocation that the probation officer may wish to use in instances where incarceration is not desired. Of course, one alternative is a verbal reprimand by the probation officer. In some cases and for some individuals, this is all that is necessary to impress upon the probationer the importance of observing the conditions of probation. In some jurisdictions, a common practice involves bringing the probationer back before the court to show cause why the probation should not be revoked, but with an understanding between the probation officer and the court that revocation is not desired. This return to court to face the judge often has a sobering effect upon the defendant to a greater degree and extent than a simple session in the probation officer's office.

Another alternative, one that is the subject of intense controversy, is that of jail therapy. *Jail therapy* consists of placing a probationer in jail without holding a subsequent revocation hearing. The period of incarceration (in jurisdictions where this practice is allowed) is usually short and is accomplished with two basic purposes in mind: (1) to impress upon the probationer the seriousness of the offense and the possible ramifications of continued violation, and (2) to provide a more realistic comparison between life in the community and that within the institution., Opponents to jail therapy reject the practice as being punitive in nature and as not contributing toward the ultimate rehabilitation of the probationer. They also believe that the relationship between the probation officer and the probationer may be permanently destroyed by such an action.

Summary of Guidelines for Revocation

Eugene C. DiCerbo, formerly chief probation officer for the United States District Court for the Eastern District of Pennsylvania, has suggested eleven guidelines to be considered by the probation officer in considering revocation actions.[60]

1. Conditions of probation should be realistic and purposive and geared to help the probationer develop into a law-abiding, self-respecting person. They must be flexible in their application. Each case should be judged on its own merits—on the basis of the problems, needs, and capacity of the individual offender. Unrealistic conditions that cannot be enforced invite violation.

2. The probation officer should make certain that the probationer fully understands the limitations placed on him or her in the general and special conditions imposed by the court. Merely signing the "Conditions of Probation"

---

59. Gagnon v. Scarpelli, 411 U.S. 778, 93 S.Ct. 1756, 36 L.Ed.2d 656 (1973).

60. Eugene C. DiCerbo, *When Should Probation be Revoked,* Federal Probation (June 1966).

form does not mean that the probationer has correctly interpreted each condition.

3. Violations of the conditions of probation do not necessarily reflect a poor probation adjustment. The conditions imposed may have been unrealistic. Perhaps too much was expected in requiring some probationers to live up to certain conditions. The customs, feelings, attitudes, habit patterns, and moral and social values of the cultural group of which a probationer is a part should be considered in assessing his noncompliance with the conditions. Probationers differ in their ability to comply or conform. It is entirely possible we are imposing a standard of conduct that is realistic for us but not for the probationer.

4. In offenses where a fine and/or restitution are being considered by the court, the probation officer should explain in detail the defendant's financial obligations and resources in order that the fine or restitution imposed will be commensurate with the defendant's ability to pay. In too many instances an automatic fine or restitution is imposed without knowledge of the financial burden it places on the probationer and the probationer's family.

5. While revocation of probation is not advocated merely for failure to keep appointments, to submit monthly reports, to observe a curfew, or to remain within the district, a generally unfavorable attitude and deliberate noncompliance with the conditions of probation and instructions of the probation officer should be grounds for revocation.

6. Although all convictions for new offenses should be brought to the court's attention, it does not follow that probation should automatically be revoked. No violation should result in automatic revocation. It may be more beneficial to society, and also to the probationer and the probationer's family, to have the probationer continue on probation than be sentenced to imprisonment.

7. Where a probationer is arrested on a new charge and held in jail, that person should be regarded as a violator until a conviction has been reached. There is always the possibility of an acquittal, and we must keep in mind that in some local jurisdictions considerable time elapses between arrest and trial.

8. Lest the probation officer be guilty of usurping the power of the court, all unfulfilled conditions of probation—for example, not paying a fine or restitution in full by the terminal date—should be brought to the court's attention in advance of the termination date. Recommendations for a course of action should be included in the report.

9. To assist the court at the revocation hearing, the probation officer should prepare a formal report containing the details of the alleged violation, factors underlying the violation, the probationer's attitude toward the violation, a summary of the probationer's conduct during supervision, and the probationer's general attitude and outlook.

10. The probationer should be present at the revocation hearing. It would seem that the United States attorney and also the counsel for the probationer should be present. But it must be remembered that the revocation hearing is not a new trial.

11. Where it is necessary to revoke probation, imprisonment should serve a constructive purpose and not be used merely for the sake of punishment. In certain cases, particularly where an indifferent probationer deliberately fails to comply with conditions of probation, it may be necessary to revoke probation so that the public—and other probationers, too—will have a fuller appreciation of probation and realize that the primary purpose of probation is the protection of the public, that the court means what it says, and that the conditions of probation are not to be flouted.

Gagnon v. Scarpelli

JOHN R. GAGNON,
Warden, Petitioner, v.
 GERALD H. SCARPELLI

411 US 778, 36 L Ed 2d 656, 93 S Ct 1756
[No. 71–1225]

Argued January 9, 1973. Decided May 14, 1973.

Summary

After the petitioner had pleaded guilty to a charge of armed robbery in Wisconsin and the trial court had sentenced him to 15 years' imprisonment, the judge suspended sentence, placed the petitioner on probation for 7 years in the custody of the Wisconsin Department of Public Welfare, and authorized him to reside in Illinois, where, pursuant to an interstate compact, he was accepted for supervision by Illinois probation authorities. Subsequently, he and a companion were arrested in Illinois for a burglary. Several days later, the Wisconsin Department, without affording him either a hearing or counsel, revoked his probation on the grounds that by being involved in and arrested for the burglary, and by associating with his companion, a known criminal, he had violated his probation. Shortly thereafter, he was incarcerated in a Wisconsin prison to begin serving his 15-year sentence. In habeas corpus proceedings in the United States District Court for the Eastern District of Wisconsin, the petitioner contended that the revocation of his probation without affording him a hearing or counsel was a denial of due process. The District Court agreed with this contention and granted a writ of habeas corpus (317 F Supp 72), and the Court of Appeals for the Seventh Circuit affirmed (454 F2d 416).

On certiorari, United States Supreme Court affirmed in part, reversed in part, and remanded the case. In an opinion by **Powell, J.**, it was held (1) expressing the unanimous view of the court, that the petitioner was entitled to both a preliminary hearing to determine whether there was probable cause to believe that he had violated his probation and a final hearing prior to the ultimate decision whether his probation should be revoked, and (2) expressing the view of eight members of the court, that the state was not under a constitutional duty to provide counsel for indigents in all probation revocation cases, but that the decision as to the need for counsel must be made on a case-by-case basis in the exercise of a sound discretion by the state authority charged with responsibility for administering the probation system, and that certain general guidelines as to whether the assistance of counsel was constitutionally necessary should be applied in the first instance by those charged with conducting the revocation hearing.

Opinion of the Court

[411 US 779]

Mr. Justice **Powell** delivered the opinion of the Court.

This case presents the related questions whether a previously sentenced probationer is entitled to a hearing when his probation is revoked and, if so, whether he is entitled to be represented by appointed counsel at such a hearing.

I

Respondent, Gerald Scarpelli, pleaded guilty in July 1965, to a charge of armed robbery in Wisconsin. The trial judge sentenced him to 15 years' imprisonment, but suspended the sentence and placed him on probation for seven years in the custody of the Wisconsin Department of Public Welfare (the Department).[1] At that time, he signed an agreement specifying the terms of his probation and a "Travel Permit and Agreement to Return" allowing him to reside in Illinois, with supervision there under an interstate compact. On August 5, 1965, he was accepted for supervision by the Adult Probation Department of Cook County, Illinois.

On August 6, respondent was apprehended by Illinois police, who had surprised him and one Fred Kleckner, Jr.

[411 US 780]

in the course of the burglary of a house. After being apprised of his constitutional rights, respondent admitted that he and Kleckner had broken into the house for the purpose of stealing merchandise or money, although he now asserts that his statement was made under duress and is false. Probation was revoked by the Department on September 1, without a hearing. The stated grounds for revocation were that:

> "1. [Scarpelli] has associated with known criminals, in direct violation of his probation regulations and his supervising agent's instructions;
>
> "2. [Scarpelli] while associating with a known criminal, namely Fred Kleckner, Jr., was involved in, and arrested for, a burglary . . . in Deerfield, Illinois." App 20.

On September 4, 1965, he was incarcerated in the Wisconsin State Reformatory at Green Bay to begin serving the 15 years to which he had been sentenced by the trial judge. At no time was he afforded a hearing.

Some three years later, on December 16, 1968, respondent applied for a writ of habeas corpus. After the petition had been filed, but before it had been acted upon, the

---

1. The Court's order placing respondent on probation provided, among other things, that "[i]n the event of his failure to meet the conditions of his probation he will stand committed under the sentence all ready [sic] imposed." App. 10. The agreement specifying the conditions of the probation, duly executed by respondent, obligated him to "make a sincere attempt to avoid all acts which are forbidden by law. . . ." App 12.

Department placed respondent on parole.[2] The District Court found that his status as parolee was sufficient custody to confer jurisdiction on the court and that the petition was not moot because the revocation carried "collateral consequences," presumably including the restraints imposed by his parole. On the merits, the District Court held that revocation without a hearing and counsel was a denial of due process. 317 F Supp 72 (ED Wis 1970). The Court of Appeals affirmed sub nom. Gunsolus v Gagnon, 454 F2d 416 (CA 7 1971),

[411 US 781]

and we granted certiorari, 408 US 921, 33 L Ed 2d 331, 92 S Ct 2490 (1972).

II

Two prior decisions set the bounds of our present inquiry. In Mempa v Rhay, 389 US 128, 19 L Ed 2d 336, 88 S Ct 254 (1967), the Court held that a probationer is entitled to be represented by appointed counsel at a combined revocation and sentencing hearing. Reasoning that counsel is required "at every stage of a criminal proceeding where substantial rights of a criminal accused may be affected," id., at 134, 19 L Ed 2d 336, and that sentencing is one such stage, the Court concluded that counsel must be provided an indigent at sentencing even when it is accomplished as a part of a subsequent probation revocation proceeding. But this line of reasoning does not require a hearing or counsel at the time of probation revocation in a case such as the present one, where the

probationer was sentenced at the time of trial.

Of greater relevance is our decision last Term in Morrissey v Brewer, 408 US 471, 33 L Ed 2d 484, 92 S Ct 2593 (1972). There we held that the revocation of parole is not a part of a criminal prosecution.

> "Parole arises after the end of the criminal prosecution, including imposition of sentence. . . . Revocation deprives an individual, not of the absolute liberty to which every citizen is entitled, but only of the conditional liberty properly dependent on observance of special parole restrictions." Id., at 480, 33 L Ed 2d 484.

Even though the revocation of parole is not a part of the criminal prosecution, we held that the loss of liberty entailed is a serious deprivation requiring that the parolee be accorded due process. Specifically, we held that a parolee is entitled to two hearings, one a

[411 US 782]

preliminary hearing at the time of his arrest and detention to determine whether there is probable cause to believe that he has committed a violation of his parole and the other a somewhat more comprehensive hearing prior to the making of the final revocation decision.

[1] Petitioner does not contend that there is any difference relevant to the guarantee of due process between the revocation of parole and the revocation of probation, nor do we perceive one.[3] Probation revocation, like parole revocation, is not a stage of a criminal prosecution, but does result in a

---

2. Respondent was initially paroled to a federal detainer to serve a previously imposed federal sentence arising from another conviction. He was subsequently released from federal custody, but remains a parolee under the supervision of the Department.

3. Despite the undoubted minor differences between probation and parole, the commentators have agreed that revocation of probation where sentence has been imposed previously is constitutionally indistinguishable from the revocation of parole. *See, e.g.,* Van Dyke, *Parole Revocation Hearings in California: The Right to Counsel,* 59 Calif L Rev 1215, 1241–1243 (1971); Sklar, *Law and Practice in Probation and Parole Revocation Hearings,* 55 J Crim LC & PS 175, 198 n. 182 (1964).

loss of liberty.[4] Accordingly, we hold that a probationer, like a parolee, is entitled to a preliminary and a final revocation hearing, under the conditions specified in *Morrissey v Brewer, supra.*[5]

[411 US 783]

III

The second, and more difficult, question posed by this case is whether an indigent probationer or parolee has a due process right to be represented by appointed counsel at these hearings.[6] In answering that question, we draw heavily on the opinion in *Morrissey.* Our first point of reference is the character of probation or parole. As noted in *Morrissey* regarding parole, the "purpose is to help individuals reintegrate into society as constructive individuals as soon as they are able. . . ." 408 US, at 477, 33 L Ed 2d 484. The duty and attitude of the probation or parole officer reflect this purpose:

While the parole or probation officer recognizes his double duty to the welfare of his clients and to the safety of the general community, by and large concern for the client dominates his professional attitude.

[411 US 784]

The parole agent ordinarily defines his role as representing his client's best interests as long as these do not constitute a threat to public safety.[7] Because the probation or parole officer's function is not so much to compel conformance to a strict code of behavior as to supervise a course of rehabilitation, he has been entrusted traditionally with broad discretion to judge the progress of rehabilitation in individual cases, and has been armed with the power to recommend or even to declare revocation.

In *Morrissey,* we recognized that the revocation decision has two analytically distinct components:

---

4. It is clear at least after Morrissey v Brewer, 408 US 471, 33 L Ed 2d 484, 92 S Ct 2593 (1972), that a probationer can no longer be denied due process, in reliance on the dictum in Escoe v. Zerbst, 295 US 490, 492, 79 L Ed 2d 1566, 55 S Ct 818 (1935), that probation is an "act of grace."

5. Petitioner argues, in addition, that the Morrissey hearing requirements impose serious practical problems in cases such as the present one in which a probationer or parolee is allowed to leave the convicting State for supervision in another State. Such arrangements are made pursuant to an interstate compact adopted by all of the States, including Wisconsin. Wis.Stat.Ann. § 57.13 (1957). Petitioner's brief asserts that as of June 30, 1972, Wisconsin had a total of 642 parolees and probationers under supervision in other States and that incomplete statistics as of June 30, 1971, indicated a national total of 24,693 persons under out-of-state supervision. Brief for Petitioner.

Some amount of disruption inevitably attends any new constitutional ruling. We are confident, however, that modifications of the interstate compact can remove without undue strain the more serious technical hurdles to compliance with *Morrissey.* An additional comment is warranted with respect to the rights to present witnesses and to confront and cross-examine adverse witnesses. Petitioner's greatest concern is with the difficulty and expense of procuring witnesses from perhaps thousands of miles away. While in some cases there is simply no adequate alternative to live testimony, we emphasize that we did not in *Morrissey* intend to prohibit use where appropriate of the conventional substitutes for live testimony, including affidavits, depositions, and documentary evidence. Nor did we intend to foreclose the States from holding both the preliminary and the final hearings at the place of violation or from developing other creative solutions to the practical difficulties of the *Morrissey* requirements.

6. In *Morrissey v Brewer,* we left open the question "whether the parolee is entitled to the assistance of retained counsel or to appointed counsel if he is indigent." 408 US, at 489, 33 L Ed 2d 484. Since respondent did not attempt to retain counsel but asked only for appointed counsel, we have no occasion to decide in this case whether a probationer or parolee has a right to be represented at a revocation hearing by retained counsel in situations other than those where the State would be obliged to furnish counsel for an indigent.

7. F. Remington, D. Newman, E. Kimball, M. Melli and H. Goldstein, Criminal Justice Administration, Materials and Cases 910–911 (1969).

"The first step in a revocation decision thus involves a wholly retrospective factual question: whether the parolee has in fact acted in violation of one or more conditions of his parole. Only if it is determined that the parolee did violate the condition does the second question arise: should the parolee be recommitted to prison or should other steps be taken to protect society and improve chances of rehabilitation?" *Morrissey v. Brewer, supra,* at 479–480, 33 L Ed 2d 484.[8]

[411 US 785]

The parole officer's attitude toward these decisions reflects the rehabilitative rather than punitive focus of the probation/parole system:

"Revocation .... is, if anything, commonly treated as a failure of supervision. While presumably it would be inappropriate for a field agent *never* to revoke, the whole thrust of the probation-parole movement is to keep men in the community, working with adjustment problems there, and using revocation only as a last resort when treatment has failed or is about to fail."[9]

[2] But an exclusive focus on the benevolent attitudes of those who administer the probation/parole system when it is working successfully obscures the modification in attitude which is likely to take place once the officer has decided to recommend revocation. Even though the officer is not by this recommendation converted into a prosecutor committed to convict, his role as counsellor to the probationer or parolee is then surely compromised.

When the officer's view of the probationer's or parolee's conduct differs in this fundamental way from the latter's own view, due process requires that the difference be resolved before revocation becomes final. Both the probationer or parolee and the State have interests in the accurate finding of fact and the informed use of discretion—the probationer or parolee to insure that his liberty is not unjustifiably taken away and the State to make certain that it is neither unnecessarily interrupting a successful effort at rehabilitation nor imprudently prejudicing the safety of the community.

[411 US 786]

[3, 4] It was to serve all of these interests that Morrissey mandated preliminary and final revocation hearings. At the preliminary hearing, a probationer or parolee is entitled to notice of the alleged violations of probation or parole, an opportunity to appear and to present evidence in his own behalf, a conditional right to confront adverse witnesses, an independent decision maker, and a written report of the hearing. *Morrissey v. Brewer, supra,* at 487, 33 L Ed 2d 484. The final hearing is a less summary one because the decision under consideration is the ultimate decision to revoke rather than a mere determination of probable cause, but the "minimum requirements of due process" include very similar elements:

---

8. The factors entering into these decisions relate in major part to a professional evaluation, by trained probation or parole officers, as to the overall social readjustment of the offender in the community, and include consideration of such variables as the offender's relationship toward his family, his attitude toward the fulfillment of financial obligations, the extent of his cooperation with the probation officer assigned to his case, his personal associations, and—of course—whether there have been specific and significant violations of the conditions of the probation. The importance of these considerations, some factual and others entirely judgmental, is illustrated by a Wisconsin empirical study which disclosed that, in the sample studied, probation or parole was revoked in only 34.5% of the cases in which the probationer or parolee violated the terms of his release. S. Hunt, *The Revocation Decision: A Study of Probation and Parole Agents' Discretion 10* (unpublished thesis on file at the library of the University of Wisconsin 1964), cited in Brief for Petitioner, Addendum 106.

9. Remington, Newman, Kimball, Melli and Goldstein, *supra,* n. 7, at 910.

(a) written notice of the claimed violations of [probation or] parole; (b) disclosure to the [probationer or] parolee of evidence against him; (c) opportunity to be heard in person and to present witnesses and documentary evidence; (d) the right to confront and cross-examine adverse witnesses (unless the hearing officer specifically finds good cause for not allowing confrontation); (e) a "neutral and detached" hearing body such as a traditional parole board, members of which need not be judicial officers or lawyers; and (f) a written statement by the factfinders as to the evidence relied on and reasons for revoking [probation or] parole. *Morrissey v. Brewer, supra,* at 489, 33 L Ed 2d 484.

[5] These requirements in themselves serve as substantial protection against ill-considered revocation, and petitioner argues that counsel need never be supplied. What this argument overlooks is that the effectiveness of the rights guaranteed by *Morrissey* may in some circumstances depend on the use of skills which the probationer or parolee is unlikely to possess. Despite the informal nature of the proceeding and the absence of technical

[411 US 787]

rules of procedure or evidence, the unskilled or uneducated probationer or parolee may well have difficulty in presenting his version of a disputed set of facts where the presentation requires the examining of cross-examining of witnesses or the offering or dissecting of complex documentary evidence.

[6] By the same token, we think that the Court of Appeals erred in accepting respondent's contention that the State is under a constitutional duty to provide counsel for indigents in all probation or parole revocation cases. While such a rule

has the appeal of simplicity, it would impose direct costs and serious collateral disadvantages without regard to the need or the likelihood in a particular case for a constructive contribution by counsel. In most cases, the probationer or parolee has been convicted of committing another crime or has admitted the charges against him.[10] And while in some cases he may have a justifiable excuse for the violation or a convincing reason why revocation is not the appropriate disposition, mitigating evidence of this kind is often not susceptible of proof or is so simple as not to require either investigation or exposition by counsel.

The introduction of counsel into a revocation proceeding will alter significantly the nature of the proceeding. If counsel is provided for the probationer or parolee, the State in turn will normally provide its own counsel; lawyers, by training and disposition, are advocates and bound by professional duty to present all available evidence and arguments in support of their clients' positions and to contest with vigor all adverse evidence and views. The role of the hearing body itself, aptly described in *Morrissey* as being "predictive and discretionary" as well as factfinding, may become more akin to that of a judge at a trial, and less attuned to the

[411 US 788]

rehabilitative needs of the individual probationer or parolee. In the greater self-consciousness of its quasi-judicial role, the hearing body may be less tolerant of marginal deviant behavior and feel more pressure to reincarcerate rather than to continue nonpunitive rehabilitation. Certainly, the decision-making process will be prolonged, and the financial cost to the State—for appointed counsel, counsel for the State, a

---

10. *See* Skar, *supra,* n. 3, at 192 (parole), 193 (probation).

longer record, and the possibility of judicial review—will not be insubstantial.[11]

[5, 7] In some cases, these modifications in the nature of the revocation hearing must be endured and the costs borne because, as we have indicated above, the probationer's or parolee's version of a disputed issue can fairly be represented only by a trained advocate. But due process is not so rigid as to require that the significant interests in informality, flexibility and economy must always be sacrificed.

In so concluding, we are of course aware that the case-by-case approach to the right to counsel in felony prosecutions adopted in Betts v Brady, 316 US 455, 86 L Ed 1595, 62 S Ct 1252 (1942), was later rejected in favor of a per se rule in Gideon v Wainwright, 372 US 335, 9 L Ed 2d 799, 83 S Ct 792, 93 ALR 2d 733 (1963). *See also* Argersinger v Hamlin, 407 US 25, 32 L Ed 2d 530, 92 S Ct 2006 (1972). We do not, however draw from *Gideon* and *Argersinger* the conclusion that a case-by-case approach to furnishing counsel is necessarily inadequate to protect constitutional rights asserted in varying types of proceedings: there are critical differences between criminal trials and probation or parole revocation

[411 US 789]

hearings, and both society and the probationer or parolee have stakes in preserving these differences.

In a criminal trial, the State is represented by a prosecutor; formal rules of evidence are in force; a defendant enjoys a number

of procedural rights which may be lost if not timely raised; and, in a jury trial, a defendant must make a presentation understandable to untrained jurors. In short, a criminal trial under our system is an adversary proceeding with its own unique characteristics. In a revocation hearing, on the other hand, the State is represented, not by a prosecutor, but by a parole officer with the orientation described above; formal procedures and rules of evidence are not employed; and the members of the hearing body are familiar with the problems and practice of probation or parole. The need for counsel at revocation hearings derives, not from the invariable attributes of those hearings, but rather from the peculiarities of particular cases.

[8, 9] The differences between a criminal trial and a revocation hearing do not dispose altogether of the argument that under a case-by-case approach there may be cases in which a lawyer would be useful but in which none would be appointed because an arguable defense would be uncovered only by a lawyer. Without denying that there is some force in this argument, we think it a sufficient answer that we deal here, not with the right of an accused to counsel in a criminal prosecution, but with the more limited due process right of one who is a probationer or parolee only because he has been convicted of a crime.[12]

[411 US 790]

[10] We thus find no justification for a new inflexible constitutional rule with re-

11. The scope of the practical problem which would be occasioned by a requirement of counsel in all revocation cases is suggested by the fact that in the mid-1960's there was an estimated average of 20,000 adult felony parole revocations and 108,000 adult probation revocations each year. President's Commission on Law Enforcement and Administration of Justice, Task Force Report: The Courts 56 n. 28 (1967).

12. *Cf. In re* Gault, 387 US 1, 18 L Ed 2d 527, 87 S Ct 1428 (1967), establishing a juvenile's right to appointed counsel in a delinquency proceeding which while denominated civil, was functionally akin to a criminal trial. A juvenile charged with violation of a generally applicable statute is differently situated from an already-convicted probationer or parolee, and is entitled to a higher degree of protection. *See In re* Winship, 397 US 358, 25 L Ed 2d 368, 90 S Ct 1068 (1970) (the standard of proof in a juvenile delinquency proceeding must be "proof beyond a reasonable doubt").

spect to the requirement of counsel. We think, rather, that the decision as to the need for counsel must be made on a case-by-case basis in the exercise of a sound discretion by the state authority charged with responsibility for administering the probation and parole system. Although the presence and participation of counsel will probably be both undesirable and constitutionally unnecessary in most revocation hearings, there will remain certain cases in which fundamental fairness—the touchstone of due process—will require that the State provide at its expense counsel for indigent probationers or parolees.

[11, 12] It is neither possible nor prudent to attempt to formulate a precise and detailed set of guidelines to be followed in determining when the providing of counsel is necessary to meet the applicable due process requirements. The facts and circumstances in preliminary and final hearings are susceptible of almost infinite variation, and a considerable discretion must be allowed the responsible agency in making the decision. Presumptively, it may be said that counsel should be provided in cases where, after being informed of his right to request counsel, the probationer or parolee makes such a request, based on a timely and colorable claim (i) that he has not committed the alleged violation of the conditions upon which he is at liberty; or (ii) that, even if the violation is a matter of public record or is uncontested, there are substantial reasons which justified or mitigated the violation and make revocation inappropriate, and that the reasons are complex or otherwise difficult to develop or present. In passing on a request for the appointment of counsel, the responsible agency also should consider,

[411 US 791]

especially in doubtful cases, whether the probationer appears to be capable of speaking effectively for himself. In every case in which a request for counsel at a preliminary or final hearing is refused, the grounds for refusal should be stated succinctly in the record

IV

[13, 14] We return to the facts of the present case. Because respondent was not afforded either a preliminary hearing or a final hearing, the revocation of his probation did not meet the standards of due process prescribed in *Morrissey,* which we have here held applicable to probation revocations. Accordingly, respondent was entitled to a writ of habeas corpus. On remand, the District Court should allow the State an opportunity to conduct such a hearing. As to whether the State must provide counsel, respondent's admission to having committed another serious crime creates the very sort of situation in which counsel need not ordinarily be provided. But because of respondent's subsequent assertions regarding that admission, see supra, at 780, 36 L Ed 2d at 660, we conclude that the failure of the Department to provide respondent with the assistance of counsel should be re-examined in light of this opinion. The general guidelines outlined above should be applied in the first instance by those charged with conducting the revocation hearing.

Affirmed in part, reversed in part, and remanded.

Mr. Justice **Douglas,** dissenting in part.

I believe that due process requires the appointment of counsel in this case because of the claim that respondent's confession of the burglary was made under duress. See Morrissey v. Brewer, 408 US 471, 498, 33 L Ed 2d 484, 92 S Ct 2593 (opinion of Douglas, J.)

II

INTRODUCTION TO PAROLE

At present, forty-one states and the federal government have some form of parole statutes and procedures for the discretionary release of most adult felony offenders from prisons and correctional institutions. Almost all jurisdictions have at least nominal methods of supervision of offenders released to the community and procedures for their return to incarceration should they fail in community adjustment.

The actual structure of the paroling process, including the composition and selection of the parole board, case loads, training, and authority of field staff and procedures used for the parole grant or revocation varies considerably from jurisdiction to jurisdiction. So does the comparative use of parole. Some states parole virtually all adult prisoners, while in others discretionary release on parole has been abolished by legislative action.

These variations in the structure and use of the parole process, as well as the accompanying variations in sentencing structures from one jurisdiction to another, account in good part for the lack of agreement about the legal status of parole across the country. Where parole is the common, almost universal, method of release from prison, it comes to be viewed as a right—where it is granted reluctantly and rarely, and in jurisdictions with long statutory sentences and no other alternatives to mitigation of sentences, parole becomes crucially important to inmates.

This section focuses upon parole as a subsystem of the entire field of criminal justice. The history and philosophy of parole are discussed in detail, as are current practices and legal issues, and attempts to clarify the contemporary issues of controversy involving parole and other forms of early release from incarceration. Parole is viewed in its relationship to sentencing, imprisonment, and other aspects of the correctional continuum.

7

The History
and Concept of Parole

The procedure known as parole was first tried in the United States one hundred years ago. During the years that have intervened since its first official sanction at Elmira Reformatory in 1876, its use has been expanded into all parts of the country and today has become the major device by which offenders are released from prisons and correctional institutions. Even after a century of use, there is much misapprehension and misunderstanding about parole, and much of this arises from a confusion in terminology. The general public often considers parole to be based on clemency or leniency and seldom distinguishes parole from probation and pardon. These three terms are used indiscriminately, not only by the public, but even by officials, judges, and in some state statutes. Because of the confusion in terminology and administration, parole is often charged with all the shortcomings of other release procedures, for which it is in no way responsible. It is evident, therefore, that the prerequisite for an analysis of parole is a clear definition of the term. *Parole is the conditional release of an individual from a prison or correctional institution after having served part of the imposed sentence.*

Probation as Distinguished from Parole

Probation and parole are two different methods of dealing with offenders, although the two terms are often used interchangeably. While parole is a form of release granted to a prisoner who has served a portion of a sentence in a correctional institution, probation is granted an offender without requiring incarceration. Parole is an administrative act of the executive or an executive agency, while probation is a judicial act of the court. Therefore, so-called bench parole, which is nothing more than a suspension of sentence without supervision, is not parole at all, but a form of probation; and the use of the word parole in this connection is improper, misleading, and should be eliminated.

151

Parole as Distinguished from Pardon

Wilcox distinguished between pardon and parole as follows:

> Pardon involves forgiveness. Parole does not. Pardon is a remission of punishment. Parole is an extension of punishment. Pardoned prisoners are free. Parolees may be arrested and re-imprisoned without a trial. Pardon is an executive act of grace; parole is an administrative expedient.[1]

The distinction between parole and pardon was clearly drawn in an address before the American Prison Association in 1916:

> The whole question of parole is one of administration. A parole does not release the parolee from custody; it does not discharge or absolve him from the penal consequences of his act; it does not mitigate his punishment; it does not wash away the stain or remit the penalty; it does not reverse the judgment of the Court or declare him to have been innocent or affect the record against him. Unlike a pardon, it is not an act of grace or of mercy, of clemency or leniency. The granting of parole is merely permission to a prisoner to serve a portion of his sentence outside the walls of the prison. He continues to be in the custody of the authorities, both legally and actually, and is still under restraint. The sentence is in full force and at any time he does not comply with the conditions upon which he is released, or does not want to conduct himself properly, he may be returned, for his own good and in the public interest.[2]

It has been pointed out that there is no similarity between pardon and parole, except that in both cases the person has been released from an institution:[3]

> In all other respects—the theory upon which he is released, the method used in selecting him for release, the treatment of him after his release, his return if he violates his parole—are all different than those which exists in the case of pardon. Some of these considerations are entirely foreign to the very idea of pardon. The idea involved in the granting of pardon is that society is taking the blame for what it has done to a man by sending him to prison. He is sent out on his own without any conditions of supervision being imposed.

Release on parole is not based upon any concept of clemency. Nor is it regarded as a lenient treatment of prisoners, even though they are released prior to the expiration of their sentence. Parole, as it functions today, is an integral part of the total correctional process. As such, it is a method of selectively releasing offenders from the institution and placing them under supervision in the community, whereby the community is afforded continuing protection while the offender is making adjustments and beginning to contribute to society.

---

1. Wilcox, *Theory of Parole* (1927), 20; *quoted in* Att'y Gen. Survey of Release Procedures, Parole, vol. 4.

2. Spaulding (1916) Proceedings American Prison Association, 548.

3. Miller, *Evils of Confusion Between Pardon and Parole* (1932), Proceedings American Prison Association.

The Origins of Parole

The word is derived from the French *parole* and is used in the sense of "word of honor" *parole d'honneur*. The choice of word was a very unfortunate one, inasmuch as most people distrust a word of honor given by a released prisoner. It is not surprising, therefore, that the French prefer the term "conditional liberation" to the one borrowed from them.

In penal philosophy, parole is a part of the reformatory idea in the general trend in nineteenth century criminology in which the emphasis shifted from punishment to reformation. In 1791, during the French Revolution, Mirabeau anticipated modern penal theories by publishing a report based upon the idea of reformation and founded on the principles of labor, segregation, rewards under a mark system, conditional liberation, and aid on discharge.[4] A Frenchman, de Marsangy, in 1847 published a book in which he discussed the pardoning power, conditional liberation, police supervision of discharged convicts, aid upon discharge, and rehabilitation. This book was distributed by the government to the members of both chambers of Parliament. In 1864, in a further work on this subject, he used the following simile in his argument for what is now called parole:

> As a skillful physician gives or withholds remedial treatment according as the patient is or is not cured, so ought the expiatory treatment imposed by law upon the criminal to cease when his amendment is complete; further his detention is inoperative for good, an act of inhumanity, and a needless burden to the state. Society should say to the prisoner "Whenever you give satisfactory evidence of your genuine reformation, you will be tested, under the operation of a ticket of leave; thus the opportunity to abridge the term of your imprisonment is placed in your own hands."[5]

Parole, as a practice, originated almost simultaneously with three European prison administrators: a Spaniard, Montesinos; a German, Obermaier; and an Englishman, Maconochie.

> In 1835, Col. Montesinos was appointed governor of the prison at Valencia, containing about 1,500 convicts. He organized the institution on the basis of semimilitary discipline and encouraged vocational training and primary education of the prisoners. The novelty of his plan consisted in the fact that there were practically no guards to watch the prisoners, who, nevertheless made few, if any, attempts to escape. The main reason for this probably was that each could earn a one-third reduction from the term of his sentence by good behavior and positive accomplishments. The number of recommitments while Montesinos was governor fell from 35 percent to "a figure which it would be imprudent to name, lest is should not be believed."

The law that allowed this program was subsequently repealed and the system collapsed. Montesinos resigned, and in a pamphlet published in 1846 drew the following conclusions from his experiment:

> What neither severity of punishment nor constancy in inflicting them can secure, the slightest personal interest will obtain. In different ways, therefore, during my

---

4. Att'y Gen. Survey, vol. 4, Parole, p. 6.

5. *Quoted in* Wines, *Punishment and Reformation* (1895) 219.

command, I have applied this powerful stimulant; and the excellent results it has always yielded, and the powerful germs of reform which are constantly developed under its influence, have at length fully convinced me that the most inefficacious methods in the prison, the most pernicious and fatal to every chance of reform, are punishments carried to the length of harshness. The maxim should be constant and of universal application in such places, not to degrade further those who come to them already degraded by their crimes. Self respect is one of the most powerful sentiments of the human mind, since it is the most personal; and he who will not condescend, in some degree, according to circumstances, to flattery of it, will never attain his object by any amount of chastisement; the effect of ill treatment being to irritate rather than to correct, and thus turns from reform instead of attracting to it. The moral object of penal establishments should not be so much to inflict punishment as to correct, to receive men idle and ill-intentioned and return them to society, if possible, honest and industrious citizens.[6]

The German, Obermaier, became governor of a prison in Munich in 1842.[7] He found approximately 700 prisoners in a state of rebellion kept in order by over 100 soldiers. In a short time he had gained the confidence of the men, taken off their chains, discharged nearly all the guards, and appointed a convict superintendent of each of the industrial shops. His succession in reforming prisoners was so great that only a reported ten percent relapsed into crime after their discharge. He was aided by two favoring circumstances of which the first was that many of the men were sentenced to simple imprisonment with no fixed term; and the second that there was a thorough supervision of discharged inmates through the labors of numerous prison aid societies.

Chief credit for developing an early parole system, however, is due to Alexander Maconochie, in charge of the English penal colony at Norfolk Island in New South Wales, and to Sir Walter Crofton, who as director of the Irish Convict Prisons, further developed the scheme originated by Maconochie and known today as the ticket-of-leave, or Irish system. Inasmuch as the earliest plan of conditional liberation is found in the Australian convict colonies, and since present day parole is closely linked to these experiments, their tragic history is worthy of consideration.

Transportation to America

The transportation of English criminals to the American colonies began in the early seventeenth century. The system evolved from a 1597 law that provides for the banishment of those who appeared to be dangerous. As early at 1617, reprieves and stays of execution were granted to persons convicted of robbery who were strong enough to be employed in the colonies. The government devised a plan to transport convicted felons to the American colonies as a partial solution to the acute economic conditions and wide spread unemployment in England, and the shortage of labor in the colonies. The London, Virginia, and Massachusetts companies and similar organizations supported the plan. The king approved the proposal to grant reprieves and stays of execution to the convicted felons who were physically able to be employed in the colonies.

---

6. *Id.* at 194.

7. *Id.* at 195.

Initially, no specific conditions were imposed upon those receiving pardons. Consequently, many of them evaded transportation and returned to England prior to the expiration of their terms, and it became necessary to impose certain restrictions upon the individuals to whom pardons were granted. About 1655, the form of pardon was amended to include specific conditions and to provide for the nullification of the pardon if the recipient failed to abide by the conditions.

Until 1717, the government paid a fee to the contractor for each prisoner transported. However, during that year a new procedure was adopted. Under the new procedure, the contractor was given "property in service" and the government took no interest in the welfare or behavior of the offender unless he or she violated the conditions of the pardon by returning to England prior to the expiration of the sentence. Upon arrival in the colonies, the "services" of the prisoner were sold to the highest bidder and thereafter the prisoner was an indentured servant.

The system of indenture dates to 1512, and originally had no relation to persons convicted of crimes. It applied usually to apprentices who were indentured to their masters for a number of years. The indenture consisted of a contract that stipulated the conditions of indenture. The conditions bore some similarity to the parole agreement of today.

Transportation to Australia and Ticket-of-Leave

The Revolutionary War brought an end to the system of transporting criminals to America; however, the transportation law was not repealed. Detention facilities became over crowded, resulting in the more liberal granting of pardons. During a serious crime wave, the English public demanded enforcement of the transportation law and Australia was designated for use as a convict settlement, with the first load arriving there in January 1788. Transportation to Australia differed from transportation to the colonies in that the government incurred all expenses of transportation and maintenance, and the prisoners remained under government control instead of being indentured. The governor was given "the property and service" for the prisoners, and he assigned them to the free settlers who assumed the property and service agreement. As early as 1790, the governor of New South Wales had been given the right of conditional pardon. He could set the convicts free and give them grants of land, afterward even assigning newcoming convict laborers to them. Such was the original ticket-of-leave system that was regulated by statute in 1834.[8] Originally there were no provisions for governmental supervision of those on ticket-of-leave.

In 1811, a policy was adopted requiring that prisoners serve specific periods of time before being eligible to receive ticket-of-leave. Strict enforcement of this policy was not seen until 1921, when a regular scale was formulated. Those prisoners serving a sentence of seven years became eligible for the ticket-of-leave after serving four years; those serving sentences of fourteen years, after serving six years; and those serving life sentences, after eight years. In 1837,

---

8. Archibald, *The Parole System*, 6 Can.L.Rev. 222 (1967).

Alexander Maconochie devised a system whereby the duration of the sentence would be determined by the industry and good conduct of the prisoner. He made his proposal to the House of Commons. Marks were to be accredited to the prisoner daily in accordance with the amount of labor performed and the type of conduct exemplified. His system saw the prisoners passing through a series of stages from strict imprisonment through conditional release to final and complete restoration of liberty, with promotions being based upon marks accredited. In 1840, Maconochie was appointed governor of the Norfolk Penal Colony, but remained there only four years. While his ideas were progressive and his experiments successful, there were no revolutionary effects due to the short duration of his tenure and the limitation of his experiences in Norfolk.

As the free settlers in Australia increased their numbers, they protested the use of the country as a dumping ground for prisoners. In response to the protest, England initiated a selection system whereby prisoners would undergo an eighteen-month training process prior to transportation to Australia. The selection experiment failed, but it saw the beginning of the utilization of trained, experienced individuals who were made responsible for the selection of prisoners who had profited by the training program. Three prison commissioners were appointed to make the selections and the membership of the group may well have been the precedent to three member parole boards later established by prison reformers in America. In 1867, transportation of prisoners to Australia terminated.

England's Experience with Ticket-of-Leave

Although England did not terminate the transportation of prisoners to Australia until 1867, the English Penal Servitude Act of 1853, governing English and Irish prisoners substituted imprisonment for transportation. In accordance with the Act, prisoners sentenced to 14 years or less were committed to prison, but the judge was given the option of ordering transportation or imprisonment for prisoners with sentences in excess of 14 years. The law also specified the length of time prisoners were required to remain incarcerated before becoming eligible for conditional release on ticket-of-leave. The Act of 1853 related to conditional release and gave legal status to the system of ticket-of-leave.

Prisoners released on a ticket-of-leave in England were released under three general conditions:

1. The power of revoking or altering the license of a convict will most certainly be exercised in the case of misconduct.

2. If, therefore, he wishes to retain the privilege, which by his good behavior under penal discipline he has obtained, he must prove by his subsequent conduct that he is really worthy of Her Majesty's clemency.

3. To produce a forfeiture of the license, it is by no means necessary that the holder should be convicted of a new offense. If he associates with notoriously bad characters, leads an idle or dissolute life, or has no visible means of obtaining an honest livelihood, etc., it will be assumed that he is about to relapse

into crime, and he will at once be apprehended and recommitted to prison under his original sentence.[9]

The British policy falsely assumed that the prison program would be reformative; that the prisoners released on ticket-of-leave would have indicated positive response to prison training programs; and that those released would be adequately supervised. Such was not the case. The three years following the enactment of the Servitude Act saw an outbreak of serious crime which was attributed to a lack of supervision of the ticket-of-leave men. The British public thus believed the ticket-of-leave system to be a menace to public safety and an absolute failure.

A series of prison riots in 1862, accompanied by another serious crime wave, again focused attention on prison administration and the ticket-of-leave system. A Royal Commission was appointed to investigate both areas. The final report that was delivered stressed the poor programs and gave the opinion that prisoners were released on ticket-of-leave without having been given reliable proof of their reformation.

The report of the Royal Commission resulted in policemen providing supervision of the released prisoners. Later, a number of prisoners aid societies, supported in part by the government, were established. These agencies aligned their methods of supervision with the method that had proven effective in Ireland.

The Irish System of Ticket-of-Leave

Sir William Crofton became the administrator of the Irish Prison System in 1854, one year after the Penal Servitude Act was passed. He believed that the intent of the law was to make the penal institution something more than houses of incarceration. Crofton felt that the prison program should be designed more toward reformation and that tickets-of-leave should be awarded only to prisoners who had shown definite achievement and had exemplified positive attitude changes.

Under Crofton's administration, the Irish system became renowned for its three stages of penal servitude—especially the second stage, where the prisoner's classification was determined by marks awarded for good conduct and achievement in industry and education, a concept borrowed from Maconochie's experience on Norfolk Island. So-called indeterminate sentences were employed and institutional conditions were made as near to normal as possible. The restraint exercised over the prisoner was no more than that required to maintain order. The ticket-of-leave in Ireland was different than the one in England. The written conditions of the Irish ticket were supplemented with instructions designed for closer supervision and control and very much resembled the conditions of parole presently used in the United States.

Ticket-of-leave men residing in rural areas were under police supervision, but those living in Dublin were supervised by a civilian employee called the Inspector of Released Prisoners. He had the responsibility of securing employment for the ticket-of-leave man, visiting the residence, and verifying employ-

---

9. Parker, Parole—Origins, Development, Current Practices and Statutes, American Correctional Association, Corrections—Parole—MDT–Project, Resource Document No. 1, 1972.

ment. It was the Inspector of Released Prisoners to whom the ticket-of-leave man periodically reported. The Irish system of ticket-of-leave had the confidence and support of the public and the convicted criminal.

Development in the United States

Three concepts underlie the development of parole in the United States: (1) a reduction in the length of incarceration as a reward for good conduct, (2) supervision of the parolee, and (3) imposition of the indeterminate sentence.

Release as a result of a reduction in the time of imprisonment was always accompanied by an agreement between the prisoner and the authority authorizing the release or what would be considered now as a parole agreement. The agreement normally stipulated that any violation of the conditions would result in a return to the institution. The first legal recognition of shortening the term of imprisonment as a reward for good conduct was the 1817 "Good Time" Law in New York.

Supervision of those released from prison was originally accomplished by volunteers. Masters of indentured children from houses of refuge undertook guardianship and supervision at their own volition. Members of prison societies were also among the first volunteer supervisors of adult offenders. The Philadelphia Society for Alleviating the Miseries of Public Prisons recognized the importance of caring for released prisoners as early as 1822. In 1851, the society appointed two agents to assist those prisoners discharged from the Philadelphia County Prison and the penitentiary. The first public employees paid to assist released prisoners are believed to have been appointed by the State of Massachusetts in 1845.

By 1865, American penal reformers were well aware of the successful achievements in the European systems of prison reformation followed by conditional release, particularly the Irish system. As a result, the first indeterminate sentence law was passed in Michigan in 1869 at the instigation of Z.E. Brockway. However, the Michigan law was subsequently declared unconstitutional. After becoming superintendent of the newly constructed Elmira Reformatory in New York, Brockway succeeded in having an indeterminate sentence law adopted in that state and the first parole system had come into being.

The system established at Elmira included grading inmates on conduct and achievement, compulsory education, and careful selection for parole. Volunteer citizens, known as guardians, supervised the parolees. A condition of parole required the parolee to report to the guardian on the first of each month. Written reports became required and were submitted to the institution after being signed by the employer and the guardian.

Parole legislation spread much more rapidly than did indeterminate sentence legislation. By 1901, twenty states had parole statutes, but only eleven states had indeterminate sentence laws. By 1944, every american jurisdiction had some form of parole release, and indeterminate sentencing had become the rule rather than the exception.[10]

---

10. The historical materials in this chapter relied heavily upon two documents: the Att'y Gen. Survey of Release Procedures, vol. 4, Parole (1939), and on an unpublished M.A. thesis, Charles L. Whitehead, Adult Parole in Texas (Huntsville, Texas: Sam Houston State University, May 1975).

The Problem of Parole*

Parole occupies a central role in the sentencing and correctional system. Once an offender is sentenced to prison, it is largely the parole board which determines when he will be released, under what conditions, and whether his conduct under supervision warrants reimprisonment.

Parole was originally introduced as a reform, and until recently it commanded a strong consensus of support. Now, it is under attack. Abolition has been urged by a number of authorities, and adopted in some jurisdictions.

The recent criticism of parole has been three-fold:

- The procedures of parole decisionmaking are unguided by explicit standards and by the traditional elements of due process;
- The tasks which parole is supposed to perform—the accurate prediction of the offender's likelihood of recidivism, and the monitoring of rehabilitative progress—are beyond our present capacities; and
- Aside from questions of effectiveness, it is unjust to base decisions about the severity of punishments on what the offender is expected to do in the future.

These criticisms, in concert, have been said to warrant abolition of parole. However, they leave a number of questions unanswered. To what extent can parole be justified on grounds other than rehabilitation or prediction? Are the various functions of parole *all* without usefulness, or should some be retained? What alternatives to parole are available, and what problems would they pose?

This report attempts to answer these questions. Doing so necessarily involves value judgments, since the issues raised concern not only what is effective, but also what is fair. Rather than avoiding such value judgments, we try to deal with them as explicitly as we can.

ASSUMPTIONS

Our analysis rests on certain general assumptions and on certain (more controver-

* From Andrew von Hirsch and Kathleen J. Hanrahan, *Abolish Parole?* Law Enforcement Assistance Administration, U.S. Department of Justice, (Washington D.C., 1978). Reprinted with permission of the U.S. Department of Justice. Footnotes omitted.

sial) assumptions about the aims of punishment.

General Assumptions

First, moral assumptions. The convicted offender should retain all the rights of a free individual except those whose deprivation can affirmatively be justified by the state. A related premise is that of parsimony. Even where a given type of intrusion can be justified, its amount should be measured with stringent economy. The state has the burden of justifying why a given amount of intervention, not a lesser amount, is called for. Severe punishments bear an especially heavy burden of justification.

The basic conceptions of due process should apply to the convicted. If, for example, an offender is to be penalized for supposed new misconduct occurring after plea or verdict of guilt, there should be fair procedures for determining whether the individual did, in fact, commit that misconduct.

Minimum requirements of humane treatment should apply to all persons who become wards of the state, including convicted criminals. Cruel punishments, intolerable living conditions, and similarly severe deprivations are barred. This obligation of humane treatment should take precedence over whatever penal goals the state is assumed to be pursuing.

Second, assumptions about controlling discretion. It was long assumed that broad, standardless discretion was necessary to allow sentences to be tailored to the particular offender's treatment needs. But this claim does not bear analysis. Any theory of punishment, even a rehabilitatively oriented one, requires standards to insure that individual decision-makers will pursue the chosen purpose, and will do so in a reasonably consistent manner. The choice of penal philosophy concerns a different question: not whether there ought to be standards, but what their particular content should be.

Thus, specific, carefully drawn standards should govern the disposition of convicted offenders. The standards should set forth the type and severity of penalties with reasonable definiteness.

Third, assumptions about the severe character of imprisonment. The harshness of life in today's prisons has been too well documented to need rehearsal. Imprisonment would still be a great deprivation, even if conditions were improved—were there smaller size, better location, improved facilities, and less regimentation than is customary in prisons now.

The severity of imprisonment is important, because it makes essential a careful scrutiny of each phase of the parole process. Parole release stands in need of justification, because that decision affects the duration of confinement. Parole supervision does so likewise, because, among other reasons, it may result in revocation and reimprisonment.

Assumptions About the Aims of Punishment

One cannot examine the usefulness of parole without first asking for what purpose? At least four different conceptions have been said to underlie sentencing and corrections. Three of these—rehabilitation, incapacitation, and deterrence—have been penologists' traditional concerns and look to reduction of crime in the future. The fourth, which the present analysis emphasizes, is desert; it looks to the blameworthiness of the offender's past criminal conduct.

In punishing the convicted, we assume, the fundamental requirement of justice is the principle of *commensurate deserts:* that the severity of the punishment must be commensurate with the seriousness of the offender's criminal conduct. The rationale for the principle was described in *Doing Justice,* * * * as follows:

The severity of the penalty carries implications of degree of reprobation. The sterner the punishment, the greater the implicit blame: sending someone away for several years connotes that he is more to be condemned than does jailing him for a few months or putting him on probation. In [setting] penalties, therefore, the crime should be sufficiently serious to merit the implicit reprobation. . . . Where an offender convicted of a minor offense is punished severely, the blame which so drastic a penalty ordinarily carries will attach to him—and unjustly so, in view of the not-so-very-wrongful character of the offense . . . [Conversely] imposing only a slight penalty for a serious offense treats the offender as *less* blameworthy than he deserves.

To satisfy this requirement of justice, the seriousness of the criminal conduct must determine the penalty. Seriousness, in turn, is measured by (1) the harm done or risked, and (2) the culpability of the actor in engaging in the conduct.

The principle establishes the following constraints on penal policies: First, it imposes a rank-ordering on penalties. Punishments must be arranged so that their relative severity corresponds with the comparative seriousness of offenses. Secondly, the principle limits the absolute magnitude of punishments; the penalty scale must, at all points on the scale, maintain a reasonable proportion between the quantum of punishment and the gravity of the crimes involved. The scale should not, for example, be so much inflated that less-than-serious offenses receive painful sanctions (not even if serious crimes were punished still more harshly). Finally, the principle requires that criminal behavior of equal seriousness be punished with equal severity. A specific penalty level must apply to all instances of law-breaking which involve a given degree of harmfulness and culpability.

The commensurate-deserts principle, as a requirement of justice, constrains all phases of a state-inflicted criminal sanction, irrespective of whether carried out in prison or in the community. Most of our inquiry

will be devoted to examining whether parole satisfies or violates commensurate-desert constraints.

For our analysis of parole, two alternative conceptual models are presented. The first is the Desert Model; it is the conception of punishment which emerges when the principle of commensurate deserts is rigorously observed. The other is the Modified Desert Model: this is a penalty scheme based primarily on desert, but permitting limited deviations from desert constraints for rehabilitative, incapacitative, or deterrent ends.

The Desert Model. Under this model, all penalties must be commensurate in severity with the seriousness of the offense. No derivation from deserved severity would be permitted for such forward-looking ends as incapacitation or rehabilitation. The salient features of such a system (as proposed in *Doing Justice*) are:

• Penalties would be graded according to the gravity of the offender's criminal conduct. (This, according to *Doing Justice,* would include both the seriousness of his present crime and the seriousness of his past criminal record, if any.) For each gradation of gravity, a specific penalty would be prescribed. Variations from that specific penalty would be permitted only in unusual instances where the degree of culpability of the actor or the degree of harmfulness of his conduct are greater or less than is characteristic of that kind of criminal conduct.

• The severe penalty of imprisonment would be prescribed only for crimes that are serious—e.g., crimes of actual or threatened violence and the more grievous white-collar crimes. Penalties less severe than imprisonment would be required for nonserious crimes.

It is sometimes assumed that parole must be abandoned if the rehabilitatively-oriented theory that has sustained it is no longer accepted. But is it necessarily true that the assumptions of the Desert Model rule out parole? Even if parole were historically based on predictive-rehabilitative ideas, it is still a fair question to ask whether any of its features might be rejustified under a desert-oriented conception of sentencing.

The Modified Desert Model. This is an alternate model which gives somewhat greater scope to forward-looking considerations in deciding penalties. The commensurate desert principle, as we noted, requires equal punishment of those whose offenses are equally serious: a specified level of severity must be selected for each level of seriousness. The Modified Desert Model permits some relaxation of this requirement. *Modest* upward or downward variation from the specific (deserved) penalty would be permitted, for the purpose of enhancing the rehabilitative, incapacitative or deterrent utility of the sentence. Large deviations from the requirements of the commensurate deserts principle still would be barred, however. In that sense, the model represents a compromise: the basic structure of the penalty system is shaped by the desert principle, but crime-control considerations are given some scope in the choice of the individual offender's sentence.

Of the two models, the authors strongly prefer the Desert Model. Because the commensurate deserts principle is a requirement of justice, we feel that deviations from it are undesirable even when small. The Modified Desert Model is useful, however, as a heuristic device. It furnishes a more complex conceptual framework, in which both desert and forward-looking considerations have a role in deciding the particular offender's punishment. This allows an analysis of parole which is of wider scope than would have been possible using only the Desert Model, with the preeminence the latter gives to the single idea of desert. Besides considering whether desert requirements are met, the Modified Desert Model requires us to inquire whether and to what extent parole does actually serve the reha-

bilitative and incapacitative aims that traditionally were thought to provide its rationale. Yet the model shows some concern for fairness, by making the blameworthiness of the criminal conduct the primary (although not exclusive) determinant of penalties.

Limits on Discretion. Earlier, the need for dispositional standards was noted. Under either of these models, it is essential that there be rules governing how serious various categories of crimes are deemed to be, and how much punishment they are considered to deserve.

The Desert Model calls for a definite disposition for each gradation of gravity, in order to satisfy the principle of punishing equally serious infractions equally. A proposed method of accomplishing this is through a system of "presumptive sentences." Each seriousness-gradation would be assigned a specific penalty, and that would be the disposition applicable in the normal case. However, departures from the presumptive disposition would be permitted in unusual circumstances where mitigating or aggravating circumstances were present. The standards would define what kind of circumstances qualified as mitigating or aggravating (and, under the Desert Model, only those which affected the harm or the culpability involved in the conduct could qualify). The standards would also determine how much variation from the presumptive disposition was permitted in such cases. Uniform treatment would thus be given to the unexceptional cases that make up the bulk of sentencers' caseloads—while still allowing variation in extraordinary cases where the harmfulness of the particular offender's conduct or the extent of his culpability is greater or less than is characteristic for that kind of offense.

A Modified Desert Model may require some adjustment in the manner of drafting the standards, since the model allows limited consideration of factors other than the seriousness of the offense. One method would be to prescribe narrow presumptive ranges, instead of specific presumptive sentences.

Let us emphasize that in recommending such standards, we are not presupposing that the legislature should be the agency to set them. The question of which agency— the legislature, the courts, the parole board, or a special rule-making agency—should bear the standard-setting responsibility merits a separate section. We shall be arguing, in fact, that a body other than the legislature is preferable for the task.

Prosecutorial Discretion. Albert Alschuler and others have suggested that adoption of presumptive sentencing standards is not likely successfully to limit discretion, but rather, merely to cause the loation of that discretion to shift to the prosecutor. Others, such as James Q. Wilson, disagree. Standards are capable of influencing dispositions, Wilson argues, provided that the prescribed penalties are perceived as reasonable by the participants in the process. Wholesale shifts in discretion to the prosecutor will only occur "at the extremes," when the stated penalties are viewed as excessively lenient or severe.

Since sentencing standards are a recent development, there is little empirical evidence to support or refute either position. Disparities will, doubtless, persist as long as there are no guidelines governing the prosecutor's discretion, but the dimensions of the problem are unknown. The severity of penalties may, however, be important: Arthur Rosett has pointed out that the harsher the stated penalties, the greater the incentive for both prosecution and defense to bypass them through the plea-bargaining process.

Our view of sentencing standards is that they are a necessary first step. It would be extremely difficult to address the issue of prosecutorial discretion, without first attempting to bring some order into the formal sentencing system. Some have argued, for example, that a system of sentencing standards will also require controls on plea-bargaining decisions that are designed to help insure consistency between those decisions and the standards themselves. But it is hard to describe what form the controls should take, until one has more fully developed the sentencing standards—and until experience provides some indication of the manner of prosecutors' response to those standards.

8

Administration and Organization of Parole

The first element of parole is the decision by a duly constituted authority to determine the portion of the sentence that an inmate must complete before being released to finish the sentence outside the institution. This authority is granted to a parole board that is charged with the administration of parole policy. The board must work within the statutes of that jurisdiction but may adopt its own rules and regulations insofar as they do not conflict with the statutes.

Newman delineates four functions of a parole board: (1) to select and place prisoners on parole; (2) to aid, supervise, and provide continuing control of parolees in the community according to previously established conditions; (3) to discharge the parolee from parole status when supervision is no longer necessary or when the sentence is complete; and (4) to determine if revocation and return to prison is necessary.[1]

Elements of an Effective Parole System

The American Correctional Association regards the essential elements of an effective parole system to be: [2]

1. Flexibility in sentencing and parole laws.
2. A qualified parole board.
3. A qualified parole staff.
4. Freedom from political or improper influences.

---

1. C. Newman and T. Bielen, *Work Release: An Alternative in Correctional Handling,* (Pennsylvania State University, 1968).

2. American Correctional Association, *Manual of Correctional Standards,* (Washington, D.C., 1966), 115–116.

5. Parole assigned to a workable position in the governmental administrative structure.

6. Proper parole procedures.

7. Prerelease preparation within the institution.

8. Parole research.

9. A proper attitude by the public toward parole.

In our discussion of the administration of parole, we will deal with each of these issues separately:

1. Flexibility in Sentencing and Parole Laws. Many offenders are still released outright upon completion of their sentences, but a growing number—now more than 70 percent of the nation as a whole—are released on parole prior to the expiration of their sentence.[3] Basically, the parole decision for adult offenders may depend on statutes, sentences imposed by the courts, or on the determination of correctional authorities or an independent parole board. The President's Commission on Law Enforcement and Administration of Justice observed:[4]

> For certain offenses some statutes require that various amounts of time must be served before parole can be considered, or they prohibit parole entirely. The basic trouble with such restrictions is that they allow no consideration of individual circumstances. Consistently, correctional authorities have found that they interfere with effective decision making; at times they cause unnecessary confinement; and at times they result in substantial inequities.
>
> If minimum sentences are to be imposed, clearly the law needs to provide that they can be neither excessively long nor set so close to the maximum as to make discretion in the granting parole illusory. In a few states, indeterminate sentencing is authorized, permitting consideration for parole at any time, without service of a minimum term. Good-time or other credits earned by conduct during imprisonment may reduce the time that must be served in some jurisdictions prior to eligibility for parole.
>
> Under any such variant, eligibility for parole does not, of course, mean that parole will in all cases be granted. In some, offenders may be released outright at the end of their term. The requirement of mandatory supervision in force in the federal system and several states is one attempt to deal with this problem. In general, mandatory supervision laws require that any prisoner released prior to the expiration of his term by reason of having earned good time or other credits during imprisonment, must be released to a parole officer subject to parole supervision and conditions. Since virtually all prisoners earn good time credits, which may amount to a substantial fraction of their term of sentence, such a provision insures supervision for a period on release unless it is explicitly waived by a parole authority as being unnecessary. The limitation of mandatory supervision to the period of good time credit is one means of insuring that supervision does not become a mere extension of sentence, but obviously it is a rule-of-thumb standard that may bear no relation to the need for supervision.

The Parole Release Decision. Most authorities agree that it is not possible to obtain agreement on a form of sentencing and parole law that would permit the release of a prisoner at the

---

3. American Correctional Association, *Standards for Adult Parole Authorities,* 1980.

4. President's Commission on Law Enforcement and Administration of Justice, *Task Force Report: Corrections,* (Washington, D.C., 1967), 60.

optimum time. In the past, wide latitude and discretion was advocated; however, the last ten years has seen a movement toward the use of quantifiable guidelines in the release decision. The National Advisory Commission stated: "The absence of written criteria by which decisions are made constitutes a major failing in virtually every parole jurisdiction."[5]

The commission recommended that parole decisions be made visible and parole authorities accountable for those decisions through the use of explicit parole selection policy to govern the decision-making process.[6]

In an attempt to provide more rational and consistent parole selection decisions, many paroling jurisdictions have established decision guidelines for parole selection that structure discretion without removing it. By making explicit the primary factors considered in parole selection, as well as the weight given to each, the paroling authority provides judges, the public, and the inmates concerned with a clearer idea of the manner in which it generally intends to exercise its discretion.[7]

The National Advisory Commission on Criminal Justice Standards and Goals suggests a sentencing system that it feels is practical and is the most consistent with parole objectives. The system has the following characteristics: [8]

• Sentence limits set by legislation with the sentencing judge having discretion to fix the maximum sentence, up to legislative limits.

• No minimum sentences, either by mandate or by judicial sentencing authority.

• Comparatively short sentences for most offenses, with a legislative maximum not to exceed five years for most offenders.

• Mandatory release with supervision for offenders ineligible for parole, so that they are not held in an institution until their absolute discharge date.

• All parole conditions set by the paroling authority but with opportunity for sentencing judge to suggest special conditions.

• Legislative prohibition of offenders' accumulating consecutive sentences if it interferes with minimum parole eligibility.

• Legislative provisions for alternatives to reimprisonment upon parole revocation.

• No offense for which parole is denied by legislation.

2. A Qualified Parole Board.

2. A Qualified Parole Board. The American Correctional Association concludes that members should have:

(a) Personality—They must be of such integrity, intelligence, and good judgment as to command respect and public confidence. Because of the importance of their quasi-judicial functions, they must possess the equivalent personal qualifications of a high judicial officer. They must be forthright, courageous, and independent. They

---

5. National Advisory Commission on Criminal Justice Standards and Goals, *supra,* at 397.

6. *Id.*

7. Peter B. Hoffman and Lucille K. DeGostin, *Parole Decision-Making: Structuring Discretion,* Federal Probation (Dec. 1974).

8. National Advisory Commission, at 393.

should be appointed without reference to creed, color, or political affiliation. (b) Education—Board members should have an educational background broad enough to provide them with a knowledge of those professions most closely related to parole administration. Specifically, academic training, which has qualified board members for professional practice in a field such as criminology, education, psychiatry, psychology, law, social work, and sociology is desirable. It is essential that they have the capacity and desire to round out their knowledge as effective performance is dependent upon an understanding of legal processes, the dynamics of human behavior, and cultural conditions contributing to crime. (c) Experiences—They must have an intimate knowledge of common situations and problems confronting offenders. This might be obtained from a variety of fields, such as probation, parole, the judiciary, law, social work, a correctional institution, a delinquency prevention agency. (d) Other—They should not be officers of a political party or seek to hold elective office while members of the board.[9]

In most jurisdictions the governor appoints parole board members and it is not unusual to have a new board appointed when a new governor takes office. On some occasions this has resulted in appointments on the basis of political affiliations rather than qualifications necessary for making parole decisions. Many states, to avoid this, have adopted civil service or merit systems for appointment of parole board members.

Any parole decision is influenced in part by the qualifications of the board member to make the decision and the expertise he or she possesses. Therefore, it is important that the board member be qualified and possess expertise. Many parole officials are able and knowledgeable; however, some have neither the qualifications nor the expertise.

Many authorities view the part-time board of parole often found in smaller states as one of the most severe problems in corrections. Able to give only a limited amount of time to the job because of business or professional concerns consuming a major amount of their energies, part-timers cannot participate effectively in correctional decision making. Approximately one-half the states have part-time boards.[10]

3. Qualified Parole Staff. According to minimum standards adopted by the National Probation and Parole Association, the parole officer's job involves four main groups of functions: (1) The parole officer will be required to make investigations and written reports, and to evaluate, interpret, and present data for the guidance of the court, the institution, or the paroling authority; (2) the officer will keep informed about the conduct and enforcement of parolees by personal contacts and will report to the court or paroling authority any violation; (3) the officer will be responsible for interpreting his or her work to the community by active participation in civic and community organizations.[11]

On the basis of these functions a parole officer must possess certain basic qualifications and specialized knowledge. The minimum qualifications should

9. American Correctional Association, *Manual of Correctional Standards,* (Washington, D.C., 1966), 117, 118.

10. Henry Burns, *Corrections: Organization and Administration,* (St. Paul: West Publishing Company, 1975), 282.

11. Giardini, *The Parole Process,* (Springfield, Illinois: Charles C. Thomas, Publishers, 1959), 377.

be (a) a working knowledge of the principles of human behavior; (b) knowledge of the laws of the jurisdiction in which the officer will work and with the powers and limitations of the position; and (c) familiarity with the operation of related law enforcement agencies in the officer's jurisdiction.

The minimum qualifications should also include: (a) a bachelor's degree from a college or university with course work in the social sciences; (b) one year of paid full-time experience in employment for the welfare of others, or one year of graduate work beyond the baccalaureate; and (c) a good character and well-balanced personality.

The qualifications of parole officers with regard to philosophy, education, and previous experience relate directly to the selfsame qualifications for probation officers discussed in Chapter 2. If the jurisdiction is one in which the traditional view of parole prevails, the profile of the typical parole officer will be social case-work dominated and will differ greatly from the profile of a parole officer in a "broker of services" or "justice model" jurisdiction.

4. Freedom from Political or Improper Influences. A parole system should be entirely free, not only from political control, manipulation, or influence, but also from improper influences brought from pressure groups of any type. The law should forbid parole board or staff participation in partisan political activities and coerced contributions to party campaign funds, and should give the parole authorities the independence and security of tenure that they must have to be able to resist interference successfully.[12]

5. Parole Assigned a Workable Position in the Governmental Administrative Structure. The parole system should be administered within the type of organization structure that will assure the most effective coordination of parole with other correctional services, such as institutional programs and community-based correctional agencies such as probation halfway houses, drug and alcohol treatment agencies, the courts, and police.

Basically, four major parole structures exist in the varying states and federal system.

1. The parole board serves as the administrative and policy-making board for a combined probation and parole system (the majority of states utilize this structure).

2. The parole board administers parole services only.

3. Parole services are administered by the department that administers the state correctional institutions.

4. Parole services are administered by the state correctional agency, which also administers the probation and institutional services.

The two dominant organizational patterns are the *institutional model* and the *autonomous model*. The institutional model is most prevalent in the juvenile field and centers parole decision making primarily in the institutions, whereas the autonomous model prevails in the adult field and centers parole decision making around the independent authority. Advocates of the institutional model believe that the institutional staff are more familiar with the offender and the offender's

12. American Correctional Ass'n, *supra* n. 9, at 124.

response to institutional programs, and are more sensitive to the optimum time for release. They see the autonomous board as (1) unconcerned or insensitive to problems of the institutional programs and goals of the staff, (2) too preoccupied with issues other than the rehabilitative aspects of the offender's treatment to make appropriate case decisions, and (3) lending unnecessary complications to decision making and infringing on the professional judgment of competent institutional staff. On the other hand, proponents of the autonomous model believe that the institutional staff places undue emphasis on the offender's institutional adjustment. They see the institutional board as (1) being tempted to set release policies to fit the needs of the institution, to control population size, and to rid itself of problem cases; (2) extending confinement as a penalty for petty rule violations; and (3) having decision-making procedures that are so informal and lacking in visibility that questions arise concerning the board's capability to maintain fairness or even an appearance of fairness. Although both the institutional and autonomous models are in practice, a consolidation model has gained popularity.[13]

The *consolidation model* is a result of the trend toward consolidation of all correctional services into a single department responsible for institutional and field programs. In the consolidation model, parole decisions are made by a central authority with independent powers, yet organizationally situated in the overall department of corrections. Advocates of this model contend that it (1) promotes an increased concern for the entire corrections system; (2) provides greater sensitivity to institutional programs; and (3) separates the parole decision from immediate control of the institution, thereby giving appropriate weight to parole decision-making considerations beyond management of the institution.[14]

Regardless of the organizational or administrative structure adopted by the various jurisdictions, it is essential that the structure foster close coordination between the parole decision makers and all the correctional programs. In so doing, sufficient autonomy should be retained to permit the parole board to serve as a check on the system.

6. Improved Parole Procedures: *The Release Decision.* Under traditional parole practice, the decision regarding when a prisoner will be released is often deferred until well into the prisoner's sentence. A prisoner is given a parole hearing shortly before completion of the minimum term. If the prisoner is not granted parole, further consideration after an additional period of time is often scheduled. Consequently, a prisoner may receive several parole hearings before learning whether he or she will be granted parole and when he or she will actually be released.

From the perspective of the traditional rehabilitative model, this practice is both necessary and desirable. Under a treatment philosophy, parole release decisions are to be based primarily upon rehabilitative concerns. The goal of the parole release authority is to identify the optimum time for release. Thus,

---

13. President's Comm'n on Law Enforcement and Administration of Justice, *Task Force Report: Corrections, supra.*

14. Nat'l Advisory Comm'n on Criminal Justice Standards and Goals, *supra,* at 397.

deferral of the release decision is necessary to enable rehabilitative progress to be monitored.[15]

Current thought is that empirical evidence has failed to demonstrate that institutional rehabilitative programs are effective or that the optimum time for release can be ascertained. Behavior in prison does not appear to be a good indicator of future criminal behavior.

More and more jurisdictions are moving by statute or voluntarily toward the use of parole guidelines to provide explicit visible standards by which the length of a prisoner's sentence may be determined without reference to the prisoner's institutional record, length of time served before parole, or other factors that have not proved to be predictive of the prisoner's ability to adjust in the world outside prison. These guidelines and other factors affecting parole release are discussed in detail in the chapter on Parole Selection.

The Parole Plan. When a tentative or definite parole date has been set by the board, a parole plan involving a satisfactory home or living arrangement and potential for employment should be developed. This plan is usually investigated and approved by the parole field staff.

Graduated Release. Direct and sudden release from confinement, from a controlled environment to the free community, often results in psychological and cultural shock to the releasee, and may very well be an important factor in that person's ability to adjust. Whenever possible, the inmate should be transferred to a minimum security or open-type institution a few months prior to release. In such a setting the inmate may begin to exercise the necessary self-direction for living in free society.

Work release and furloughs are also helpful as means of gradually allowing the inmate short, yet all important, opportunities to function without the strict regimen and all-encompassing discipline of the closed institution.

The use of halfway houses or prerelease centers is becoming increasingly prevalent and preliminary research indicates that inmates released to those settings are considerably less prone to recidivism.[16]

Release Under a Firm and Helpful Supervisor. Parole supervision is a continuation of the correctional process and relies upon the knowledge and experience of the field officer in aiding the parolee in the reintegrative process. This topic is more fully discussed in the chapter on Supervision of Probationers and Parolees.

7. A Proper Public Attitude Toward the Parolee. The American Correctional Association states, "The parole board and the institution have a large part to play in the matter of the parolee's return to society; however, the manner in which the public receives the parolee and the attitude it assumes is vital to that person's success." [17]

The Manual for Probation Officers of the U.S. Probation System addresses the issue of community attitude. It directs U.S. probation officers to "do all they can to increase public understanding of probation and parole and recogni-

---

15. Peter B. Hoffman and Michael A. Stover, 7 Hofstra L.R. 1, (1978).

16. Corrections in the Community: Alternatives to Imprisonment (ed.) George G. Killinger & Paul Cromwell, Jr., (St. Paul: West Publishing Company, 1974) 492.

17. American Correctional Ass'n, *Manual of Correctional Standards, supra,* at 132.

tion of their advantages .... They should take advantage of radio and television facilities to foster public understanding of probation and parole and to explain their own responsibilities and objectives."[18]

8. Research and Statistics on Board's Effectiveness. Full public acceptance of parole as a means of release from prisons or correctional institutions depends upon the demonstrated effectiveness of parole. There is virtually no subject connected with crime or criminal justice into which further research is unnecessary. In 1927, Felix Frankfurter observed that the subject of crime was "overlaid with shibboleths and cliches" and that it was essential to "separate the known from the unknown, to divorce fact from assumption, to strip biases of every sort from their authority."[19] This statement is no less true today.

Parole research is needed in development and validation of parole prediction tables, recidivism outcome indices and other instruments that provide the board with an indication of the future behavior of those being considered for parole. Research into causes of recidivism and subsequent revocation could be invaluable in equipping the parole officer with the necessary tools to aid parolees in avoiding the pitfalls they encounter. Many questions remain to be answered in this area, most importantly: what factors in an inmate's background and present circumstances are predictive of success or failure on parole?

Preconceived or outmoded prejudices and concepts on the part of the parole board members or staff can often be modified or eliminated through the use of statistical analysis of the outcome of board decisions. Parole authorities realize that the system needs improvement. As a springboard for the introduction of new methods, there must be professional research. It should be a continuing program with staff assigned full time for this specific purpose.

Clearly, an effective parole system is the result of legislative foresight, careful selection of board and staff members, judicial concern, and knowledgeable sentencing practices. It is equally the result of close cooperation between the parole system and other segments of the correctional process as well as with the general public. Parole, as a subsystem of the criminal justice process, is dependent upon the inextricable interrelationships it has with all other aspects of the system.

In the final analysis, the success of any parole system, however well conceived, will depend upon how it is administered.

---

18. U.S. Probation System, *Manual for Probation Officers* (Washington D.C.: Administrative Offices of the U.S. Courts).

19. Quoted in *The Challenge of Crime in a Free Society*, A Report by the President's Commission on Law Enforcement and Administration of Justice (1967), 273.

Parole: A Survey*

The objectives of parole systems vary widely. Without clearly stated and understood objectives, the administrator cannot make the most basic decisions regarding effective resource allocation. Even a casual attempt to clarify the purposes of parole will reveal that objectives frequently are in conflict. One of the parole administrator's chief tasks is to minimize this conflict.

A Basic Purpose: Reduction of Recidivism

Few things about parole evoke consensus, but there is some agreement that one objective and measure of success is reduction of recidivism. Even this consensus quickly becomes less firm when two specific functions are examined: (1) provision of supervision and control to reduce the likelihood of criminal acts while the offender is serving his sentence in the community (the "surveillance" function), and (2) provision of assistance and services to the parolee, so that noncriminal behavior becomes possible (the "helping" function).[1]

To the extent that these concerns can be integrated, conflicts are minimized, but in the day-to-day activity of parole administration they frequently clash. Decisions constantly must be made between the relative risk of a law violation at the present time and the probable long-term gain if a parolee is allowed freedom and opportunity to develop a legally approved life style. Resources are needed to clarify the choices and risks involved. Key requirements for this kind of assistance are development of clear definitions of recidivism and creation of information systems that make data available about the probabilities of various types of parole outcome associated with alternative decisions.

Varied Concerns of Parole Boards

Reducing the risk of further criminality is not the sole concern. In fact, it actually may be secondary in some instances. A wider variety of concerns was expressed in a questionnaire completed by nearly half the

---

* The National Advisory Commission on Criminal Justice Standards and Goals, *Report on Corrections*, (Washington, D.C., 1973).

1. American Correctional Association, *Manual of Correctional Standards* (Washington, D.C. 1966), 114.

parole board members in the United States in 1965, who were asked to indicate what they considered the five most important factors to be weighed in deciding on parole. Table 1 shows the items selected by at least 20 percent of those responding as being among the five most important considerations. The first three items selected as the most important were related to the risk of violation. However, the next four related to three other concerns: equitable punishment, impact on the system, and reactions of persons outside the correctional organization.

A number of other studies have noted the same phenomenon.[2] Most parole board members consider risk a paramount concern, but other factors assume such importance in certain cases that risk becomes secondary. A well-known inmate convicted and sentenced for violation of a public trust may be denied parole repeatedly because of strong public feelings, even though he might be an excellent risk. In another type of case, an offender convicted of a relatively minor crime may be paroled even though a poor risk, because in the opinion of the board he has simply served enough time for the offense committed. To some analysts, these other-than-risk considerations are viewed simply as contingencies that arise from time to time; to others they involve objectives

Table 1. Items Considered by Parole Board Members to be Most Important in Parole Decisions

Item	Percent Including Item as One of Five Most Important
1. My estimate of the chances that the prisoner would or would not commit a serious crime if paroled.	92.8
2. My judgment that the prisoner would benefit from further experience in the institution program or, at any rate, would become a better risk if confined longer.	87.1
3. My judgment that the prisoner would become a worse risk if confined longer.	71.9
4. My judgment that the prisoner had already been punished enough to "pay" for his crime.	43.2
5. The probability that the prisoner would be a misdemeanant and a burden to his parole supervisors, even if he did not commit any serious offenses on parole.	35.3
6. My feelings about how my decision in this case would affect the feelings or welfare of the prisoner's relatives or dependents.	33.8
7. What I thought the reaction of the judge might be if the prisoner were granted parole.	20.9

Source: National Parole Institutes, Selection for Parole (New York: National Council on Crime and Delinquency, 1966).

2. See Robert Dawson, Sentencing: The Decision as to Type, Length, and Conditions of Sentence (Little, Brown, 1969).

central to parole decisionmaking. In either case, considerations other than risk assessment figure prominently in parole decisionmaking and must be accounted for in any discussion of objectives. To judge from questionnaires returned by parole board members and from studies in the field, there seem to be at least three core sets of concern other than reducing recidivism, which significantly and regularly impinge upon most parole decisionmakers.[3]

Fairness and Propriety

Parole programs are part of larger systems of criminal justice. They are governed by concepts of propriety and modes of conduct arising from American culture and law. Especially in recent years, parole systems have been expected to conform with practices that enhance the ideals of fairness and reflect hallmarks of American justice such as procedural regularity, precedent, and proof.

Most recently these issues have been reflected in increased sensitivity to inmates' or revokees' rights to counsel, the right of a hearing on parole grant and revocation, and disclosure of information used in decisionmaking. Reflecting this emphasis, some parole board members may even refuse to consider at a parole violation hearing evidence that might have been secured by questionable search procedure. Comparable issues also arise in establishing conditions for parole supervision, which are expected to meet the tests of relevance, reasonableness, and fairness.

Appropriate Sanctions and Public Expectations

Though it seldom is stated openly, parole boards often are concerned with supporting a system of appropriate and equitable sanctions. This concern is reflected in several ways, depending upon a jurisdiction's sentencing system. One of the most common is through decisions seeking to equalize penalties for offenders who have similar backgrounds and have committed the same offense but who have received different sentences.

Alternatively, decisions to grant or deny parole, particularly in well-known cases, often may hinge on the question, "Has this person served enough time for the act he committed?" Considerable differences in these matters exist from one system to another, as well as among individuals in the same system. Such concerns usually are less apparent in, and perhaps less relevant to, juvenile agencies. However, in many parole systems, maintaining an appropriate system of sanctions directly or indirectly underlies most decisionmaking. How significant these considerations are depends on the kind of sentencing framework in which the parole system is operating.

In addition to issues of equity, parole decisionmakers sometimes respond to actual or anticipated public attitudes. Such concerns for public acceptance of parole generally, and case decisions specifically, govern the kinds of risks that are acceptable and the actions considered feasible by parole decisionmakers. This public reaction issue is particularly acute in cases affecting society's core beliefs. Criteria having little to do with the question of risk may be used by parole officials in dealing with certain cases, particularly those involving crimes seen as "heinous." The concern is more for meeting general social norms and responding according to public expectations.

Maintenance of the Justice System

A third set of concerns that influences parole decisionmaking relates to support of other criminal justice operations. Parole

---

3. Keith Hawkins, "Parole Selection: The American Experience," (unpublished, Cambridge University, 1971).

boards play a crucial role as a kind of system regulator, influencing other parts of the justice system, from police to prisons. For example, in some systems where a parole board has extensive control over the amount of time a large proportion of inmates will serve, institutional populations can change dramatically depending on board policy. Not only do parole board decisions influence institutional size, but they also reinforce behavior that can have profound effects on the kinds of programs sustained. Inmates are more likely to participate in a program the parole board explicitly values than in one to which the board pays no attention.

Institutional staff members have an obvious stake in the programs in which inmates are involved. Hence they too are affected by parole decisions. Various parole officials are sensitive to the correctional impact of their decisions and some take this factor into account in their decisions.[4] In some instances, boards will be reminded forcefully of their effect on inmates and institutions. For example, it is not uncommon during times of high prison tension (as after riots), when parole policy is under attack by inmates and sympathizers, for boards to become more "liberal." In such instances, the degree of risk acceptable for parole, conditioned by pressures within the institutions, shifts perceptibly. Parole boards directly affect parole supervision staff by the kind of offenders they release and revoke, and by the policies surrounding these actions.

System maintenance and other basic concerns cited clearly influence parole decisionmaking. However, questions of risk, fairness, public expectation, and system maintenance are not the only considerations affecting parole authorities. Of great importance as well are the beliefs they hold concerning the sources of criminality, strategies for changing offenders, and the nature of the relationship between the correctional system and the offender.

ORGANIZATION OF PAROLING AUTHORITIES

Most persons concerned with parole decisionmaking for juveniles are full-time institutional personnel. Only a few juvenile jurisdictions have noninstitutional personnel determining parole releases.

Different circumstances prevail in the adult area. For example, adult boards tend to carry many more direct state-level administrative responsibilities than do releasing authorities for juveniles.

Although there is considerable variety in the organizational settings in which parole decisionmakers work, at least two dominant organizational strains can be identified—the institutional model, which largely predominates in the juvenile field, and the independent model, the most common in the adult field. Considerable controversy has arisen around these two models.[5]

The Institutional Model
In general, the institutional model perceives parole as being bound closely to institutional programs. It places the release decision with the correctional facility's staff. Parole is simply one more of a series of decisions affecting the offender. The persons most familiar with the cases make the releasing decision; and this makes it possible to develop a rational and consistent set of decisions that affect the inmate. The Crime

---

4. Keith Hawkins, *"Some Consequences of a Parole System for Prison Management,"* in D.F. West, ed., *The Future of Parole* (London: Gerald Duckworth, 1972).

5. *Task Force Report: Corrections,* pp. 65–66.

Commission reported that thirty four of fifty states used this form of organization in the juvenile field.

The major arguments raised against the institutional model is that too often institutional considerations, rather than individual or community needs, influence the decisions. Overcrowding in the institution, desire to be rid of a problem case or to enforce relatively petty rules, or other concerns of institution management easily become the basis of decisionmaking. Institutional decisionmaking also lends itself to such informal procedures and lack of visibility as to raise questions about its capacity for fairness or, what may be as important, the appearance of fairness.

The Independent Authority

In the adult field, a good deal of reform was associated with removing parole decision-making from institutional control to an independent authority. Undoubtedly, much of the basis for his reform came from the view that paroling authorities were being swayed too easily by institutional considerations or were not being objective enough.[6] The change was so complete that today no adult parole releasing authority is controlled directly by the operating staff of a penal institution.

Whatever its merits in fostering objectivity, the independent parole board also has been criticized on several counts. First, the claim is made that such boards tend to be insensitive to institutional programs and fail to give them the support they require. Second, independent boards are accused of basing their decisions on inappropriate considerations, such as the feelings of a local police chief. Third, their remoteness from the institutional program gives independent boards little appreciation of the dynamics in a given case; their work tends to be cursory,

with the result that too often persons who should be paroled are not, and those who should not be paroled are released. Fourth, the argument is made that independent systems tend to place on parole boards persons who have little training or experience in corrections.

Lack of knowledge about corrections, combined with the distance of the parole board from institutional programs, builds unnecessary conflicts into the system. The rapid growth of part-way release programs and halfway houses has increased the probability of those conflicts. In short, critics of the independent model assert that important decisions are being made concerning the correctional system, its programs, and the offenders in it by persons far removed from the system who have little appreciation of its true nature.

The Consolidation Model

While these arguments and their rebuttals continue, an alternate system has gained considerable support in recent years, tending to cut the ground away from both major models. This system is linked with a general move toward consolidation of all types of correctional services into distinctive departments of corrections that subsume both institution and field programs. The consolidation model, emerging from the drive toward centralized administration, typically results in parole decisions being made by a central decisionmaking authority organizationally situated in an overall department of corrections, but possessing independent powers. The director of corrections may serve on such a releasing authority, or may designate a staff member to do so. In the youth field, the centralized board may have policy responsibilities for institutions as well as parole decision making.

Proponents of the consolidation model argue that there is increased concern for the

---

6. *Atty Gen.'s Survey of Release Procedures,* vol. 49.

whole correctional system in departments where parole releasing authority is part of a centralized system. They claim that sensitivity to institutional programs seems more pronounced in consolidated systems than in completely autonomous ones. They also contend that removal of parole decision-making from the immediate control of specific correctional institutions tends to give greater weight to a broader set of considerations, a number of which are outside direct institutional concerns.

Although variations in organizational or administrative arrangements may be required to meet special circumstances, certain general organizational requirements seem clear. Among the most essential requisites is that the organizational structure of parole authorities should foster close coordination between parole decision makers and the increasingly complex set of programs throughout the correctional network. Yet, sufficient autonomy should be preserved to permit parole boards to act as a check on the system.

The trend in this country clearly is in the direction of consolidation. More than 60 percent of the state parole boards responsible for release of adult offenders now function in common administrative structures with other agencies for offenders. This trend enhances integration of correctional operations. If parole boards are to function as useful and sophisticated decision-making units that balance a wide set of concerns, they also must achieve and maintain some degree of autonomy from the systems with which they interface. This issue involves appointment and tenure methods, as well as the tasks and functions for which parole authorities take responsibility.

9

Critical Issues in Parole

For fifty years, the predominant goal of corrections has been to rehabilitate the offender. This rehabilitative ideal, or "medical model," assumed that criminal behavior had its roots in environmental and psychosocial aspects of the offender's life and that corrections could, in fact, correct. Inherent within the medical model of corrections is the indeterminate sentence and the concept of parole. Indeterminacy of sentencing provides the flexibility and discretion for the rehabilitative ideal to function. The judge at the time of sentencing can "tailor make" a sentence to the particular needs of the offender and provide, by means of an indeterminate sentence, an opportunity for release at the optimum time in the rehabilitative process. The release decision is thus shared between the court, which sets a minimum and a maximum period of incarceration, and the correctional system—usually a parole board. The parole board's responsibility is to determine, with the assistance of prison authorities, the optimal release moment—the time at which the inmate is most ready to reenter the community as a responsible citizen.

This philosophy assumes that correctional specialists have the ability to diagnose an offender's problems and develop a means of curing those problems. Since at the time of diagnosis, one cannot know how long it will take to effect a cure, the indeterminate sentence makes it possible, in theory at least, to confine an offender as long as is necessary and to follow up that confinement with community supervision. Through almost consensual use of indeterminate sentencing in the United States since the middle 1930s, parole has played a major role in the American correctional system. Once an offender is sentenced to prison, it is largely the parole authorities who determine when the offender will be released and under what conditions, and whether the offender's conduct after release warrants continued freedom or reimprisonment.

The motives for the development and spread of parole were mixed. They were: partly humanitarian, to offer some mitigation of lengthy sentences; partly to control in-prison behavior by holding out the possibility of early release; and partly rehabilitative, since supervised reintegration into the community is more effective and safer than simply opening the gates.

Although parole has drawn support from many sources and generally has a history of consensual acceptance, it has on occasion been subject to vigorous criticism and reexamination. In the early years of the twentieth century, particularly after World War I, parole administration came under attack. Critics claimed that parole was not fulfilling its promise. Antiparole groups believed that parole release was used primarily as a means of controlling inmates and that it failed to encourage changes in their behavior and attitudes after their release from prison. This was a severe criticism in an age of an increasing acceptance of the rehabilitative ideal and a commensurate emphasis on treatment and cure in criminal corrections.[1]

Other critics of the system pointed out that release was granted only after a cursory review of the records of inmates, and that paroling authorities had no criteria by which rehabilitation could be measured and upon which release decisions could be based.

These criticisms led to two major changes in parole administration and organization. First, increasing emphasis was placed upon postrelease supervision of parolees, with a corresponding increase in the number of parole conditions. Second, there was a shift away from giving parole authority to prison personnel, and toward parole boards with independent authority and statewide jurisdiction.[2]

By the mid-1930s the parole system was again being scrutinized as to its continuance as a viable part of the justice system. The Attorney General's Survey of Release Procedures, a monumental study of the correctional process, was essentially established to review the efficacy of parole. The survey stated:

> While there has never been a time when the functions and purpose of parole have been clearly understood, at no period has the entire institution been the object of so much controversy and attack or viewed with as much suspicion by the general public as it has been during the past four of five years.[3]

Mounting prison population and rising recidivism rates aggravated the general uneasiness concerning early release via parole. Questions regarding the value of rehabilitation itself were making themselves heard, and without the philosophical underpinnings of reform and rehabilitation as a purpose of punishment, parole has no meaning in the criminal justice system.

Both the concept of rehabilitation and the practice of parole survived the criticism, and in 1940, President Franklin D. Roosevelt declared, "We know from experience that parole, when it is honestly and expertly managed, provides

---

1. Lawrence F. Travis III and Vincent O'Leary, *Changes in Sentencing and Parole Decisionmaking: 1976–1978,* (National Institute of Corrections, 1979). A Publication of the National Parole Institutes and Parole Policy Seminars. (Washington D.C.: National Institute of Corrections, 1979).

2. *Id.* at 6.

3. U.S. Department of Justice, *Parole,* vol. 4 of *Attorney General's Survey of Release Procedures* (Washington, 1939).

better protection for society than does any other method of release from pris-on."[4]

Perhaps a bit optimistically, Sanford Bates, in 1941 in a speech entitled "The Next Hundred Years", stated:

> Parole, as a method of release, will soon have become an indispensable part of this correctional process. We shall speak more accurately of *subjecting* a prisoner to parole than of *granting* him parole. We shall learn to speak of recidivists, not as parole failures, but as unreformed inmates. We shall not shrink from the word, parole, as something involving weakness or venability, but shall recognize institution aftercare and supervision as a necessary sequel to a prison term. *Nevermore shall we talk about abolishing parole* any more than about abolishing police or commitment or discipline.[5] [Emphasis added.]

The treatment or medical model of corrections was born during these years of the late 1930s and early 1940s. The rehabilitative ideal viewed corrections as corrective and reformative as opposed to punitive.

By 1967 (at the height of the reformative era), a Harris Poll, using a nationwide sample, found that 77 percent of the population believed that prisons should be *mainly corrective,* while only 11 percent believed prisons should be *mainly punitive.*[6]

The years between World War II and 1970 saw the advent and development of classification systems, vocational training, academic training, group and individual therapy, conjugal visitation in some prisons, work release, and numerous other reforms. The belief that criminals could be changed if given the opportunity and if sufficient skills, funds, and personnel were available, was the central philosophy of the rehabilitative ideal. Parole was once again considered a viable and necessary aspect of the American system of corrections.

A PHILOSOPHICAL CHANGE

In the middle seventies, with a suddenness remarkable in social change, there was a dramatic turnabout. Individualization, rehabilitation, sentence indetermi-nacy, and parole all seemed to fall from grace and, indeed, appeared to be on their way out.[7]

By 1978, a Law Enforcement Assistance Administration monograph stated: "One of the movements we are currently witnessing in the criminal justice field

---

4. Quoted by Sanford Bates in his speech, "The Next Hundred Years," at the Thirty-Fifth Annual Conference of the National Probation Association, Atlantic City, N.J., 1941.

5. Sanford Bates, then the commissioner of parole for the State of New York, became the director of the U.S. Bureau of Prisons. Bates reorganized the Bureau of Prisons, introduced psychologists and psychiatrists into the system, and is often recognized as being the father of the "New Prison."

6. Harris Poll, *Los Angeles Times,* Aug. 14, 1967.

7. National Advisory Commission on Criminal Justice Standards and Goals, *A National Strategy to Reduce Crime* (Washington: Law Enforcement Assistance Administration, 1973).

is the trend toward the establishment of determinate or 'fixed' sentencing of criminal offenders."[8]

The failure of the correctional system to reduce the steadily increasing crime rate and the system's obvious inability to reduce recidivism, rehabilitate offenders or make predicative judgments about offenders' future behavior, brought about public disillusionment, disappointment and resentment. The pendulum began to swing, and by the late seventies seemed to have moved 180 degrees from the rehabilitative ideal to the "just deserts" approach to criminal correction.

In contrast to the rehabilitative ideal, the just deserts or "justice model" denies the efficacy of rehabilitation and changes the focus of the system from the offender to the offense. The September 1977 issue of *Corrections Magazine,* for example, was devoted to the debate regarding the justice model and determinacy of sentencing. Even a brief review of the contents of this journal indicates that determinate sentences and abolition of parole were embraced by liberals and conservatives alike. Prison reformers and police chiefs seemed to be in almost complete agreement.

The general aim of those favoring determinate sentencing was to abolish, or at least tightly control, discretion. This included the discretion of the prosecutor to choose charges and plea bargain; the discretion of judges to choose any sentence within a broad range of time; the discretion of prison administrators to decide what kind of treatment a prisoner needed to become law-abiding; and the discretion of parole boards to release or not release prisoners without ever having to justify their decision or render their decisions consistent. Determinate sentencing was the reformers' answer to this problem.[9] The proposals of the mid-1970s called for clear, certain, uniform penalties for all crimes, either through legislative action or the promulgation of guidelines to which prosecutors, judges, and parole boards would be required to adhere.

Origins of Modern
Concepts of Determinacy

Where did all this talk of determinate sentencing begin? John Irwin, an ex-prisoner and now author and college professor, contends that inmates themselves, particularly inmates of California prisons in the 1960s, were the original advocates of determinacy.[10]

California, Irwin believes, had the most indeterminate of all indeterminate sentencing structures and a parole board that was very "stingy with its favors." The situation in California prisons prompted the formation of a working group of the American Friends Service Committee, which produced the book *Struggle for Justice* in 1971. It denounced the very existence of American prisons and denounced the rehabilitative model of corrections, declaring coercion of prisoners for any purpose to be immoral. Although *Struggle for Justice* declared that all

---

8. *Id.*

9. David B. Griswold and Michael D. Wiatrowski, *The Emergence of Determinate Sentencing,* Federal Probation (June 1983).

10. Reported in Michael S. Serrill, *Determinate Sentencing: The History, the Theory, the Debate,* Corrections Magazine (September 1977).

prisons should be shut down, it recognized that such a proposal was unrealistic. The book declared that the least that should be done was to repeal all indeterminate sentencing laws and design a system in which offenders convicted of similar crimes served roughly equal terms in prison.

One of the primary authors of the Friends' Book was David Greenberg, who was also a member of a group called the Committee for the Study of Incarceration. Greenberg, together with Andrew von Hirsch, the Committee's executive director, persuaded the committee that the most important subject to study was not the conditions of incarceration, but the haphazard and irrational manner in which offenders ended up—or did not end up—in prison, and the equally chaotic system of release.

The committee's final report was published in 1976 under the title, *Doing Justice: The Choice of Punishments.* Written by von Hirsch, it is a heavily philosophical tract that has as its thesis that the motives underlying the treatment of criminal offenders are all wrong.

The principal goals of the correctional system at the time were to rehabilitate and restrain offenders based upon predictions of their future criminality or dangerousness. The result was that the sanctions prescribed for particular crimes had little to do with the severity of criminal behavior. In fact, large numbers of widely disparate crimes were often punishable by the same indeterminate term, with the actual setting of a release date left to parole boards, which made judgments about the rehabilitation and dangerousness of particular offenders.

Doing Justice suggested that the goal of sentencing should be to punish offenders and that it is proper to punish the criminal because the criminal "deserves" to be punished, and each punishment should be made commensurate with the gravity of the last offense or series of offenses.

The committee recommended the adoption of a *presumptive sentence* for each crime or category of crimes, with the presumptive sentences graded according to the severity of the crime. The severity of the crime was to be graded on two scales: (1) the harm done by the offense, and (2) the culpability of the offender. The degree of culpability would be judged based partly on the offender's prior record. The reasoning behind this was that a succession of criminal acts would imply calculation or deliberate defiance of the law, thus making the offender more culpable for the current offense.

Having proposed punishment as the main goal of sentencing, the committee then ruled out prison as the punishment for all but the most serious offenses— meaning those in which bodily harm is threatened or done to the victim. The committee proposed alternatives such as periodic imprisonment, increased use of fines, and other lesser sanctions. In those cases where prison is deemed necessary, the committee recommended that no prison sentence ever exceed five years except in some murder cases.

At about the same time *Doing Justice* was making the academic rounds, another determinate sentencing model was published in David Fogel's book, ". . . *We Are The Living Proof . . ." The Justice Model for Corrections.* Fogel, former Commissioner of Corrections in Minnesota, former head of the Illinois Law Enforcement Commission, and then a university professor, is considered by many to be the father of determinate sentencing. He had been actively urging a narrowing of sentencing and parole discretion as early as 1970, and of all the determinate sentencing advocates, has been the most influential in the drafting of legislation in different states.

One of the main goals of Fogel's sentencing reforms was to humanize the internal operation of correctional institutions by extending much more freedom to inmates and "unhooking" their release dates from their progress or participation in programs. He advocated the abolition of parole boards and the establishment of "flat time" sentencing—a single sentence for each class of felonies that could be altered slightly if there were aggravating or mitigating circumstances.[11]

In June 1977, University of Chicago Law School Dean Norval Morris, speaking at a symposium on criminal sentencing, addressed the issues of determinacy and parole by asking, "Should the indeterminacy of parole discretion be preserved?"[12] Morris cited the six most common justifications for the parole board fixing the precise release date rather than the judge. The parole board can:

1. find the optimum moment for release;

2. provide an incentive for rehabilitation;

3. facilitate prison control and discipline;

4. share sentencing responsibility to maximize deterrence while reducing time served;

5. control the size of the prison population; and

6. rectify unjust disparity in sentencing.[13]

Morris stated that the first justification—prediction of the optimum moment of release—has repeatedly failed to be proved empirically. The second justification, provision of an incentive for the offender's rehabilitation, has as its net effect the reliance on compulsory rehabilitation in the prison setting. "This type of coerced curing of crime is ineffective," Morris said, "and is wasteful of resources. We don't know enough to make that second purpose work."

The third justification, facilitation of prison control and discipline, is an important, latent, pragmatic justification of parole. But it is vulnerable to attack on grounds of injustice.

The fourth claimed justification of parole is the sharing of sentencing responsibility between the court and the parole board in order to maximize deterrence. While it is true that parole allows for judicial pronouncements of larger punishments that are in fact served, the charade, Morris claims, is so well known that court systems compensate for it. Judges and juries (where jury sentencing is applicable) routinely take parole laws into consideration when handing down sentences, knowing that, in most cases, the offender will serve less time than the sentence publicly announced. There still exists the question,

---

11. ". . . We Are The Living Proof . . ." The Justice Model for Corrections, second edition, David Fogel (Anderson Publishing Company, 1979).

12. *Id.* The foregoing material on the history of the determinate sentencing movement drew liberally and heavily from the excellent Serrill article cited here.

13. *Conference Takes a Hard Look at Proposals,* Corrections Magazine (September 1977), 65–66.

however, of whether the parole experience has increased or reduced times served in America.

The fifth justification, the control of the size of the prison population, has occasionally been useful. Generally speaking, however, in times of community anxiety about crime and of pressures for law and order, there has also been great pressure on the parole boards to be more conservative in granting parole. When this has occurred, parole boards, rather than solve the problem of prison overcrowding by tightening requirements, have compounded the problem.

To the last claimed justification of parole, that of rectifying unjust sentencing disparities, Morris replies:

> In Illinois, and I believe the same is true in many states, crime for crime and criminal for criminal, sentences imposed by courts in Chicago are subsequently less severe than those imposed in downstate, small town, and rural areas. The Illinois Parole Board, not incorrectly, in my view, exercises its releasing discretion so as to minimize the grosser disparities—it moves toward a regression to the mean.[14]

The question arises, however, should we not develop other mechanisms for that purpose rather than parole? Morris believes we should and views the ultimate abolition of parole as inevitable. What alternatives are available and what problems do these alternatives pose?

The trend of the 1978 symposium and of the public attitude prevalent at the time seemed inevitably to point toward increasing determinacy in sentencing and ultimately abolishing parole as a release mechanism. However, many theorists of the sentence reform movement urged caution before abolishing parole outright and reinstituting "real time" sentences. In their book, *The Question of Parole,* Andrew von Hirsch and Kathleen Hanrahan warned:

> Our culture has historically thought of prison time in huge quantities and this has made it harder to justify the more modest actual confinements meted out by parole boards. The long run objective should be the creation of a system that speaks in terms of moderate real sentences and banishes the long, fictional prison terms— through a gradual—slow phase out of parole release.[15]

Parole, however, did not disappear from the correctional scene, and by 1981 the American Correctional Association's publication, *Standards for Adult Parole Authorities,* stated that "parole accounts for 70 percent of all releases from prison in the United States."[16]

Indeed, at the present time and in most states, the parole board retains the power to alter the amount of time served in prison by releasing prisoners to community supervision before the completion of the maximum sentence. In some jurisdictions, the legislature has limited the releasing power of the parole board by requiring that prisoners must serve a flat minimum or proportion of the maximum sentence before becoming eligible for parole. In other jurisdic-

---

14. Law Enforcement Assistance Administration, *Determinate Sentencing* at 7.

15. *The Question of Parole: Retention, Reform, or Abolition?* (Cambridge, Mass.: Ballinger Publishing) 81.

16. American Correctional Association, *Standards for Adult Parole Authorities* (College Park, Maryland: American Correctional Association, 1980).

tions, parole board discretion is extensive—relatively unconstrained by law or not constrained at all. In cases where the discretion available to the parole board by law is broad, the board may nonetheless choose to exercise its discretion narrowly.

Forty-one states, the federal system, the District of Columbia, and the California Youth Authority allow some degree of discretion in the release of prisoners to the parole board.[17] Where the parole board has this power, persons entering prison may have no clear idea of exactly when they will be released. Two persons receiving the same sentence may actually serve different lengths of time in prison. Thus, the power of the parole board to release prisoners may diminish the role of the judge in setting prison terms. In the seven jurisdictions where judicial discretion is already relatively restricted—Arizona, California (CYA), Iowa, Ohio, Pennsylvania, Utah, and West Virginia—this parole board discretion further limits the power of the courts to influence time served in prison.[18]

The American Corrections Association's Standards continue to recommend parole as the preferred release mechanism and that such power be given to:

> . . . (a) single authority provided by statute which has parole decisionmaking power with respect to all offenders convicted of a felony who are sentenced to a term of imprisonment and are eligible for discretionary parole.[19]

Although the very active movement toward determinacy and abolition of parole has lost momentum in the 1980s, the movement has by no means disappeared. By late 1983, nine states—California, Colorado, Connecticut, Illinois, Indiana, Maine, Minnesota, New Mexico, and North Carolina—had abolished the power of their parole boards to release persons early. Under the sentencing statutes in these nine states, commonly known as the determinate sentencing states, prisoners receive fixed sentences, which they must serve in full, minus any time off for good behavior.

In all determinate sentencing states, parole boards continue to handle revocations and good-time decisions. Discretionary paroling may also continue in these states to a limited extent, for persons sentenced to life imprisonment, persons sentenced before the current structure went into effect, or for youthful offenders.

Determinate sentencing first appeared in Maine in 1976. By 1979, six other states (California, Colorado, Illinois, Indiana, Minnesota, and New Mexico) had eliminated the discretionary releasing power of the parole board for all, or most, state prisoners. During the last four years, however, only two states—North Carolina and Connecticut—have abolished parole board discretion. The nine determinate sentencing states differ considerably in the size and nature of their

---

17. In some instances, the California Department of the Youth Authority (CYA) has been distinguished from the California Department of Corrections (CDC). These two state agencies have separate parole boards.

18. Jim Galvin, *Dramatic Changes Seen In Sentencing, Parole,* Justice Assistance News, (U.S. Department of Justice, September 1983).

19. *American Correctional Association, supra,* at XIX.

correctional populations and the procedures under which prison terms are imposed.

In Maine, Connecticut, Illinois, and Indiana, the judge has great power to determine time served in prison. In Maine, statutes provide very broad ranges for four general classes of offenses—each carries a maximum but no minimum. The judge selects a single term from within that broad range, a flat sentence that must be served by the inmate. In Illinois, sentencing ranges are provided for seven classes of offenses. Extended ranges are provided for cases where aggravating factors are present. The judge selects one term from these ranges. The more serious the felony, the broader the sentencing options. For a less serious felony, such as shoplifting, the regular sentencing range is one to three years with an extended range of three to six years. For a more serious felony, such as armed robbery, the regular term range is four to fifteen years with an extended term range of fifteen to thirty years.

By contrast, in the five determinate sentencing states where judicial discretion is narrow—California (CDC), Colorado, Minnesota, New Mexico, and North Carolina—the sentence prescribed by law becomes the most powerful factor in determining actual time served in prison. California law provides three specific sentencing terms for each offense or group of offenses. The middle term must be chosen in the absence of either mitigating or aggravating factors, the latter of which must be charged and proven in court. The prison term imposed must be justified by the proven facts of the case, and each case is reviewed by the Board of Prison Terms. In California, persons convicted of the same offense are likely to serve very similar periods of time in prison. Consequently, plea bargaining to negotiate the offense for which a defendant will be charged becomes particularly crucial in determining sentence lengths.

One aspect of parole—that of postrelease supervision—has been maintained in most jurisdictions, even in those that have effectively abolished the parole board's discretion in release decisions.

Good Time Policies

Most of the new laws have retained good-time or discretionary reduction of sentence, ranging from one-fifth to *more* than one-half (Texas) off of inmates' time in prison. All but four states (Hawaii, Pennsylvania, Tennessee, and Utah) award prisoners days off their minimum or maximum terms for maintaining good behavior or participating in various prison activities or programs. The amount of good-time that can be accrued varies widely among states—from five days a month to forty-five days a month in several states. Good-time, because it can result in a major reduction of the sentenced term, can be an incentive to encourage cooperative behavior.

Good-time policies are often written into state statutes, but may also be nonstatutory, system-wide correctional policies. Good-time is typically awarded and administered by a state's department of corrections or by individual prison wardens.

Forty-one states, the federal system, and the District of Columbia award good-time credit to prisoners for good behavior. Typically, this credit is automatically awarded and subtracted from a prisoner's sentenced term at the time of prison entry and then rescinded in whole or in part for unsatisfactory behavior. In Oregon, good-behavior credit is subtracted from the maximum sentence and does not affect a prisoner's parole eligibility date or actual time served unless the prisoner is not paroled and serves the maximum term. But more often, the minimum sentence is reduced by good-time, so that good-time policies become a significant element in prison-term length. This is particularly relevant for states that have eliminated discretionary parole release.

A few states award good-time in ways that do not reduce sentence length. In New Hampshire, for example, a number of disciplinary days are automatically added to the minimum term, and it is from this number that good-behavior days are subtracted. If the prisoner accrues all of his or her good-time, the disciplinary days will be canceled out, and the parole eligibility date will occur, as scheduled, on the completion of the minimum sentence. Otherwise, the prisoner is penalized by a delay in the eligibility date.

Good-time reductions based on positive actions of the prisoner are in effect in thirty-three states and the federal system. These reductions result from participating in various programs (such as work, school, rehabilitative counseling, medical research, or blood donation) or from meritorious conduct (including success under minimum security). In January 1983, the California Department of Corrections eliminated automatic time off for good behavior; prisoners sentenced after that date must earn all their good-time through work or school participation.[20]

Postrelease Supervision

Only three states have completely abolished postrelease supervision: Maine, Connecticut, and Washington. This aspect of the Washington law will not take effect until 1988.[21]

Krajick points out that in Maine and Connecticut, many judges, unhappy with the abolition of postrelease supervision, are sentencing large numbers of prisoners to *split sentences* —that is, terms of jail or imprisonment to be followed by probation—in an effort to assure that inmates will not be released without some kind of supervision.[22] In Maine, the proportion of split sentences has doubled since the abolition of parole supervision.[23]

These means of circumventing the legislation were forecast by former U.S. Parole Board Chairman Maurice Sigler in 1975 when he spoke of the criminal justice system as having "hydraulic properties."[24] Sigler stated that when discretion is artificially compressed from one level of the system, it is increased at another level in order that the decision makers, be they policemen, prosecutors, judges, or parole boards, are capable of individualizing justice and "reduc-

---

20. *Justice Assistance News, supra,* at 6.

21. *Id.* at 8.

22. Kevin Krajick, *Abolishing Parole: An Idea Whose Time Has Passed,* Corrections Magazine (June 1983).

23. *Id.*

24. Maurice Sigler, *Abolish Parole?* Speech given at Law Day Ceremonies, Culver-Stockton College, Canton, Missouri (May 1976).

ing injustice caused by ill-conceived laws."[25]   He spoke of a state that had introduced a mandatory sentence for nighttime burglary. Within the next year the filings by police and prosecutors for daytime burglary had increased by 90 percent and nighttime burglary had all but disappeared. Had the burglars, in response to the new legislation, changed their nocturnal habits, or were the police and prosecutors maintaining their discretion by filing the cases as daytime burglary? The danger in this situation is that the discretion, formerly out in the open, becomes less visible and not subject to scrutiny.

SENTENCING GUIDELINES

Sentencing reformers have criticized current sentencing practices as abusive and as rooted in untenable assumptions. While many different approaches have been suggested, none have yet satisfied the need to reduce or eliminate unjustifiable and unfair disparity in sentencing. Just what does constitute inequity or unjustified disparity in sentencing? The point is arguable, depending upon one's philosophy, and may be stated for the sake of brevity and simplicity that "inequity exists when significant differences in sentencing occur which cannot be justified on the basis of the severity of the crime, the defendant's prior criminal history or characterological considerations which have a demonstrable bearing upon the appropriate penalty or disposition."[26] In other words, it is not uniformity in sentencing that should be the goal, but rather a fair and rational approach at arriving at a sentence that allows for variability within a constantly applied framework.

A considerable body of opinion exists favoring the so-called just deserts model of sentencing. Under that model, penalties are meted out in proportion to the actual harm done in the offender's current crime, with prior criminal history factored in as a rule.[27]

Other, less restrictive reform efforts would narrow judicial and administrative discretion and place possible sentence choices within a structured framework. James Stanfiel developed the concept of *target sentences,* based upon the just deserts philosophy and derived specifically from objective determinations of current offense and cumulative criminal history.[28] Stanfiel's system would allow judicial discretion in departing from the target sentence, but only with cogent written justification, and only according to established criteria for such departures. Specifically, the approach advocates the use of the statutory minimum as the *base* penalty for all offenders convicted of a given offense, with the possibility of enhancements (a higher level of penalty) by clearly defined gradations according to either or both of two conditions: (1) an objective

---

25. Maurice Sigler *Abolish Parole?* Speech given at Law Day Ceremonies, Culver-Stockton College, Canton, Missouri (May 1976).

26. James D. Stanfiel, *Criminal Justice Decisionmaking: Discretion vs. Equity,* Federal Probation (June 1983).

27. *Id.*

28. *Id.* at 40–41.

analysis of the nature and severity of the instant offense, based upon clear
written criteria for making such determinations; and (2) the number, severity,
and recency of prior convictions, measured according to an objective formulation.

> Suppose, for example, that a young offender is convicted of second degree
> burglary on the basis of entering an unoccupied residence through an open window
> and stealing $50 lying on a table. Assuming no complicating conditions, an analysis
> of the crime would presumably indicate that minimal harm had been done and would
> point to the statutory penalty—provided there were no enhancements through prior
> criminal history. Would the victim or society be better served by damaging the
> young offender's life, and causing the taxpayers enormous expense, by locking up this
> person in prison for, say, two years (the "mid-base" term in California for second
> degree burglary)? On the other hand, given the same circumstances for the current
> offense, but also given that it was the offender's third burglary conviction in five
> years, there would be a greater demonstrated need for incapacitation and thus an
> enhancement (a specific addition to the base penalty) because of prior criminal
> history. In this way, a more rational and equitable system of criminal accountability
> could be established with a wide base in time (i.e., cumulative social harm). How-
> ever, some authorities believe, and I agree, that it would be desirable to build in a
> gradual "forgiveness" or decay factor in order that an offender not be caught forever
> in the web of prior criminal history.[29]

This approach is clearly not without problems in conceptualization, execution, and philosophy, but does represent one effort to inject equity, justice, and
predictability into the problem of sentencing. Three states—Minnesota (1980),
Pennsylvania (1982), and Utah (1979)—have established statewide sentencing
guidelines with specific recommendations on the in/out decision as well as the
length of prison terms. In Minnesota and Pennsylvania, sentencing guidelines
have been approved by the state legislature and written into law. In Utah, the
state court system has guidelines formulated by administrative policy. In
Washington, Florida, and Maryland, statewide guidelines have been legislatively
ratified, but in January 1983 were not yet in effect.

While the criminal statutes in virtually all states detail a general range of
sentencing options deemed appropriate for any particular crime, sentencing
guidelines attempt to direct the court to the available options it should choose in
a given case. In each of the sentencing-guidelines states, a sentence range is
specified for most offenses, based on the seriousness of the offense and the
extent of the criminal history of the offender.

The range and form of the prescribed sentence can vary significantly from
state to state, as the cases of Minnesota and Pennsylvania demonstrate. In
Minnesota, a nonimprisonment alternative is the recommended sentence for
most property crimes in which the offender's criminal history is not extensive.
Pennsylvania guidelines, in contrast, generally specify nonconfinement only for
misdemeanor offenses where mitigating circumstances are involved. For normal
misdemeanor cases, minimum ranges of zero to six or zero to twelve months are
specified, regardless of an offender's prior record. Furthermore, Minnesota
sentencing guidelines provide judges with a relatively narrow sentence range for
a given level of offense according to severity combined with a given history of

---

29. *Id.* at 40.

criminal activity. From this range, one fixed term is chosen. Pennsylvania sentencing guidelines, however, are broad and specify a minimum range, an aggravated minimum range, and a mitigated minimum range from which the judge chooses a minimum term (the maximum term is set by statute).

A sentencing commission in each state monitors the use of the guidelines and departures from the recommended sentences by the judiciary. Written explanations are required from judges who depart from guidelines ranges. The Minnesota Sentencing Guidelines Commission state that while the sentencing guidelines are advisory to the sentencing judge, departures from the presumptive sentences established in the guidelines should be made only when substantial and compelling circumstances exist. Pennsylvania sentencing guidelines stipulate that court failure to explain sentences deviating from the recommendations shall be grounds for vacating the sentence and resentencing the defendant. Furthermore, if the court does not consider the guidelines, or inaccurately or inappropriately applies them, an imposed sentence may be vacated upon appeal to a higher court by either the defense or the prosecution.

Six other court systems—Maryland, Massachusetts, Rhode Island, Vermont, Washington, and Wisconsin—have sentencing guidelines that currently apply only in certain jurisdictions or to a limited range of offenses. In some cases, these selectively applied guidelines represent the pilot phase of a study that may eventually lead to the establishment of a statewide sentencing guideline policy.[30]

PAROLE GUIDELINES

In fourteen states, the District of Columbia, and the federal system, the discretion of the parole board to release prisoners is limited by explicit parole guidelines enacted by the legislature or voluntarily adopted by parole boards. In California, parole release has been eliminated for all prisoners under the authority of the California Department of Corrections, except for those prisoners serving life imprisonment terms. The Board of Prison Terms applies parole guidelines to determine prison term lengths for those prisoners. In Minnesota, parole guidelines are used only for prisoners sentenced before the advent of determinate sentencing in 1980.

Although nearly all states have legislation that defines general criteria for parole release, formal parole guidelines attempt to make these criteria explicit and measurable. Parole guidelines are used by parole boards to measure the presumed risk that an offender will commit additional crimes while on parole, based on such factors as the offender's prior convictions, substance abuse history, and prison behavior. A decision on when to release an offender (i.e., on how long a term should be served) is then made by the parole board, based upon both the presumed risk and the severity of the current offense. Most guidelines allow for exceptions to specify term lengths if mitigating or aggravating circumstances are involved. Prison behavior, either good or bad, is often considered.[31]

---

30. *Justice Assistance News, supra,* at 7–8.

31. *Id.*

SUMMARY

Although the mid-1980s finds the criminal justice system embroiled in controversy, engaged in self-examination, and subjected to scrutiny by the public and
the courts, the issues involved—overcrowding of prisons, the efficacy of probation and parole, sentencing disparity, parole release decision making, and indeed,
the very continued existence of parole—are not new, and neither are the
proposed solutions.   The inertia of the criminal justice system is as great as is its
failure to learn the lessons of history.

Over 110 years ago, the leading penologists of the time met in Cincinnati to
form the National Prison Association, now known as the American Correctional
Association.   The main objective of that first meeting in 1870 was to attempt to
resolve the conflict between the advocates of the punishment-centered Pennsylvania and Auburn Prison Systems and the proponents of a progressive new
system recently imported from Ireland.   The new system, which appealed to
progressive prison administrators, consisted of three main factors: (1) trade
training, (2) the indeterminate sentence, and (3) parole.

What emerged was the remarkable "Declaration of Principles," a blueprint
for the future of American corrections.   The concepts of vocational training,
indeterminacy of sentencing, and parole were established, and for the most part
embraced by the leadership of the newly emerging discipline of corrections.
Since that time, these same issues have been studied, scrutinized, rejected,
embraced, modified, codified, outlawed, and reincarnated under new labels.
Presidential commissions, over a period of fifty years, have alternately recommended the extension of parole and indeterminacy of sentencing and the
outright abolition of the same.   The answer is not yet at hand.   History has
taught us that all too often the unenvisioned and unintended consequences of
reform have aggravated rather than mitigated the problems leading to their
enactment.   Prudence in reform efforts is advisable and such lessons as can be
learned from past efforts should be carefully assessed.

The Case for an Early Time-Fix*

Parole typically involves the deferral of the decision on how long the prisoner will remain confined. At the time the offender is sent to prison, he ordinarily does not know what portion of his judicially-imposed sentence he will actually serve: that is decided at a later date by the parole board. This deferral of the duration-of-confinement decision is sometimes known as "indeterminacy" of sentence. But as that expression has been used with a variety of other connotations, we will refer to the practice as the "deferred time-fix."

Recently, deferral has become a much criticized feature of parole. It is said to rest on outdated assumptions, and to subject prisoners to the needless cruelty of waiting for a decision. A number of penologists and study commissions have proposed moving toward an early decision on the duration of confinement.

To resolve whether the time-fix should be early or late, we should examine what, if anything, is learned by waiting. We must look at the items of information that are relevant to deciding the duration of confinement. If any of those items can be known only late—well after sentence is imposed—that would be reason for delaying the time-fix. If all such information is known or can be determined at the time of sentence, that would support an early fix.

What information is germane depends, of course, on the assumed goals of punishment. We therefore will consider successively (1) the Desert Model, (2) the Modified Desert Model, and (3) more strongly utilitarian assumptions. With respect to each conception, we shall ask what kinds of information would be relevant to deciding the duration of prisoners' confinement, and when that information is available.

Our conclusion is that on *any* of these assumptions the decision should occur early. We shall advocate that each prisoner should be notified, at the time he is sentenced or shortly thereafter, of when he is to be released from prison. Then, in the next section, we will consider whether this conclusion needs to be altered in order to deal

---

* From Andrew von Hirsch and Kathleen J. Hanrahan, *Abolish Parole?*, A report submitted to the Law Enforcement Assistance Administration, U.S. Dept. of Justice (Washington, D.C., 1978). Reprinted with permission of the U.S. Department of Justice.

with the practical problems of prison discipline and prison overcrowding.

The Time-Fix Under the Desert Model. Under the Desert Model, the duration of an individual's confinement would be based only on an assessment of the gravity of his criminal conduct, without reference to forward-looking considerations of treatment, prediction, or deterrence. To decide how much imprisonment the offender deserves, the time-fix need not be delayed. The concept of desert looks to the past: to the gravity of the crime or crimes of which the offender was convicted. The seriousness of the past crime—that is, the extent of the harm done or risked and the degree of the offender's culpability—is normally as well ascertainable at the time of conviction as at a later date. By waiting longer to fix the time in prison, one ordinarily learns nothing new.

The Time-Fix Under the Modified Desert Model. The analysis becomes more complicated if we adopt a Modified Desert Model, for that model permits more factors to influence the penalty and, hence, more items of information to affect the time-fixing decision. We must attempt to determine, then, whether any of these added items of information could be known only later.

Incapacitation. The Modified Desert Model allows some room for incapacitive considerations. It thus could permit risk-of-recidivism to be taken into account to a mofest extent in deciding the dispostion. Assuming this much scope for prediction, does it require deferral of the time-fix?

At present, there would be little reason to defer the time-fix on predictive grounds. Currently available statistical prediction methods have had a limited degree of success in forecasting recidivism, if success is defined as the ability to identify the "true positives" with better than random accuracy. (They achieve this success at the expense of considerable overprediction: many

of those identified as recidivists will be "false positives"—those who would not have offended again.) The existing prediction devices rely on *pre*-conviction information such as past criminal history, age, prior drug or alcohol abuse, and record of employment, and do not make significant use of postconviction information. Prisoners' behavior inside the institution does not seem much correlated with subsequent recidivism. And, while it has been suggested that offenders' behavior on furlough or partial release might be useful in assessing risk of recidivism, there is little information to confirm this.

Rehabilitation. It was conventionally believed that rehabilitation required deferral of the time-fix. Since the sentencing judge cannot know in advance how quickly the offender will respond to treatment, the date of release (to the extent determined by rehabilitative considerations) should be set later, after observing the inmate's progress in the program. But to delay the time-fix for treatment presupposes that the treatment works. Reviews of treatment efforts (while some have challenged their conclusions) have not found much evidence of success.

Suppose, however, one were to assume that some of today's treatments were capable of succeeding at least for certainly carefully selected subgroups of prisoners. That still would not suffice to justify deferral for several reasons.

First, even if a few categories of offenders were thought amenable to treatment, the entire population of inmates certainly is not. Why, then, routinely defer the time-fix for all prisoners?

Second, a successful treatment program would not necessarily affect the duration of imprisonment. If the offender is deemed to deserve a certain period of imprisonment, it may be possible to treat him without accelerating or postponing release. The question of duration of treatment, however, has been largely ignored in existing research.

Third, even if the treatment were of approximately known length and were to require some addition or reduction in the period of imprisonment, that would not necessarily call for deferral. We still would have to ask the same kind of question as we did about incapacitation: What kind of information germane to the duration of treatment is gained by waiting? It may be that the information needed to place the offender in a suitable program and to estimate its duration is largely known at the time of sentence. Again, there has been no empirical research on the question of the usefulness of "late" information for these decisions.

General Deterrence. We doubt that the timing of the offender's time-fix would affect the deterrent effect of his punishment on the general public.

It has sometimes been suggested that deferral enhances deterrence by permitting the system, Potemkin-like, to *seem* to punish more severely than in fact it does. The usefulness of this strategy depends, however, on which segment of the public would be fooled. Persons with the greatest potential for offending may be most familiar with the actual workings of the system.

The Modified Desert Model would theoretically permit limited adjustments in duration of confinement to enhance the penalty's deterrent impact. But the technology does not now exist to calculate deterrent returns with any precision—and there is some reason to believe that crime rates are not particularly sensitive to modest variations in severity. Finally, there is little reason to expect that one will gain new information about deterrent effects by delaying the time-fix. Certainly, "late" information about what has befallen the prisoner himself would be irrelevant, since general deterrence depends on how much others are intimidated, not on the prisoner's own responses.

Deferral of the time-fix thus is unnecessary, even when one considers the compli-cating factors which a Modified Desert Model introduces. The addition of these factors has made our conclusions depend somewhat on the state of empirical knowledge; but based on current knowledge, we can say that the relevant information is available early.

Why Defer?—On Other Models. Our conclusion favoring an early time-fix would appear to hold, even if one were to reject the Modified Desert Model in favor of a still more strongly utilitarian penal philosophy. Suppose, for example, that one held the view that duration of confinement should be based *primarily* on the offender's predicted likelihood of offending again. If one asks what information is needed for making such forecases, the answer remains: information known at the time of sentence. It is true that this conclusion would depend still more on the state of empirical knowledge than under the Modified Desert Model—since predictive technology rather than desert considerations would occupy the central role. But given the current state of the art, there till would seem to be no need for delay.

Changes in Empirical Knowledge. What if empirical knowledge were to change, however? Consider prediction. While existing prediction methods rely on information available at sentence, that may have been due in part to its having been more readily at hand. Were "late" information more carefully recorded than it is today, and where a systematic effort made to explore its predictive usefulness, instances might be discovered where it did enhance prediction. To what extent would that alter our conclusions about the early time-fix?

On a Desert Model, it would make no difference—for there, prediction is not a factor in the time-fix at all. It is only on a Modified Desert Model—or other assumptions stressing prediction still more—that the question arises.

Even then, prisoners would not have to routinely be kept ignorant of when they will be released. Were new research to find instances where items of "late" information enhanced prediction, such cases could be accommodated through a limited modification in what we have recommended: namely, an early *presumptive* time-fix. Each prisoner would be informed immediately of his expected release date, based on the seriousness of his offense and (to the extent one's assumptions permit) on his estimated risk of recidivism. That release date could be altered on the basis of "late" information *only* when there was strong evidence that the information did, in fact, alter the estimated probability of the offender's returning to crime. Imprisoned offenders would thus know, immediately after sentence, when they would be likely to leave prison. That date could change only in those special circumstances when "late" information *did* tell one something new. (And, if one assumes a Modified Desert Model, the amount of the change could not be very great since the model permits incapacitative considerations to affect the disposition only to a limited extent.)

Moreover, this suggested modification—if ever necessary—would be called for only at some possible future date, when the predictive technology has altered substantially.

The Time-Fix and Institutional Problems
Aside from questions of the aims of punishment, it has been asserted that the deferred time-fix has important practical uses relating to the prison itself.

Overcrowding. Overcrowding is perhaps the most serious problem facing prisons today. Crowding could remain a problem, even on our assumptions. Those assumptions permit imprisonment only for serious crimes, but if the number of convictions for serious crimes grows, the prison population will also increase. Prison capacity, however, is not readily expanded, given the costs of construction and operation.

It is commonly believed that parole boards respond to overcrowding by releasing more prisoners as population levels climb. Empirical evidence on this is scarce, and it appears that the board's responsiveness varies by jurisdiction.

We think that it is proper to adjust prison terms to alleviate overcrowding. While we have assumed desert to be the preeminent penal aim, certain minimum constraints of a civilized society take precedence over any aim of punishment, even desert. One such constraint, is that persons in the state's custody should not suffer inhumane treatment. Since overcrowding in prisons can create intolerable living conditions, the obligation to punish as deserved must give way to a still more fundamental obligation of the state not to treat its wards with brutality.

Assuming that it is proper to shorten stays in prison to alleviate overcrowding, such actions should be governed by explicit standards or guidelines. Those guidelines should define what constitutes overpopulation for various types of facilities, and should contain provisions designed to ensure that, when crowding occurs, adjustments in terms of confinement are carried out in as evenhanded a manner as possible.

Such adjustments, when necessary, will complicate a system with an early time fix. Were it possible to predict prison population trends with reasonable accuracy, the adjustments could be made when the release date was initially set. But the techniques for projecting population levels are still quite rudimentary. Until there has been a substantial improvement in projection methods, therefore, adjustments to alleviate overcrowding will have to be made at a point close to the release date. This, in turn, would mean modifying the early time-fix procedure roughly as follows:

• At or shortly after sentence, the time-fixer would set the anticipated release date, taking into account how much time in prison the offender deserves and all permitted additional factors *other* than crowding.

• The crowding issue would be dealt with later, at a time near enough to the expected release date to allow population estimates to be made more accurately. The time-fixer would determine whether there was overcrowding that was severe enough to require acceleration of the release date; and if so, would set an altered date pursuant to the guidelines on crowding.

Discipline. If the state punishes by imprisoning, there must be sanctions to preserve order in the prison. The parole system can provide such a sanction, throught the threat of denying release to prisoners who do not abide by the rules.

There are, however, means other than parole denial for extending the terms of violent or disruptive prisoners. One method is, of course, a new criminal trial. This squares better with desert: a prisoner who intentionally injures another person, for example, has committed an offense that is serious and deserving of some added incarceration. But for obvious reasons, it is not easy to prosecute crimes in prison.

The alternative would be to adjust the duration of confinement administratively. The judgment of whether an infraction occurred would be made not through the ordinary criminal process, but in a hearing by an administrative fact finder (e.g., the parole board or a special disciplinary board). Such an administrative proceeding, however, increases the risk that some inmates will serve added time for infractions they did not commit or have valid excuses for committing, since the strict standards of proof and the other procedural safeguards of a new trial would not be present.

A possible solution would be to have the stringency of the procedure depend on the amount of potential punishment. A limited amount of time could be added in an administrative hearing; but large adjustments of time-in-confinement would call for a full criminal prosecution.

The problem of devising standards and penalties for institutional misconducts is not unique to the early time-fix. Irrespective of when the release decision occurs, the drafters of the standards for duration of confinement will have to decide how much adjustment should be made for misbehavior in prison.

How such adjustments are to be made in a system having an early time-fix should readily be apparent. When the offender is notified of his release date at or shortly after sentence, he would also be informed that the date could be altered by specified amounts, either downward for satisfactory institutional behavior, or upward for unsatisfactory behavior.

Even with these modifications, the procedure we recommend differs markedly from traditional parole release practice. Instead of a largely discretionary release decision, the time-fix would be guided by explicit standards. Instead of the decision being delayed as it is today in most jurisdictions, the decision would occur early: all prisoners would swiftly be informed of their release date. In most cases, that early decision would be final. In the exceptions just discussed, where overcrowding or disciplinary infractions are involved, it would be subject to limited subsequent alteration. But even so, prisoners would have a much more definite idea of when they would be likely to leave the institution.

10

Parole Selection

Who is to be paroled? This question was asked by the *Attorney General's Survey of Release Procedures* in 1939, and it is a question of vital importance today. The process and procedure of parole selection is of serious consequence to the effectiveness, perhaps even the survival, of the entire parole system. Since the selection process determines to a great extent the character of the system as a whole, it has inevitably become the target of more criticism than any other phase of parole procedure.

The decision to grant parole is a complicated one, and the consequences of the decision are of the gravest importance, both for society and for the inmate. A decision to grant parole results in conditional release prior to the expiration of the maximum term of imprisonment; a denial results in continued imprisonment. The parole release decision is often more important than the sentence of the court in determining how long prisoners actually spend incarcerated. In the absence of clear legislative or judicial guidelines for parole release decision making, vast responsibility has been placed upon parole boards. Parole decisions traditionally have been considered matters of special expertise, involving observation and treatment of offenders and release under supervision at a time that maximizes both the protection of the public and offenders' rehabilitation. This idealistic correctional aim, of protecting society and rehabilitating the offender, has served as an additional justification for the broad discretionary powers vested in parole authorities.[1]

Statutes have usually directed parole boards to make decisions based upon one or more of the following criteria: (a) the probability of recidivism, (b) the welfare of society, (c) the conduct of the offender while in the correctional institution, and (d) the sufficiency of the parole plan. As such statutory language does not lend itself to a workable decision-making scheme, the parole

---

1. William J. Genego, Peter D. Goldberger and Vicki C. Jackson, *Parole Release Decision Making and the Sentencing Process,* 84 Yale L.J. 810 (1975).

board must interpret and determine the best means by which to turn the legislative mandate into functioning administrative machinery. This broad discretion has brought criticism upon the paroling authority for arbitrary, capricious, and disparate decision making. The lack of published standards to guide decision making, combined with the lack of written reasons for decisions, contribute to this perception.[2]

TRADITIONAL PAROLE
DECISION MAKING

Traditionally, the hearing stage of parole decision making was thought to provide decision makers with an opportunity to speak with and observe the prospective parolee, to search for such intuitive signs of rehabilitation as repentance, willingness to accept responsibility, and self-understanding. Parole decisions were not based upon formally articulated criteria or policies, but on the discretionary judgments of individual decision makers.[3] The courts, to the extent that they were willing to review the parole decision at all, agreed with the contentions of paroling authorities that to impose even minimal due process constraints on the decisional process would interfere with fulfillment of its duty to engage in diagnosis and prognosis.

In *Menechino v. Oswald,* the U.S. Court of Appeals held:

> The Board has an identity of interest with (the inmate) . . . . It is seeking to encourage and foster his rehabilitation and readjustment to society . . . . In making this determination the Board is not restricted by rules of evidence developed for the purpose of determining legal or factual issues. It must consider many factors of a nonlegal nature (such as) medicine, psychiatry, criminology . . . psychology and human relations.[4]

However, in 1973 the National Advisory Commission on Criminal Justice Standards and Goals spoke to the issue of parole decision making, stating:

> The sound use of discretion and ultimate accountability for its exercise rests largely in making visible the criteria used in forming judgments. . . . The absence of written criteria by which decisions are made constitutes a major failing in virtually every parole jurisdiction.[5]

Development of Parole Guidelines
In 1973 the U.S. Board of Parole, now called the U.S. Parole Commission, took a major step in the direction recommended by the National Advisory Commission. As a part of a general reorganization plan, case decision making authority was

---

2. Elizabeth L. Taylor, *In Search of Equity: The Oregon Parole Matrix*, An unpublished monograph (1981).

3. 84 Yale L.J. 810, 820.

4. Menechino v. Oswald, 430 F.2d 403, 407–08 (2d Cir.1970), *cert. denied,* 400 U.S. 1023 (1971).

5. Nat'l Advisory Comm'n, 397.

delegated to panels of hearing examiners, using explicit parole selection guidelines established by the Board.[6] The guidelines attempted to structure discretion without removing it. By making explicit the primary factors considered in parole selection, as well as the weight given to each, the parole board provided judges, the public, and inmates with a clearer idea of the manner in which it intended to exercise its discretion.[7]

Previously, in a 1972 study of patterns in federal parole release decisions, three focal concerns were identified as explaining a large number of the board's decisions.[8] The research made it clear that each case was not decided strictly on its own merits; rather, decisions could be predicted by using specific variables. The variables or focal concerns were shown to be: (1) the seriousness of the offense, (2) the risk posed by the inmate (probability of recidivism), and (3) the institutional behavior of the inmate, a variable that was relatively less important than the first two. The researchers produced a chart that linked seriousness of offense and risk of recidivism to suggested terms of imprisonment. Based on this chart, the parole board constructed a matrix by plotting the two dimensions—seriousness of offense and risk of recidivism—on a graph. Range of sentence length was determined by the position of both dimensions on the graph. If prospective parolees were not granted release within the range appropriate to their offense and history, the reasons were required to be articulated by the decision maker.[9]

The Salient Factor Score

This actuarial device has been continually validated and evaluated over the past ten years and has gone through several changes, the latest in 1981. Known as the Salient Factor Score (SFS), it provides explicit guidelines for release decision making based upon a determination of the potential risk of parole violation. The 1981 version of the SFS measures six offender characteristics and assigns a score to each.

As noted in Table 1, the first offender characteristic considered in the Salient Factor Score is *Prior Convictions/Adjudications*. This offender characteristic has a score range of zero to three. Offenders with no prior convictions are assigned a score of three, one prior conviction results in a score of two, and two to three prior convictions a score of one, etc. Each of the six offender characteristics is scored in a similar manner and the sum of the six items yields the *predictive score*. The higher the score—maximum of ten—the more favorable the prognosis (a lower probability of recidivism).

---

6. Peter B. Hoffman and Lucille K. DeGostin, *Parole Decision-Making: Structuring Discretion*, Federal Probation (Dec. 1974).

7. *Id.*

8. Don M. Gottfredson, et al., *The Utilization of Experience in Parole Decision Making: Summary Report* (Washington: U.S. Parole Board, U.S. Dept. of Justice 1974).

9. National Council on Crime and Delinquency "*Changes in Sentencing and Parole Decision Making*, A monograph prepared for national parole institutes and parole seminars sponsored by the National Institute of Corrections (Jan. 1979).

Table 1. Salient Factor Score (SFS 81)

Item A. PRIOR CONVICTIONS/ADJUDICATIONS (ADULT OR JUVENILE).................. ☐

    None .... = 3
    One .... = 2
    Two or three .... = 1
    Four or more .... = 0

Item B. PRIOR COMMITMENT(S) OF MORE THAN THIRTY DAYS (ADULT OR JUVENILE) .... ☐

    None .... = 2
    One or two .... = 1
    Three or more .... = 0

Item C. AGE AT CURRENT OFFENSE/PRIOR COMMITMENTS .... ☐

    Age at commencement of the current offense:
     26 years of age or more..................... = 2 *
     20–25 years of age .... = 1 *
     19 years of age or less .... = 0

   * EXCEPTION: If five or more prior commitments of more than thirty days (adult or juvenile), place an "x" here _____ and score this item .... = 0

Item D. RECENT COMMITMENT FREE PERIOD (THREE YEARS)............................. ☐

    No prior commitment of more than thirty days (adult or juvenile) or released to the community from last such commitment at least three years prior to the commencement of the current offense ....= 1

    Otherwise .... = 0

Item E. PROBATION/PAROLE/CONFINEMENT/ESCAPE STATUS VIOLATOR THIS TIME... ☐

    Neither on probation, parole, confinement, or escape status at the time of the current offense; nor committed as a probation, parole, confinement, or escape status violator this time ....=1

    Otherwise .... = 0

Item F. HEROIN/OPIATE DEPENDENCE .... ☐

    No history of heroin/opiate dependence .... = 1

    Otherwise .... = 0

 TOTAL SCORE .... ☐

Note: For purposes of the Salient Factor Score, an instance of criminal behavior resulting in a judicial determination of guilt or an admission of guilt before a judicial body shall be treated as a conviction, even if a conviction is not formally entered.

Source: U.S. Parole Commission.

Table 1. Guidelines for Decision Making and Customary Total Time to be Served before Release (including jail time).

OFFENSE CHARACTERISTICS: Severity of Offense Behavior	OFFENDER CHARACTERISTICS: Parole Prognosis (Salient Factor Score 1981)			
	Very Good (10–8)	Good (7–6)	Fair (5–4)	Poor (3–0)
CATEGORY ONE [formerly 'low severity']	Adult Range			
	<= 6 months	6–9 months	9–12 months	12–16 months
	Youth Range			
	<= 6 months	6–9 months	9–12 months	12–16 months
CATEGORY TWO [formerly 'low moderate severity']	Adult Range			
	<= 8 months	8–12 months	12–16 months	16–22 months
	Youth Range			
	<= 8 months	8–12 months	12–16 months	16–20 months
CATEGORY THREE [formerly 'moderate severity']	Adult Range			
	10–14 months	14–18 months	18–24 months	24–32 months
	Youth Range			
	8–12 months	12–16 months	16–20 months	20–26 months
CATEGORY FOUR [formerly 'high severity']	Adult Range			
	14–20 months	20–26 months	26–34 months	34–44 months
	Youth Range			
	12–16 months	16–20 months	20–26 months	26–32 months
CATEGORY FIVE [formerly 'very high severity']	Adult Range			
	24–36 months	36–48 months	48–60 months	60–72 months
	Youth Range			
	20–26 months	26–32 months	32–40 months	40–48 months

Table 1. Guidelines for Decision Making and Customary Total Time to be Served before Release (including jail time). (Continued)

OFFENSE CHARACTERISTICS: *Severity of Offense Behavior* (Continued)	OFFENDER CHARACTERISTICS: *Parole Prognosis (Salient Factor Score 1981)*			
	Very Good (10–8)	Good (7–6)	Fair (5–4)	Poor (3–0)
CATEGORY SIX	Adult Range			
	40–52 months	52–64 months	64–78 months	78–100 months
	Youth Range			
	30–40 months	40–50 months	50–60 months	60–76 months
CATEGORY SEVEN	Adult Range			
	52–80 months	64–92 months	78–110 months	100–140 months
	Youth Range			
	40–64 months	50–74 months	60–86 months	76–110 months
CATEGORY EIGHT *	Adult Range			
	100 + months	120 + months	150 + months	180 + months
	Youth Range			
	80 + months	100 + months	120 + months	150 + months

Source: U.S. Parole Commission.

* For category eight, no upper limits are specified due to the extreme variability of the cases within this category. For decisions exceeding the lower limits of the applicable guidelines category *by more than forty-eight months*, the pertinent aggravating case factors considered are to be specified in the reasons given (i.e., that a homicide was premeditated or committed during the course of another felony, or that extreme cruelty or brutality was demonstrated).

While the salient factor score provides a method of summarizing knowledge of the relationship between offender characteristics and likelihood of recidivism, its use with a guidelines system does not mean the elimination of clinical judgment. No prediction device can take into account all the variations in human behavior. Thus, provision is made to allow the decision maker to override the salient factor score, but only for articulated, written reasons. If the decision maker chooses to make a clinical judgment outside the guidelines, he or she must articulate the specific factors considered in coming to the conclusion to override the SFS.[10]

Basically following the lead of the federal parole system, other states adopted guidelines for use in release decision making. While some states (Florida, Maryland, Minnesota, Oklahoma, Colorado, Georgia, New York, Oregon, Washington, Texas, North Carolina, and Missouri) adopted a matrix guideline system similar to the U.S. Parole Commission's Salient Factors, others (Hawaii, Massachusetts, Ohio, Pennsylvania, Rhode Island, South Carolina, and West Virginia) adopted different types of guidelines. Most often, they involve a list of factors to be considered in making a parole release decision. Unlike the matrix system, time served is not directly associated with the other factors.[11] Four of the original guidelines states (Minnesota, Washington, North Carolina, and Colorado), eventually passed laws that abolished parole, guidelines and all.[12]

Regardless of the form parole release guidelines take, their goal is to structure the exercise of discretion. Parole boards are free to deviate from their guidelines, but generally must give reasons for doing so. Parole authorities are guided in their decision making, while retaining broad powers; deviations from these guides are checked by the possibility of appeal.[13]

Research indicates that guidelines have performed one of their intended functions, which is to even out obvious disparities and make prison time more predictable. But the main argument against them is that they do not address the question of who is to go to prison in the first place, nor of how wide the sentence ranges should be. This is done mostly by the courts, and many critics have pointed out that court sentencing is just as capricious, unpredictable, and fraught with disparities as are parole decisions.[14]

Whether length of incarceration before granting parole is any more predictable in guideline states or in the federal system is still speculative. James Beck studied the perceptions of prisoners of parole decision making in the U.S. parole system, which used a justice model guideline jurisdiction, and in Pennsylvania, which used a rehabilitative nonmatrix guideline system.[15] The Pennsylvania board was generally treatment oriented and strongly considered institutional behavior, recommendations of institutional staff, and parole release plans. The

10. Peter B. Hoffman and Sheldon Adelberg, *The Salient Factor Score: A Non-Technical Overview*, Federal Probation (March, 1980).

11. Nat'l Council on Crime and Delinquency, National Parole Institutes, *supra* at 20, 21

12. Krajick, *supra,* at 34. Florida has passed legislation that will replace parole with sentencing guidelines by 1987.

13. National Parole Institutes, *supra*.

14. Krajick, *supra,* at 34.

15. James L. Beck, *Offender Perceptions of Parole Decisionmaking*, An unpublished monograph (1981).

federal system, as we have already discussed in detail, considers primarily offense severity and offender characteristics, such as prior criminal history.

Contrary to expectations, Beck found no significant difference in the inmates' ability to predict parole decision making, and found that a significantly greater percentage of state inmates considered the parole procedure "basically fair" (48 percent of Pennsylvania inmates and only 20 percent of the federal inmates). The major conclusion of the study was that the justice approach to parole does not result in greater perceived certainty for the offender, even though the criteria were made concrete and more sharply defined. The treatment model—based upon institutional adjustment—allowed the offender a greater perceived influence over the parole decision, and thus was viewed as basically more fair. Beck concluded that the justice approach to parole is still a useful tool for reducing sentence disparity and the rehabilitation model must always be suspect until some method of rehabilitating offenders has been proven effective. From the viewpoint of the offender, however, the rehabilitative model of parole seems to be the preferred method of deciding when an offender should be released from prison. Any system that totally ignores positive institutional behavior may run the risk of alienating the offender and increase the possibility of poor adjustment.[16]

Despite criticism leveled at the use of guidelines, this procedure appears to be the one that offers the greatest degree of fairness to the parole-granting process. By making explicit the primary factors that the board should consider in parole selection, and the weight that should be given to each, the unfettered discretion traditionally allowed parole boards should, at the very least, be structured and more predictable.

Due Process

One of the most striking aspects of the traditional parole release process has been the virtual inability to review parole decisions.[17] In recent years, courts have provided some procedural protections and articulated criteria for reviewing the conditions that parole boards have set upon parolees' conduct, and for revoking parole and returning parolees to prison. Until very recently, federal and state courts almost invariably rejected claims that the denial of parole was subject to review because of procedural or substantive defects in the parole release decision process.[18]

The parole grant has long been analogized by courts to the grant of executive pardon, which is essentially an "act of grace" or the conferring of a "privilege," and which does not give rise to rights or expectations in need of due process.[19] In addition to the act of grace and privilege rationales, another theory for judicial passivity in this area has been the argument that parole constituted a mere

16. *Id.* at 12.

17. 84 Yale L.J. 810, at 842.

18. *Id.*

19. French v. Ciccone, 308 F.Supp. 256, 257 (W.D.Mo.1969).

change in the nature of custody, and that therefore the parole release decision lay in the area of administrative decision making.[20]

However, the theories of grace or privilege are inconsistent with the view that parole is merely a change in custody status, since the former theories recognize that a substantial benefit of conditional freedom is being conferred. The custody theory ignores the fact that a major purpose of parole is to provide a halfway point between incarceration and total freedom in the community in order to promote rehabilitation and to protect society.[21]

Another rationale used to justify the vast and unreviewable discretion is that parole boards are acting as *parens patriae* with respect to the inmates; as such, they are concerned only with promoting the inmates' own rehabilitation through the exercise of their expert knowledge and judgment, which obviates any need for procedural protection.[22] This rationale reflected the pervasive judicial view that release decisions were part of the rehabilitation process. In support of this view, courts emphasized that parole boards possessed an administrative expertise in evaluating "nonlegal" factors relevant to the release decision.[23] They acquiesced in the board's assertion that the proper moment for parole can only be determined after an inmate has been observed for a period of time and attempts have been made to treat the inmate within the rehabilitative institutional context.[24]

In *Menechino v. Oswald*,[25] a prisoner argued that the New York State Board of Parole's denial of his application for parole was illegal because he had not received notice of the information to be considered, a fair parole hearing with a right to counsel, the right to cross-examination and to produce favorable witnesses, or a specification of the grounds and underlying facts upon which the denial was based. The court offered two reasons in holding that these due process rights did not apply to parole release hearings. First, the court ruled that the inmate had no legally cognizable "interest" in his parole grant, since he did not enjoy a status that was being threatened or taken away. Second, the parole board's interest in the proceeding was not adverse to that of the inmate [26] because the "board . . . is seeking to encourage and foster his rehabilitation and readjustment into society.[27]

Although the prevailing view of the courts has been one of noninterference in parole release decisions, it has not been the absolute view. Abuses of discretion have been judicially reviewed and parole boards have been found

---

20. Anderson v. Coral, 263 U.S. 193 (1923).

21. C. Newman, *Sourcebook in Probation, Parole and Pardons,* 3d ed. *(Springfield: Charles C. Thomas, 1968), 206–207, 84 Yale L.J. 810, 843 and 45 Minn.L.Rev. 803, 827 (1961).*

22. Scarpa v. United States Bd. of Parole, 477 F.2d 278, 281 (5th Cir.1972 *vacated as moot,* 414 U.S. 809 (1973); Menechino v. Oswald, 430 F.2d 402, 407 (2d Cir.1970), *cert. denied,* 400 U.S. 1023 (1971).

23. Scarpa, *supra,* at 281.

24. 84 Yale L.J. 810, 843.

25. 430 F.2d 403 (2d Cir.1970), *cert. denied,* 400 U.S. 1023 (1971).

26. *Id.* at 407–08.

27. *Id.*

abusing their discretion, committing capricious acts, and conducting practices contrary to the general notions of fairness.[28]

In 1979 the U.S. Supreme Court addressed directly the issue of due process in parole release decision making. In *Greenholtz v. Inmates of the Nebraska Penal and Correctional Complex*[29] the inmates of a Nebraska prison brought an action alleging they had been unconstitutionally denied parole by the Nebraska Board of Parole. The inmates contested, among other things, (1) the state's hearing process, (2) the board's practice when it denies parole of informing the inmate in what respect he or she falls short of qualifying for parole, and (3) a notice procedure of informing inmates, in advance, of the month during which the parole hearing will be held, and then posting, on the day of the hearing, notice of the exact time for the hearing.

After the lower federal courts held in favor of the inmates, the U.S. Supreme Court reversed the decision of the court of appeals. The Court stated:

> Like most parole statutes, it (the Nebraska statute) vests broad discretion in the Board. No ideal, error-free way to make parole release decisions has been developed. The whole question has been, and will continue to be, the subject of experimentation involving analysis of psychological factors combined with fact evaluation guided by the practical experience of the actual parole decision makers in predicting future behavior.[30]

The Court continued the trend of past decisions by discussing the "ultimate purpose of parole . . . rehabilitation,"[31] and stated:

> The fact that anticipations and hopes for rehabilitation programs have fallen short of expectations of a generation ago need not lead states to abandon hopes for those objectives; states may adopt a balanced approach in making parole determinations, as in problems of administering the correctional systems.[32]

The Court in *Greenholtz* refused to require a hearing in all cases for every inmate as prescribed by the court of appeals, holding that such a requirement would provide, at best, a negligible decrease in the risk of error.

In sum, the Court held that "The Nebraska procedure affords an opportunity to be heard and when parole is denied it informs the inmate in what respect he falls short of qualifying for parole; this affords the process that is due under these circumstances. The Constitution does not require more."[33]

The Importance of Greenholtz

Although the *Greenholtz* case did not extend due process as far as desired by the plaintiffs, nor as extensively as did the court of appeals, it did establish that

---

28. *See* United States *ex rel.* Campbell v. Pate, 401 F.2d 55 (7th Cir.1968); *Palermo v. Rockefeller,* 323 F.Supp. 478 (S.D.N.Y.1971); *Monks v. New Jersey State Parole Board,* 55 N.J. 238, 277 A.2d 193 (1971).

29. 442 U.S. 1, 60 L.Ed.2d 668, 99 S.Ct. 2100 (1979).

30. Greenholtz v. Inmates of the Nebraska Penal and Correctional Complex, 442 U.S. 1, 14, 60 L.Ed.2d 668; 99 S.Ct. 2100 (1919).

31. *Id.*

32. *Id.*

33. *Id.* at 16.

some due process protections were available in the parole-granting process. The Court held that the methods provided for in the Nebraska statute—providing the right to an initial hearing, notice of the hearing, and articulation of the reasons for denial—were sufficient. It differentiated parole release decision making from parole revocation decision making and refused to apply the due process provisions of *Morrissey v. Brewer,* which prescribe a panoply of rights available to a parolee in a revocation hearing. The Court concluded that parole release and parole revocation "are quite different" because "there is a . . . difference between losing what one has and not getting what one wants." [34]

Greenholtz, then, appears to require reasonable notice of a hearing, an initial hearing wherein the prisoner is allowed to present the case, and if parole is denied, a recitation of the reasons for denial. On the other hand, the requirement depends upon the wording of the state or federal statute being interpreted:

> We can accept respondent's view that the expectancy of release provided in this statute is entitled to some measure of constitutional protection. However, we emphasize that this statute has unique structure and language and thus whether any other state statute provides a protectable entitlement must be decided on a case by case basis.[35]

The American Correction Association (ACA) Standards require parole hearings to be conducted as fairly and equitably as possible with due process conditions maintained and all procedural safeguards assured.[36] The ACA Standards do not differentiate (with regard to due process) between parole release hearings and revocation hearings. Further, ACA Standards require written criteria for decision making in enough detail to permit consistent application in individual cases. Standard 2–1085 requires that the decision regarding parole release and the reasons for it be communicated to the prisoner orally and explained to agree with written criteria. Applicants denied parole must be informed of an approximate future hearing date and must receive suggestions for improving their chances to receive parole by the time of the next hearing.

The American Correctional Association Standards far exceed the due process requirements established by the courts, although it must be noted that the standards are not binding upon any paroling authority, and rather are only guidelines or models.

As there is considerable disagreement regarding the amount and type of due process necessary at the parole-granting hearing, it is instructive to note that in *Greenholtz* there was division on the Court and that separate concurring opinions were written. Of particular interest is the separate opinion of Justice Powell. Powell agreed that the inmates had a right to some due process in the consideration of their release on parole, but disagreed that the due process was conditioned upon the wording of the state statute governing the deliberations of the parole board. Powell wrote that substantial liberty from legal restraint is at

---

34. *Id.* at 9–10.

35. *Id.* at 12.

36. American Correctional Association Standards for Adult Parole Authorities, second edition published by ACA, College Park Maryland, June 1982, at 242–248. Standards 2–1080 through 2–1085 (1981).

stake when the state makes decisions regarding probation or parole. "Although still subject to limitations not imposed or citizens never convicted of a crime, the parolee enjoys a liberty comparably greater than whatever minimal freedom of action he may have retained within prison walls, a fact that the Court recognized in *Morrissey v. Brewer* . . . ." [37]

Because this liberty is valuable and its termination inflicts a grievous loss on the parolee, the Court concluded in *Morrissey v. Brewer* [38] that the decision to revoke parole must be made in conformity with due process standards. Powell wrote that the prisoner should justifiably expect that parole will be granted fairly and that the mere existence of a parole system is sufficient to create a liberty interest in the parole release decision protected by the Constitution. [39]

Justice Marshall, joined by Justices Brennan and Stevens, dissenting in part wrote:

"I must register my opinion that all prisoners potentially eligible for parole have a liberty interest of which they may not be deprived without due process, regardless of the particular statutory language that implements the parole system. [40]

Considering the lack of unanimity in the *Greenholtz* case, it is not only possible but probable that a future case will further extend due process to the parole release hearing and that the due process rights in *Morrissey v. Brewer* and *Gagnon v. Scarpelli* will be incorporated into the parole selection process.

SUMMARY

The parole selection process, for all its importance to the prisoner, society, and the justice system as a whole is a confused procedure with little consensus regarding the proper means by which the decision is to be made, upon what grounds the decisions should be made, and about whether or not minimal due process should be allowed.

From the intuitive approach of the rehabilitative parole board to the justice model system with its guidelines and parole matrices, the system has not yet evolved a consistent decision making base. Even the prisoners who are at the complete mercy of the system do not agree upon what method is preferable. One study seems to indicate that inmates may prefer mercy to justice as they overwhelmingly favored the intuitive approach of the Pennsylvania parole system to the guidelines approach of the federal system.

The courts too, are at odds, although at present there seems to be a rather consistent theme that due process, if allowed at all, will be minimal and determined by the statutes of the jurisdiction; however, it will not be protected by the fourteenth amendment and therefore will not be a constitutional issue.

---

37. Greenholtz v. Inmates of the Nebraska Penal and Correctional Complex, *supra,* at 18.

38. Morrissey v. Brewer, 408 U.S. 471, 92 S.Ct. 2593, 33 L.Ed.2d 484 (1972).

39. *Id.* at 19.

40. *Id.* at 22.

The Manual of Correctional Standards perhaps summarizes the issue of due process at the release hearing as well as possible:

> To an even greater extent than in the case of imprisonment, probation and parole practice is determined by an administrative discretion that is largely uncontrolled by legal standards, protections, or remedies. Until statutory and case law are more fully developed, it is virtually important within all of the correctional field that there should be established and maintained reasonable norms and remedies against the sort of abuses that are likely to develop where men have great power over their fellows and where relationships may become both mechanical and arbitrary.[41]

---

41. American Correctional Association, *Manual of Correctional Standards* (College Park, Maryland) 1980, 500. *See also* Justice Douglas separate opinion in Morrissey v. Brewer, 408 U.S. 471.

Presumptive Parole Dates: The Federal Approach*

An overview of the goals and structure of the U.S. Parole Commission's approach to parole release decisionmaking is presented in this article; and the relationship of this approach to the philosophical concerns of equity and determinacy is highlighted.[1]

The statute governing federal parole release consideration sets forth the following criteria for parole release: (1) that an eligible prisoner has substantially observed the rules of the institution(s) to which he has been confined; (2) that release would not depreciate the seriousness of his offense or promote disrespect for the law; and (3) that release would not jeopardize the public welfare. In addition, the statute mandates the use of paroling policy guidelines as a flexible means of structuring decisionmaking discretion to provide equity among groups of similar offenders without removing the

opportunity to consider individual case factors.[2]

In developing the guidelines and other rules and procedures to implement this statutory mandate, the Parole Commission has attempted to pursue three general objectives. First, the specific guidelines established must reflect the parole release criteria set forth in the statute. Second, to provide equity, the guidelines established must be sufficiently explicit and detailed to permit consistent decisionmaking among similarly situated offenders. Third, unnecessary uncertainty as to the date of the prisoner's eventual release is to be avoided through early notification of the tentative date of release from prison; yet this procedure must be flexible enough to permit modification of a release date should there be significant change in circumstances. The Parole Com-

---

* Barbara Stone-Meierhoefer and Peter B. Hoffman, *Federal Probation* (June 1982.) Reprinted with permission.

1. U.S. Parole Commission regulations are published at 28 C.F.R. §§ 2.1–2.60 (1981) [as amended by 46 *Federal Register* 35635–35640 (July 10, 1981)].

2. 18 U.S.C. §§ 4201 et seq. *See particularly,* 18 U.S.C. §§ 4203 and 4206.

mission has attempted to reach these objectives through the development of a system of explicit guidelines for decisionmaking combined with a presumptive release date procedure.

SETTING A PRESUMPTIVE RELEASE DATE

The first stage of the decisionmaking process takes place within 120 days after incarceration when almost all federal prisoners are eligible for an initial parole hearing.[3] At this hearing, the paroling policy guidelines are calculated, the case is assessed against these guidelines, and the prisoner is notified of a presumptive date of release.[4]

The Concern of Equity

The paroling policy guidelines calculated at the initial hearing are an important tool in the overall parole decisionmaking process.[5] These guidelines provide a scheme for classifying offenders into groups which are similar in relation to (1) the seriousness of the offense they committed, and (2) the risk of recidivism presented to society.

The determination of offense seriousness is accomplished with reference to a severity scale which classifies examples of common

federal offense behaviors into seven categories of seriousness. A "risk" of recidivism determination is then made with the aid of an actuarial device containing six items (primarily concerning prior criminal record), which, taken together, have been found to relate to the likelihood of recidivism. This device, known as the "salient factor score," is used to classify cases into one of four risk categories.[6] The guideline matrix then sets forth a customary range of months to be served in prison for the applicable combination of offense severity and parole prognosis assessments. This guideline range presumes good institutional behavior.

Calculation of the appropriate guideline range is the necessary first step in decisionmaking; however, the actual release decision rests on an assessment of each individual prisoner's case against the guideline parameters. The guidelines do not prescribe the *only* factors which are to be taken into account at the initial parole hearing. Rather, they specify that offense severity and risk are primary factors that must be considered in *every* case. Other case-specific factors are then used to place the actual release decision at a point either within or outside of the appropriate guideline range. If the circumstances surrounding an individual case contain no substantial aggravating or mitigating circumstances, a decision within the guidelines will be chosen. If,

---

3. The procedures governing initial parole hearings are at 28 C.F.R. §§ 2.12, 2.13 (1981). The exception to the early hearing provision of the presumptive date plan is that prisoners with minimum sentences of ten years are not heard until just prior to their eligibility date. This stems from the regulation which prohibits the setting of a presumptive release date in excess of ten years from the date of the hearing.

4. The only prisoners not given a presumptive release date at the initial hearing are those for whom the commission does not feel release within ten years from the date of the hearing would be appropriate. These prisoners are continued for a ten-year reconsideration hearing at which all of the facts of the case are reevaluated against the guidelines calculated at the initial hearing for possible setting of a presumptive release date. It is to be noted that any presumptive release date must be set within the limits of the judicial sentence imposed (i.e., it may not be set earlier than the judicial minimum sentence, if any, nor later than the mandatory release date).

5. 28 C.F.R. §§ 2.20 and 2.21 as amended by 46 Federal Register 35635–35640 (July 10, 1981). For an overview of the development of the paroling policy guidelines, *see:* D.M. Gottfredson, L.T. Wilkins, and P.B. Hoffman, *Guidelines for Parole and Sentencing (Lexington, Mass:* Lexington Books 1978).

6. For a summary of the method used in construction and validation of the salient factor score, *see:* P.B. Hoffman and S. Adelberg, *The Salient Factor Score: A Non-Technical Overview,* 44 FEDERAL PROBATION (1980), 44–53.

however, there are significant aggravating or mitigating circumstances surrounding the case, departure from the guideline range—either above or below—would not only be permitted but would be called for.[7] When aggravating or mitigating factors sufficient to warrant a decision outside of the guideline range are found, specific written reasons for the departure must be provided.[8]

The Concern of Determinacy

The outcome of the initial parole hearing is the setting of a presumptive date of release, the aim of which is to place a particular offender in fair relation to other prisoners with respect to offense severity and risk of recidivism. This presumptive release date may be set up to ten years from the date of the hearing, and may be either a presumptive parole date or a decision to continue the prisoner to the expiration of his/her sentence less institutional good time (when the prisoner's sentence is not long enough to accommodate the particular time-served decision deemed appropriate).[9] If confinement of more than ten years is indicated, the prisoner will be rescheduled for a full reconsideration hearing in ten years. Actual release upon the presumptive parole date is contingent upon maintenance of a good conduct record and development of an acceptable release plan.

By making a presumptive release decision early in the parole process, the prisoner is given certainty to the extent that a release date has been set which cannot be taken away except for specified reasons. However, the early notification provision also has the effect of limiting the information considered in making this initial decision to that which is known at the time of commitment. Those relevant release factors which come to light during the course of imprisonment are the focus of subsequent reviews.

MODIFICATION OF A PRESUMPTIVE RELEASE DATE

After a presumptive release date is set, there are two types of regularly scheduled parole considerations. First, approximately six months prior to a previously set presumptive parole date, a record review is conducted to ascertain whether or not the conditions of the presumptive date (i.e., satisfactory conduct and an acceptable release plan) have been met. Second, by statute, prisoners are given an in-person parole review hearing every eighteen months (prisoners with sentences of less than seven years) or twenty-four months (prisoners with sentences of seven years or more).[10] In addition to these regularly scheduled considerations, there is provision for the reopening of a case at any time upon receipt of new and significant information.[11]

Decisionmaking at these subsequent considerations focuses on whether there have been any changes in circumstances since the previous hearing significant enough to warrant a change in the presump-

---

7. The U.S. Parole Commission's Procedures Manual (Appendix 4, Section V) provides examples of the more common factors which may warrant a decision outside the guidelines.

8. 18 U.S.C. 4206(c).

9. When a prisoner is denied parole, this does not mean that he or she will serve the entire sentence imposed by the court in prison. Release from prison in the absence of parole is effected upon expiration of the full term sentence less statutory good time (up to ten days a month) and earned extra good time (up to an additional five days a month). Upon release, a prisoner denied parole will be supervised as if on parole up to the full term date of the sentence (less six months).

10. 28 C.F.R. § 2.14 (1981).

11. 28 C.F.R. § 2.28 (1981).

tive release date. In designing the presumptive date process, the commission has attempted to balance the sometimes competing aims of determinacy and equity. That is, allowance of any change in a presumptive date, by definition, decreases the certainty of the initial release decision. However, it is the commission's position that offenders, through institutional behavior or other changes in circumstance, may need to be differentiated from those to whom they were considered "similar" when the presumptive date decision was originally made. It would therefore be inequitable if the previously set release date could not be adjusted to reflect these differences when they occur.

To consider all of the relevant information demanded by equity, while still eliminating unnecessary uncertainty, the commission has specified the factors which may be relied upon to modify a presumptive date, and has established decisionmaking guidelines for the two most commonly occurring change factors: institutional misconduct and superior program achievement.

POSTPONEMENT OF A PRESUMPTIVE DATE

Disciplinary Infractions

As stated earlier, the commission's paroling policy guidelines assume good conduct while confined. A record of serious disciplinary infractions does not meet this presumption, nor would it meet the statutory requirement that the commission consider whether the prisoner has substantially obeyed the rules of the institution in which confined. Therefore, poor discipline is con-

sidered by the commission as good cause to rescind a previously set presumptive parole date provided the infraction(s) has been adjudicated under the Bureau of Prison's Institutional Disciplinary Committee procedures.[12]

The purpose of the commission's rescission guidelines[13] is to facilitate consistent decisionmaking in sanctioning rule infractions. These guidelines specify the customary period of prison time to be added to the original presumptive release date for prisoners who commit various types of disciplinary infractions. It should be noted that rescission guidelines only apply to those prisoners to whom the commission has given a presumptive or effective date of parole. If the commission has continued a prisoner to the expiration of his/her sentence less institutional good time, the sanctioning of disciplinary infractions is within the authority of the Bureau of Prisons which may take away the prisoner's institutional "good time" and, thus, delay the prisoner's mandatory release date.

The Parole Commission's rescission guidelines classify infractions into three categories. The first category, "administrative infractions," includes conduct prohibited by institutional rule, but which is not a criminal law violation.

A second category includes escape or attempted escape. The rescission penalty for escape depends on the type of institution from which the prisoner escaped and the length of time in escape status. The "escape" penalty is separate from that to be applied for any other criminal acts that may be committed during the escape.

A third category includes conduct which constitutes new criminal behavior (other than escape). A distinction is made as to

---

12. 28 C.F.R. § 2.34 (1981). The Bureau of Prisons may handle disciplinary infractions in an informal manner (through which only minor sanctions may be imposed) or may refer consideration of infractions to an Institutional Disciplinary Committee hearing. Only the latter method of adjudicating infractions provides the standard of due process required of the Parole Commission when considering rescission of a parole date.

13. 28 C.F.R. § 2.36 (1981).

whether the new criminal behavior occurred in an institutional setting, or whatever it occurred while the prisoner was actually in the community (e.g., on furlough, on work status from a community treatment center, or in escape status). In each case, the rescission penalty is determined by assessing the seriousness of the new criminal conduct using the severity scale of the paroling policy guidelines such that the more serious the rescission behavior, the more time is added to the previously set date. If the criminal behavior occurred while the prisoner was in the community, the risk of recidivism dimension (salient factor score) is also recalculated. The result is that the rescission guidelines for new offenses committed in the community call for the most additional prison time to be served.

Failure to Establish a Suitable Release Plan

A previously set presumptive parole date may also be retarded if the prisoner fails to establish an acceptable release plan. A release plan is initially proposed by the prisoner and his/her caseworker. It is then sent to the probation office located in the proposed area of release for verification of the details of the plan and the probation officer's recommendation as to its suitability. The plan is then submitted to the Parole Commission for approval. An acceptable plan will generally include a place to live and a place of employment (or schooling). If a prisoner has limited community resources, an effort is made to release such prisoner through a community treatment center (halfway house) for the purpose of obtaining employment and housing.

If an acceptable release plan has not been approved by the time of the parole date, the parole date may be retarded while efforts are made to secure an approved plan. If, after 120 days, the prisoner is still without an approved plan, a hearing must be held to discuss the problem and explore alternative solutions.[14] The case must then be reviewed at least every thirty days so that continuing efforts to secure release can be monitored.

Prior to actual release, the prisoner must sign the release certificate agreeing to the general, and any special, conditions of parole supervision. Failure to sign this certificate will result in waiver of parole.

New Adverse Information

A presumptive parole date is given under the assumption that all relevant information is known and has been accurately presented to the commission. If any significant information adverse to the prisoner comes to the attention of the commission subsequent to the granting of a presumptive date, the case may be reopened for another hearing, from which a more adverse parole decision may result.[15]

ADVANCEMENT OF A PRESUMPTIVE DATE

Superior Program Achievement

In addition to assuming good conduct, the paroling policy guideline range also assumes good program performance. However, where a prisoner subsequently demonstrates exceptional positive institutional achievements over a sustained period of time, the previously set presumptive date may be reduced according to a schedule of limited rewards under the superior program achievement guidelines.[16]

14. 28 C.F.R. §§ 2.12(d) and 2.28(e) (1981).

15. 28 C.F.R. § 2.28(c), (d), and (f) (1981).

16. 28 C.F.R. § 2.60 (1981). It should also be noted that the Parole Commission does not punish lack of program achievement. The previously set presumptive date sets the outside release decision assuming the discipline

The superior achievement guidelines provide a specified normal maximum limit (in months) by which a previously set presumptive date may be advanced. This maximum limit is purposely kept small so as not to reintroduce the gross uncertainty which the presumptive date system was designed to eliminate. Additionally, keeping the potential reward small reduces the likelihood of prisoners participating superficially in programs merely to impress the Parole Commission in the hope of obtaining a substantially earlier release date.[17] By limiting the impact of positive institutional achievements, the commission is also stating a philosophical position that, although positive institutional behavior is appropriately considered in making the ultimate release decision, considerations of offense severity and risk should remain primary.

The objective of the superior program achievement guidelines is to specify small but meaningful incentives to reward prisoners who choose to spend their prison time in an exceptionally constructive manner. While in some respects the superior program achievement guidelines represent the counterpart to the rescission guidelines, there are several important differences between the two.

First, the size of the potential reductions is tied to the total length of prison time to be served as established by the original presumptive date. This tie is important because the perceived size of the reward is, of course, relative. For example, in light of the above discussion a potential six-month reduction may seem an appropriate incentive for a prisoner with a fifty-month presumptive date. But the same potential six-month reduction would appear excessive for a prisoner with a twelve-month presumptive date. This relationship between the superior program achievement guidelines and the length of time required by the original presumptive date is in contrast to the structure of the rescission guidelines, which set customary penalties for specific misconducts to be served in addition to, and independent of, the length of time required by the previously set presumptive date.

Second, the superior program achievement standards state that accomplishments in any area of activity or job performance can be considered, and that a clear conduct record is, in itself, not sufficient. The guidelines do not, however, describe the specific types of behavior which can be considered by the commission to be "superior." To do this would be an overwhelming task because the definition of what is considered "superior program achievement" for one prisoner may not be considered "superior" for another. Prisoners enter the federal prison system with a wide array of talents and weaknesses. To complete five college courses while in prison may not be that exceptional for a prisoner who already has a law degree. However, this accomplishment may indeed be considered "superior" for a prisoner who previously has been unable to succeed in the educational system.

---

and release plan conditions are met. However, a prisoner, while incarcerated, may not remain idle. In addition to elective activities, a prisoner is required to perform a job assignment within the prison. A prisoner's refusal to work may be cited as a disciplinary infraction. If serious enough to be referred by the Bureau of Prisons to an Institutional Disciplinary Committee, the Parole Commission may consider this behavior under its rescission guidelines for administrative infractions.

17. While the Commission is cognizant of the potential for problems with "game-playing," it is believed that this potential is much reduced under the now published procedures of Federal parole decisionmaking which allocates only limited weight to institutional program participation. Furthermore, the atmosphere with gave rise to the initial critiques of consideration of program participation in release decisionmaking was one where prisoners were given virtually no idea of when they might be paroled until right before their actual release. In addition, no specific criteria were published and available as to how parole decisions were actually being made. This informational vacuum is not present in current Federal parole procedures.

Therefore, application of the superior program achievement guidelines involves a substantial amount of subjective judgment. Yet, by limiting the maximum amount of time to be awarded, potential inconsistency is minimized; and program participation, while encouraged, is not coerced.

Other Exceptional Circumstances

In addition, a previously set presumptive date may be reduced for other exceptional factors such as severely deteriorating health; isolated acts of unusual responsibility or courage, which though not "sustained" nonetheless merit recognition (e.g., helping others during a fire); or the receipt of new favorable information concerning the circumstances of the case not previously known.[18]

SUMMARY

The U.S. Parole Commission's procedures have evolved over the years from a system which a decade ago made parole decisions on a case by case basis with essentially no structure, through a period where structure was developed for paroling decisions in the form of paroling policy guidelines, to the current system which combines the use of guidelines with the setting of presumptive dates.

Throughout this evolution, a change in one part of the process has allowed for or necessitated changes in other parts of the system. The development of guidelines based on preincarceration factors allowed the development of the presumptive date procedures. Presumptive date procedures, in turn, necessitated a restructuring of the process used to consider institutional (and other postincarceration) factors in the release decision.

The current federal parole procedures have developed in a piecemeal fashion. Yet what has emerged is a conceptually simple system which provides for the early setting of a tentative date of release based on factors known at the time of commitment (offense severity and risk assessment) with provision for the modification of that release date based on factors of significance which become known during the period of confinement (e.g., retardation for disciplinary infractions; advancement for exceptionally positive accomplishments). Furthermore, the system is designed to contain sufficient structure to provide consistent decisionmaking for similarly situated offenders, yet to be flexible enough to accommodate significant differences among individual offenders.

---

18.   28 C.F.R. §§ 2.14(a)(2)(ii) and 2.28(a) (1981).

11

Supervision in Probation and Parole

Probation and parole conditions are imposed primarily to furnish a means of controlling the offender's conduct during the supervision period. Whether the probation or parole period becomes anything more than a mere interim of law observances and minimum good behavior depends upon the degree and quality of supervision that is exercised by the probation or parole officer.

In its simplest terms, supervision may be defined as the oversight that an officer exercises over those committed to his or her custody. Whether, in practice, it becomes more meaningful than mere oversight depends upon many conditions. Few offenders can be expected to transform themselves into law-abiding citizens without some degree of assistance.

Probation or parole cannot, moreover, become a constructive force in the administration of criminal justice if supervision amounts only to discipline that is directed toward holding in check antisocial tendencies during the period of probation or parole. Merely observing conditions or lack of arrests for new offenses does not indicate an offender has changed for the better.

It is the element of *constructive* supervision that places the concepts of probation and parole beyond the definition of either leniency or punishment.

In 1939 the authors of The Attorney General's Survey of Release Procedures defined supervision as follows:

> In the conventional attitudes of the criminal law, it is a form of punishment, but the purpose back of it is reformative, reconstructive, and educational; to use a scientific term, it is therapeutic.[1]

Supervision, in more modern terms, might be defined as planned guidance based upon a careful study of the needs, problems, capabilities, and limitations

---

1. Att'y Gen. Survey, vol. 2, Probation, 261.

of the client. It utilizes all available community resources—social, educational, recreational, and religious—to aid offenders to change their patterns of behavior and become law abiding citizens.

Supervising the probation or parole client must be goal oriented, and directed toward removing or reducing individual and social barriers that may result in recidivism.

Judging by the practices followed and the results achieved in some of the more highly developed probation or parole agencies throughout the country, it can safely be said that probation or parole supervision is capable of accomplishing the social reintegration and adjustment of many offenders. Carrying out a supervisory process that can accomplish this end is an extraordinarily difficult task. Since supervision deals with variable and unpredictable human nature, much of its application must be by trial and error, but it need not be purposeless or planless.

RELATIONSHIPS IN SUPERVISION

Offenders can be dealt with effectively if on an individual basis and according to their special conditions and needs. Much of the effectiveness of supervision depends upon the personal relationship between the officer and the offender, and for this reason the prescribed qualifications for probation and parole officers, while necessary to maintain service of professional caliber, do not constitute the entire equipment of a good probation or parole officer. Without the element of human understanding, the highly educated and trained probation officer will fail because a purely scientific outlook tends to see the individual, not as an individual who is measurably unique, but as a "case" that has resulted from the intertwined effects of many causal factors.

While specific and generally reliable techniques of supervision have been developed, their successful application demands tact, sympathy, and understanding on the part of the officer. The officer cannot be controlled by sentiment and cannot function merely as a policeman. An officer who employs harsh and repressive methods and who holds an attitude of distrust and suspicion can only hinder constructive relationships and thus the potential for the offender's successful adjustment in the community.

While an offender under supervision must accept the structure and control inherent in his or her status as probationer and parolee, an offender cannot be expected to respond readily to the suggestions and plans of an officer who harbors only attitudes of dislike and distrust toward the offender. The relationship established, while one of respect, should be, when possible, amicable. The authoritative nature of the relationship should be made clear to the offender, but the predominating spirit should be one of encouragement and helpfulness. With admonition and firmness should also go tact and understanding.

However, the custodial or enforcement aspect of the officer's duties cannot be overlooked. Probation and parole is expected to provide a means of ascertaining whether those released under its oversight live up to the conditions imposed by the court or the parole board. The officer must supply not only a guiding and helping hand, but also a watchful eye. The officer cannot allow the offender to drop out of sight by the simple expedient of changing an address; it is the officer's duty to know the whereabouts and conduct of his or her charges at all times, and failure to maintain proper vigilance can only bring the officer and the system into disrepute. Furthermore, an officer's failure to require the offender to adhere to the terms of release complicates the officer's task. Supervision cannot exist in a lax, haphazard manner without arousing the contempt of the offender. In addition, public support and cooperation are difficult to obtain for any probation or parole system that does not assure the community of at least minimum protection against renewed criminal activities on the part of those under supervision. The discipline required for this purpose need not amount to police surveillance, but rather a discriminating oversight calculated to achieve the safety of the community without unduly restricting or harassing the offender.

It is not expected that the role of any probation or parole officer can be spread so thinly as to require the officer to be all things to all persons. The officer must be considered as an analyst and organizer, prepared to draw upon all the vocational, educational, recreational, medical, and social resources in the community to assist in the task of rehabilitation and reintegration.

The Probation and Parole Officer as a Manager of Resources

In an era of diminishing resources, we must recognize that the organization of services for offenders requires fundamental restructuring in the way its services are delivered. Organizational patterns that are based on the notion of a single officer attempting to provide all the necessary services to the offender is a narrow and outdated concept doomed to failure.[2] The National Advisory Commission states:

> To obtain these resources, available parole staff must gear their attention to other community service agencies and develop greater competence in acting as resource managers as well as counselors. A parole staff has a specific task: to assist offenders in availing themselves of community resources and to counsel them regarding their obligations. The staff must take responsibility for finding needed resources in the community for those under their supervision.[3]

IDENTIFYING NEEDS OF OFFENDERS

Proper supervision in a probation or parole system must be initiated by determining the needs of the target group. This assessment of needs must be ongoing because needs change. An inventory of needs should be developed by involving offenders in the identification process rather than relying solely on

---

2. Nat'l Advisory Comm'n Report on Corrections, (1973), 431.

3. *Id.*

probation or parole staff to identify what it believes the problems are. More specifically, the National Advisory Commission has specified what it believes is required for this assessment to be accomplished:

1. Knowledge of the target group in terms of such factors as age, race, education, employment, family status, and availability of transportation.

2. Identification of what services the offender most wants and needs to remove individual and social barriers.

3. Identification of services available and conditions under which they can be obtained.

4. Determination of which needed and wanted services do not exist or are inadequate.[4]

From such an assessment of needs, problem areas can be highlighted and priorities determined. This process makes it possible to specify how the various identified needs are to be met, whether they are to be met directly through the probation system or through other social institutions. The process also allows the number or percentage of the target group to be determined, the period of time to be established, and the purpose to be clearly identified. Specifying objectives provides a means of evaluating whether the system is able to accomplish what it sets out to achieve. If an objective is not met, the basis for pinpointing possible reasons is provided.[5]

Differentiating Internal and External Services

Direct probation services should be defined clearly and differentiated from services that can be met by other social institutions.

Needs of probationers related to employment, training, housing, health, and so forth are the responsibility of social institutions other than probation and parole agencies and should be provided by those institutions.

Employment is an example. Some probation and parole agencies have created positions of job developers or vocational counselors. The system should not attempt to duplicate services that are already available in the community, but rather should work to enable the offender to take full advantage and receive assistance from such social institutions as state and private employment commissions. The responsibility of the probation and parole agency in this area is to aid offenders in cutting through the barriers often barring or restricting them from using available services, and to monitor and evaluate those services to insure that they are, in fact, being provided and that they meet the specified objective.[6]

The traditional concept of the probation and parole officer serving as a sole treatment agent no longer meets the needs of either the criminal justice system or the offender. The goals of most probation and parole agencies can better be carried out where the officer becomes a community resource manager. This

---

4. *Id.* at 320–325.

5. *Id.* at 321.

6. *Id.*

means that the officer will have the primary responsibility of meshing an offender's needs with a range of available services and supervising the delivery of those services. This change in role and responsibility should enable the probation and parole officer to have a greater impact upon those individuals under the officer's supervision. As a community resource manager, the officer can utilize a wide range of free sources rather than act as the sole provider of services—a role that until now has been an impossible one to fulfill.

THE WORKING PHILOSOPHY OF THE PROBATION AND PAROLE OFFICER

Klockars found that the broadest component of the concept of probation supervision is the role that officers set for themselves and the logic and rationale they develop to explain what they do or what they ought to do. He developed a typology of probation officers that falls roughly between the polar concepts of "probation is not casework" and "probation is casework." His typology revealed four basic roles: [7]

1. *The law enforcers.* At the "probation is not casework" pole, we find officers who stress the legal authority and enforcement aspects of their position. One may find officers at this pole with philosophies that dictate firmness, authority, and rule abidance as essentials of social life. Of prime importance to such officers is (a) the court order; (b) authority, and (c) decision-making power.

2. *The time servers.* Time-serving officers are nearly the functional equivalent of the law enforcers. They see their jobs as having certain requirements to be fulfilled until their retirement and they have little aspiration to improve their skills. Their conduct on the job is to abide by the rules and their job responsibilities are met minimally but methodically. Rules and regulations are upheld but unexamined. They don't make the rules; they just work there.

3. *The therapeutic agent.* At the other pole are officers who consider themselves as therapeutic agents. Their role is emphasized in administering a form of treatment, introducing the probationer or parolee to a better way of life, and motivating patterns of behavior that are constructive. They give guidance and support to those who are unable to solve their problems by themselves and provide them an opportunity to work through their ambivalent feelings. The philosophy of the therapeutic agent may be summarized as follows:

    (1) We take conscious pains in our every contact with offenders to demonstrate our concern about them and our respect for them as human beings.

    (2) We seize every opportunity to help offenders come to understand the nature of the shared, problem solving, helping process by actually experiencing it.

    (3) We recognize, bring into the open, and deal directly with offenders' negative attitudes toward us and as the representatives of social authority.

7. Carl B. Klockars, Jr., *Journal of Criminal Law, Criminology and Police Science,* vol. 63, no. 4 (1974).

(4) We partialize the total life problem confronting offenders.

(5) We help individuals perceive the degree to which their behavior has and will result in their own unhappiness.

4. *The synthetic officer.* The fourth and final officer type in Klockars's typology is distinguished by his recognition of both the treatment and law enforcement components of probation officers' roles. Their attempts at supervision reflect their desire to satisfy the arguments of both the therapeutic and law-enforcing agents. Thus, they set for themselves the active task of combining the paternal, authoritarian, and judgmental with the therapeutic. Theirs is a treatment-controlled dilemma; one that is found throughout the field of corrections.

From the foregoing, it is obvious that probation and parole supervision is a multifaceted problem that depends to a great extent not only upon the quality of administrative organization and the educational and experience qualifications of the officers, but also—and to a great degree, more importantly—upon the way in which the officers view their job and their role within the system.

Other Factors Influencing Supervision.

In 1939 the Attorney General's Survey of Release Procedures stated, "Both the scope of the supervisory process and the character of the oversight given are influenced directly by the number of probationers placed in the custody of the individual supervising agent. The larger the number of probationers assigned to a single officer, the more he must depend upon purely mechanical means of supervision." [8] That report recommended a caseload of fifty units as a desirable goal. This figure is still the standard.

More recent studies have addressed the question of how increasing or decreasing case-load size impacts the performance of probationers and parolees under supervision. Two of these studies are of particular interest in our discussion of supervision.

The SIPU Study

The California Division of Adult Parole developed a research project known as the Special Intensive Parole Unit (SIPU).[9] This unit set up case loads of fifteen men in experimental groups paired with regular case loads of ninety men in controlled groups. The fifteen-man case loads were supervised closely and intensely for the first three months after release—presumably the most vulnerable months for failure. After three months, these intensive case load parolees were reassigned to regular ninety-man case loads. After reviewing the progress of the parolees in the experimental groups, the data did not show that fifteen-man intensive supervision units were superior to ninety-man case loads.

Subsequent SIPU projects utilized thirty-man case loads for periods of six months; thirty-five-man case loads for twelve months, and thirty-man case loads for twenty-four months respectively. The project as a whole did not

8. *Att'y Gen. Survey, Probation, supra,* at 310.

9. Stuart Adams, *Some Findings from Correctional Caseload Research,* Federal Probation (December 1967).

show significant results on the part of intensive case loads as opposed to standard case loads.[10]

The San Francisco Project

In a study of federal probation in the northern district of California, an attempt was made to determine the relative effectiveness of minimum, regular, ideal, and intensive case loads.[11]

The minimum case load, nominally the largest in size, called for reporting by mail and service upon demand.

The regular case load contained eighty-five persons. The ideal caseload was a fifty-unit work load, and the intensive case load was twenty-five units.

New probationers were assigned randomly to these various case loads. At the end of two years, the performance on the minimum cases was not significantly different from that of the regular load. The regular and ideal case loads showed violation rates of 22 percent and 24 percent respectively. The intensive case load had a violation rate of 38 percent. This inflated rate contained a high proportion of technical violations, presumably a consequence of the higher level of supervision provided. If technical violations were excluded from the analysis, there were no significant differences in violation rates between minimum, regular, ideal, and intensive case loads.

All of the studies conducted in case load size give point to one of the most frequently voiced criticisms of early research—the case loads were reduced but the supervising officers were not told or taught what to do with the extra time available to them. The conclusions drawn in the San Francisco project to explain why intensive supervision did not seem to reduce the rate of violation included the possibility that it is not the number of contacts but rather the quality of work that is vital. The authors stated, "If at the outset of supervision, a climate of trust and confidence is established, it seems more likely the clients will seek the assistance of a probation officer before permitting their personal adjustment to deteriorate to the point of probation or parole violation. No available evidence documents that routine contacts without goals will increase such a possibility. Clearly needed is a closer attention to understanding and measuring the quality, not the quantity of supervision.[12]

It should become apparent that the success of probation or parole supervision depends upon personal relationships and acquaintances brought about by the frequent contact of the client and the probation or parole officer. The officer must be able to study the client, to plan effective treatment for the client's rehabilitation, and to render practical service to that end. Of paramount importance is the necessity of developing an atmosphere of mutual respect and understanding.

---

10. *Id.* at 54.

11. Joseph V. Lohman, G. Albert Wahl and Robert M. Carter, *The San Francisco Project,* (Berkeley: University of California, April 1965).

12. William P. Adams, Paul M. Chandler and M.G. Neithercutt, Federal Probation (December 1971).

CASE LOAD CLASSIFICATION

It is safe to say that even the largest case loads should be so organized that at least most of those cases in particular need of assistance would find it forthcoming.

Most probation and parole agencies have established some form of case classification as a means of identifying the level of perceived risk posed by the offender, as a guide for allocating officer time, and as a measurement of work loads carried by officers, both individually and collectively. While various names are used to differentiate the levels of supervision, most are essentially restatements of the traditional maximum/medium/minimum supervision classes.

Some systems place almost all new cases in the highest supervision class. Others categorize primarily in terms of seriousness of the committed offense and length of prior record, or occasionally, the kind and extent of services required. Practically all systems specify a schedule of contact requirements for each classification. Unfortunately, such contacts are almost universally described in terms of their number (i.e., per month or other time interval) or the type and location (i.e., home, office, telephone, or collateral). Few reveal the quality or content of the contact.

In most instances, the work plan optimistically looks toward gradual reduction of the level of supervision if the client manages to avoid further transgressions of rules or laws (or at least avoids apprehension for any transgressions). In many instances, the final or minimum level amounts to no supervision or a level of assistance other than that specifically requested by the client or made necessary by rearrest.

While most classification processes provide some reasonably objective though generalized guidelines for initial category assignment, none of those observed processes extend such guidelines to the reclassification process. There, passage of time and avoidance of violation are supplemented by the subjective hunches of the field officer or first-line supervisor to carry out a status change.

1. *Suggested strategy.* Case classification should be perceived as the initial phase of case management planning. Specific objectives to be achieved by the offender and the agency should be identified. Ideally, such planning should involve the investigating officer, the officer responsible for case supervision, the first-line supervisor, any specialist involved in the case assessment, and the offender.

Case classifications should also determine control requirements, treatment needs, and the administrative categorization of the case. *Control requirements* can include placing restrictions on movement, residence, and associations; on frequency of contact with the probation or parole officer; or on reporting requirements. *Treatment needs* often arise concerning employment, training, education, residence, and finances; and specific problems such as counseling and guidance to address drug or alcohol abuse, or treatment of any other psychological or emotional inconsistencies. The *administrative categorization* of the case generally involves the extent and nature of time to be allocated by staff, possible assignment of the offender to a specification of the degree of perceived risk posed by the offender. In this classification, it is essential to identify strategies and resources to meet the offender's needs.

Classification is an ongoing process. It should provide for periodic review (probably quarterly) of actions initiated and completed by both the offender and the agency. Reviews provide opportunity for reclassification or change of plan as indicated by changing circumstances or reassessments of needs for control and treatment. Achievement of defined objectives should trigger a reduction in controls and restraints, as well as staff time invested, and should look toward the earliest possible release from supervision that is also consistent with public safety.

Developing specific objective norms or guidelines for categorizing risk and intensity of supervision can permit more consistent handling of cases and provide a more rational basis for determining staff time requirements. The development and consistent use of a logical classification process provides a basis for rational management of probation or parole case loads and is a prerequisite for determining the numbers and kinds of staff and other resources needed.

Classification of case load or work load is ideally a management tool to aid in setting priorities within the agency and case load. Classification, then, is an aid to effective supervision rather than a substitute for it. It is not like a crystal ball in terms of having an ability to accurately predict an individual's future behavior. However, it does enable an officer to quickly and consistently get a handle on an individual case with only limited information, and to focus on the degree to which an individual's behavior fits a behavioral profile that corresponds to a prescribed level of supervision. The initial assessment is then expanded by a more detailed supervision plan that is regularly reassessed and modified.

In addition to assisting officers in identifying needs and risks, a classification system should provide a rationale for deploying agency resources and enabling administrators to make efficient use of them.

Wisconsin pioneered the development of a comprehensive classification and case management system. Many parole and probation agencies have adopted the Wisconsin system wholly or in part, and the National Institute of Corrections (NIC) chose the system as the model for probation and parole agencies. The components of the Wisconsin system are:

• Classification based on risk of continued criminal activity and the offender's need for services.

• A parallel case management classification system designed to help officers develop effective case plans and select appropriate casework strategies.

• A management information system designed to enhance planning, monitoring, education, and accountability.

• A work load system to allow an agency to equitably, effectively, and efficiently allocate limited resources.

CLASSIFICATION SYSTEM

Four levels of supervision are used—maximum, medium, minimum, and mail-in—with requirements varying from two contacts per month to receipt of a monthly report by mail. The risk and needs assessment forms the core of system, as it determines the level of supervision for each client.

Within thirty days of admission to probation or parole, all cases are assessed according to their need for services and their risk of the offender committing a new offense. Reclassification is then done at subsequent six-month intervals. At reclassification, the emphasis shifts from prior criminal history items to measures that reflect adjustment during supervision. This allows clients to move between supervision levels based upon their performance.

Although the assessment of risk and needs provides a measure of the client's propensity to further criminal activity, it is also an indication of the amount of agent intervention required to deal with a client's problem. It can determine the *level* of supervision for each client, but does not address the question of supervision strategy.

Case Management

An officer often needs considerable experience with a client to formulate an appropriate casework strategy. This can create problems when dealing with involuntary clients where time is often limited, and the first few months of supervision are often critical to achieving successful completion of probation and parole. Therefore, a method that would reduce time required to develop casework strategies would be beneficial. To this end, the Wisconsin model includes a process (termed client-management classification) that consists of a forty-five-minute semistructured interview and utilizes a forced-choice rating instrument. Four groups of clients are identified, based on supervision techniques used in working with each. Such techniques indicate the following:

1. Selective Intervention
2. Casework/Control
3. Environmental Structuring
4. Limit Setting

This classification process helps officers anticipate the behavior and problems clients may present and provides recommendations for dealing with each type of client. It does not contribute to the assignment of a level of supervision; it deals generally with how a particular client can best be supervised and does not specifically deal with the amount of supervision needed. Maximum, medium, and minimum supervision clients may be found in all four client-management classification categories.

Management Information System

A unique feature of the Wisconsin program was the use of classification data as an integral part of the management information system.

The information system contains data collected on probationers and parolees at admission, at reevaluation and at termination. A comprehensive client profile is completed for each offender at the time of admission to probation or parole. Data collected at reevaluation and termination are then merged with admission data, providing a before, during. and after record of each client.

Analysis of data falls into three categories: routine reports to management, evaluation of the system, and answers to special requests. Comprehensive periodic reports are prepared for various levels of management, and these are used to identify trends, project populations, examine usage of community resources, and plan future purchase of service priorities.

Workload Computation

As we have stated, the traditional "ideal case load" of fifty units has not been empirically found to be valid. Many administrators have maintained that any standard client-to-agent ratio is an inadequate method of staff deployment because it assumes that all other work loads are distributed equally. The number and difficulty of presentence reports written by a probation officer, the number of drug or alcohol offenders, or the geographic distribution of a case load all mitigate against standardized case load size. One author, while employed as a United States probation officer in west Texas during the early 1970s, supervised a case load dispersed geographically from San Antonio to Midland, Texas, a distance of over 300 miles one way. A colleague in New York City could visit his entire case load within the confines of twelve city blocks. A case load consisting primarily of drug addicts differs greatly from one involving white-collar tax evaders or violators of Securities and Exchange Commission rules.

A classification system is designed to identify differences in offenders that will have an impact on the amount of supervision required. It is then possible to ascertain the total work load of probation or parole officers rather than the total caseload.[13]

Wisconsin Model in Summary

Recently, the National Institute of Corrections (NIC) modified the Wisconsin system by adding objective-based case planning to the supervision process. This technique sets specific behavioral objectives for each client to accomplish during an explicit time frame. Currently, NIC is involved with implementing this "model system" in various jurisdictions around the country for supervising clients in the community. This system represents the state of the art in probation and parole supervision.[14]

The Case Record and Case Recording

An essential aspect of supervision is maintaining an accurate and valid case record through chronological entries. The case record may be defined as a

---

13. Much of the foregoing discussion of the Wisconsin model is based upon articles in the professional literature by S. Christopher Baird, particularly, *Probation and Parole Classification: The Wisconsin Model*, Corrections Today (May-June 1981).

14. Kenneth W. Gallagher, *The Generalizability of the Wisconsin Case Management Model* (Paper presented to the Academy of Criminal Justice Sciences, San Antonio, Texas, 1983).

conveniently organized and readily accessible accumulation of all data that relates to the study and treatment of offenders. It constitutes a permanent file of pertinent information that the probation or parole officer has gathered in a preliminary investigation and during supervision of the client. The record should reflect the progress of probationers or parolees from the time of their first contact until the period of supervision is terminated. This record should contain the kind of information that will help the officer determine the problems and needs of probationers, to determine what types of services and help is required, and to evaluate the results of the service rendered. Information about family relations, religious interest and expression, health, education, finances, employment, and the character and personality of a client, as well as about the client's attitudes and outlook in general, is essential in developing a program of reintegration and change. The quality of the work of the probation and parole officer in its overall plan in helping the client is reflected in the facts, observations, and situations that the officer has documented in the narrative record.

Each entry should give 1) the purpose, nature and circumstances of the contact and the action taken; 2) the problems and needs of the probationer or parolee at the time of the interview, how the probationer or parolee is affected by them, and how they are being met; 3) the specific action taken to help resolve the client's needs, 4) an evaluation of the progress or success achieved as a result of earlier contacts, and 5) any modification in the treatment plan in order to cope with the changing needs of the client.

The probation or parole officer should record as objectively and as accurately as possible what transpired during the interplay of the personalities of the officer and the client, what decisions were reached and in what manner, and what accomplishments were achieved.

Objective and accurate recording of the client's emotional makeup, attitudes, wishes, desires, aspirations, prejudices, likes and dislikes, predispositions, conflicts, and sense of values is essential to understanding the client's problems and needs. Skills in observation, enrichment of vocabulary, and clarity of expression are requisites in recording these relatively subjective elements of the probationer or parolee's character and personality.

Periodic evaluations of the case record should be made. The periodic summary encourages the officer to give diagnostic thinking to his or her work and to reflect on the progress of the case. It is particularly useful in cases under supervision for periods of a year or more and is helpful in gaining a quick summary of the case. A periodic summary should show what actions have been attempted but failed, what has been accomplished, and what plan for the future is indicated.

SUMMARY AND CONCLUSIONS

The most vital aspect of probation and parole as a process in the criminal justice system is supervision. In its simplest terms, supervision is the oversight that is exercised over those who have been placed on probation or parole. Only a supervisory process that is, in effect, highly individualized and purposefully reconstructive can meet the needs of an adequate probation or parole system. The personality, training, and experience of the supervising officer in a large manner determines the adequacy of the process. Lax supervision and failure to deal firmly with those who persistently violate the terms of release can only bring an entire system into disrepute. Adequate probation or parole supervision must deal with all phases of the offender's life including the offender's family and the community in which the offender lives. Although there is controversy as to the value and propriety of many specific techniques of supervision, all recognize the usefulness of a plan of treatment based upon the needs, capacities, and limitations of each offender. The physical and mental health, capacities, and limitations of the offender; the offender's home and family, his leisure time activities, education, vocational training, economic status and work habits, as well as the offender's capacity for discipline and self-control must all be considered by those who are attempting to aid the offender in becoming a law-abiding citizen.

In order to deal affirmatively with all aspects of the probationer or parolee's life that require aid, the officer cannot act entirely alone. The officer must, whenever possible, endeavor to secure the assistance and cooperation of community agencies and facilities. Responsibility for securing the assistance and monitoring and evaluating the results of these agencies rests with the probation and parole officer. This is an indispensable part of an officer's duty, and where it is neglected the officer's work will remain unsatisfactory.

Probation and parole supervision necessitate frequent and continuous contact between the offender and the officer. This contact should be based upon a positive relationship of mutual respect and trust, the willingness of the officer to see his or her role as being a multi-faceted one, not a singularly therapeutic or enforcement-oriented one.

Good probation service is not easily accomplished where officers are compelled to handle too many cases. A case load of fifty offenders per officer for supervision has been suggested as desirable; however research has indicated that work load, based upon a properly classified case load, should be the factor determining the ratio of clients to agent.

Our discussion of supervision in probation and parole may be summarized by paraphrasing from the American Bar Association's project on Standards for Criminal Justice, Standards Relating to Probation:

"The basic idea underlying probation and parole is to help the offender learn to live productively in the community that has been offended.[15]"

---

15. American Bar Association Project on Standards in Criminal Justice, Standards Relating to Probation, approved draft (1970) 1.

Parole Supervision and Services*

PAROLE SUPERVISION

Besides facing a different adjudication system if accused of a new crime, a parolee is subjected to a system of supervision which supposedly will make him more likely to lead a law-abiding life. Parole conditions regulate conduct which is not criminal in itself, but is thought linked with possible future criminality. To ensure compliance with these conditions, a parole agent is assigned to and maintains contact with the parolee. Violation of any condition—even in the absence of a new substantive criminal offense by the parolee—is grounds for revocation of parole and reimprisonment.

Does Supervision Work?

The ostensible purpose of parole supervision is preventive: to reduce the likelihood of further law violations by the parolee. Given this purpose, there are threshold criteria concerning whether supervision works, that must be satisfied before even a *prima facie* case for this device can be made.

One such criterion may be called *"rationality."* It requires that parole conditions be reasonably and directly related to the prevention of future crimes by the parolee. If the aim is to encourage law-abiding behavior, the means—namely, the conditions and techniques of parole supervision—should be rationally suited to that aim. Before parolees may be subjected to behavior constraints not applicable to the general population, the burden should lie on the state to give specific reasons why the behavior is linked to recidivism.

Even the most rational-seeming condition may fail when tested, however. Thus a second criterion should be empirical evidence of effectiveness. If, for example, parolees are to be routinely required to seek and hold jobs, however plausible that may seem as an incentive for law-abiding behav-

---

* From Andrew von Hirsch and Kathleen J. Hanrahan, *Abolish Parole?* Law Enforcement Assistance Administration, U.S. Department of Justice (Washington, D.C., 1978). Footnotes omitted. Reprinted with permission of the U.S. Department of Justice.

ior, there should be empirical confirmation that former prisoners do offend at a lower rate when subjected to this condition.

The rationality criterion would call much of present day supervision practice into question. Many of the conditions of parole have little or no perceptible relevance to criminal behavior. Periodic visits between the parole agent and the parolee—the mainstay of parole supervision—customarily are brief and superficial. Little effort is made to verify in any systematic fashion what kind of behavior in the community is, in fact, connected with future criminality and to relate parole conditions to such behavior. And, treatment programs are seldom made available to parole agents who wish to refer their charges to treatment.

The effectiveness of parole is also open to question. A number of studies have compared the recidivism rates of parolees with those of offenders released at expiration of sentence. Some of these are inconclusive because they do not control for possible differences in the selection of the two groups. (The parolees may have recidivated less often not because of any virtues of supervision, but because the parole board has selected the better risks for release on parole.) A few studies do attempt to control for such differences in selection. Of these, some report favorable results, others less favorable (albeit mixed) results.

The research is too scanty and its results are too equivocal to warrant the inference that supervision succeeds—at lease, if the burden of proving success rests on the proponents of supervision, as we think it should. Since there have been so few studies, it is possible that further empirical inquiry might show success, or at least, success among certain selected subcategories of offenders. But that is not what can be concluded now.

Were further research to yield positive results, empirical data on what specific components of the supervision accounted for the outcome would also be necessary. It is

possible, for example, that any successes are due to the lower standard of proof in revocation proceedings: e.g., parolees may be more reluctant to risk new crimes because they can be reimprisoned more easily. This would be a troublesome result because, as we pointed out in the previous section, a low standard of proof—whatever its usefulness as an inducement to law abiding behavior—entails greater danger of penalizing the innocent.

Is Supervision Just?
—Desert Constraints

Can supervision be squared with the requirements of desert? Although preventive in aim, supervision is unpleasant, and so we must ask whether it enhances the severity of the punishment in ways prohibited by the commensurate-deserts principle.

In assessing supervision, one should distinguish between (1) the contribution of supervision *per se* to severity, and (2) the contribution of the revocation sanction. Supervision may not (depending upon its content) enhance severity by much; and any such enhancement in severity could, in any event, be offset by appropriately scaling down the duration of the original confinement. Revocation, on the other hand, presents the following, more serious difficulty.

Revocation can result in substantial periods of reimprisonment, although no new criminal act has been committed. (Not all revocations result in lengthy terms, of course. But the potential exists, since the parolee can be reconfined, at the board's discretion, until his sentence expires.) As a result of revocation, offenders sentenced for the same original crime and serving initial terms of the same duration ultimately may serve very disparate terms of confinement, depending on whether or not they are reimprisoned for parole violations that are not in themselves criminal acts. And the additional confinement can render the total punishment inflicted disproportionately severe in relation to the seriousness of the original crime. This objection holds not only under the strict Desert Model, but under the Modified Desert Model as well. The latter, as we saw, permits a limited amount of variation from deserved severity for crime-control ends, and this could conceivably allow a modest amount of added confinement. But revocation could involve a *large* amount of extra imprisonment.

We have spoken only of whether the revocation sanction can be justified as deserved for the original offense. But might not the sanction be defended instead as a penalty deserved for the parole violation itself? If a parole condition is imposed as part of one's punishment ᶠor a crime, why shouldn't the flouting of that requirement be deserving of extra punishment? There are two reasons why this argument will not sustain parole revocation:

• *Standards of liability and proof.* A willful refusal to abide by the terms of supervision might, perhaps, be defined as a new crime, as escape is now declared a crime. But then, the parolee would be entitled to demand a full trial, in which proof beyond a reasonable doubt and other procedural safeguards would apply. These safeguards are missing when a parolee is reimprisoned through a revocation hearing.

• *Severity of the revocation penalty.* Even were parole violations declared crimes, they would not deserve severe punishment unless they can be shown to be serious. Yet how reprehensible are technical parole violations? There is no immediate injury to others, such as occurs when the parolee commits most ordinary crimes. The parolee is not "getting away with" substantially less punishment than he deserves for his original crime—as occurs in prison escapes—since he has largely paid the price for that crime already, through his sojourn in prison before being released on parole. Of course, it is difficult to give a definitive rating to such

conduct in the absence of a fuller theory of what constitutes seriousness. But on these common-sense grounds alone, we would be skeptical of claims that a parole violation is so blameworthy in itself as to deserve the long durations of reconfinement that parole revocation potentially entails.

Try to Reform Supervision?

If the severity of the revocation sanction creates the problem, could supervision be salvaged by scaling down that sanction? Would supervision, thus reformed, meet the desert requirements? And could it be effective, with such limited sanctions? The answers depend on which of the two models—Desert or Modified Desert—one chooses.

On a Modified Desert Model: Here, modest backup sanctions would be permissible. Even if such sanctions are viewed as deviations from the amount of the deserved punishment for the original offense, this model expressly allows such deviations, provided their extent is limited.

Effectiveness could, however, become more difficult to achieve. Through the revocation sanction, parole can now operate as a method of incapacitation: parolees who seem headed for new crimes can be taken out of circulation. Using parole supervision in this manner requires only that one identify empirically which kinds of behavior after release are indicative of enhanced risk of recidivism. If one limits the power to reconfine parole violators, however, supervision will have to change from an incapacitative to a rehabilitative technique: it will have to be capable of rendering parolees more law-abiding while they remain in the community. The task becomes the harder one of changing behavior, not just forecasting it.

We are, therefore, not optimistic about the prospects of success. The question of effectiveness can only be resolved, however, by empirical research. The research should examine not only the effect of supervision of recidivism rates, but also a second factor: cost. Parole supervision is unquestionably an expensive process, but little is known about how expensive it is, where the greatest costs lie, and how much money could be saved through elimination of needless procedures. Even if supervision were shown to have some effect on recidivism, it is important to consider whether those effects are sufficiently great to warrant the expense.

On a Desert Model. By requiring strict adherence to the commensurate deserts principle, this model would, in our opinion, rule out parole supervision, even with modest sanctions for parole violations.

Such sanctions could not be justified as part of the deserved punishment for the original offense, since they would impose on violators an added amount of punishment not suffered by nonviolators whose original crimes were of equal seriousness. Treating the violation itself as deserving of punishment is likewise problematic—since ordinarily, only *crimes* are punishable acts.

Keep Supervision
Under Other Models?

Were someone to reject our desert-oriented models of justice, how would the conclusions differ?

One could no longer object to the potentially severe revocation sanction as undeserved. A more utilitarian sentencing philosophy might permit the added severity of parole revocation, if useful in reducing recidivism.

But there remains the question of the effectiveness of conventional parole supervision. For the past 75 years, supervision has been routinely imposed, with negligible efforts to ascertain its effectiveness and cost. At least, this institution should be forced to undergo a period of rigorous testing, and should be discontinued if its utility is not demonstrated. One way this could be accomplished would be by setting a "sunset" date: existing authority to supervise would be made to expire in (say) 5 years. During that period parole agencies would be expected to devote much of their resources to the empirical testing of supervision methods (both as to effectiveness and cost). At the end of the period, the results would be evaluated, and unless substantial positive results emerged, the authority to supervise should be terminated.

Were supervision so tested, we venture to guess that if it survives at all, it will emerge with much smaller dimensions than it has today. Conceivably, supervision could be found effective (and worth its expense) for certain carefully selected categories of offenders. But we would be surprised if this elaborate and costly process needs to be imposed on all released offenders.

During the period of testing (and afterward, to the extent supervision survives), guidelines would also be needed. They should specify such matters as the type of intensity of supervision, the types of violations warranting reimprisonment rather than lesser sanctions and the duration of imprisonment upon revocation. This could help somewhat in reducing disparities in handling similarly situated parole violators.

SERVICES TO PAROLEES

Even if parole supervision is abolished or restricted, there remains the question of providing services to ex-prisoners. Imprisonment severs many of the prisoner's links to the outside world. When released, he will have to reestablish these links, and that will be made harder by the stigma of his criminal record. Furlough and work-release programs may ease this process somewhat, by providing the prisoner a "halfway out" status for a time before he leaves prison. But it will still be a difficult transition. The problems encountered by recently-released prisoners have been cataloged by a number of researchers. Not surprisingly, most report that the most pressing needs are material: financial aid, housing, employment, and obtaining credentials.

Provision of services has been one of the supposed functions of parole supervision. However, the services tend to be rudimentary, since the parole agent seldom has any resources for assistance at his disposal. Moreover, the helping and policing functions tend to conflict. It has thus been suggested that services could better be performed were they made the sole focus of the state's involvement after the prisoner's release. This would, it is said, allow more resources to be put into the provision of services, by freeing those now devoted to trying to control supervisees. And it could make ex-prisoners less reluctant to accept the help offered, because assistance would be separated from enforcement.

Which Objective: Crime Control or Help? In speaking earlier of programs for offenders, we were referring to those that were rehabilitative in the conventional sense: that is, those whose objective was to reduce participants' rate of return to crime. The criterion for success was whether individuals enrolled in the program recidivated less often than similar samples of nonparticipants.

It is sometimes claimed that voluntary services would succeed better in this rehabilitative task. This claim would have to be tested empirically, but hopes for much success may be disappointed. Those volunteering for treatment programs may well be the best risks: those who might not recidivate even without programs. Moreover, it is not merely compulsion that tends to interfere with treatment, but more fundamental problems such as the lack of understanding of the causes of criminal behavior.

We think service programs should, instead, seek a different goal: helping ex-prisoners reestablish a tolerable life for themselves in the community. The criterion of success would not be recidivism control, but the programs' ability to alleviate suffering and disorientation among ex-inmates. Programs for ex-prisoners would thus be judged as social service.

Meeting the Needs. The services for releasees should include provision of financial support during the difficult first weeks after the offender leaves prison; job placement and job training services, aid in locating housing; and "status clearance" services such as assistance in obtaining credentials, and psychological counseling.

When should assistance be provided? Many authorities report that the period of greatest stress for releasees is the weeks and months immediately following release. Priority should be given to providing assistance during this difficult early period. More specific answers about timing depend on the particular needs involved. A few are quite short-term and could be met through furlough or other prerelease programs—status clearance being an example. Most services, however, may have to continue for a time after release.

Parole systems now have a staff of parole agents working to carry out the traditional supervision function. If the recommendations of the last section were adopted, these agents may have little or no supervision left to do. Could the agents assume the service-providing function?

At present, the parole agency has few services at its disposal. However, the services could be obtained by having the parole agency contract for them with specialized community agencies. Then the individual agent could act as a broker or "resource manager." He would inform his clients of the available resources, channel them to the program of choice, and followup to insure that the parolee receives the service. The agent could also act as a conduit to any programs offered to members of the community generally, such as welfare or adult education programs.

What remains to be seen is how well the parole agency and its agents would be suited to this new function. Parole agents have not been trained in locating and arranging social services and many tend to view their role as chiefly law enforcement. Whether this change of mission could successfully be accomplished, and what retraining programs and other steps would be needed for the change, can be determined only by experimenting.

Voluntary or Compulsory Services? If the ex-prisoner does not wish to accept the services, should there be any penalty for refusal? We think not, for both pragmatic and moral reasons.

One objection concerns how participation could be policed if it were made obligatory. Because offenders would be living in the community rather than in the controlled environment of a prison, procedures would have to be developed for monitoring participation, reasserting control over nonparticipants, and imposing penalties—in short, something akin to a miniature system of supervision. As such a system of enforcement expands, the agency offering the services is likely to find its energies increasingly absorbed by administering the policing system, rather than providing services.

Compulsory services are questionable on moral grounds as well. We assign a high value to preserving the liberty of the individual. Given this goal, we think that forcing the ex-offender to accept services thought to be beneficial only (or primarily) to himself cannot be justified.

Our view, therefore, is that the services should be voluntary. They should be offered to any offender who needs them, but he should be free to reject them. Participation should not be made a condition of release, nor should there be penalties (even mild ones) for refusal.

12

Parole Conditions, Revocation and Discharge

CONDITIONS OF PAROLE

In General

The statutes may require that certain conditions be imposed upon parolees,[1] and typically they give the paroling authority the right to impose such other conditions "as it may deem proper." Usual conditions direct that upon release parolees will report to their parole supervisor, that they not change their county of residence without approval, that they work at gainful employment and support their dependents, that they make regular reports, that they refrain from the use of alcohol and narcotics, that they avoid association with former inmates of penal institutions and other individuals of bad character, that they obey all municipal, county, state, and federal laws and ordinances, that they conduct themselves as good citizens, and that they cooperate with their parole supervisor and the parole board.[2] Special conditions may prohibit the possession of firearms or the use of a motor vehicle.[3]

---

1. The Texas provision reads: * * * The Board may adopt such other reasonable rules not inconsistent with law as it may deem proper or necessary with respect to the eligibility of prisoners for parole, the conduct of parole hearings, or condition to be imposed upon parolees. Whenever an order for parole is issued it shall recite the conditions thereof in clear and intelligible language. * * Tex.Code Crim.Proc.Ann. art. 42.12, § 15 (Vernon).

The Board shall have the power and duty to make rules for the conduct of persons placed on parole by the Board. *Id.* at art. 42.12, § 20.

2. Model Penal Code, § 305.13.

See also N.Y.Correct.Law § 215 (McKinney).

3. Jones v. Allen, 185 Cal.App.2d 278, 8 Cal.Rptr. 316 (1960).

As in the case of probation conditions, the courts will uphold reasonable conditions but will strike down illegal conditions or those considered impossible to fulfill.[4] The courts also frown upon the imposition of unusual or exotic conditions. However, generally speaking, courts will uphold more stringent conditions imposed upon a parolee than upon a probationer. The reason is that the parolee is "constructively a prisoner of the state."[5] Another reason is that by accepting parole, a prisoner is deemed to have accepted the conditions and entered a form of contract with the state to comply with them.[6] For this reason, it is generally held that a prisoner may refuse parole if he or she does not want to accept the conditions.[7]

In addition to the usual conditions, the following conditions of parole have been upheld: that parolee forfeit good time credits on revocation;[8] that parolee obtain psychiatric care;[9] that an offender convicted of statutory rape and who was syphilitic be sterilized. The grounds were that it would prevent transmission of the venereal disease to his children.[10]

Conditions that have been struck down include a requirement that the parolee obtain permission from his parole officer before giving any public speech,[11] and banishment from the state.[12] A condition that has the effect of enlarging the sentence is illegal.[13] The standard condition that the released offender refrain from use of alcohol has been challenged in one case where a probationer claimed that he should have had a psychiatric examination, which would have disclosed that he was a chronic alcoholic and hence not responsible for his acts when he violated probation by drinking alcoholic beverages. The court stated that to impose such condition upon a person who could not keep it might amount to infliction of "cruel and unusual punishment."[14]

---

4. The tests applied to probation conditions in the case of People v. Dominguez, 236 Cal.App. 623, 64 Cal.Rptr. 290 (1967), are often cited as a proper measure of the reasonableness of parole conditions as well. The court said in that case that a condition of probation, which (1) has no relationship to the crime of which the offender was convicted; (2) relates to conduct which is not of itself criminal; and (3) requires or forbids conduct which is not reasonably related to future criminality, does not serve the statutory ends of probation and is invalid.

5. *Ex parte* Heckman, 90 Cal.App. 700, 266 P. 585 (1928).

6. *Ex parte* Peterson, 14 Cal.2d 82, 92 P.2d 890 (1939); Marshall v. Hiatt, 73 F.Supp. 471 (M.D.Pa.1947); People *ex rel.* Martin v. Martin, 266 App.Div. 695, 40 N.Y.S.2d 118 (1943); *Ex parte* Falconi, 22 Cal.App.2d 604, 71 P.2d 948 (1937); Richetti v. New York State Board of Parole, 300 N.Y.S. 357, 90 N.E.2d 893 (1950).

7. *Ex parte* Peterson, 14 Cal.2d 82, 92 P.2d 890 (1939).

8. *Ex parte* Borgfeldt, 75 Cal.App.2d 83, 170 P.2d 94 (1946).

9. People v. Ainsworth, 32 A.D.2d 839, 302 N.Y.S.2d 308 (1969).

10. People v. Blankenship, 16 Cal.App.2d 606, 61 P.2d 352 (1936).
The Youth Authority also is required to impose a condition that the paroled person totally abstain from the use of alcoholic liquor or beverages if he has been convicted of offenses enumerated in Cal.Penal Code § 290 (West) (certain sex offenses).

11. Hyland v. Procunier, 311 F.Supp. 749 (N.D.Cal.1970).

12. People v. Baum, 251 Mich. 187, 231 N.W. 95 (1930).

13. People ex rel. Ingenito v. Warden and Agent of Auburn Prison, 267 App.Div. 295, 46 N.Y.S.2d 72, aff'd 293 N.Y. 803, 59 N.E.2d 174 (1944).

14. Sweeney v. United States, 353 F.2d 10 (7th Cir.1965).

Rights of Parolees
During Parole Period

Parolees have a right to personal liberty so long as they comply with the conditions of parole. The California statute gives the Adult Authority the right to permit paroled persons all their civil rights except the right to act as a trustee, or hold public office, or exercise the privilege of an elector.[15]

It has been held that the premises of a parolee may be searched by his or her parole supervisor without a search warrant and without the parolee's consent.[16] Some states require that the parolee, as a condition of parole, give this permission. The condition has generally been upheld, although special problems arise when evidence of a new crime is obtained as a result of the search. In a New York case, a parole officer obtained a warrant charging the parolee with a violation; the officer went to the parolee's apartment and charged him with a parole rule violation. He then conducted a two-and-one-half hour search, which yielded narcotics. The parolee was convicted on the new charge, and the conviction was upheld. The court said:

> Defendant appellant, as a parolee, was deprived of no constitutional rights by the search and seizure which was made under the circumstances of this case.[17]

In another New York case, the court noted that the test of reasonableness of a search and seizure is not necessarily the same when applied to a parolee as when applied to a person whose rights are not similarly circumscribed.[18] Many states give a parole officer the right to arrest a parolee without a warrant.[19] Other states require a warrant that may be issued by the parole board.[20] A parolee

---

15. Cal.Penal Code § 3054 (West).

The Adult Authority makes a permanent record of the order permitting such civil rights, which becomes a public record. *Id.* at § 3055.

The parole rules given to the parolee instruct him as to his civil rights.

16. People v. Debnam, 261 Cal.App.2d 206, 67 Cal.Rptr. 692 (1968).

Several other courts, without discussing the due process implications, have held that the exclusionary rule does not apply to parole or probation revocation proceedings. *See* United States v. Frederickson, 581 F.2d 711 (8th Cir.1978); United States v. Winsett, 518 F.2d 51 (9th Cir.1975); United States v. Farmer, 512 F.2d 160 (6th Cir.), *cert. denied,* 423 U.S. 987, 96 S.Ct. 397, 46 L.Ed.2d 305 (1975); United States v. Brown, 488 F.2d 94 (5th Cir.1973); United States v. Hill, 447 F.2d 817 (7th Cir.1971); State v. Sears, 553 P.2d 907 (Alaska 1976); *In re* Martinez, 1 Cal.3d 641, 463 P.2d 734, 83 Cal.Rptr. 382, *cert. denied,* 400 U.S. 851, 91 S.Ct. 71, 27 L.Ed.2d 88 (1970); People v. Atencio, 186 Colo. 76, 525 P.2d 461 (1974); Croteau v. State, 334 So.2d 577 (Fla.1976); People v. Dowery, 62 Ill.2d 200, 340 N.E.2d 529 (1975); State v. Thorsness, 165 Mont. 321, 528 P.2d 692 (1974). *See also* Latta v. Fitzharris, 521 F.2d 246 (9th Cir.) (en banc), *cert. denied,* 423 U.S. 897, 96 S.Ct. 200, 46 L.Ed.2d 130 (1975) and United States v. Bradley, 571 F.2d 787 (4th Cir.1978). *See generally* 3 W. LaFave, *Search and Seizures* § 10.10 (1978 and 1982 supp.).

17. People v. Randazzo, 15 N.Y.2d 526, 254 N.Y.S.2d 99 (1964).

A California case reached the same result. People v. Denne, 141 Cal.App.2d 499, 297 P.2d 451 (1956).

18. People v. Langella, 41 Misc. 65, 244 N.Y.S.2d 802 (1963); DiMarco v. Greene, 385 F.2d 556 (6th Cir.1967).

19. People v. Contreras, 263 Cal.App.2d 281, 69 Cal.Rptr. 548 (1968).

20. A former provision in the Texas law which permitted arrest without a warrant was ruled unconstitutional by the attorney general. Attorney General's Opinion No. 22 (Mar. 11, 1958). The

may be arrested by the duly constituted authorities without the consent of the paroling authorities.[21]   In California, the police may arrest and search the residence of a parole violator without a warrant.[22]

California has a statute that makes it a crime to communicate the fact of a parolee's offense with the purpose of depriving the parolee of employment, or preventing the parolee from securing the same, or to extort money from the parolee.[23]

REVOCATION OF PAROLE

The term revocation refers to the formal termination of conditional freedom and the reinstatement of imprisonment.

For many years, the issue of revocation of parole has been a controversial one in the criminal justice field.   As the public views the problem, the rate of parole violation is the criterion of parole success or failure.   Criminal justice practitioners, however, recognize that what appears to be good parole results (statistically) may, in the light of the quality and extent of supervision, indicate just the opposite.

One state may report a violation rate of 8 percent; but when it is learned that the only reason for the return of a parolee as a violator is the conviction for a new crime, the violation rate does not mean very much.   On the other hand, the record of another state may indicate a much greater rate of parole violation. Upon inquiry, this state is shown to practice very close and intensive supervision and has a policy of enforcing *all* the rules of parole.   In neither instance is the reported violation rate an accurate appraisal of that jurisdiction's parole system.

What constitutes a violation of parole?   Theoretical grounds for revoking parole are related to concepts of parole as a form of grace, a contract, or a different type of custody.[24]   Advocates of the *grace* concept view parole as a matter of grace by the executive, conferring no particular rights and subject to withdrawal at any time.   The *contract* theory holds that parole is a contract between the executive and the parolee.   Under the contract, a prisoner agrees to revocation upon violation of a condition, upon commission of a new crime, and even at the whim of the grantor.   Parole as *continuing custody* means that the

---

present Texas provisions read as follows: "Upon order by the Governor, the Board is authorized to issue warrant for the return of any paroled prisoner to the institution from which he was paroled."

21. Strand v. Schmittroth, 251 F.2d 590 (9th Cir.1957); Powell v. Turner, 167 Kan. 524, 207 P.2d 492 (1949), *cert. den.* 338 U.S. 835, 70 S.Ct. 41, 94 L.Ed. 509 (1949).

22. People v. Wells, 245 Cal.App.2d 203, 53 Cal.Rptr. 762 (1966).

23. Any person who knowingly and wilfully communicates to another, either orally or in writing, any statement concerning any person then or theretofore convicted of a felony, and then on parole, and which communication is made with the purpose and intent to deprive said person so convicted of employment, or to prevent him from procuring the same, or with the purpose and intent to extort from him any money or article of value; and any person who threatens to make any said communication with the purpose and intent to extort money or any article of value from said person so convicted of a felony, is guilty of a misdemeanor.   Cal.Penal Code § 3058 (West).

24. Sol Rubin, *The Law of Criminal Correction* (1964), 559.

parolee remains in custody of either the parole board or prison warden and therefore revocation is merely a change in degree of custody.[25]

As in probation (see chapter 6), violations are either technical or criminal. Technical violation is distinguished from conviction for a crime and refers to violation of a prescribed condition of release, such as prohibitions against the use of alcoholic beverages or associating with persons with criminal backgrounds.[26]

Regardless of the theory under which parole proceeds or the nature of the violation, the central issues of the parole revocation process are the right to a fair hearing.

Until the last 1920s, procedures in many jurisdictions for the return of parole violators were so informal that the term "hearing" was a misnomer. In many instances, revocation involved no more than the parole boards *pro forma* approval of the request of the parole officer. In many areas, the revocation decision represented almost unfettered discretion of paroling authorities. In addition to minimal procedural formality, the grounds for revocation were also nonspecific, such as "poor attitude," "poor adjustment," and "failure to cooperate."[27]

This general procedure of casual and quick return of parole violators rested primarily upon the grace or privilege theory of the parole grant. Parole officials operating under the grace doctrine did not view the revocation process as warranting such matters as due process, procedural regularity, matters of proof, hearing, or review.

In 1964, a study of parole board revocations showed that there was no hearing at all in at least seven states. In jurisdictions where a hearing was provided, counsel rarely was allowed to represent the alleged violator. Any witnesses to the alleged violation were almost always seen outside the hearing at the parole board offices, rarely subject to confrontation or cross-examination. While at the time of the survey, some states allowed parolees to have assistance of lawyers, no jurisdiction assigned counsel to indigent parolees.[28]

The Parole Revocation Hearing

Within the past decade, the appellate courts have intervened considerably in the parole process generally and revocation procedures specifically. Until 1972, there was a conflict in the various jurisdictions as to whether the parolee had a constitutional right to a parole revocation hearing. Some jurisdictions provided for such a hearing by statute; in others, parole revocation could take place without either notice or hearing. Courts disagreed, as well. One of the leading cases in the federal jurisdiction was *Hyser v. Reed,* decided in the District of Columbia circuit court in 1963.[29] The appellate court generally supported the common position that revocation was strictly a withdrawal of a privilege not requiring procedural due process, such as confrontation and cross-examination

---

25. Burns, *supra,* at 308.

26. *Id.* at 308.

27. Nat'l Advisory Comm'n Report on Corrections (1973), 404.

28. *Id.* at 405.

29. 115 U.S.App.D.C. 254, 318 F.2d 225 (1963).

of witnesses or assistance of counsel. *Hyser* did, however, deal with the issue of venue, of where the revocation hearing should take place.

The court supported the U.S. Board of Parole practice of conducting a fact-finding hearing on the site of the alleged offense or violation of conditions, with review at the institution only if the first hearing determined the offender should be returned.

Subsequent to *Hyser,* however, courts in some states and federal jurisdictions departed from the first part of the decision, namely, the lack of any right, constitutional or otherwise, for due process to be applied at revocation proceedings. Most courts that departed from *Hyser* did so on the basis of a United States Supreme Court decision involving deferred sentencing or probation revocation. In *Mempa v. Rhay,* the court held in 1967 that a state probationer had a right to a hearing and to counsel upon allegations of violation of probation.[30] A number of courts interpreted the principle of *Mempa* to apply to parole as well. Since that decision, a great deal of discussion and controversy has occurred with regard to parole revocation and due process.

In 1968 a superior court judge in Washington held that a parolee has the right of access to the parole violation report and a right to confront and cross-examine witnesses. The court said that there is no substantial difference between a probation revocation and a parole revocation. The ruling prescribed that any parole violation must take place near the location of the alleged violation and that counsel be appointed for indigent parolees for the revocation process.[31]

Morrissey v. Brewer

In 1972 the United States Supreme Court dealt with several crucial issues relating to parole revocation in the case of *Morrissey v. Brewer.*[32] Two parolees appealed an appellate court's decision on the ground that their paroles were revoked without a hearing and that they were thereby deprived of due process. The appellate court, in affirming the district court's denial of relief, had reasoned that parole is only "a correctional device authorizing service of sentence outside a penitentiary" and concluded that a parolee, who is still "in custody" is not entitled to a full adversary hearing.[33]

In reversing the court of appeals' decision, the Supreme Court held that:

> * * * the liberty of a parolee, although indeterminate, includes many of the core values of unqualified liberty and its termination inflicts a "grievous loss" on the parolee and often on others. It is hardly useful any longer to try to deal with this problem in terms of whether the parolee's liberty is a "right" or a "privilege." By whatever name the liberty is valuable and must be seen as within the protection of

---

30. Mempa v. Rhay, 389 U.S. 128, 88 S.Ct. 254, 19 L.Ed.2d 336 (1967).
  Among due process requirements, the *Mempa* court held that in order for probation to be revoked and a new sentence imposed, an offender must be provided counsel.
31. *In re* Bailey, No. 57125 (Wash.Super.Ct., May 22, 1968). For a discussion of this case *see* Burns, *Corrections: Organization and Administration* (St. Paul: West Publishing Company, 1975), 311.
32. 408 U.S. 471, 92 S.Ct. 2593, 33 L.Ed.2d 484 (1972).
33. 408 U.S. 474, 92 S.Ct. 2596, 33 L.Ed.2d 487 (1972).

the Fourteenth Amendment. Its termination calls for some orderly process, however informal.[34]

The question is not merely the weight of the individual's interest, but whether the nature of the interest is one within contemplation of the "liberty or property" language of the fourteenth amendment. The court stated that the state properly subjects a parolee to many restrictions not applicable to other citizens, and the parolee is not entitled to the full panoply of rights due a defendant in a criminal proceeding. However, due process requires that a parolee be given a preliminary hearing to determine whether there is probable cause to believe that he or she committed a parole violation. At this preliminary hearing, the parolee may appear and speak in his or her own behalf, and may bring letters, documents, or individuals who can give relevant information to an independent, neutral, and detached hearing officer. The hearing officer need not be a lawyer or a judge. The parolee should receive prior notice of the inquiry, its purpose, and the alleged violation, and the hearing officer should digest the evidence on probable cause and state the reasons for holding the parolee for the parole board's decision.

At the revocation hearing, which must be conducted reasonably soon after the parolee's arrest, minimum due process requirements must be met. These are: (a) written notice of the claimed violation of parole; (b) disclosure to the parolee of the evidence against him or her; (c) opportunity to be heard in person and to present witnesses and documentary evidence; (d) the right to confront and cross-examine adverse witnesses (unless the hearing officer specifically finds good cause for not allowing confrontation); (e) a "neutral and detached" hearing body such as a traditional parole board, members of which need not be judicial officers or lawyers; and (f) a written statement by the fact finders as to the evidence relied on and the reasons for revoking parole.

The Court in the *Morrissey* case did not reach the question of the right of the parolee at each hearing to the assistance of retained counsel or of appointed counsel if indigent. However, in one of the first cases decided after the *Morrissey* decision, the California Supreme Court *en banc* held that "as a judicially declared rule of criminal procedure," a probationer was entitled to the representation of retained or appointed counsel at formal proceedings for the revocation of probation. The Court pointed to the fact that a violation of a condition of probation is often a matter of degree or quality of conduct, and the point when a violation occurs often is a matter of technical judgment. It then quoted from *Goldberg v. Kelly,* that "trained counsel in such circumstances can help delineate the issues, present the factual contentions in an orderly manner, and generally safeguard the interests of his client." [35]

In *Gagnon v. Scarpelli* the Supreme Court used similar reasoning to mandate a case-by-case determination of the need for counsel at probation and parole revocation hearings. The determination of the need for counsel was left to the sound discretion of the state authority responsible for administering the proba-

---

34. 408 U.S. 482, 92 S.Ct. 2602, 33 L.Ed.2d 493 (1972).

35. People v. Vickers, 105 Cal.Rptr. 305, 503 P.2d 1313 (1972), *quoting* Goldberg v. Kelly, 397 U.S. 254, 90 S.Ct. 1011, 25 L.Ed.2d 287 (1970).

tion and parole system. In cases where a probationer's or parolee's version of a disputed issue can be fairly presented only by trained counsel, appointment of counsel for the indigent probationer or parolee should be made "[a]lthough the presence and participation of counsel will probably be both undesirable and constitutionally unnecessary in most revocation hearings * * * ."[36]

Both the Supreme Court and the California court refused to make the rule in *Morrissey* retroactive to a parole revocation which took place prior to the date of that decision.[37]

The Decision to Revoke Parole

The *Morrissey* case has mandated an on-site probable cause hearing and due process during the revocation hearing. Failure to provide the on-site hearing required by *Morrissey* has been held to constitute a waiver of the parole violation.[38] However, if the required procedures are followed and in the absence of proof of an abuse of discretion by the paroling authority, *Morrissey* and related decisions have probably not changed the general rule that the decision of the paroling authority to revoke parole and return the parolee to prison is not reviewable by the courts.[39] Habeas corpus will not lie, nor can the prisoner obtain an order of mandamus requiring reduction of sentence.[40]

Resentencing after Parole Revocation

In some states the parolee whose parole is revoked receives no credit on his sentence for the time spent on parole. In other states, he receives credit on the

---

36. Gagnon v. Scarpelli, 411 U.S. 778, 93 S.Ct. 1756, 36 L.Ed.2d 656 (1973).

But see Lane v. Attorney General, 477 F.2d 857 (5th Cir.1973), where appointed counsel was required on equal protection grounds where retained counsel was permitted at a revocation hearing.

See also Cottle v. Wainwright, 477 F.2d 269 (5th Cir.1973), and Pannell v. Jones, 2 Prison Law Reporter 347 (Erie County, New York Sup.Ct., April 13, 1973).

37. In re Prewitt, 105 Cal.Rptr. 318, 503 P.2d 1326 (1972).

38. In re La Croix, 30 Cal.App.2d 999 (1973).

39. Johnson v. Walls, 185 Ga. 177, 194 S.E. 380 (1937); Hogan v. Zerbst, 101 F.2d 634 (5th Cir.1939).

However, a revocation ordered issued without following a statutory requirement that it record the reasons for revocation was declared a nullity. Ex parte Diehl, Mo., 255 S.W.2d 54 (1953), and evidence based on mere suspicion, belief, assumptions and conclusions alone is not sufficient to justify revocation of parole. Compagna v. Hiatt, 100 F.Supp. 74 (N.D.Ga.1951); In re Cleaver, 266 Cal.App.2d 143, 72 Cal.Rptr. 20 (1968).

The California statutes expressly provide that no parole shall be suspended or revoked without cause which must be stated in the order suspending or revoking parole. West's Ann.Penal Code § 3063.

40. The action of the Parole Board in revoking parole and in ordering parolee returned to prison is not reviewable in habeas corpus proceedings. People ex rel. De Maggio v. Bates, 36 N.Y.S.2d 64 (1942).

Revocation of a prisoner's parole by the parole board in the exercise of its discretionary power cannot be reviewed by habeas corpus. People ex rel. Schlecter v. Jennings, 130 Misc. 748, 226 N.Y.S. 98 (1927).

But see Olson v. Pope, No. 8361 [2 Prison Law Reporter 291] Solano County, Cal.Super.Ct., March 28, 1973, where court ordered California Adult Authority to reconsider prisoner's application for parole.

sentence as "straight time," i.e., without benefit of good time credits.[41] In a few states, the parolee receives credit on his or her sentence equal to the time spent on parole and also obtains reductions for good behavior earned while on parole.[42] Generally, a parolee whose parole has been revoked may be reparoled.[43] In some cases, the parolee must remain in prison for a stated time before becoming eligible to be considered for reparole.[44]

DISCHARGE FROM PAROLE

Right to Discharge

A parolee is entitled to discharge when he or she has successfully completed the parole term. The statutes of most states also make provision for early discharge on parole at the discretion of the paroling authority.[45] In New York, if the board of parole is satisfied that an absolute discharge from parole or from conditional release is in the best interests of society, the board may grant such release to any person who has been on unrevoked parole for at least five years and unrevoked conditional release for at least two years.[46] If the parolee is not

---

41. A Texas inmate does not receive credit on sentence for times spent on parole. Vernon's Ann.C.Cr.P. art. 42.12. In Illinois, the time served on parole prior to the violation is credited on the sentence. Smith-Hurd Ann.Stat. ch. 38, § 123–3. The sentence of a New York parolee, who is serving an indeterminate sentence, continues to run while he is on parole. N.Y.Penal Law § 70.40(1)(a) (McKinney). However, provision is made for a declaration of delinquency which interrupts the person's sentence as of the date of the delinquency and continues until the return of the person to the institution under the jurisdiction of the state department of corrections. Id. at § 70.40(3). The effect of this provision is to toll the service of parole. People ex rel. Rainone v. Murphy, 1 N.Y.2d 367, 135 N.E.2d 567 (1956).

A federal court found it to be a regular practice in California for the Adult Authority to resentence a California parolee who breaks parole to the maximum term allowed by law. This practice was questioned by the court which mandated individual consideration in resentencing. Hester v. Craven, 322 F.Supp. 1256 (C.D.Cal.1971). Automatically redetermining sentence at maximum following first order suspending parole was held to violate due process requirements in Anderson v. Nelson, 352 F.Supp. 1124 (N.D.Cal.1972).

Earlier California decisions upheld resentencing to a maximum term. People v. Dorado, 62 Cal.2d 280, 42 Cal.Rptr. 169, 398 P.2d 361 (1965), cert. den. 381 U.S. 937, 85 S.Ct. 1765, 14 L.Ed. 702 (1965).

42. The Model Penal Code provisions permit recommitment of the parolee whose parole has been revoked for the remainder of his maximum parole term, after credit for the period served on parole prior to the violation and for reductions for good behavior earned while on parole. See Model Penal Code, § 305.17.

43. Illinois law permits a subsequent parole. Ill.Ann.Stat. ch. 38, § 123–3 (Smith-Hurd).

44. In New York, the Parole Board may re-parole prisoner without return to prison as of the date set by the Board.
Model Penal Code, § 305.17(2).

45. N.Y.Correct.Law § 220 (McKinney); Tex.Code Crim.Proc.Ann. art. 42.12, §§ 23, 24, 25 (Vernon).
Model Penal Code, §§ 305.11 and 305.12.

46. N.Y.Correct.Law § 805(8) (McKinney). A discharge granted under this section constitutes a termination of the sentence with respect to which it was granted.

issued a discharge, he or she is discharged by operation of law.[47]   A court does not have power to grant a discharge.[48]   Once a discharge has occurred, the parole authority may not exercise jurisdiction over the parolee.[49]

---

47. In Illinois, the court held that expiration of original sentence less statutory allowance for good behavior, which would have entitled paroled convict to apply for final discharge, did not preclude his subsequent imprisonment for violation of parole, where such final discharge had not been applied for, since sentence of imprisonment for crime may only be satisfied by actual service unless remitted by some legal authority.   People *ex rel.* Ross v. Becker, 382 Ill. 404, 47 N.E.2d 475 (1943).

48. People *ex rel.* Castle v. Spivey, 10 Ill.2d 586, 141 N.E.2d 321 (1957); Tague v. Hudspeth, 171 Kan. 225, 231 P.2d 209 (1951); People v. Denecke, 279 App.Div. 824, 109 N.Y.S.2d 193 (1952).

49. People *ex rel.* Brackett v. Kaiser, 209 App.Div. 722, 205 N.Y.S. 317 (1924); People *ex rel.* Lewandowski v. Division of Parole, 139 Misc. 485, 248 N.Y.S. 511 (1931).

SUPPLEMENTAL READING 13*

Standards Relating to Conditions of Parole, Arrest, Revocation & Discharge

CONDITIONS OF PAROLE

2–1099 General conditions for release which apply to all parolees and mandatory releases under supervision are limited to requirements that a parolee observe the law, maintain appropriate contact with the parole system, and notify the parole agency of changes in residence. (Essential)

> DISCUSSION: The critics of parole have argued that the rules tend to be moralistic, or that they tend to be overly vague and unfairly invade the privacy of parolees. In most cases, general conditions which apply to all parolees should require simply that a parolee observe the law, maintain appropriate contact with the parole system, and notify the parole field agency of changes in residence.

2–1100 In addition to the general conditions of release which apply to all cases, the parole authority adds special and specific conditions for individual cases that are related to the previous offense pattern and the probability of further serious law violations by the individual parolee. (Important)

> DISCUSSION: Special conditions of release should be added only when they are clearly relevant to the parolee's compliance with the requirements of the criminal law. Conditions should not concern themselves with the lifestyle of the offender as such, but should be tested directly against the probability of serious criminal behavior by the individual parolee.

2–1101 The offender is given an opportunity to present his or her views to the parole authority about specific parole conditions which may be imposed on him or her. (Essential)

> DISCUSSION: As much as possible, the offender should be encouraged to make known to the parole authority his or her

* Reprinted from *Standards for Adult Parole Authorities,* 2d ed. (The American Correctional Association, 1980). Used by permission.

views about the conditions which will be imposed. The parolee should have an opportunity to appeal any request of a parole officer to fix a new condition of parole. The parolee should clearly understand how such an appeal can be pursued and steps should be taken to see that the parolee can avail himself or herself of such procedures.

2–1102 Written copies of the conditions of parole are furnished to the parolee, and are explained to him or her. (Essential)

DISCUSSION: Conditions of parole should be reviewed with the parolee so that he or she fully understands them. A regular program in the institution should exist to assist parolees in understanding the conditions of their release, and in dealing with any problems involved in their release plans. (See related standard 2–1020)

2–1103 The parolee acknowledges in writing that he or she has received and understands the conditions of his or her parole. (Essential)

DISCUSSION: (See related standard 2–1102)

2–1104 The parolee and/or the parole field staff may request that parole conditions be amended. If the parole authority approves, it makes needed amendments in writing. (Essential)

DISCUSSION: Parole is a dynamic process, and as the parolee's adjustment changes, so should the conditions of parole supervision. A procedure by which the parolee and/or the parole field staff can request and the parole authority review and grant changes as needed in the conditions of release best serves the interest of public protection and the welfare of the individual parolee.

2–1105 Parole authorities require that the parolee complies with all applicable provisions of the Interstate Compact for the Supervision of Probationers and Parolees or the Interstate Compact for Juveniles, and

that he or she is fully aware of the requirements of transfer under these compacts. (Essential)

DISCUSSION: Essential resources for the effective supervision of probationers and parolees are the Interstate Compact for the Supervision of Probationers and Parolees, and the Interstate Compact for Juveniles. It is important to the effective operation of these compacts that all rules governing the conditions of these compacts are carefully observed, and that parolees transferring between jurisdictions are fully advised as to their provisions and accept them.

ARREST AND REVOCATION

Determination

2–1106 Warrants for the arrest and detention of parolees, pending a determination by the parole authority as to whether parole should be revoked, or provisionally revoked, are issued only upon the affirmative approval of a parole authority member or the statewide or regional director of parole supervision services. (Essential)

DISCUSSION: The arrest and detention of a parolee on violation charges is a serious act with profound implications for the parolee. In view of the loss of liberty which results from the issuance of a detention warrant, the need for such a warrant should be reviewed by a parole authority member or the statewide or regional director of parole services. The power to issue detention warrants should be exercised by such administrative personnel, not by the parole officer involved directly in the supervision process.

2–1107 Warrants for the arrest and detention of parolees are issued only upon adequate evidence which indicates a probable serious or repeated pattern of violation of parole conditions and a compelling need for detention pending the parole authority's initial revocation decision. (Essential)

DISCUSSION: The standard for the issuance of detention warrants may not rise to the standard of probable cause required for arrest on criminal charges. However, to justify issuance of a detention warrant, sufficient evidence should be produced to indicate that parole conditions have been seriously breached and that detention is required. Detention may be required in order to prevent injury to an individual or the public, to interrupt a serious continuing violation of parole, or to assure the presence of a parolee at a preliminary hearing when it is determined that the parolee would not attend voluntarily.

2–1108 When parole violation charges are based on the alleged commission of a new crime, a detention warrant is not issued unless the parolee's presence in the community would present an unreasonable risk to public or individual safety. (Essential)

DISCUSSION: The issuance of a detention warrant often precludes a parolee who is charged with committing a new crime from the possibility of bail or other forms of pretrial release. As a general rule, parolees should be able to seek the forms of pretrial release which are available to other criminal defendants. However, the presence of other serious parole violation charges or a danger to public or individual safety may justify the issuance of a detention warrant when a parolee is charged with committing a new crime.

Preliminary Hearing

2–1109 When a parolee is arrested on a detention warrant, or when a detention warrant is lodged as a backup to bail in conjunction with pending criminal charges, a preliminary hearing is held within fourteen calendar days after the arrest and detention of the parolee or the lodging of the detention warrant; however, when there has been a conviction or a finding of probable cause on new criminal charges, the preliminary hearing is not required. (Essential)

DISCUSSION: The United States Supreme Court case of *Morrissey v. Brewer*, 408 U.S. 471 (1972), requires, as a matter of due process, that a preliminary hearing be conducted as soon as possible after a parolee is taken into custody, while evidence and sources are readily available. The purpose of the hearing is to determine whether probable cause exists to believe that parole conditions have been violated. Later cases in various jurisdictions have held that a conviction or a finding of probable cause on new criminal charges takes the place, for due process purposes, of the preliminary parole hearing.

2–1110 The preliminary hearing is held in or near the community where the violation is alleged to have occurred or where the parolee has been taken into custody. (Essential)

DISCUSSION: (See related standard 2–1109)

2–1111 The preliminary hearing may be delayed or postponed for good cause, and the parolee may waive the hearing if first informed of rights pertaining to the hearing and of the consequences of waiving the hearing. (Essential)

DISCUSSION: Due process requires that any waiver of rights by the parolee be done knowingly and voluntarily. Therefore, the parole authority should assure that no form of coercion is used to induce a waiver of the preliminary hearing, and that the parolee understands the nature and consequences of the hearing before waiving it.

2–1112 The authority may delegate to a member of the parole administrative staff or to field officers the authority to conduct a preliminary hearing and make findings as to grounds for revocation. (Essential)

DISCUSSION: The *Morrissey* case provides that the hearing officer need not be a judicial official, but may be a parole staff member, so long as that staff member is impartial.

2–1113 The preliminary hearing is conducted by an administrative staff member or officer who has not previously been involved in the case. (Essential)

> DISCUSSION: In view of the requirement that the hearing officer be impartial, it is inappropriate for the officer who supervised the parolee, or an individual who authorized the parolee's detention, to conduct the preliminary hearing.

2–1114 At least three days prior to the preliminary hearing, the parolee is notified in writing of the time and place of the hearing, and of the specific parole violation(s) charged. The parolee is also advised in writing of the right to:

> Present evidence and favorable witnesses
> Disclosure of evidence
> Confront adverse witness(es), unless the witness(es) would be subjected thereby to a risk of harm
> Have counsel of choice present, or, in case of indigent parolees who request assistance to adequately present their case, have counsel appointed
> Request postponement of the hearing for good cause
> (Essential)

DISCUSSION: Due process requires that the parolee receive notice of the hearing, of the specific acts alleged to constitute parole violations, and of all rights with respect to the hearing. Consistent with the United States Supreme Court case of *Gagnon v. Scarpelli*, 411 U.S. 778 (1973), a parole authority should decide, on a case-by-case basis, whether to appoint counsel for an indigent parolee who requests such assistance. Among the factors to be considered in making this decision are: whether the parolee denies committing the alleged violation(s); whether there are mitigating factors which are complex or otherwise difficult to develop or present; and whether the parolee appears to be capable of speaking effectively for himself. (See related standards 2–1084 and 2–1118)

2–1115 The person who conducts the preliminary hearing determines whether there is probable cause to revoke parole and hold the parolee for a revocation hearing before the parole authority. The parole authority may empower the hearing officer to make the provisional revocation decision, or merely to report his/her findings and recommendation to the parole authority for a decision as to revocation. The hearing officer issues a verbal decision or a recommendation immediately after the hearing and provides a written decision to the parolee within 21 calendar days of the hearing. (Essential)

> DISCUSSION: The hearing officer should make a summary of the documents presented and responses made at the preliminary hearing in order to make a determination as to probable cause for revocation. Although the findings need not be formal, the officer should state the reasons for the determination and indicate the evidence relied upon.

2–1116 The parolee is returned to prison only when probable cause is found at the preliminary hearing and when it is determined, after considering the appropriateness of less severe sanctions, that the clear interest of the public requires reincarceration. (Essential)

> DISCUSSION: The preliminary hearing has a usefulness that goes beyond the narrow fact-finding process. The hearing may provide an occasion to identify and reverse potentially harmful patterns of conduct, or to identify gaps in the program of supervision and recommend alternatives. The parole authority should consider not only whether a violation of parole has been committed, but also whether a less severe sanction is appropriate. (See related standard 2–1120)

Revocation Hearing

2–1117 The revocation hearing is conducted within 60 calendar days after the parolee's return to prison as a parole violator; a delay or postponement for good cause may be approved by the authority chairperson or designate. (Essential)

DISCUSSION: The *Morrissey* case requires that the revocation hearing, as well as the preliminary hearing, be timely. Subsequent cases have held that a revocation of parole will be invalidated if, without justifiable cause, a revocation hearing is not provided within a reasonable time after the return of the parolee to prison. Delays or postponements should be granted only sparingly.

2–1118 The same procedural and substantive rights which are afforded to a parolee at a preliminary hearing are afforded at a revocation hearing. In addition, a parolee is provided an opportunity at the revocation hearing to demonstrate that, even if parole has been violated, mitigating circumstances exist which suggest that the violation does not warrant revocation. (Essential)

DISCUSSION: The *Morrissey* case mandates essentially the same procedural guarantees for both hearings in the two-state revocation process, and also provides for an opportunity to present mitigating factors at the revocation hearing. This hearing also should go beyond the narrow fact-finding process and the parole authority should weigh the best interests of the parolee and the public in making its final decision. (See related standard 2–1114)

2–1119 Within 21 calendar days of the revocation hearing, the parolee is provided a written statement of the reasons for the determination made and the evidence relied upon. (Essential)

DISCUSSION: The parolee should be informed as soon as possible about the decision to revoke parole. A written statement of reasons and evidence relied upon is required under the *Morrissey* case and also promotes thoughtful decision-making.

2–1120 Alternatives other than further imprisonment are used in decisionmaking on parole violations. (Essential)

DISCUSSION: Although further imprisonment may be required, parole authorities should use warnings, short-term local confinement, special conditions, varieties of intensive supervision, referral to other community resources, and other alternatives to confinement. (See related standard 2–1116)

2–1121 In jurisdictions where the parole authority has discretion to award or forfeit good conduct deductions for time served on parole in the community, there are written guidelines for the award or forfeiture of such deductions. (Essential)

DISCUSSION: Careful review of individual cases is required in making a determination on provision of credit to the parolee for time served in the community. Written policy* should state specific criteria for allowing or disallowing credit for time served in the community when a parolee is imprisoned for a parole violation.

2–1122 If it is decided that the offender is to be reincarcerated, there is no statutory or administrative prohibition against re-parole on the original charge for which paroled. (Important)

DISCUSSION: Neither in law nor in practice should any predisposition operate to deny further parole consideration to a parole violator. The fact of parole violation should be considered in the context of an offender's total history in deciding the next appropriate action(s) after revocation of parole.

2–1123 After a revocation hearing, the parole authority immediately informs the offender of the next tentative release date. When circumstances, such as pending criminal charges or outstanding sentences to be served, prevent the setting of a tentative release date, or when the tentative release date is greater than one year after the revocation hearing, the parole authority sets a date for a review hearing within one year, and advises the offender of this date. (Essential)

DISCUSSION: In revocation decisions, no less than in release decisions, it is of paramount importance for the parole authority to minimize uncertainty in the mind of the offender. Tentative release dates should be set unless circumstances make it impossible to predict the offender's future eligibility status. The certainty of even a distant tentative release date is preferable to no date at all. When an obstacle to the setting of a date, such as pending criminal charges, is removed, the parole authority should advance the date of the review hearing to the earliest convenient time. (See related standard 2–1086)

Morrissey v. Brewer*

JOHN J. MORRISSEY and
G. DONALD BOOHER, Petitioners
v. LOU B. BREWER, Warden, et al.

408 U.S. 471, 33 L.Ed.2d 484, 92 S.Ct. 2593
[No. 71–5103]

Argued April 11, 1972. Decided June 29, 1972.

SUMMARY

Two Iowa convicts whose paroles were revoked by the Iowa Board of Parole filed habeas corpus petitions in the United States District Court for the Southern District of Iowa, alleging that they were denied due process because their paroles were revoked without a hearing. The District Court denied the petitions on the ground that due process did not require a prerevocation hearing, and the United States Court of Appeals for the Eighth Circuit affirmed (443 F.2d 942).

On certiorari, the United States Supreme Court reversed and remanded the case to the Court of Appeals for return to the District Court with directions to make findings on the procedures actually followed by the Parole Board in the two parole revocations. In an opinion by BURGER, Ch. J., expressing the views of six members of the court, it was held that the minimum requirements of due process in revoking paroles include (a) written notice of the claimed parole violations; (b) disclosure to the parolee of evidence against him; (c) opportunity to be heard in person and to present witnesses and documentary evidence; (d) the right to confront and cross-examine adverse witnesses (unless the hearing officer specifically finds good cause for not allowing confrontation); (e) a neutral and detached hearing body such as a traditional parole board, members of which need not be judicial officers or lawyers; and (f) a written statement by the fact finders as to the evidence relied on and reasons for revoking parole. The court further held that a preliminary hearing officer's determination that there is probable cause to hold a parolee for the parole board's final decision on parole revocation warrants the parolee's continued detention pending the final decision; but the court expressly pretermitted the question whether a parolee is entitled, in a parole revocation proceeding, to the assistance of retained counsel or to appointed counsel if he is indigent.

BRENNAN, J., joined by MARSHALL, J., concurred in the result on the ground that due process also requires that the parolee be allowed the assistance of retained counsel at his revocation hearings.

DOUGLAS, J., dissented on the grounds that a parolee who does not commit a new offense should not be arrested or jailed until his parole is revoked, and that a parolee is entitled to counsel in parole revocation proceedings.

BURGER, C.J., delivered the opinion of the Court, in which STEWART, WHITE, BLACKMUN, POWELL, and REHNQUIST, JJ., joined; BRENNAN, J., filed an opinion concurring in the result, in which MARSHALL, J., joined, *post,* p. 490, 33 L.Ed.2d p. 500. DOUGLAS, J., filed an opinion dissenting in part, *post,* p. 491, 33 L.Ed.2d p. 500.

Appearances of Counsel

W. DON BRITTIN, Jr., argued the cause for petitioners.

LARRY S. SEUFERER argued the cause for respondents.

Briefs of Counsel, p. 962, *infra.*

Opinion of the Court

[408 U.S. 472]

Mr. Chief Justice BURGER, delivered the opinion of the Court.

[1] We granted certiorari in this case to determine whether the Due Process Clause of the Fourteenth Amendment requires that a State afford an individual some opportunity to be heard prior to revoking his parole.

Petitioner Morrissey was convicted of false drawing or uttering of checks in 1967 pursuant to his guilty plea, and was sentenced to not more than seven years' confinement. He was paroled from the Iowa State Penitentiary in June 1968. Seven months later, at the direction of his parole officer, he was arrested in his home town as a parole violator and incarcerated in the county jail. One week later, after review of the parole officer's written report, the Iowa Board of Parole revoked Morrissey's

[408 U.S. 473]

parole, and he was returned to the penitentiary located about 100 miles from his home. Petitioner asserts he received no hearing prior to revocation of his parole.

The parole officer's report on which the Board of Parole acted shows that petitioner's parole was revoked on the basis of information that he had violated the conditions of parole by buying a car under an assumed name and operating it without permission, giving false statements to police concerning his address and insurance company after a minor accident, obtaining credit under an assumed name, and failing to report his place of residence to his parole officer. The report states that the officer interviewed Morrissey, and that he could not explain why he did not contact his parole officer despite his effort to excuse this on the ground that he had been sick. Further, the report asserts that Morrissey admitted buying the car and obtaining credit under an assumed name, and also admitted being involved in the accident. The parole officer recommended that his parole be revoked because of "his continual violating of his parole rules."

The situation as to petitioner Booher is much the same. Pursuant to his guilty plea, Booher was convicted of forgery in 1966 and sentenced to a maximum term of 10 years. He was paroled November 14, 1968. In August 1969, at his parole officer's direction, he was arrested in his home town for violation of his parole and confined in the county jail several miles away. On September 13, 1969, on the basis of a written report by his parole officer, the Iowa Board of Parole revoked Booher's parole and Booher was recommitted to the state penitentiary, located about 250 miles from his home, to complete service of his sentence. Petitioner asserts he received no hearing prior to revocation of his parole.

[408 U.S. 474]

The parole officer's report with respect to Booher recommended that his parole be revoked because he had violated the territorial restrictions of his parole without consent, had obtained a driver's license under an assumed name, operated a motor vehicle without permission, and had violated the employment condition of his parole by failing to keep himself in gainful employment. The report stated that the officer had interviewed Booher and that he had acknowledged to the parole officer that he had left the specified territorial limits and had operated the car and had obtained a license under an assumed name "knowing that it was wrong." The report further noted that Booher had stated that he had not found employment because he could not find work that would pay him what he wanted—he stated he would not work for $2.25 to $2.75 per hour—and that he had left the area to get work in another city.

After exhausting state remedies, both petitioners filed habeas corpus petitions in the United States District Court for the Southern District of Iowa alleging that they had been denied due process because their paroles had been revoked without a hearing. The State responded by arguing that no hearing was required. The District Court held on the basis of controlling authority that the State's failure to accord a hearing prior to parole revocation did not violate due process. On appeal, the two cases were consolidated.

The Court of Appeals, dividing 4 to 3, held that due process does not require a hearing. The majority recognized that the traditional view of parole as a privilege rather than a vested right is no longer dispositive as to whether due process is applicable; however, on a balancing of the competing interest involved, it concluded that no hearing is required. The court reasoned that parole is only "a correctional device authorizing service of sentence outside the penitentiary," 443 F.2d

[408 U.S. 475]

942, 947; the parolee is still "in custody." Accordingly, the Court of Appeals was of the view that prison officials must have large discretion in making revocation determinations, and that courts should retain their traditional reluctance to interfere with disciplinary matters properly under the control of state prison authorities. The majority expressed the view that "non-legal, non-adversary considerations" were often the determinative factors in making a parole revocation decision. It expressed concern that if adversary hearings were required for parole revocation, "with the full panoply of rights accorded in criminal proceedings," the function of the parole board as "an administrative body acting in the role of parens patriae would be aborted", id., at 949, and the board would be more reluctant to grant parole in the first instance—an apprehension that would not be without some basis if the choice were between a full-scale adversary proceeding or no hearing at all. Additionally, the majority reasoned that the parolee has no statutory right to remain on parole. Iowa law provides that a parolee may be returned to the institution at any time. Our holding in Mempa v. Rhay, 389 U.S. 128, 19 L.Ed.2d 336, 88 S.Ct. 254 (1967), was distinguished on the ground that it involved deferred sentencing upon probation revocation, and thus involved a stage of the criminal proceeding, whereas parole revocation was not a stage in the criminal proceeding. The Court of Appeals' decision was consistent with many other decisions on parole revocations.

[2] In its brief in this Court, respondent asserts for the first time that petitioners were in fact granted hearings after they were returned to the penitentiary. More generally, respondent says that within two months after the Board revokes an individual's parole and orders him returned to the penitentiary, on the basis of the parole officer's written report it grants the individual a hearing before the Board. At that time, the Board goes over "each of

[408 U.S. 476]

the alleged parole violations with the returnee, and he is given an opportunity to orally present his side of the story to the Board." If the returnee denies the report, it is the practice of the Board to conduct a further investigation before making a final determination either affirming the initial revocation, modifying it, or reversing it.[1] The State asserts that Morrissey, whose parole was revoked on January 31, 1969, was granted a hearing before the Board on February 12, 1969. Booher's parole was revoked on September 13, 1969, and he was granted a hearing on October 14, 1969. At these hearings, the State tell us—in the briefs—both Morrissey and Booher admitted the violations alleged in the parole violation reports.

Nothing in the record supplied to this Court indicates that respondent claimed, either in the District Court or the Court of Appeals, that petitioners had received hearings promptly after their paroles were revoked, or that in such hearing they admitted the violations; that information comes to us only in the respondent's brief here. Further, even the assertions that the respon-

dent makes here are not based on any public record but on interviews with two of the members of the parole board. In the interview relied on to show that petitioners admitted their violations, the board member did not assert he could remember that both Morrissey and Booher admitted the parole violations with which they were charged. He stated only that, according to his memory, in the previous several years all but three returnees had admitted commission of the parole infractions alleged

[408 U.S. 477]

and that neither of the petitioners was among the three who denied them.

[3] We must therefore treat this case in the posture and on the record respondent elected to rely on in the District Court and the Court of Appeals. If the facts are otherwise, respondent may make a showing in the District Court that petitioners in fact have admitted the violations charged before a neutral officer.

I

Before reaching the issue of whether due process applies to the parole system, it is important to recall the function of parole in the correctional process.

[4, 5] During the past 60 years, the practice of releasing prisoners on parole before the end of their sentences has become an integral part of the penological system. Note, *Parole Revocation in the Federal System,* 56 Geo.L.J. 705 (1968). Rather than being an ad hoc exercise of clemency, parole is an established variation on imprisonment of convicted criminals. Its purpose is to help individuals reintegrate into society as constructive individuals as soon as they are able, without being confined for the full

---

1. The hearing required by due process, as defined herein, must be accorded *before* the effective decision. *See* Armstrong v. Manzo, 380 U.S. 545, 15 L.Ed.2d 62, 85 S.Ct. 1187 (1965). Petitioners assert here that only one of the 540 revocations ordered most recently by the Iowa Parole Board was reversed after hearing. Petitioners' Reply Brief 7, suggesting that the hearing may not objectively evaluate the revocation decision.

term of the sentence imposed. It also serves to alleviate the costs to society of keeping an individual in prison.[2] The essence of parole is release from prison, before the completion of sentence, on the condition that the prisoner abide by certain rules during the balance of the sentence. Under some systems, parole is granted automatically after the service of a certain portion of a prison term. Under others, parole is granted by the discretionary action of a board, which evaluates an array of information about a prisoner

[408 U.S. 478]

and makes a prediction whether he is ready to reintegrate into society.

To accomplish the purpose of parole, those who are allowed to leave prison early are subjected to specified conditions for the duration of their terms. These conditions restrict their activities substantially beyond the ordinary restrictions imposed by law on an individual citizen. Typically, parolees are forbidden to use liquor or to have associations or correspondence with certain categories of undesirable persons. Typically, also they must seek permission from their parole officers before engaging in specified activities, such as changing employment or living quarters, marrying, acquiring or operating a motor vehicle, traveling outside the community, and incurring substantial indebtedness. Additionally, parolees must regularly report to the parole officer to whom they are assigned and sometimes they must make periodic written reports of their activities. Arluke, *A Summary of Parole Rules—Thirteen Years Later,* 15 Crime & Delinq. 267, 272–273 (1969).

[6] The parole officers are part of the administrative system designed to assist parolees and to offer them guidance. The conditions of parole serve a dual purpose; they prohibit, either absolutely or conditionally, behavior that is deemed dangerous to the restoration of the individual into normal society. And through the requirement of reporting to the parole officer and seeking guidance and permission before doing many things, the officer is provided with information about the parolee and an opportunity to advise him. The combination puts the parole officer into the position in which he can try to guide the parolee into constructive development.[3]

The enforcement leverage that supports the parole conditions derives from the authority to return the parolee

[408 U.S. 479]

to prison to serve out the balance of his sentence if he fails to abide by the rules. In practice, not every violation of parole conditions automatically leads to revocation. Typically, a parolee will be counseled to abide by the conditions of parole, and the parole officer ordinarily does not take steps to have parole revoked unless he thinks that the violations are serious and continuing so as to indicate that the parolee is not adjusting properly and cannot be counted on to avoid antisocial activity.[4] The broad discretion accorded the parole officer is also inherent in some of the quite vague conditions, such as the typical requirement that the parolee avoid "undesirable" associations or correspondence. *Cf.* Arciniega v. Freeman, 404 U.S. 4, 30 L.Ed.2d 126, 92 S.Ct. 22 (1971). Yet revocation of parole is not an unusual phenomenon, affecting only a few parolees. It has been estimated that 35% –45% of all parolees are subject to revoca-

---

2. *See* Warren, *Probation in the Federal System of Criminal Justice,* 19 Fed.Prob. 3 (Sept. 1955); *Annual Report,* (Ohio Adult Parole Authority 1964/65), 13–14; Note, *Parole: A Critique of Its Legal Foundations and Conditions,* 38 N.Y.U.L.Rev. 702, 705–707 (1963).

3. Note, *Observations on the Administration of Parole,* 79 Yale L.J. 698, 699–700 (1970).

4. *Ibid.*

tion and return to prison.[5] Sometimes revocation occurs when the parolee is accused of another crime; it is often preferred to a new prosecution because of the procedural ease of recommitting the individual on the basis of a lesser showing by the State.[6]

Implicit in the system's concern with parole violations is the notion that the parolee is entitled to retain his liberty as long as he substantially abides by the conditions of his parole. The first step in a revocation decision thus involves a wholly retrospective factual question: whether the parolee has in fact acted in violation of one or more conditions of his parole. Only if it is determined that

[408 U.S. 480]

the parolee did violate the conditions does the second question arise: should the parolee be recommitted to prison or should other steps be taken to protect society and improve chances of rehabilitation? The first step is relatively simple; the second is more complex. The second question involves the application of expertise by the parole authority in making a prediction as to the ability of the individual to live in society without committing antisocial acts. This part of the decision, too, depends on facts, and therefore it is important for the board to know not only that some violation was committed but also to know accurately how many and how serious the violations were. Yet this second step, deciding what to do about the violation once it is identified, is not purely factual but also predictive and discretionary.

If a parolee is returned to prison, he usually receives no credit for the time "served" on parole.[7] Thus, the returnee may face a potential of substantial imprisonment.

II

[7] We begin with the proposition that the revocation of parole is not part of a criminal prosecution and thus the full panoply of rights due a defendant in such a proceeding does not apply to parole revocations. *Cf.* Mempa v. Rhay, 389 U.S. 128, 19 L.Ed.2d 336, 88 S.Ct. 254 (1967). Parole arises after the end of the criminal prosecution, including imposition of sentence. Supervision is not directly by the court but by an administrative agency, which is sometimes an arm of the court and sometimes of the executive. Revocation deprives an individual, not of the absolute liberty to which every citizen is entitled, but only of the conditional liberty properly dependent on observance of special parole restrictions.

[408 U.S. 481]

[8–11] We turn, therefore, to the question whether the requirements of due process in general apply to parole revocations. As Mr. Justice Blackmun has written recently, "this Court now has rejected the concept that constitutional rights turn upon whether a governmental benefit is characterized as a 'right' or as a 'privilege.'" Graham v. Richardson, 403 U.S. 365, 374, 29 L.Ed.2d 534, 543, 91 S.Ct. 1848 (1971). Whether any procedural protections are due depends on the extent to which an individual will be "condemned to suffer grievous loss." Joint Anti-Fascist Refugee Committee v. McGrath, 341 U.S. 123, 168; 95 L.Ed. 817,

---

5. President's Commission on Law Enforcement and Administration of Justice, Task Force Report: Corrections 62 (1967). The substantial revocation rate indicates that parole administrators often deliberately err on the side of granting parole in borderline cases.

6. *See* Morrissey v. Brewer, 443 F.2d 942, at 953–954, n. 5 (C.A.8 1971) (Lay, J., dissenting); Rose v. Haskins, 388 F.2d 91, 104 (C.A.6 1968) (Celebrezze, J., dissenting).

7. Arluke, *A Summary of Parole Rules—Thirteen Years Later,* 15 Crime and Delinquency 267, 271 (1969); Note, *Parole Revocation in the Federal System,* 56 Geo.L.J. 705, 733 (1968).

852; 71 S.Ct. 624 (1951) (Frankfurter, J., concurring), quoted in Goldberg v. Kelly, 397 U.S. 254, 263; 25 L.Ed.2d 287, 296; 90 S.Ct. 1011 (1970). The question is not merely the "weight" of the individual's interest, but whether the nature of the interest is one within the contemplation of the "liberty or property" language of the Fourteenth Amendment. Fuentes v. Shevin, 407 U.S. 67, 32 L.Ed.2d 556, 92 S.Ct. 1983 (1972). Once it is determined that due process applies, the question remains what process is due. It has been said so often by this Court and others as not to require citation of authority that due process is flexible and calls for such procedural protections as the particular situation demands. "[C]onsideration of what procedures due process may require under any given set of circumstances must begin with a determination of the precise nature of the government function involved as well as of the private interest that has been affected by governmental action." Cafeteria & Restaurant Workers Union v. McElroy, 367 U.S. 886, 895; 6 L.Ed.2d 1230, 1236; 81 S.Ct. 1743 (1961). To say that the concept of due process is flexible does not mean that judges are at large to apply it to any and all relationships. Its flexibility is in its scope once it has been determined that some process is due; it is a recognition that not all situations calling for procedural safeguards call for the same kind of procedure.

We turn to an examination of the nature of the interest

[408 U.S. 482]

of the parolee in his continued liberty. The liberty of a parolee enables him to do a wide range of things open to persons who have never been convicted of any crime. The parolee has been released from prison based on an evaluation that he shows reasonable promise of being able to return to society and function as a responsible, self-reliant person. Subject to the conditions of his parole, he can be gainfully employed and is free to be with family and friends and to form the other enduring attachments of normal life. Though the State properly subjects him to many restrictions not applicable to other citizens, his condition is very different from that of confinement in a prison.[8] He may have been on parole for a number of years and may be living a relatively normal life at the time he is faced with revocation.[9] The parolee has relied on at least an implicit promise that parole will be revoked only if he fails to live up to the parole conditions. In many cases, the parolee faces lengthy incarceration if his parole is revoked.

[12] We see, therefore, that the liberty of a parolee, although indeterminate, includes many of the core values of unqualified liberty and its termination inflicts a "grievous loss" on the parolee and often on others. It is hardly useful any longer to try to deal with this problem in terms of whether the parolee's liberty is a "right" or a "privilege." By whatever name, the liberty is valuable and must be seen as within the protection of the Fourteenth Amendment. Its termination calls for some orderly process, however informal.

Turning to the question what process is due, we find that the State's interests are several. The State has found the parolee guilty of a crime against the people. That finding justifies imposing extensive restrictions on the individual's liberty. Release of the parolee before the end of his prison sentence is made with the recognition that

---

8. "It is not sophistic to attach greater importance to a person's justifiable reliance in maintaining his conditional freedom so long as he abides by the conditions of his release, than to his mere anticipation or hope of freedom." United States ex rel. Bey v. Connecticut Board of Parole, 443 F.2d 1079, 1086 (C.A.2 1971).

9. See, e.g., Murray v. Page, 429 F.2d 1359 (C.A.10 1970) (parole revoked after eight years; 15 years remaining on original term).

with many prisoners there is a risk that they will not be able to live in society without committing additional antisocial acts. Given the previous conviction and the proper imposition of conditions, the State has an overwhelming interest in being able to return the individual to imprisonment without the burden of a new adversary criminal trial if in fact he has failed to abide by the conditions of his parole.

Yet, the State has no interest in revoking parole without some informal procedural guarantees. Although the parolee is often formally described as being "in custody," the argument cannot even be made here that summary treatment is necessary as it may be with respect to controlling a large group of potentially disruptive prisoners in actual custody. Nor are we persuaded by the argument that revocation is so totally a discretionary matter that some form of hearing would be administratively intolerable. A simple factual hearing will not interfere with the exercise of discretion. Serious studies have suggested that fair treatment on parole revocation will not result in fewer grants of parole.[10]

This discretionary aspect of the revocation decision need not be reached unless there is first an appropriate determination that the individual has in fact breached

[408 U.S. 484]

the conditions of parole. The parolee is not the only one who has a stake in his conditional liberty. Society has a stake in

whatever may be the chance of restoring him to normal and useful life within the law. Society thus has an interest in not having parole revoked because of erroneous information or because of an erroneous evaluation of the need to revoke parole, given the breach of parole conditions. *See* People *ex rel.* Menechino v. Warden, 27 N.Y.2d 376, 379 and n. 2; 267 N.E.2d 238, 239 and n. 2 (1971) (parole board has less than full picture of facts). And society has a further interest in treating the parolee with basic fairness: fair treatment in parole revocations will enhance the chance of rehabilitation by avoiding reactions to arbitrariness.[11]

[13] Given these factors, most States have recognized that there is no interest on the part of the State in revoking parole without any procedural guarantees at all.[12] What is needed is an informal hearing structured to assure that the finding of a parole violation will be based on verified facts and that the exercise of discretion will be informed by an accurate knowledge of the parolee's behavior.

III

We now turn to the nature of the process that is due, bearing in mind that the interest of both State and

[408 U.S. 485]

parolee will be furthered by an effective but informal hearing. In analyzing

---

10. Sklar, *Law and Practice in Probation and Parole Revocation Hearings,* 55 J.Crim.L.C. & P.S. 175, 194 (1964) (no decrease in Michigan, which grants extensive rights); Rose v. Haskins, 388 F.2d 91, 102 n. 16 (C.A.6 1968) (Celebrezze, J., dissenting) (cost of imprisonment so much greater than parole system that procedural requirements will not change economic motivation).

11. *See* President's Commission on Law Enforcement and Administration of Justice, Task Force Report: Corrections 83, 88 (1967).

[13] 12. *See* n. 15, *infra.* As one state court has written, "Before such a determination or finding can be made it appears that the principles of fundamental justice and fairness would afford the parolee a reasonable opportunity to explain away the accusation of a parole violation. [The parolee] . . . is entitled to a conditional liberty and possessed of a right which can be forfeited only by reason of a breach of the conditions of the grant." Chase v. Page, 456 P.2d 590, 594 (Okla.Crim.App.1969).

what is due, we see two important stages in the typical process of parole revocation.

[14] (a) *Arrest of Parolee and Preliminary Hearing.* The first stage occurs when the parolee is arrested and detained, usually at the direction of his parole officer. The second occurs when parole is formally revoked. There is typically a substantial time lag between the arrest and the eventual determination by the parole board whether parole should be revoked. Additionally, it may be that the parolee is arrested at a place distant from the state institution, to which he may be returned before the final decision is made concerning revocation. Given these factors, due process would seem to require that some minimal inquiry be conducted at or reasonably near the place of the alleged parole violation or arrest and as promptly as convenient after arrest while information is fresh and sources are available. *Cf.* Hyser v. Reed, 115 U.S.App.D.C. 254, 318 F.2d 225 (1963). Such an inquiry should be seen as in the nature of a "preliminary hearing" to determine whether there is probable cause or reasonable ground to believe that the arrested parolee has committed acts that would constitute a violation of parole conditions. *Cf.* Goldberg v. Kelly, 397 U.S. at 267–271; 25 L.Ed.2d at 298–300.

[15] In our view, due process requires that after the arrest, the determination that reasonable ground exists for revocation of parole should be made by someone not directly involved in the case. It would be unfair to assume that the supervising parole officer does not conduct an interview with the parolee to confront him with the reasons for revocation before he recommends an arrest. It would also be unfair to assume that the parole officer bears hostility against the parolee that destroys his neutrality; realistically the failure of the parolee is in a sense a

[408 U.S. 486]

failure for his supervising officer.[13] However, we need make no assumptions one way or the other to conclude that there should be an uninvolved person to make this preliminary evaluation of the basis for believing the conditions of parole have been violated. The officer directly involved in making recommendations cannot always have complete objectivity in evaluating them.[14] *Goldberg v. Kelly* found it unnecessary to impugn the motives of the caseworker to find a need for an independent decision-maker to examine the initial decision.

[16] This independent officer need not be a judicial officer. The granting and revocation of parole are matters traditionally handled by administrative officers. In *Goldberg,* the Court pointedly did not require that the hearing on termination of benefits be conducted by a judicial officer or even before the traditional "neutral and detached" officer; it required only that the hearing be conducted by some person *other* than one initially dealing with the case. It will be sufficient, therefore, in the parole revocation context, if an evaluation of whether reasonable cause exists to believe that conditions of parole have been violated is made by someone such as a parole officer other than the one who has made the report of parole violations or has recommended revocation. A State could certainly choose some other independent decision-maker to perform this preliminary function.

[17, 18] With respect to the preliminary hearing before this officer, the parolee should be given notice that the hearing

---

13. Note, *Observations on the Administration of Parole,* 79 Yale L.J. 698, 704–706 (1970) (parole officers in Connecticut adopt role model of social worker rather than an adjunct of police, and exhibit a lack of punitive orientation).

14. This is not an issue limited to bad motivation. "Parole agents are human, and it is possible that friction between the agent and parolee may have influenced the agent's judgment." 4 Attorney General's Survey on Release Procedures: Parole 246 (1939).

[408 U.S. 487]

will take place and that its purpose is to determine whether there is probable cause to believe he has committed a parole violation. The notice should state what parole violations have been alleged. At the hearing the parolee may appear and speak in his own behalf; he may bring letters, documents, or individuals who can give relevant information to the hearing officer. On request of the parolee, persons who have given adverse information on which parole revocation is to be based are to be made available for questioning in his presence. However, if the hearing officer determines that the informant would be subjected to risk of harm if his identity were disclosed, he need not be subjected to confrontation and cross-examination.

[19, 20] The hearing officer shall have the duty of making a summary, or digest, of what occurs at the hearing in terms of the responses of the parolee and the substance of the documents or evidence given in support of parole revocation and of the parolee's position. Based on the information before him, the officer should determine whether there is probable cause to hold the parolee for the final decision of the parole board on revocation. Such a determination would be sufficient to warrant the parolee's continued detention and return to the state correctional institution pending the final decision. As in *Goldberg,* "the decision-maker should state the reasons for his determination and indicate the evidence he relied on

. . ." but it should be remembered that this is not a final determination calling for "formal findings of fact and conclusions of law." 397 U.S. at 271; 25 L.Ed.2d at 300. No interest would be served by formalism in this process; informality will not lessen the utility of this inquiry in reducing the risk of error.

[21] (b) *The Revocation Hearing.* There must also be an opportunity for a hearing, if it is desired by the parolee, prior to the final decision on revocation by the parole

[408 U.S. 488]

authority. This hearing must be the basis for more than determining probable cause; it must lead to a final evaluation of any contested relevant facts and consideration of whether the facts as determined warrant revocation. The parolee must have an opportunity to be heard and to show, if he can, that he did not violate the conditions, or, if he did, that circumstances in mitigation suggest that the violation does not warrant revocation. The revocation hearing must be tendered within a reasonable time after the parolee is taken into custody. A lapse of two months, as the State suggests occurs in some cases, would not appear to be unreasonable.

[22, 23] We cannot write a code of procedure; that is the responsibility of each State. Most States have done so by legislation, others by judicial decision usually on due process grounds.[15] Our task is limited to deciding the

---

15. Very few States provide no hearing at all in parole revocations. Thirty States provide in their statutes that a parolee shall receive some type of hearing. *See* Ala.Code, Tit. 42, § 12 (1959); Alaska Stats. § 33.15.220 (1962); Ariz.Rev.Stats.Ann. § 31–417 (1956); Ark.Stat.Ann. § 43–2810 (Supp.1971); Del.Code.Ann., Tit. 11, § 4352 (Supp.1970); Fla.Stats.Ann. § 947.23(1) (Supp.1972); Ga.Code Ann. § 77–519 (Supp.1971); Haw.Rev.Stats. § 353–66 (1968); Idaho Code §§ 20–229, 20–229A (Supp.1971); Ill.Ann.Stat. §§ 204(e), 207 (Supp.1972); Ind.Ann. Stats. § 13–1611 (Supp.1972); Kan.Stat.Ann. § 22–3721 (1971); Ky.Rev.Stats.Ann. § 439.330(1)(e) (1962); La.Rev. Stats.Ann. § 15:574.9 (Supp.1972); Me.Rev.Stats.Ann., Tit. 34, § 1675 (Supp.1970–1971); Md.Ann.Code, Art. 41, § 117 (1971); Mich.Comp.Laws § 791.240a, Mich.Stats.Ann. § 28.2310(*l*) (Supp.1972); Miss.Code Ann. § 4004–13 (1956); Mo.Ann.Stats. § 549.265 (Supp.1971); Mont.Rev.Codes §§ 94–9838, 94–9835 (1969); N.H.Rev.Stats.Ann. § 607:46 (1955); N.M.Stat.Ann. § 41–17–28 (1972); N.Y.Correc.Law § 212, subd. 7 (Supp.1971); N.D.Cent.Code § 12–59–15 (Supp.1971); Pa.Stats.Ann., Tit. 61, § 331.21a(b) (1964); Tenn.Code Ann. § 40–3619 (1955); Texas

[408 U.S. 489]

minimum requirements of due process. They include (a) written notice of the claimed violations of parole; (b) disclosure to the parolee of evidence against him; (c) opportunity to be heard in person and to present witnesses and documentary evidence; (d) the right to confront and cross-examine adverse witnesses (unless the hearing officer specifically finds good cause for not allowing confrontation); (e) a "neutral and detached" hearing body such as a traditional parole board, members of which need not be judicial officers or lawyers; and (f) a written statement by the fact finders as to the evidence relied on and reasons for revoking parole. We emphasize there is no thought to equate this second stage of parole revocation to a criminal prosecution in any sense. It is a narrow inquiry; the process should be flexible enough to consider evidence including letters, affidavits, and other material that would not be admissible in an adversary criminal trial.

We do not reach or decide the question whether the parolee is entitled to the assistance of retained counsel or to appointed counsel if he is indigent.[16]

[408 U.S. 490]

[24] We have no thought to create an inflexible structure for parole revocation procedures. The few basic requirements set out above, which are applicable to future revocations of parole, should not impose a great burden on any State's parole system. Control over the required proceedings by the hearing officers can assure that delaying tactics and other abuses sometimes present in the traditional adversary trial situation do not occur. Obviously a parolee cannot relitigate issues determined against him in other forums, as in the situation presented when the revocation is based on conviction of another crime.

In the peculiar posture of this case, given the absence of an adequate record, we conclude the ends of justice will be best served by remanding the case to the Court of Appeals for its return of the two consolidated cases to the District Court with directions to make findings on the procedures actually followed by the Parole Board in these two revocations. If it is determined that petitioners admitted parole violations to the Parole Board, as Iowa contends, and if those violations are found to be reasonable grounds for revoking parole under state standards, that would end the matter. If the procedures followed by the Parole Board are found to meet the standards laid down in this opinion that, too, would dispose of the due process claims for these cases.

We reverse and remand to the Court of Appeals for further proceedings consistent with this opinion.

Reversed and remanded.

Code Crim.Proc. Art. 42.12, § 22 (1966); Vt.Stat.Ann., Tit. 28, § 1081(b) (1970); Wash.Rev.Code §§ 9.95.120 through 9.95.126 (Supp.1971); W.Va.Code Ann. § 62–12–19 (1966). Decisions of state and federal courts have required a number of other States to provide hearings. *See* Hutchison v. Patterson, 267 F.Supp. 433 (Colo.1967) (approving parole board regulations); United States *ex rel.* Bey v. Connecticut State Board of Parole, 443 F.2d 1079 (C.A.2 1971) (requiring counsel to be appointed for revocation hearings); State v. Holmes, 109 N.J.Super. 180, 262 A.2d 725 (1970); Chase v. Page, 456 P.2d 590 (Okla.Crim.App.1969); Bearden v. South Carolina, 443 F.2d 1090 (C.A.4 1971) (North Carolina and Virginia also subject to fourth circuit rule); Baine v. Beckstead, 10 Utah 2d 4, 347 P.2d 554 (1959); Goolsby v. Gagnon, 322 F.Supp. 460 (E.D.Wis.1971). A number of states are affected by no legal requirement to grant any kind of hearing.

16. The Model Penal Code § 305.15(1) (Proposed Official Draft 1962) provides that "[t]he institutional parole staff shall render reasonable aid to the parolee in preparation for the hearing and he shall be permitted to advise with his own legal counsel."

COLLATERAL ISSUES IN
PROBATION AND PAROLE

INTRODUCTION

Because such overwhelming importance is attributed to the direct consequences of a criminal conviction—which include imprisonment, often followed by a term of parole or mandatory supervision; probation for a specified period, with the possibility of imprisonment for failure to adjust properly; or even execution in capital cases—the routine loss of civil rights that accompanies a criminal conviction is often not considered at all. This is both understandable and unfortunate. It is understandable that the criminal defendant and those who come into contact with the defendant on behalf of the state would be more concerned with the immediate and drastic sanctions that may result from an adjudication of guilt for a criminal offense. It is unfortunate because the civil disabilities that follow from such a conviction may have long-term detrimental effects upon the ability of the offender to successfully reintegrate into society.

The routine loss of civil rights that also may be referred to as the routine imposition of civil disabilities—upon convictions of a felony, of a "crime of moral turpitude," or of "an infamous crime," as the case may be—carries serious effects that may be of lifetime duration. It is impossible for probation and parole officers to render adequate services to probationers or parolees unless the officers are knowledgeable about the legal restrictions that follow a declaration of guilt for a criminal offense. Officers may also function inadequately if they are unfamiliar with the methods and stratagems available for minimizing these harmful effects.

For probationers, minimizing the detrimental effects of conviction begins at the time of adjudication, since the type of adjudication may determine whether any significant collateral consequences will follow. Thus, if an offender is placed on probation after a suspension of imposition of sentence, as opposed to suspension of execution of sentence, that person may not be regarded as "convicted" in the sense in which collateral consequences would attach. This can depend upon a number of factors, primarily, whether the law of the state where conviction occurs recognizes a broad or narrow definition of the term conviction. The probationer who has not been convicted can normally expect his or her full civil rights to be automatically restored upon successful completion of the period of probation, usually by operation of the statute under which the individual was placed on probation.

For the parolee who has been incarcerated in prison as a direct consequence of a criminal offense, there is normally no question of whether there has been a conviction for the purposes of imposing civil disabilities both during and after the period of confinement. Thus the only hope for that person to regain any such forfeited civil rights is via some legal restoration process. Probationers who are convicted for the purposes of the law of the state in which they were placed on probation must also look to such legal restoration of forfeited rights if they are not to be permanently affected by such losses.

Probation and parole officers need to be aware of the collateral consequences of conviction, not only to assist the probationer or parolee to regain lost rights upon discharge, but also to become cognizant of the realities of probation or parole status as they daily confront the releasee.

This chapter focuses upon the initial forfeiture of civil rights, when and under what circumstances that forfeiture occurs, and the specific rights that are affected. The chapter also discusses the collateral consequences of conviction that are not based strictly on the loss of legal rights—the so-called social stigmatization of ex-offenders and the often irreparable damage that may be done to one's "good moral character" by virtue of a criminal conviction. The various methods of restoring forfeited civil rights are discussed in the next chapters.

13

Direct and Collateral Consequences of Conviction

The distinction between the direct and collateral consequences of conviction deserves consideration. Conviction is customarily followed by the imposition of sanctions, in the form of both criminal penalties and civil disabilities. The direct or collateral sanctions that may be imposed are normally fixed by the legislature, but may also be provided for in the constitution of the jurisdiction in question. *Direct sanctions* are normally determined by the sentencing authority acting in the case, pursuant to statute. Usually, this authority is held by the judge, although in some states the jury decides the penalty, and in others the sentence is fixed by an administrative body. The sentence directly imposed by the sentencing authority largely determines where, how long, and under what conditions the convicted offender will be subjected to correctional supervision, even though the sentence may be reduced by an operation of good-time statutes, a commutation received by the governor, or the operation of the probation and parole laws.

We normally think of direct sanctions in terms of a fine, a commitment to a penal or correctional institution, a commitment to an institution or program for specialized treatment, a probationary term, or some combination of these.[1] In certain homicide cases, a number of states may impose the death penalty. Some states provide for unconditional discharge—conditional discharge that does not involve supervision—and intermittent or periodic imprisonment. The permissible direct sanctions are set out in the statutes of the state.

Penalties or restraints associated with probation or parole are included when referring to the direct consequences of punishment for the instant offense and

---

1. The word "punishment" as used in connection with the criminal law is sometimes held to be any evil or inconvenience consequent on crime or misdemeanor. *Thompson v. Bunton*, 117 Mo. 83, 22 S.W. 863 (1893). Punishment includes deprivation or suspension of any right, civil or political. *Harris v. Terry*, 98 N.C. 131, 3 S.E. 745 (1887).

are classified as criminal sanctions. The most common of these are: requiring the probationer or parolee to report regularly to a probation or parole officer; requiring that the releasee remain in a specified locality or obtain permission prior to leaving; requiring the probationer or parolee to make restitution or reparation to the victim of the crime or to engage in some form of community service; requiring the individual to abstain from the use of narcotics or intoxicants; restricting the releasee's right to operate a motor vehicle; and requiring the payment of a supervision fee.

Collateral consequences refer to disabilities that follow a conviction and which are not directly imposed by the sentencing authority. As such, they stem from the fact of conviction but are imposed either by operation of law, the decisions of licensing or other administrative bodies, or by private individuals, as when an employer refuses to hire an ex-convict. Such adverse decisions of licensing bodies and private individuals are often based upon the fact that the offender is no longer of "good moral character." Since benefits under licensing laws are customarily restricted to persons of good moral character, one of the most damaging effects of conviction is the perceived loss of good character.

Certain incidental criminal and quasi-criminal sanctions that may follow a conviction should also be considered as collateral consequences. Common examples of these include restrictions on the ownership, control, or possession of firearms; supervision or revocation of a driver's license; dishonorable discharge from the armed forces; certain criminal registration requirements; impeachment as a witness; and special requirements relating to application for pardon or other forms of executive clemency.

Thus, while collateral consequences are normally considered as the loss of *civil* rights or the imposition of civil disabilities, they may actually involve effects that are of a criminal nature, or which are very closely related to the criminal rather than the civil realm.

The overall effects of a conviction upon an offender—which include direct *and* collateral consequences—are the criminal and civil disabilities or penalties that the person actually suffers. This "real" sentence is the result of fixed legislative penalties, the sentence imposed by the sentencing authority, the operation of good-time statutes and of suspended sentence and probation and parole laws, and the disabilities that result from decisions of licensing bodies and the actions of private individuals, including the disabilities that follow upon loss of "good moral character."

CIVIL AND POLITICAL RIGHTS DEFINED

A civil right is a right that belongs to a person by virtue of citizenship. Political rights are those that have relation to the establishment, support, or management of government. Civil rights usually include political rights, but on occasion the two kinds of rights are distinguished. For example, an alien may not exercise political rights such as the right to vote or to hold political office. However, the resident alien has full enjoyment of civil rights.

In common usage, and in some statutes, the word "citizenship" is sometimes used to mean "civil rights." It will then be stated that conviction deprives the offender of citizenship, or that a pardon restores the convicted person to citizenship. This is an unfortunate use of words, for in point of fact a conviction does not deprive a natural-born citizen of citizenship.

In 1958, the U.S. Supreme Court, in the case of *Trop v. Dulles,* declared that to deprive a man of his citizenship and thus condemn him to "statelessness" is "a penalty more cruel and punitive than torture, for it involves a total destruction of the individual's status in organized society."[2] The *Trop* case involved the application of a statute that denationalized citizens convicted of desertion in time of war. A statute that attempted to deprive of their citizenship persons who leave the United States to avoid the draft was likewise declared unconstitutional.[3]

Although a person cannot be deprived of citizenship as a result of conviction, that person can and does lose civil and political rights and suffers from certain civil disabilities. The civil penalties and disabilities are usually not mentioned in the sentence of the court, but are incurred by the offender as a collateral consequence of conviction.

History of Civil Disabilities

Civil disabilities as a consequence of crime have been traced back to ancient Greece.[4] The Greeks called the disability "infamy," a word that found its way into Anglo-American criminal law in the term "infamous crimes." Infamous crimes not only carried more severe criminal penalties than noninfamous crimes, but they subjected the offender to additional penalties as well. The two main ways of imposing these additional penalties were *outlawry* and *attainder.*

A person who was outlawed was deemed out of the protection or aid of the law. In effect, this established a kind of "open season" on the offender, who could be hunted down and killed by any citizen. The person who was "attaint" lost all civil rights and forfeited all property to the Crown. The individual's entire family was declared corrupt, which made them unworthy to inherit his or her property. The theory behind both outlawry and attainder was that since the offender had declared war upon the community by committing an infamous crime, the community had the right of retaliation and retribution against the offender.

The Constitution of the United States forbids "bills of attainder,"[5] and similar provisions against the attainder or its effects are found in the constitutions and statutes of various states.[6] Although the outlaw was a familiar figure in pioneer society, particularly in western pioneer society, outlawry as a form of punishment was expressly forbidden. For example, both the Constitution and

---

2. Trop v. Dulles, 356 U.S. 86, 78 S.Ct. 590, 2 L.Ed.2d 630 (1958).

3. Kennedy v. Mendoza-Martinez, 372 U.S. 144, 83 S.Ct. 554, 9 L.Ed.2d 644 (1963).

4. Damaska, *Adverse Legal Consequences of Conviction and Their Removal: A Comparative Study,* 59 J.Crim. L.C. & P.S. 347 (1968).

5. U.S. Const. art. 1, § 9, cl. 3.

6. Tex.Code Crim.Proc.Ann. art. 1–19 (Vernon).

Code of Criminal Procedure of Texas provide that "No citizen shall be outlawed, nor shall any person be transported out of the state for any offense committed within the same."[7]

Civil Disabilities Today

In spite of constitutional and statutory provisions against outlawry and certain aspects of attainder, every state has enacted civil disability laws that affect the convicted offender. The loss of rights and civil disabilities that results from such laws varies from state to state and crime to crime.[8] They range from "civil death," which deprives the criminal of all or almost all civil rights while serving a prison sentence,[9] through loss of political rights, revocation of occupational licenses, and denial of employment opportunities. Such things as pension rights, rights under worker's compensation acts, and benefits under insurance policies may be lost, and marital status and the right to prevent the adoption of one's children may be affected.

Some of the rights are automatically lost upon conviction. Others can be lost according to judicial or administrative discretion. Still others are denied by the decisions and actions of private individuals.[10] In some cases, only conviction within the state can result in the loss of rights; in other situations, the disability can follow a conviction in a sister state or for a federal offense. According to some statutes, a conviction must be followed by incarceration for a specified period before the right is lost; in such cases, the right would not be lost upon conviction followed by probation, or where the sentence to probation is not considered as a conviction. Other statutes provide that conviction alone leads to forfeiture. Some rights are permanently lost and cannot be restored; some are automatically restored upon completion of the sentence or may be restored by action of the executive or of a court. *To determine the status of the rights of a particular convicted offender requires an analysis of the statutory provisions, judicial decisions, administrative rulings and practices, and actions of individuals of both the state of conviction and the state in which a particular right is sought to be enforced.*

Extent of Loss of Rights

The civil penalty may amount to a complete denial of the right, or may merely impose restrictions and conditions upon its exercise. For example, the right to vote or the right to hold public office are usually denied for life, unless restored

---

7. *Id.* at art. 1.18.

8. For the definitive study on collateral consequences of a conviction, *see, The Collateral Consequences of a Criminal Conviction,* Vanderbilt Law Review, vol. 23, no. 5 (Oct. 1970). The authors acknowledge their substantial obligation to that publication for the material set out in this chapter.

9. These statutes often apply only to persons serving a life sentence or sentenced to death, though some civil death statutes affect persons serving a term of years in a state penitentiary.

10. Paul Tappan, at a time when he was chairman of the United States Board of Parole, identified four main ways in which an ordinary political or civil right of the individual may be taken away as a direct or indirect consequence of a criminal conviction. These ways were (1) civil death statutes; (2) suspended rights; (3) permanent deprivation; and (4) deprivations by commissions or boards. Paul Tappan, *Loss and Restoration of Civil Rights of Offender,* National Probation and Parole Association Yearbook, (1952), 86–107; and *The Legal Rights of Prisoners,* 293 The Annals 90–112 (1954).

by pardon or special proceeding. On the other hand, a conviction, except a conviction for perjury, does not generally completely disqualify the offender as a witness—the effect is to permit the proof of the conviction to be shown in impeachment of the individual's testimony. The statutes concerning marital status may result in automatic divorce, give the spouse grounds for divorce, or give the spouse grounds for divorce only if the conviction is accompanied by imprisonment for a specified length of time. The extent of the loss of rights may also be determined by the meaning given to the word conviction, and whether the disability is determined to result only from conviction in the forum state or also to convictions in sister states and the federal courts.

The majority rule seems to be that specific disability statutes extend to convictions in sister states and in the federal courts.[11] Some courts, however, have decided that the legislature did not intend that the statutes be applied to convictions in other states or in the federal courts. The majority rule is based upon the reasoning that disability statutes are designed to protect the public, and that the public needs protection from felons convicted in other states just as it needs protection from offenders convicted in the home state. The states holding to the minority view argue that a conviction can have no effect beyond the limits of the state where the offender's guilt was determined.

As is generally true in the matter of civil disabilities, the particular right must be considered in order to determine the extent of the loss. Variations may come from the wording of particular statutes as well as from contrasting theories as to the effect of a foreign judgment of conviction.

LOSS OF RIGHTS DURING PROBATION PERIOD

The rights of the probationer during the probation period are determined basically by whether the probationer has been convicted. If the probated offender is deemed to have been convicted, he or she loses the same rights as any other convicted person in that jurisdiction; however, as we shall see, there may be special statutory provisions for expunging the conviction and restoring those rights. On the other hand, if probation has intervened prior to imposition of sentence, application of the narrow definition of conviction in particular situations may serve to protect the probationer from loss of civil rights. In a state where power of the court to grant probation may be exercised in either of two ways—by suspending imposition of sentence, or by imposing sentence and thereafter suspending its execution—the result may be that some probationers have lost their civil rights and others have not.

The statutory provisions with reference to license revocation and the application of the broad or narrow definition of conviction may also bring about different results with respect to different classes of probationers. For example, in California a teacher's credentials are revoked when a conviction becomes

---

11. David Rudenstine, *The Rights of Ex-Offenders* (New York: Avon Books, 1979), 20.

final.[12] The attorney general of that state has ruled that as to offenses not related to sex where probation was granted without imposition of sentence, there is no final judgment of conviction upon which to base a mandatory revocation of a teacher's license.[13] With respect to certain sex offenses, however, a plea, finding, or verdict of guilty is sufficient to require a mandatory revocation of a teacher's license because other sections of the education code except these offenses from the general requirement for a final conviction.[14] Thus, application of the broad definition of conviction protects the teacher who is convicted of a non-sex-related offense, while the teacher convicted of a sex offense loses his or her job because the law requires that the narrow definition of conviction be applied in this case.[15]

Differences in notions as to what is and is not a penalty may make a practical difference as to whether the probationer is, for example, subject to registration requirements; and whether the probationer has been found guilty of a felony or misdemeanor will affect such things as voting rights and liability to impeachment as a witness.[16]

As was suggested by a presidential commission, the problem with much of the present law concerning the civil rights and liabilities of offenders is not inherent in the concept of imposing various disabilities and disqualifications as consequences of a conviction of a crime, but rather results from the misuse of that concept.[17] Many deprivations during imprisonment can be justified in that they are appropriate to punitive aims of imprisonment; for example, to hold public office, to serve as a juror, or to carry on one's business are obviously incompatible with the nature of imprisonment, and certain deprivations may be useful as independent sanctions for criminal behavior. Suspending or revoking a driver's license for convictions involving dangerous driving is an appropriate sanction and perhaps more appropriate than a fine or term of imprisonment. For one reason, it is likely to be a highly effective deterrent. It proposes to protect society from a particular kind of danger that that person poses. Little in the present law can be so justified. As a general matter it has simply not been rationally designed to accommodate the varied interest of society and the individual convicted person.[18]

Such consideration prompted the American Bar Association Standards Relating to Probation to suggest that most civil rights be retained by the probationer:

---

12. De Veau v. Braisted, 5 N.Y.2d 236, 183 N.Y.S.2d 793, 157 N.E.2d 165 (1959), aff'd 363 U.S. 144, 80 S.Ct. 1146, 4 L.Ed.2d 1109 (1960). But the word "conviction" as used in the Correction Law was held to mean imposition of sentence, not plea of guilty. Richetti v. New York State Board of Parole, 300 N.Y. 357, 90 N.E.2d 893 (1950).

13. Cal.Educ.Code Ann. § 13206 (West).

14. Attorney General's Opinion No. 61–50, Sept. 14, 1961.

15. Kelly v. Municipal Court, 160 Cal. App. 2d 38, 324 P.2d 990 (1958).
The Ninth Circuit ruled as "not a penalty" a registration requirement for citizens entering and leaving the country. Adams v. United States, 299 F.2d 327 (9th Cir.1962).

16. Truchon v. Toomey, 116 Cal. App. 2d 736, 254 P.2d 638 (1953).

17. President's Commission on Law Enforcement and Administration of Justice, Corrections, pp. 88–89, 171.

18. Id.

Every jurisdiction should have a method by which the collateral effects of a criminal record can be avoided or mitigated following the successful completion of a term on probation and during its service.[19]

The commentary accompanying the standard points out that at the very least the statutes that authorize a sentence of probation should also address the problem of collateral disabilities and provide a method by which their effect can be individualized in a particular case. The status of a probated offender, including the basis on which that person can participate in normal community life, should be a prime concern in the sentencing court and should be a factor, which, like other conditions of probation, can be tailored in a manner best calculated to effect the rehabilitation of the offender. The standard recommends that the court be given not only authority to deal with collateral disabilities following the successful completion of probation, but also the authority to avoid or mitigate their imposition during the probated term.[20]

Let us now consider some specific civil and political rights that may be lost, or whose exercise may be restricted upon conviction.

CIVIL AND POLITICAL RIGHTS AFFECTED BY CONVICTION

The following list, which is discussed in detail in the succeeding sections of this chapter, sets out the civil and political rights that may be forfeited, restricted, or otherwise affected by virtue of conviction or imprisonment in a state penitentiary in one or more states. The forfeiture or abridgement in question may be limited in effect to the state in which the offender was convicted, or it may extend to sister states or be based upon a conviction in federal court. The civil and political rights that may be affected by conviction include:

- All civil rights (civil death).
- The right to claim good moral character.
- The right to hold public office.
- The right to vote.
- The right to serve on a jury.
- The right to be a witness.
- The right to hold a position of trust.
- The right to full and free enjoyment of property.
- The right to purchase insurance.
- The right to enjoy pension benefits.
- The right to marry and have children.
- The right of citizenship or residency in the U.S. (for aliens).

---

19. ABA, Probation Standard 4.3.
20. ABA, Probation, pp. 54–56.

- Employment-related rights, such as the right to an occupational license, the right to public sector employment, the right to private sector employment, and the right to be bonded.
    - The right to manage one's own affairs.
    - The right to inherit property or make a will.

Civil Death

By far the most severe civil penalties are suffered by the offender who is declared "civilly dead."[21] Civil death statutes are gradually being repealed or their more drastic provisions eliminated.[22] At one time, some seventeen states provided by law that the offender convicted of a felony and sentenced for life (or in some instances, sentenced to death) suffered civil death. In a few states, civil death statutes apply to persons imprisoned for a term of years in a state penitentiary. Persons placed on probation do not suffer the penalties associated with civil death unless probation is revoked and the offender becomes subject to the penalties imposed on persons committed for a term of years and committed in a civil death state.

Loss of Good Character

One of the most inclusive and damaging consequences of a conviction is loss of "good character," or, as it is sometimes phrased, "good moral character." Because good character is not a civil or political right, loss of good character is not customarily included in a list of rights lost upon conviction. In practical effect, however, the loss of good character forms the basis for denying the offender licenses and other employment benefits. The loss is serious because there is considerable doubt that pardon or other proceedings to expunge a conviction restore the offender to good character.

The Right to Hold Public Office

A public office has been defined as an "agency for the state, the duties of which involve in their performance the exercise of some portion of the sovereign power, great or small."[23] The laws of the federal government and of most states and municipalities disqualify convicted persons in general or persons convicted of certain crimes from holding public office. In this context, most courts apply

---

21. One author makes this comment about civil death statutes: "Since conviction of a felony at early common law resulted in the death penalty, the effect of civil death was normally unnecessary. Although the convicted felon was considered dead by law, it mattered little which rights were lost and which were retained, for his natural state was soon to coincide with that of his legal state by means of execution. Thus, civil death was a practical way of settling the earthly affairs of a convicted felon soon to be executed." Harry David Saunders, *Civil Death—A New Look at an Ancient Doctrine,* 2 Wm. & Mary L.Rev. 988 (1970).

22. The following states had civil death statutes in 1979: Arizona, Idaho, Missouri, Rhode Island and South Dakota, David Rudenstine, *The Rights of Ex-offenders,* 16, 22.

23. Yaselli v. Goff, 12 F.2d 396 (2d Cir.1926). The first element of public office is that it must be created by the Constitution or legislature or by a municipality or other body with authority conferred by the legislature.

the narrow definition of conviction. Thus, a person who has pleaded guilty or against whom a verdict of guilty has been returned, and a person placed on probation are barred from office.[24] The federal statutes also contain provisions that exclude certain offenders from holding positions in the government of the United States. The disqualifying statutes affecting federal offices are passed by Congress; state statutes and municipal ordinances disqualify the offender from state and local offices.[25]

The thrust of the standards developed by the National Advisory Commission would seem to prohibit holding public office only during a period of actual confinement, but presumably permit the holding of a public office during a period of probation that did not involve confinement.[26]

The Right to Vote

Although the right to vote is considered to be a fundamental right of citizenship, it is generally held that it can be denied to convicted felons. The provisions of the constitutions and laws of fifty states that remove or limit the right of the convicted offender to vote vary widely.[27] Disfranchisement may follow conviction of a felony, conviction of an infamous crime, conviction of a crime involving moral turpitude, or conviction for a specified list of offenses.

The California Supreme Court, in a case decided in 1973, declared that the provisions of the California constitution and statutes that deprived the convicted felon of a right to vote violated the equal protection clause of the United States Constitution.[28] The case was overruled by the United States Supreme Court, which held that a state may strip ex-felons who have fully paid their debt to

---

24. Pope v. Commissioner, 138 F.2d 1006 (6th Cir.1944).

25. For example, the Michigan employment application contains a provision which reads as follows:

Arrest and Conviction Record. If you were ever fined, or jailed, or placed on probation, or received a suspended sentence, or paid court costs, or forfeited bond or collateral for violation of any law, give the full facts of the trouble. You may omit only minor traffic violations. Other minor violations must be listed. Drunk driving, reckless driving, hit and run driving, and revocation of driver's license are not minor traffic violations and must be included. If you are in doubt as to whether a traffic violation not mentioned above is a major violation, list it on the application. You will be fingerprinted and investigated before being hired.

In evaluating arrest records we consider the kind of offense, the number and recency of offenses, the penalty imposed, your age at the time, and your prior and subsequent conduct and work record. If you have been in trouble, be sure you have given us a full explanation. The fact that you admit an arrest record does not necessarily mean that your examination will be rejected nor that you will be rejected nor that you will be barred from state employment.

Be sure to tell us the full truth about yourself, and your background * * *. If a materially false answer is found after you are on the job, you will be dismissed. As quoted in Herbert S. Miller, *The Closed Door: The Effect of a Criminal Record on Employment with State and Local Public Agencies,* Appendix E. (Springfield, Va., National Technical Information Service 1975). A report prepared for the Manpower Administration, U.S. Department of Labor, under Research Contract No. 81–09–70–02, authorized by Title I of the Manpower Development and Training Act. (Hereafter referred to as *The Closed Door.*)

26. Nat'l Advisory Comm'n Standard 16.17.

27. Rudenstine, *supra* at 161–170.

28. Ramirez v. Brown, 9 Cal. 3d 199, 107 Cal.Rptr. 137, 507 P.2d 1345 (1973).

society of their fundamental right to vote without running afoul of the fourteenth amendment.[29]

There is nothing in the *Richardson v. Ramirez* case that *requires* a state to deny the vote to the person on probation or parole or to the convicted felon. Thus, some states disqualify persons only during a period of imprisonment, which may have the result of preserving the right of a person on probation to vote. The Model Penal Code would disqualify an offender from voting only during the period of confinement in prison.[30]

The Uniform Act on the Status of Convicted Persons takes the position that a person on probation or parole should be entitled to vote in an election or become a candidate for or hold public office during the period that the person is on probation or parole. The provision reads:

> A person sentenced for a felony from the time of his sentence until his final discharge may not vote in an election, but if execution of sentence is suspended with or without the defendant being placed on probation or he is paroled after commitment to imprisonment, he may vote during the period of the suspension or parole; or become a candidate for or hold public office.[31]

The Right to Serve on a Jury

Exclusion of convicted persons from jury service has its origin in the common law. Most of the states have enacted the common law rule and exclude persons from jury duty if they have been convicted of felonies, infamous crimes, crimes involving moral turpitude, or of certain specified crimes.[32] Conviction for any crime will disqualify in New Jersey; in Maine, an individual convicted of any "scandalous crime or gross immorality" cannot serve. The federal rule is that citizens are not competent to serve on a federal grand or petit (trial) jury if they have been convicted of a crime punishable by imprisonment for more than one year.[33]

A statute that provides that only citizens having "good character" can serve on a jury also serves to disqualify the person with a criminal record.[34] If the law requires that only persons who are qualified electors can serve on the jury, loss of the right to vote following a conviction carries with it the right to serve on a jury.[35]

---

29. Richardson v. Ramirez, 418 U.S. 24, 94 S.Ct. 2655, 41 L.Ed.2d 551 (1974).

30. Model Penal Code § 306.1.

31. National Conference of Commissioners on Uniform State Laws, The Uniform Act on the Status of Convicted Persons [Rights Lost]. Section 2.

32. Rudenstine, *supra* at 120, 121.

33. 28 U.S.C.A. § 1865(b)(5).

34. Calif.Civ.Code § 205 (West); Ill.Ann.Stat. ch. 78 § 2 (Smith-Hurd); N.Y.Jud. Law § 504(4) (McKinney); Tex.Rev.Civ.Stat.Ann. art. 2133(2) (Vernon).

35. There is disagreement on the question of whether a pardon removes the ban on jury service. Texas has held that a pardon removes the disability; Easterwood v. State, 34 Tex.Crim. 400, 31 S.W. 294 (1895). In a much later case, Alabama reached the opposite conclusion. Anderson v. State, 40 Ala.App. 509, 120 So.2d 397 (1959), reversed on other grounds 366 U.S. 208, 81 S.Ct. 1050, 6 L.Ed.2d 233 (1961).

If a convicted person becomes a member of the jury, the effect may be to render the verdict of the jury illegal and require a new trial.[36] Other courts hold that the disqualification is waived if the juror is not questioned and challenged before the verdict is rendered. The juror who answers falsely to conceal his or her criminal record is, of course, subject to prosecution for perjury.

Although the National Advisory Commission Standards restrict the right of the convicted person to serve on a jury only during the period of confinement, it is very doubtful that the court would permit a person on probation to be a member of a jury. Typically, statutes setting up qualifications for jurors provide that no person who is charged with or has been indicted for a felony may be a member of a jury. Such a provision would effectively exclude a probationer whether or not that person has been convicted and irrespective of the fact that the person is not in confinement.[37]

The Right to Be a Witness

The common law disqualified as a witness any citizen convicted of treason, felony, or crimes involving fraud or deceit. This absolute disqualification extends today in a few states to persons convicted of perjury or subornation of perjury.[38] However, the usual situation today is that the person who is convicted of a crime is permitted to testify, but the fact of conviction may be shown to impeach (discredit) that person's testimony.[39] The theory behind both absolute disqualification and impeachment is that a person who has been convicted cannot be trusted to give truthful testimony; thus, the court and the jury are entitled to take the conviction into account. The witness can be asked if he or she has been convicted of a felony or other crime, which according to the laws of the state permits impeachment. The witness must answer truthfully as to any such conviction. Counsel is then at liberty to argue that because the witness is a convicted offender the testimony should not be believed. This does not mean, of course, that the jury (or the court) must disbelieve the witness. The jury—or the judge who is trier of the fact—may in its wisdom decide that the convicted offender is indeed telling the truth and give the individual's testimony the weight accorded to the testimony of any other witness.

When the question is impeachment of testimony of a convicted witness, some of the decisions apply the broad definition and require a final conviction and judgment. Thus, when a witness had not been sentenced, the conviction could not be shown in impeachment.[40] Another court insisted upon a judgment (a verdict or plea being insufficient), but permitted the impeachment of a

---

36. Texas extended this rule to include a foreman of the jury who had been convicted in federal court. Amaya v. State, 87 Tex.Crim. 160, 220 S.W. 98 (1920).

37. *See, for example,* Tex.Code Crim.Proc.Ann. art. 35.16 (Vernon), which permits a juror to be challenged for cause who has been convicted of theft or any felony, or is under indictment or other legal accusation for theft or any felony.

38. "Subornation of perjury" means to procure or induce another to commit perjury.

39. The New York statute is illustrative of statutory provisions which permit proof of a prior conviction to be shown in impeachment. N.Y.Civ.Proc.Law § 60.40 (McKinney).

40. Burnett v. State, 83 Tex.Crim. 97, 201 S.W. 409 (1918).

witness who had been put on probation.[41]   A similar result was reached in California. Impeachment was permitted during the period when the appeal was pending where judgment had been suspended and the offender was on probation.[42] But a reversal on appeal entitled a witness to deny he was convicted.[43] A pardon may or may not prevent impeachment of a convicted witness.[44]

A recent Supreme Court case places the constitutional right of confrontation by a defendant in a criminal case above any considerations that might protect the offender on probation against impeachment.[45] At issue in the *Davis* case was whether an adjudication of delinquency could be shown against a prosecution witness, although the statutes of Alaska, as do the statutes of many states, provide that an adjudication of delinquency is not a conviction. The Court held that the right of the defendant to confront the witness and to inquire into all circumstances that might affect the witness's credibility was paramount over the statutory policy against permitting the use of an adjudication of delinquency for impeachment purposes.[46]

Many of the recent standards that prohibit in one way or another the showing of a status of probation for impeachment purposes have been rendered moot by the *Davis* case. At least in criminal cases, the law is now settled that the right of the criminal defendant to confrontation is paramount over the right of the adjudicated delinquent or the convicted person who is a prosecution witness to conceal his or her status. This same right of confrontation would also prevail in favor of the criminal defendant who wishes to impeach a probationer-witness on the grounds of that person's existing status as a probationer, regardless of the technicalities of whether the person was actually convicted.

The defendant with a previous conviction who elects to testify in a second criminal trial is subject to the same rules as any other witness. The effect is to put the defendant in the unenviable position of having to disclose a prior conviction during the trial, or to decline to take the stand, and thus deprive the jury of important testimony that only he or she can supply. Also, in spite of routine court admonitions to the contrary, juries often infer guilt from the defendant's failure to deny the charges against him or her.[47]

Suggested modification in the rule would permit impeachment by proof of a prior conviction and would apply the rule only if the offender had been convicted of an offense that involved dishonesty or a false statement. It has been pointed out that acts of violence have little to do with veracity, but crimes such as perjury, fraud, cheating, and stealing do.[48] However, regardless of the nature of the offense, the *Davis* case would probably not permit concealment of

---

41. Commonwealth v. Palarino, 168 Pa.Super. 152, 77 A.2d 665 (1951).

42. People v. Clapp, 67 Cal. App. 2d 197, 153 P.2d 758 (1944).

43. People v. Van Zile, 80 Misc. 329, 141 N.Y.S. 168 (1913).

44. Rudenstine, *supra,* at 128.

45. Davis v. Alaska, 415 U.S. 308, 94 S.Ct. 1105, 39 L.Ed.2d 347 (1974).

46. *Id.*

47. *To Take the Stand or Not to Take the Stand: The Dilemma of a Defendant with a Criminal Record.*   4 Colum. J.L. & Soc. Prob. 215 (1968).

48. Gordon v. United States, 127 U.S.App.D.C. 343, 383 F.2d 936 (1967).

the prior conviction or concealment of an individual's existing status as a probationer or parolee.

The Right to Hold a Position of Trust

Several positions of trust that are derived from court appointment are denied to the convicted offender. These denials may result from the express wording of disqualification statutes or more often, from the discretionary power of the court to appoint only "suitable persons" to such positions. Thus, convicted persons are denied the right to act as an executor of a will or administrator of an estate, to be a guardian, guardian *ad litem,* or a trustee.

An *executor* is a person named in a will to administer the estate of a deceased person.

An *administrator* is a court-appointed representative of a deceased person who dies without a will.

A *guardian* is a person appointed by the court to handle the property and affairs of a minor or an incompetent person.

A *guardian ad litem* is a person who represents a minor or an incompetent person in a legal action.

A *trustee* is a person who administers a trust. A trustee holds property in his or her own name as trustee, but manages the property and affairs for the benefit of another person. Being incarcerated makes it almost impossible for a person to act as a trustee, since that person is not free to move about, meet with others, physically inspect the property, and do other things that may be necessary to properly handle the assets of the trust. A probationer who is required to remain within a stated geographical area suffers from a similar handicap. The laws of several states expressly or by interpretation exclude a convict or ex-convict from holding a position of trust. The inability to furnish a bond also often prevents the convicted offender from acting in a position of trustee.

Great latitude is given a court to remove an executor, administrator, guardian, or trustee who is "unfit" or "unsuitable" or not a "proper person" to act in the fiduciary capacity. A court may also remove a person who is not of good moral character.[49] The courts will revoke the appointment of any fiduciary who is convicted of a felony or a crime involving moral turpitude, or who is dishonest in the way the person handles the property given over to his or her care.

The Right to Enjoyment of Property

Generally, a conviction does not divest the offender of property. The Constitution of the United States specifically prohibits bills of attainder,[50] and most states have similar constitutional or statutory provisions. Even in civil death

---

49. The Illinois statutes require guardians to be "fit" persons. Ill.Ann. Stat. ch. 37, §§ 705, 706, 707 (Smith-Hurd).

Texas laws refer to a "proper" person. Tex.Prob.Code Ann. § 114(c) (Vernon).

The courts in Oklahoma must find that the guardian of a minor is a "suitable" person. Coats v. Benton, 80 Okl. 93, 194 P. 198 (1920).

50. U.S.C. art. 1, § 9, cl. 3.

states, the convict does not lose rights to property unless there is an express statutory provision to that effect.[51]   Many states, including some civil death states, have express provisions against forfeiture of estate by reason of conviction.[52]

A felon at common law did not lose the right to inherit, although under the doctrine of attainder the property that person did inherit could be expropriated by the Crown.   Today, in most states, the convict has the right to inherit property.

The Right to Purchase Insurance

The person with a criminal record may find it difficult, if not impossible, to obtain insurance.   Particularly during the period of imprisonment, that person may be uninsurable, or if he or she can obtain insurance, it will be at a higher rate.   The probationer or parolee suffers from the same disability.   An applicant whose offenses have been relatively minor and who shows substantial proof of rehabilitation may be able to get insurance at standard rates.

Information about a prior criminal record is usually not sought on insurance application forms.   However, the investigations of the insured's background may uncover the criminal conviction or the probation status.

Some policies of life insurance, particularly those issued by fraternal organizations, contain forfeiture clauses that authorize the life insurance company to cancel the policy if the insured is convicted of a serious offense.   The courts uphold such forfeitures but usually apply the broad definition of conviction that requires judgment and sentence as well as plea or verdict of guilty.

The convicted person who is the beneficiary of a life insurance policy can generally receive the proceeds of the policy.

A conviction impairs the ability of the convicted person to obtain automobile insurance.   The denial is based upon the contention by the insurance industry that the mere existence of a criminal record adversely affects the company's chances of successfully defending any action brought against the offender-insured.   The criminal record gets before the jury often enough to make the problem a real one, according to the insurance companies.

Not only does a criminal record make it difficult to obtain automobile insurance, conviction may result in cancellation of an existing policy.   Moreover, once a person has had a cancellation, the cancellation itself is an obstacle to subsequent insurance.[53]   An ex-convict may be able to obtain automobile insurance at higher rates in an "assigned risk" insurance pool or from a company that writes high-risk insurance, but these avenues will probably be closed to the ex-convict who has two or more convictions.   No-fault insurance plans may be of benefit to ex-convicts.[54]

---

51. Hawaii has an express divestment statute, however it apparently is not enforced.   Rudenstine, *supra,* at 104.

52. Cal.Penal Code § 2604 (West); N.Y.Penal Law § 79–b (McKinney).

53. Cal.Ins.Code § 669 (West); Pruitt v. Allstate Ins. Co., 92 Ill.App.2d 236, 234 N.E.2d 576 (1968).

54. New York's Rockefeller-Stewart plan improves the status of the ex-convict in that state.   *See* Ghiardi and Kircher, *Automobile Insurance: The Rockefeller-Stewart Plan,* 37 Ins. Counsel J. 324 (1970).

The Right to Enjoy Pension Benefits

A pension has been defined as "a state allowance out of the public treasury granted by government to an individual, or his representatives, or in compensation for loss or damage sustained by him in the public service."[55]   Although today there are many private pensions paid out of the treasuries of corporations and unions, the great majority of pensions are for the benefit of public employees.   Such pensions are created by the federal and state governments and also by municipalities.   The funds for the payment of pensions are built up by contributions of the governmental agency and by deductions from the salaries of the employees.

Federal statutes disqualify social security recipients and members of its uniformed services from annuity or retirement programs if they have been convicted of specific crimes,[56] and veteran's benefits may also be denied. Several states also disqualify convicted criminals from participation in pension funds.   For example, policemen and firemen in California; policemen in Florida; firemen, municipal employees, county employees, laborers, park employees, sanitary district employees, university employees, teachers, judges, house of correction employees, library employees in Illinois; teachers, policemen, and sanitary officers in Indiana; policemen and firemen in Kansas; all members of the state retirement system in Massachusetts; and state and county pensioners in Texas.[57]

The Right to Marry and Have Children

Conviction of a crime may be deemed to show unfitness as a spouse and parent. The marriage of a person who conceals the fact of a former conviction from his or her intended spouse may be annulled on the grounds of fraud.   Since marriage is generally held to be a contract as well as (to some) a sacrament, the inability to contract may affect the right to marry in a civil death state.[58]   At least one state prohibits the marriage of habitual criminals on the apparent theory that criminal tendencies may be transmitted to the offspring.[59]   Some states provide for the compulsory sterilization of certain offenders, sometimes

---

55. Black's Law Dictionary, revised fourth edition.

5 U.S.C.A. §§ 8372–8315.

56. 42 U.S.C.A. § 402(u). Crimes involving national security such as sabotage, treason, aiding the enemy.

57. Cal.Gov't Code § 50883 (West). (policemen and firemen).

Fla. Stat. Ann. § 185.18(3)(b) (West).

Ill. Ann. Stat. ch. 108.5, § 4–138 (policemen); § 8–251 (municipal employees); § 9–235 (county employees); § 11–230 (laborers); § 12–191 (park employees); § 13–221 (sanitary district employees); § 15–187 (university employees); § 16–199 (teachers); § 18–163 (judges); § 19–103 (house of correction employees); § 19–203 (library employees) (Smith-Hurd).

§ 28–4514 (teachers); § 48–6405 (policemen); § 48–6655 (sanitary officers) (Burns).

Tex.Rev.Civ.Stat.Ann. art. 6220 (state and county pensioners); art. 6243e § 17 (firemen) (Vernon).

58. Jandro v. Jandro, 246 S.W. 609 (Mo.App.1923).

59. Wash.Rev.Code Ann. § 26.04.030. However, one commentator has suggested that this statute is unconstitutional. Rudenstine, *supra,* at 56.

referred to as "eugenic sterilization." However, the enforcement of such statutes is of dubious constitutional validity.[60]

The right to adopt a child has been denied to the ex-offender,[61] and requirements in adoption statutes that the prospective parent be of good moral character or a "suitable person" likewise disqualify the applicant with a criminal record.

At common law, neither criminal conviction nor imprisonment were grounds for divorce. Under modern law, a criminal conviction may (1) automatically dissolve a marriage in some civil death states,[62] (2) constitute grounds for divorce, or (3) constitute grounds for divorce if accompanied by imprisonment. The most usual situation is that the conviction gives the spouse grounds for divorce. The conviction alone, if for a felony or infamous crime, may constitute such grounds,[63] or the conviction may be accepted as proof of "intolerable conduct" or "irreconcilable differences" where the statute grants divorce for these reasons. In other states, to constitute grounds for divorce, the conviction must be accompanied by imprisonment, or by imprisonment for a specified number of years.[64] The theory behind the latter statutes is that a conviction followed by probation, for example, does not interfere with the ability of the convicted person to fulfill any marital and parental responsibilities.

In a few jurisdictions, a convicted offender may forfeit his or her parental rights. They may be awarded to the innocent spouse in case of divorce, or the children may be taken into the custody of the state under dependency and neglect statutes. Some states provide that a convicted criminal's children may be adopted without his or her consent,[65] or that the necessity of consent is waived if the parent is imprisoned for a stated number of years.[66] In New York, the parent deprived of civil rights as a result of a criminal conviction need not consent to the adoption.[67]

General statutes, which dispense with the necessity of consent from a parent who has been judicially deprived of the right to custody of his or her children, have been applied to the convicted parent,[68] although the requirement in some

---

60. Rudenstine, *supra*, at 56–60. Skinner v. Oklahoma, 316 U.S. 365 (1942).

61. Petition of Berkowitz, 88 Ill.App.2d 1, 232 N.E.2d 72 (1967). The applicant had committed forgery.

62. *In re* Lindewall's Will, 287 N.Y. 347, 39 N.E.2d 907 (1942).

The spouse of a convict sentenced to life imprisonment is free to remarry immediately. Zizzo v. Zizzo, 41 Misc.2d 928, 247 N.Y.S.2d 38 (1964).

But in Rhode Island, the spouse must file for divorce and the marriage must be dissolved by the court.

63. Conviction of a felony or infamous crime is grounds for divorce, irrespective of imprisonment is some sixteen states, including Illinois. Ill.Ann.Stat. ch. 40, § 1 (Smith-Hurd).

64. Rudenstine, *supra*, at 50–55.

65. All that is required in Iowa is imprisonment for a felony. Iowa Code Ann. § 600.3 (West).

66. Imprisonment for three or more years is required in Massachusetts, Oregon, and Rhode Island. A parent convicted of adultery, offense punishable by imprisonment for one or more years, or moral turpitude offense, need not give consent in South Dakota.

67. N.Y.Dom.Rel.Law § 111 (McKinney).

The rule is the same in Washington. Wash.Rev.Code Ann. § 26.32.040.

68. Calif.Civ.Code § 224 (West).

states is that the loss of custody must be due to the parent's unfitness or wrongdoing.[69] Abandonment, desertion, failure to support, failure to communicate, neglect, and unfitness often obviate the necessity of obtaining the consent of the guilty parent to the adoption of his or her children.[70] A few cases hold that conviction and imprisonment do not of themselves demonstrate a parent's unfitness so as to permit the adoption of children without the parent's consent.[71] Most courts, however, permit adoption against the parent's wishes where the offense shows unfitness, as for example, when the conviction was for child abuse.[72].

The Right of Citizenship or Residency (for aliens)

Although aliens as well as citizens are entitled to protection under the due process and equal protection clauses of the Constitution, and are protected in their exercise of the first amendment rights to freedom of speech and religion, an alien who is convicted of certain crimes may be denied admission into the United States. An alien already in the United States who is convicted of a criminal offense may be denied the right to become a citizen, and in some cases may be deported.

An alien who has been admitted into the United States may be unable to obtain naturalization under the rules established by Congress, which provide that no person shall be naturalized as a citizen unless that person has demonstrated good moral character for at least five years preceding the date when the petition for naturalization was filed.[73] Conviction within that five-year period of any offense that would exclude that person from admission to the United States deprives the individual of good moral character,[74] as does conviction of two or more gambling offenses,[75] confinement in a penal institution for 180 days or more regardless of the offense,[76] or conviction for murder at any time.[77] Habitual drunkards,[78] persons who have committed adultery,[79] and sexual psychopaths do not possess good moral character, regardless of a conviction. Arrests and traffic violations are also taken into account in determining good moral character for purposes of naturalization.[80]

---

69. N.Y.Dom.Rel.Law § 111 (adultery) (McKinney).

70. Calif.Civ.Code § 224 (West); Ill.Ann.Stat. ch. 4, § 9.1–8 (Smith-Hurd).

71. *In re* Adoption of Baby Boy, 10 Ariz.App. 47, 455 P.2d 997 (1969). The consent of the natural mother who had been convicted of forgery was required.

72. Petition of Kelley Minors, 6 Ariz.App. 299, 432 P.2d 158 (1967).

Casper v. Huber, 85 Nev. 474, 456 P.2d 436 (1969). Conviction of murder with penalty of imprisonment for 25 years.

73. 8 U.S.C.A. § 1427(a).

However a finding by the Attorney General that an alien is not deportable is not conclusive evidence that the alien possesses good moral character. *Id.* at § 1427(d).

74. *Id.* at § 1101(f)(3).

75. *Id.* at § 1101(f)(5).

76. *Id.* at § 1101(f)(7).

77. *Id.* at § 1101(f)(8).

78. *Id.* at § 1101(f)(1).

79. *Id.* at § 1101(f)(2).

80. United States v. Chandler, 152 F.Supp. 169 (D.Md.1957); *In re* Petition for Naturalization of Odeh, 185 F.Supp. 953 (D.Mich.1960).

The attorney general of the United States may order the deportation of an alien who has been convicted of a crime involving moral turpitude within five years after his or her entry into the United States and who has been sentenced to or confined in a prison for a year or more.[81] Conviction of two or more crimes involving moral turpitude at any time after entry and regardless of confinement may lead to deportation.[82] Congress has authorized the deportation of aliens convicted of violating laws relating to illicit possession of or traffic in narcotics or marijuana.[83] It has been held that deportation statutes are not designed to punish aliens, but to rid the country of persons whose presence might be detrimental to the safety and welfare of society.[84]

The Right to an Occupational License

Federal, state and local governments throughout the United States restrict entry into more than 350 occupations or professions through licensing requirements.[85] These restrictions—of which there are in excess of 2000—affect more than 10 million people.[86] For example, the state of California has passed legislation requiring the licensing of automobile mechanics.[87]

The following occupations are among those affected by state licensing regulations: embalmer, junk dealer, midwife, liquor dealer, taxicab operator, solicitor and canvasser, vocational nurse, watchmaker, guide dog trainer, tourist camp operator, inhalation therapist, dental hygienist, operator of a massage parlor, water well contractor, operator of a "public cart," psychiatric technician, trading stamp dealer, night clerk, practical nurse, seller of horse meat, minnow dealer, fur dealer, sewage work operator, florist, photographer, seller of lightning rods, weigh master, fish and game guide, surveyor, manicurist, milk dealer, operator of hotel, lodge, or home for the aged, anthracite coal mine inspector, mine foreman, policeman, oil and gas inspector, forester, money lender, motor car dealer, manufacturer of narcotics, seller of hearing aids, operator of driver training school, hospital administrator, threshing machine operator and dealer, tile layer, yacht salesman, tree surgeon, pest controller, well digger, potato grower, hypertrichologist (hair remover), dealer in scrap tobacco, landscape architect, and billiard hall owner and operator.[88]

---

81. 8 U.S.C.A. § 1251(a)(4). *Supra* note 162 (which says: There is a little known provision in the law that the court at the time of sentencing or within 30 days thereafter can recommend against deportation if it gives notice to the interested parties, including the Immigration and Naturalization Service, and they have an opportunity to oppose the recommendation).

82. Cubbels v. Del Guercio, 152 F.Supp. 277 (S.D.Cal.1957).

83. 8 U.S.C.A. § 1251(a)(11).

84. Mahler v. Eby, 264 U.S. 32, 44 S.Ct. 283, 68 L.Ed. 549 (1923).

85. Rudenstine, *supra*, at 82–83.

86. *Id.*

87. In 1980, some sixty occupations required a license in California.

88. H. Miller, *The Closed Door: The Effect of a Criminal Record on Employment with State and Local Public Agencies*, distributed by National Technical Information Service (1972); Rudenstine, *supra*, at 88–96, 171–195.

In all of the states and in the federal government, the right to obtain or hold an occupational license is affected by a criminal record, and similar provisions restrict the right of the convicted offender to hold jobs covered by the licensing regulations of cities and towns. Disqualification may result from the express words in general statutes, as for example, in the business or professional code, or the licensing acts governing the particular trade or profession. Both the renewal and initial granting of a license are affected by a criminal record, and power to revoke an existing license is granted to the licensing agency as well as to the courts. Even without express words, statutory or even administrative requirements that a license may be issued only to persons of good moral character effectively exclude the convicted person.[89]

The exact provisions of licensing statutes vary from state to state, from occupation to occupation, and even within an occupation. The criminal record that disqualifies may be a felony, a misdemeanor, a felony with moral turpitude, a crime with moral turpitude, or an infamous crime. The conviction that disqualifies may be interpreted according to the narrow or broad definition of conviction.

An analysis of the licensing statutes set out in *The Closed Door* discloses that a felony record affected 225 occupations; a felony with moral turpitude, an additional twenty-seven.[90] A misdemeanor record was a barrier to licensing in fifteen occupations, while a misdemeanor record involving moral turpitude disqualified in twenty-four others. A crime involving moral turpitude was sufficient to prevent licensing in some 166 occupations. Over one-half of the licenses required good moral character, a requirement that virtually closes the door to persons with a criminal record.

Unfortunately, rehabilitation, whether evidenced by a pardon, successful completion of probation, certificate of good conduct, expungement proceedings, "sealing" of the record of conviction, or otherwise, does not effectively open the door to professional and occupational licenses.[91] This situation occurs not only within the imprisoning state; it also is inevitable if the offender moves to a different part of the country. The lack of uniformity in the laws and practices of the various states and localities makes it almost impossible for persons with a criminal record to determine where they can utilize their training and skills, whether they acquired them in or out of prison.

The Requirement of Good Character. The most serious obstacle to the offender who seeks to enter a licensed occupation arises from two facts. The first is that many, if not most, licensing statutes require that the licensee must possess good character. The second is that there is an almost universal assumption that the person who has been convicted of a criminal offense is not of good character. The obstacles created by the provisions and assumptions about good character

---

89. Rudenstine, *supra,* at 83–85.

90. *Id.*

91. *See* George A. Pownall, *Employment Problems of Released Prisoners,* a report prepared for Manpower Administration, U.S. Department of Labor, under research contract No. 81–19–37, with the University of Maryland, authorized by Title I of the Manpower Development and Training Act.

are all the more serious because there is considerable doubt that there is any way for the convicted person to restore his or her good character. Although pardon and other forms of wiping out a conviction may remove particular civil disabilities and, for example, permit the convicted person to vote or serve on a jury, such a pardon or expungement proceeding does not necessarily, or even by implication, restore good character.[92]

Most, if not all, professions require that the applicant for licensing prove good character. This requirement is usually statutory, but even when the provision is not expressed, courts have found that the licensing authority has the implied power to bar persons who are morally unfit from being licensed.[93] Conviction of a crime is generally held to be evidence that the offender lacks the requisite character for the professional license.[94] The same rule is also applied to nonprofessional occupations, as for example, a merchant[95] and a taxicab operator.[96] In some instances, however, the rule is that the fact of conviction is only evidence of loss of good character. Additional inquiry is made into the circumstances to determine if the offense involved moral turpitude.

Moral turpitude has been defined as "an act of baseness, vileness, or depravity in the private and social duties which a man owes to his fellow men, or to society in general, contrary to the accepted and customary rule of right and duty between men."[97] Another definition is that moral turpitude is "conduct contrary to justice, honesty, modesty, or good morals."[98] Both felonies and misdemeanors are included if their commission is contrary to the public's moral standards.[99]

Because the public's moral standards may differ from place to place and change from time to time, it is impossible to know just what crimes do and what crimes do not involve moral turpitude. The terms good moral character or good character are also susceptible of changing meanings. Thus, as a practical matter, licenses are refused or revoked according to the meaning placed on these terms by the licensing agency. In general, however, a conviction is accepted by the licensing agency as conclusive evidence of bad character, and such decisions are seldom overruled by the courts.[100]

---

92. New York issues a Certificate of Good Conduct to convicted persons after five years of good conduct. A few New York licensing statutes require recognition of the Certificate. For example, N.Y.Gen.Bus.Law § 74 (McKinney), covering private investigators.

93. Dorf v. Fielding, 20 Misc.2d 18, 197 N.Y.S.2d 280 (1948). A person convicted for running a house of prostitution was denied a license to sell second-hand goods.

94. Application of Brooks, 57 Wash.2d 66, 355 P.2d 840 (1960), *cert. den.* 365 U.S. 813, 81 S.Ct. 694, 5 L.Ed.2d 692 (1961).

95. Hirsch v. City and County of San Francisco, 143 Cal. App. 2d 313, 300 P.2d 177 (1956).

96. Kaufman v. Taxicab Bureau, 236 Md. 476, 204 A.2d 521 (1964), *cert. den.* 382 U.S. 849, 86 S.Ct. 95, 15 L.Ed.2d 88 (1965).

97. Traders and General Ins. Co. v. Russell, 99 S.W.2d 1079 (Tex.Civ.App.1936); Jordan v. De George, 341 U.S. 223, 71 S.Ct. 703, 95 L.Ed. 886 (1951), reh. den. 341 U.S. 956, 71 S.Ct. 1011, 95 L.Ed. 1377 (1951).

98. Marsh v. State Bar of California, 210 Cal. 303, 291 P. 583 (1930).

99. Raphalides v. New Jersey Department of Civil Service, 80 N.J.Super. 407, 194 A.2d 1 (1963).

100. Some decisions require a hearing before denial of license particularly if the criminal record is remote. Peterson v. State Liquor Authority, 42 A.D.2d 195, 345 N.Y.S.2d 780 (1973).

The courts have also upheld revocation of professional licenses for "unprofessional conduct." Some licensing statutes list specific acts that are considered to be unprofessional conduct. "Conviction of a felony" is often so listed. Revocations may be upheld by the courts even though the criminal proceedings are dismissed.[101]

In the application of licensing statutes, both the narrow and broad definition of conviction are used. Differences in application occur from occupation to occupation within the same state, or as to the same occupation in different states. In at least one state, the statute permits the denial or revocation of a license upon a mere *commission* of a felony.[102] And a conviction may mean an action of a court or a finding of violation by the licensing agency itself.[103]

In the majority of cases it is up to the courts to apply either the narrow or broad definition. With regard to disbarment of an attorney, the tendency seems to be to apply the narrow definition, which means that disbarment may follow a plea of guilty, irrespective of judgment and sentence.[104] But the opposite result has been reached in cases concerning the removal of a license to practice medicine. Applying the broad definition, a doctor in Arkansas, upon whom sentence had not been imposed, and a doctor in Florida who had been placed on probation, were held not to have been convicted. There was thus no authority in the board of medical examiners to remove their licenses.[105] The Missouri laws require the suspension of a real estate broker's license upon conviction of forgery, embezzlement, and similar crimes. The word conviction was interpreted in "the most comprehensive sense, which includes judgment of a court upon a verdict or confession of guilt."[106]

When the question is the granting, renewal, or revocation of a professional or occupational license, both the wording of the statutory provisions and the court decisions must be resorted to in order to determine the circumstances under which the narrow or broad definition will be applied.

The Right to Public Employment

The term "public employment" is often used interchangeably with the term "public office," although there are certain technical distinctions between the two. An elective position in the federal, state, or municipal government is generally held to be a public office, and some appointive positions are also public offices. Public employment is a broader term. Membership in the armed forces and positions involving chiefly clerical functions are public employment, although they are not generally referred to as public office. A public office may

---

101. Meyer v. Board of Medical Examiners, 34 Cal.2d 62, 206 P.2d 1085 (1949).

102. Ariz.Rev.Stat.Ann. § 32–1263. Mandatory revocation of dentist's license.

103. *See, e.g.,* Calif.Bus. & Prof.Code § 6101 (West). If the act constitutes a felony or misdemeanor, conviction thereof in a criminal proceeding is not a condition precedent to disbarment or suspension from practice therefore.

104. *In re* Hickman, 18 Cal.2d 71, 113 P.2d 1 (1941); *In re* Clark, 52 Cal.2d 332, 340 P.2d 613 (1959).

105. State Medical Board v. Rodgers, 190 Ark. 266, 79 S.W.2d 83 (1935); Page v. State Board of Medical Examiners of Florida, 141 Fla. 294, 193 So. 82 (1940).

106. Meyer v. Missouri Real Estate Commission, 238 Mo.App. 476, 183 S.W.2d 342 (1944).

not be compensated, as for example, positions on a school board or even positions on a municipal council. Public employment, on the other hand, is paid employment with some type of governmental agency.

In most states, loss of political rights following a conviction includes loss of the right to hold public office, or the disqualification may be the right to hold office. Either term usually encompasses the right to be a public official, but may or may not be extended to mean the right to be a public employee. The restrictions that exclude convicted criminals from public employment affect a large number of job opportunities.

Restrictions against the hiring of a convicted offender for public employment are found in constitutional and statutory provisions, in civil service regulations, and in the administrative rulings of governmental agencies. The policy of the United States military services is to exclude or strictly condition the enlistment of persons with a criminal record.[107] In practice, few ex-convicts are given jobs in the public sector. A study of the types of jobs in governmental agencies held by persons with criminal records reveals that the government generally employs persons with criminal records in unskilled positions.[108] An acquittal on a criminal charge may not prevent denial of employment if the public agency regards the prospective employee as "unfit."

Federal, state, and municipal employment is affected by statutory enactments and governmental policy against the hiring of an ex-convict. Promoting insubordination in the armed forces disqualifies the offender from employment in the United States government or any department or agency for a period of five years after conviction. Conviction of advocating the overthrow of the government or inciting a riot or civil disorder, followed by imprisonment for one year, likewise disqualify the offender from employment for five years.[109]

Felons are ineligible to serve as officers or directors of any labor organization.[110] Persons convicted of an offense involving dishonesty or breach of trust cannot be employed by the Federal Deposit Insurance Corporation. It is almost impossible for a convicted criminal to obtain a position in a defense-related industry, since a criminal record, or a dishonorable discharge, precludes the issuance of a security clearance.[111]

Civil Service Regulations

The regulations of the United States Civil Service Commission provide that "criminal, infamous, dishonest, immoral, or notoriously disgraceful conduct" may disqualify a person from federal service.[112] The commission will accept applicants from ex-convicts at any time, and the decision about employment takes into consideration the seriousness and circumstances of the crime, the

---

107. Rubin, *supra,* at 626.

108. H. Miller, *supra,* at 82.

109. 5 U.S.C.A. § 7313; Rudenstine, *supra,* at 76.

110. 29 U.S.C.A. § 504(a); Rudenstine, *supra,* at 76.

111. 32 C.F.R. § 155.5.

112. 5 C.F.R. § 731.201(b).

offender's age, the individual's social and economic environment, and his or her rehabilitation.[113]

The bulk of public employees of states, counties, and municipalities are covered by civil service statutes and regulations. Some of the statutes and regulations provide for mandatory exclusion of persons with criminal records; in almost all instances, the authority to exclude the ex-offender is given to the civil service commission or the hiring authority. In addition, the regulations permit the denial of employment to persons not of good moral character or who are deemed unfit, as well as to persons who are guilty of "infamous" or "notoriously disgraceful" conduct. "Guilty" in this case does not necessarily imply a conviction in a legal sense; thus, an arrest, or even a report of the proscribed conduct may be an accepted basis for disqualification. In some cases, the term "not qualified" is sufficient to exclude persons with a criminal record although their training or education may be adequate for the job sought.

Civil service statutes routinely contain provisions that require or permit the firing of an individual for "misconduct" or for "cause." This may include misstatements in the original application. Thus, a person who conceals a conviction is subject to discharge if the fact later comes to light.[114] The language in some statutes, permitting discharge for a crime or violation is broad enough to include minor offenses and even an arrest without conviction.[115] A few jurisdictions have a policy of not automatically excluding applicants with criminal records. Illinois protects the misdemeanant and the person merely arrested,[116] and provides for automatic restoration of licenses unless the licensing agency holds an investigation and hearing and determines that the restoration is not in the public interest.[117]

Rules and regulations of civil service commissions sometimes make an effort to relate the offense to the kind of job sought. Thus, Nevada provides that persons convicted of crimes against property may not be considered for positions involving merchandise; persons convicted of a crime against persons will not be considered for positions involving the care or custody of individuals; persons convicted of crimes such as forgery will not be considered for positions that require the handling of money, and persons convicted of serious traffic infractions will not be considered for positions involving motor vehicle operation.[118]

As in the federal government, in some cases the disqualification involves a time-delay factor. Thus, a person convicted of a felony may be considered after

---

113. *See, Employment of the Rehabilitated Offender in the Federal Service,* Federal Probation (Sept.1971), 52–3.

114. 18 U.S.C.A. § 4082.

Employees who conceal a criminal charge may be discharged even though the charges were subsequently dismissed. *The court in* Sumeracki v. County of Wayne, 354 Mich. 377, 92 N.W.2d 325 (1958), upheld a suspension, declaring, that however harsh the present rule may be, all were cognizant of it when they started to work. In any case, such rules reflect an awareness that public policy may exclude not only a convicted felon from civil service employment, but also one accused of a felony.

115. *Id.*

116. Ill.Ann.Stat. ch. 127, § 63b108b1 (Smith-Hurd).

117. Section 1005–5–5, Illinois Unified Corrections.

118. H. Miller, *supra,* at 42–43.

a lapse of five years; of a misdemeanor, after a lapse of one year; with increasing delays if there are several offenses within the time period.[119]

A Model Civil Service Criminal Conviction Statute proposed by the author of *The Closed Door* (see note) proposes that a conviction will not automatically disqualify a person for civil service employment, and mandates consideration of the following factors by the hiring authority: (a) the nature of the crime and its relationship to the job for which the person has applied; (b) information pertaining to the degree of rehabilitation of the convicted person; and (c) the time elapsed since the conviction.

Private Employment

A job applicant with a criminal record faces almost insurmountable barriers to private employment.[120] It is difficult to identify the nature and extent of these barriers because of the complexity and diversity of private employment and because of the reluctance of some private employers to admit to job discrimination directed toward the ex-convict. Two surveys of private employers showed that 60 percent had reservations about employing ex-offenders. Some totally refused to hire the ex-offender; some hired offenders only for certain (usually unskilled) positions.[121] Even when the refusal to hire the ex-offender is based upon previous unhappy experiments in such hiring, the employer will not disclose either the unhappy experience nor the resulting decision to not employ any more "ex-cons." The employer simply finds a person with a criminal record "not qualified" for the job in question and lets it go at that.

Several projects are underway to update employers' attitudes and to determine the nature and extent of the refusal of the private sector to employ convicted offenders. In spite of the lack of documentation, it is generally agreed that many employers flatly reject applicants who have criminal records, and most employers will not hire a released convict if other personnel are available.[122] When ex-convicts are hired, they will be offered only low-skilled and poorly paid jobs.[123]

Discrimination based upon age, sex, or race is unlawful, and it has been held that the refusal of a private employer to hire a job applicant because of his arrest record violated his civil rights.[124] The protection, however, does not extend to persons who have been convicted of a criminal offense. In the case of a private employer, the definition of conviction and of criminal offense is almost completely within his or her discretion. The probationer, regardless of his or her technical legal status, is a convicted person as far as the general public is concerned.

---

119. H. Miller, *supra,* at 43.

120. Rudenstine, *supra,* at 77–80.

121. J. Ryan, R. Webb, and N. Mandel, Offender Employment Resource Survey. Minnesota Department of Corrections (1966).

122. Rudenstine, *supra,* at 77.

123. Harris, *Changing Public Attitudes Toward Crime and Corrections,* 32 Fed.Prob. 12 (1968).

124. Gregory v. Litton Systems, Inc., 316 F.Supp. 401 (C.D.Cal.1970). An employer was enjoined from denying a job to applicant because of his arrest record on the ground that blacks are arrested more frequently than whites.

There are, of course, business and trade organizations and private employers who make a point of providing jobs to convicted offenders. The Solution to Employment Problems (STEP) program of the National Association of Manufacturers is one such effort.[125] In this and similar programs, the employers provide equipment and instructors to train inmates while they are in prison and then guarantee them a job upon their release.

The Right to Be Bonded

A bond is the certificate or evidence of an obligation. A simple bond is signed only by the principal; a surety bond is signed by the principal and by other persons, known as sureties. The sureties undertake to pay money in the event that the assured, the party in whose favor the bond is written, suffers damage because the principal fails to perform as agreed. A bail bond, for example, guarantees the appearance of the accused (the principal) for trial. If the accused (the principal) fails to appear, the bail bondsman (the surety) must locate the principal and return that person for trial or forfeit the amount of the bond to the state (the assured).

Almost any kind of job where the employee handles money or merchandise may require a bond. Thus, a person who cannot furnish bond cannot work in a bank, a mercantile institution, or a warehouse. That person cannot become a truck driver, responsible for valuable shipments of goods, if the job specifications require the posting of a bond. Similarly, collection agents, bookkeepers, door-to-door canvassers, ticket-takers, ice-cream vendors, and holders of a milk route may need a bond before they will be allowed to enter upon their duties.

Private individuals are sometimes sureties on bonds for friends or relatives, but most surety bonds are written by insurance and bonding companies that are in the business of writing bonds. In the typical situation, the employee (or sometimes the employer) pays a fee for the bond, in return for which the insurance company agrees to pay any losses to the employer occasioned by the dishonesty or unlawful acts of the employee.

No bonding company is required by law to furnish a bond to all applicants. The decision to write or deny a bond is with the surety. The company makes a careful investigation of all persons who request bonds and refuses to bond persons whom they consider to be poor risks. Since they refuse to bond poor risks, the saying goes that "bonding companies bond only those who don't need it." The loss of the right to be bonded that follows upon a criminal conviction is not so much a loss of the *right* to be bonded as it is the loss of the *ability* to get a bond. This is because almost without exception a person with a criminal record is considered to be a poor risk. Irrespective of any other obstacle, this inability to get a bond may constitute the final barrier to employment.

The Manpower Administration of the Department of Labor offers fidelity bonding coverage for qualified job applicants. The coverage is available to persons who cannot obtain suitable employment because they have police, credit, or other records that prevent their being covered by the usual commercial

---

125. The National Association of Manufacturers operates its S.T.E.P. (Solutions to Employment Problems) in correctional institutions as part of the Work Release programs in certain federal institutions.

bonds. Ex-offenders are eligible for the bonds if (a) they are qualified and suitable for the employment in question, and (b) they are not commercially bondable under ordinary circumstances. The bonds are issued in units of $500. Maximum coverage is twenty units, or $10,000. The usual coverage is one year, but this term may be extended if the employer cannot make other arrangements at the end of the period. The applicant makes application for the bond through a state employment office, and the bond becomes effective when the applicant has begun work and the manager of the local employment service office or other authorized personnel of the state agency has certified the bond.

Unfortunately, it does not appear that a substantial number of ex-offenders seek to take advantage of this program. Both employers and prospective employees seem to lack information about the fact that bonding is available through the state employment agencies. There is the additional fact that ex-offenders generally refrain from making application for jobs that require bonding.

The Right to Manage
One's Own Affairs

The Latin phrase *sui juris* means having capacity to manage one's own affairs, or not being under legal disability to act for one's self. Conviction for a criminal offense renders the offenders *non-sui-juris,* because it deprives them of their full capacity to act with reference to their own affairs. The disabilities are more severe during imprisonment. In all states, one of the collateral consequences of conviction is to deny prisoners and ex-convicts full participation in the judicial process and unhampered ability to manage their own affairs.

A contract has been defined as a "promise or a set of promises for the breach of which the law gives a remedy * * *." [129] Today, in the majority of states, the convicted person can contract and can resort to the courts to enforce those contracts. A distinction is sometimes made between the right to contracts conveying property and other types of contracts.[130] Also, some statutes authorize a convict to contract for necessities, such as for legal services.[131]

The Right to Make a Will

At common law, since the convict was without property, he or she did not need to make a will. However, the right to make a will may be an important right to the convict who retains his or her rights to property. Generally in the United States, prisoners have this testamentary capacity to make a will. In most states, a prisoner is also a competent witness to a will made by another.

---

126. The Federal Bonding Program, *Questions and Answers,* (U.S. Department of Labor, Manpower Administration, 1971). *See also* Rudenstine, *supra,* at 79.

127. *Id.*

128. *Id.*

129. Restatement of Contracts, § 1 (1932).

130. Rosman v. Cuevas, 176 Cal.App.2d Supp. 867, 1 Cal.Rptr. 485 (1959). The decision in this case upheld the validity of a conveyance made by a convict.

131. Byers v. Sun Sav. Bank, 41 Okl. 728, 139 P. 948 (1914).

THE EFFECT OF AN ADJUDICATION OF DELINQUENCY

We have seen how a conviction for a criminal offense affects the civil rights of the adult offender. Now let us consider the collateral consequences of an adjudication of delinquency upon the juvenile offender.

At the outset, we should note that it was not the intention of the founders of the juvenile court that an adjudication of delinquency impose or imply any negative collateral consequences whatever. The juvenile court operates under the doctrine of *parens patriae,* a Latin phrase meaning literally "father of his country." As applied to the juvenile court, the doctrine means that the state has a responsibility toward its neglected, dependent, and errant children. In the event that a child's own parents fail or neglect to train him or her properly, then it is the duty of the state to take the place of the parents. In exercising this duty, the court acts toward the child as "a kind of loving father."

Since the stated objective of the juvenile court is to provide the conditions under which a child brought before it can grow up as a useful citizen, the right of the court to act with respect to the child does not depend upon the child's having committed an act, which, if committed by an adult, would be a crime. The juvenile court is given the power to declare a child delinquent and to take the child under its protection for such things as habitual truancy, frequenting places of ill repute, keeping bad company, running away, and engaging in conduct harmful to the child and others. A juvenile court may exercise jurisdiction over a juvenile for a much wider span of misconduct than that which will give a criminal court jurisdiction over an adult.[132]

Some states make a distinction between a juvenile delinquent, who has committed an act that if committed by an adult would be a crime, and a minor in need of supervision.[133] A person in need of supervision is a child who has committed a strictly juvenile offense, such as running away, truancy, or ungovernable behavior. One of the purposes of this distinction, as we shall see, is to protect the child from the effects of an adjudication of delinquency. However, the distinction between the juvenile delinquent and the child in need of supervision is not observed in most states. Thus, an adjudication of delinquency may be made upon a finding of either criminal or noncriminal misconduct within the juvenile court age.

Direct Consequences of an Adjudication of Delinquency

The dispositional alternatives of the juvenile judge exceed those available to the judge who must pronounce sentence in an adult criminal court. The juvenile judge has authority even after adjudication of delinquency to dismiss the

---

132. Even where there is an invasion of protected freedom, the powers of the state to control the conduct of children reaches beyond its scope of authority over adults. Ginsberg v. New York, 390 U.S. 629, 88 S.Ct. 1274, 20 L.Ed.2d 195 (1968).

133. Thus we have PINS (Persons In Need of Supervision); MINS (Minors In Need of Supervision); and CHINS (Children In Need of Supervision).

petition or return the child to its parents without imposing sanctions of any kind. The Standard Juvenile Court Act [134] states that following adjudication the court may:

• Place the minor on probation in his or her own home or in the custody of a suitable person elsewhere, upon conditions determined by the court.

• Vest legal custody of the minor in a governmental or nongovernmental agency or institution licensed or approved by the state for the care of minors.

• Order whatever care or treatment is authorized by law.

• Order the parents or other persons having custody of the child to do or omit any acts deemed harmful to the child. This may include a decree for support or an order requiring either spouse to stay away from the other spouse or children.

• Dismiss the petition or otherwise terminate its jurisdiction at any time.

• Make any order or judgment authorized by law.[135]

Collateral Consequences of an Adjudication of Delinquency

It was clearly the intent of the sponsors of the juvenile court movement to protect the child from any adverse consequences arising out of appearances in court. This objective appears in modern juvenile court legislation. Five basic types of protection are set out in the statutes: (1) provisions limiting access to law enforcement and juvenile court records relating to the handling of the juvenile by the police and the court—these provisions may prohibit publication of the names of juveniles taken into custody or appearing before the court; (2) provisions against fingerprinting or photographing the juvenile, or if fingerprinting or photographing are permitted under special circumstances, directions that the fingerprints and photographs be removed from the files and destroyed after the particular purpose has been served or a stated period of time has elapsed; (3) provisions for permanent sealing of files and records relating to the juvenile court proceedings within a stated period after the final discharge of the juvenile from the jurisdiction of the court; (4) provisions declaring that an adjudication of delinquency is not a conviction; and (5) statutes declaring that a juvenile proceeding is not a disqualifying factor for civil service.[136] Unfortunately, these statutory protections have not been successful in practice. As a result, an adjudication of delinquency may carry with it many of the collateral consequences of a conviction in an adult criminal court.

However, neither the adjudication of delinquency nor a commitment ordered by a juvenile court judge is a conviction. The charge in a juvenile proceeding is

---

134. National Council on Crime and Delinquency, Standard Juvenile Court Act, sixth edition (1959), § 24.

135. In general the decisions are split as to whether it is constitutional to impose a longer "placement" on a juvenile than the maximum sentence which could be imposed on an adult for the same crime. Constitutionality upheld in Packnett v. United States, 435 F.2d 693 (5th Cir.1970); R.R. v. State, 448 S.W.2d 187 (Tex.Civ.App.1969). *But contra,* Matter of Brown, 439 F.2d 47 (3rd Cir.1970).

136. Standard Juvenile Court Act, *supra* n. 134.

that the minor is a delinquent child.   The purpose of such proceedings is not to punish juveniles but to reform them from their state of delinquency.   The proceedings are not criminal cases and their disposition should not be considered conviction of a crime.

The Standard Juvenile Court Act section dealing with the legal effect of an adjudication of delinquency is entitled, "Adjudication of Child Noncriminal," and reads:

> No adjudication by the court of the status of any child shall be deemed a conviction; no adjudication shall impose any civil disability ordinarily resulting from conviction; no child shall be found guilty or be deemed a criminal by reason of adjudication; and no child shall be charged with crime or be convicted in any court except as provided in Section 13 of this Act.   The disposition made of a child, or any evidence given in the court, shall not operate to disqualify the child in any civil service or military application or appointment.[137]

Some twenty-four states have statutes providing that juvenile records may not serve to disqualify the applicant for civil service employment.[138]   Other states, on the other hand, expressly allow examination of the record by the Civil Service Commission.   The practical effect of such statutes is largely determined by the character of the inquiries on job application forms.

Juvenile Protective Statutes in Practice

In spite of statutory provisions that seek to protect the confidentiality of juvenile court records and shield the juvenile from the adverse effects of adjudication and commitment, knowledge of juvenile court proceedings is widely available for a variety of purposes.[139]   Legal restrictions on the press are stoutly resisted by editors and reporters, although some news media have cooperated with the juvenile authorities to the extent of establishing a *policy* against disclosing the names of juveniles in the court.   Law enforcement officers are also reluctant to set up special records and procedures for the arrest and booking of juveniles, although, like the news media, some police departments work out cooperative agreements on confidentiality with the juvenile court.   There is also a considerable body of opinion against confidentiality of juvenile court proceedings, based either on the belief that confidentiality statutes are unfair to the public, which is entitled to know the nature and extent of juvenile crime,[140] or on the belief that attempts to seal and destroy juvenile records are

---

137. Standard Juvenile Court Act, *supra,* § 25.

138. N.Y.Fam.Ct. Act § 782 (McKinney).

See also, In re Smith, 63 Misc.2d 198, 310 N.Y.S.2d 617 (1970) and Hambel v. Levine, 243 A.D. 530, 275 N.Y.S. 702 (1934), where it was said that judgment of delinquency will not operate to the detriment of the defendant in his desire to enter the civil service.   Ill.Ann.Stat. ch. 37, § 702–9(3) (Smith-Hurd).

Tex.Fam.Code Ann. Title 3, § 51.13(a) (Vernon).

139. One such purpose is the consideration of the juvenile record when sentencing the convicted adult.   *See for example,* N.Y.Fam.Ct. Act § 783 (McKinney).

140. Iowa Code Ann. § 232.54 (West).

unfair to the juvenile because, as one author states, "the record comes out inevitably."[141]

Employers obtain access to juvenile court records by two simple expedients— they require persons seeking employment to obtain a court clerk's certificate of their recent record in court, or they request a waiver of confidentiality. The armed forces secure juvenile and family court records in the same manner. In some cases, statutory restrictions on disclosure of arrest records (including those of juveniles) make exceptions for the release of the records to certain official agencies. As to private employers, a great many courts permit inspection simply because they consider them to be persons with a legitimate interest in the juvenile records.[142] The most telling blow against the protective statutes is struck by job application forms that require the job seekers to disclose information about their juvenile record. Only a few job application forms specifically advise applicants not to include juvenile records when answering questions concerning conviction and arrest, although the forms routinely instruct the applicant not to include minor traffic violations. Occasionally applicants are permitted to exclude offenses committed under a certain age—16, 17, or 18 are usual, although one state uses the age 21.[143] On the other hand, it is not uncommon to require the applicant to report an arrest "at any time in your life,"[144] or instructions may be made to include juvenile offenses *unless sealed.*[145]

Research discloses that there is a wide discrepancy between the stated policy of protecting juveniles from any adverse consequences arising out of juvenile court proceedings and the actual practice as revealed by an analysis of job application forms.

Social Stigmatization of Adult and Juvenile Ex-offenders

Stigmatization and loss of social status are probably the most severe of the collateral consequences of an adjudication of delinquency, and they also constitute a significant problem for adult offenders. The status degradation that follows a person with a court record outlasts the discharge of an offender from

---

Tex.Rev.Civ.Stat.Ann. art. 2338–1 § 15(A) (Vernon). If a child has been charged with the violation of the penal law of the grade of felony and if the child has previously been declared delinquent, officials concerned with the case shall release upon request information as to the name and address of the child and the alleged offense. Hearings on the case in juvenile court shall be open to persons having a legitimate interest in the proceedings, including representatives of the news media; and juvenile court records shall be open to inspection by representatives of the news media.

141. Kogon and Loughery, *Sealing and Expungement of Criminal Records—The Big Lie,* 61 J.Crim.L.C. & P.S. 378 (1970).

142. A juvenile in California against whom charges were subsequently dismissed obtained a court order sealing the arrest record as provided in West's Ann.Calif.Pen.Code § 851.7. He subsequently noted on a job application that he had no prior arrests. Nevertheless, the employer was able to obtain the arrest record and the individual was fired for having falsified the employment application. The Closed Door, op. cit., pp. 24–25.

143. State law provides for a cut-off at age 18 in Massachusetts. The United States Civil Service Commission does not require applicants to disclose information concerning convictions by juvenile authorities that occurred prior to age 21, nor consider arrest records that were not followed by conviction.

144. H. Miller, *supra,* at 16.

145. *Id.*

the correctional process. This is particularly true if the adjudication or conviction has been followed by commitment to a state correctional institution.

A kind of circular effect can be observed in the assignment of such a status. Ex-offenders suffer from civil disabilities that bar them from jobs and entry into professions. Society thus limits their occupational choices to jobs considered menial. The public then views all ex-offenders as holding menial jobs and characterizes them as members of a lower strata of society. Membership in the lower strata of society forecloses opportunities for more prestigious jobs, and movement into the upper levels of society is restricted. The result is "management of status," [146] or, as one author puts it, "Civil disabilities trigger a societal response that groups all offenders together and ostracizes them from the community." [147]

In spite of the philosophy stated in juvenile court statutes that the appearance of a juvenile in the juvenile court shall in no way produce adverse consequences, it is clear that a juvenile record consigns juveniles to an inferior status. Their education, their training, their employment opportunities, and their place in the community are all endangered. They suffer from civil disabilities [148] and from the inferior status directly promoted by civil disabilities. [149] Civil disabilities then become the "badge of 'convict' " and "the brand of iniquity." [150] Sealing and expungement statutes are of limited value in removing the more direct consequences of adjudication or conviction. They are of even less value in reducing or eliminating the stigmatization that the community imposes upon its offenders.

That civil disabilities following conviction directly and indirectly affect the ability of the released offender to make his way in the society is generally recognized. The adjustment of the offender into society is further impeded by his belief that these disabilities prevent such adjustment. According to a 1949 survey, 88 percent of ex-offenders believed that loss of voting rights would hinder them. Some 93 percent believed that the conviction would increase their difficulty in getting an occupational license such as barber, plumber, bartender; 92 percent expected difficulty in getting a driver's license. All of these things, in the opinion of the offenders, would keep them from becoming "good citizens" and securing a "decent living." [151]

The convicted person, including the probationer, goes back into a society which treats him with suspicion and hostility. The imposition of continuing civil disabilities imposes an inferior status on the convicted person, and contributes to this distrust and hostility. [152] One author states that the result is to create a permanent class of outcasts who can never be assimilated into the mainstream of community life. [153]

---

146. Schrag, *The Correctional System: Problems and Perspectives,* 381 Annals 11–20 (1969).

147. Gough, *The Expungement of Adjudication Records of Juvenile and Adult Offenders: A Problem of Status,* 1966 Wash.U.L.Q. 147.

148. Carafas v. LaVallee, 391 U.S. 234, 88 S.Ct. 1556, 20 L.Ed.2d 554 (1968).

149. United States v. Pendergast, 28 F.Supp. 601 (W.D.Mo.1939).

150. Webb v. County Court of Raleigh County, 113 W.Va. 474, 168 S.E. 760 (1933).

151. "Crime Prevention Through Treatment," Survey reported in Yearbook of the National Probation and Parole Association, (1952), 86, 89.

152. United States v. Morgan, 346 U.S. 502, 74 S.Ct. 247, 98 L.Ed. 248 (1954).

It is, of course, an open question whether the removal of continuing civil disabilities would change community attitudes toward the offender. Attention must also be paid to the proposition that the public has a right to knowledge of the previous criminal record to protect itself against the recidivist offender. It is probable that removal of civil disabilities will not of itself change the public attitude toward the offender. But distinctions must be made. The imposition of civil disabilities should bear some rational relationship to the offense committed and to the function to be performed. Different treatment must be accorded the hard-core recidivist offender and the rehabilitated offender, and a way found to distinguish one from the other. Procedures for removing disabilities must be simplified and provide for a restoration of "good character" when circumstances warrant. Most important of all, affirmative educational efforts must involve the public in corrections and in the welfare of the ex-offender. Professionals in law enforcement and corrections and the leaders of the bench and bar must concern themselves with the removal of the inconsistencies and inequities which today characterize the consequences of conviction.

14

Pardon and Restoration of Rights

The Problem

We have seen that a conviction for a criminal offense or an adjudication of delinquency are followed by direct consequences in the form of criminal sanctions and collateral consequences in the form of widespread loss of civil rights, the many rights affected by a conviction can include: voting rights, rights to hold public office, employment opportunities, and judicial rights, such as the rights to sue, execute legal instruments, serve on a jury, and testify without impeachment. Certain marital and parental rights may be lost, and rights relating to property—including insurance, worker's compensation, and pension benefits—may be impaired.

The direct consequences of conviction—the criminal sanctions—come to an end with the completion of the sentence. Generally, a sentence is completed on the day of release from an institution or the date of discharge from probation or parole supervision. In the case of a juvenile, the right of the juvenile court or the youth authority to control the juvenile's actions terminates upon discharge from probation or parole or from an institution, or when the juvenile reaches a certain age, usually twenty-one years.

The collateral effects of a conviction or adjudication—the loss of civil rights or of employment opportunities—continue for the lifetime of the offender [1] or until some affirmative act takes place that by law prevents the civil disabilities from attaching or serves to "wipe out" or reduce them. As we shall see, these affirmative acts are of limited value; some because there is no intention that they be completely effective in reducing or wiping out the conviction, others

---

1. A direct attack on all constitutional and statutory provisions depriving criminal offenders of various civil rights in California was unsuccessful. Morrison v. California, 238 F.Supp. 22 (S.D.Cal. 1964).

because they cannot reach occupational licenses or the private employer. Almost all procedures for restoring civil rights have an additional fatal weakness as far as the objective of wiping out a criminal conviction or adjudication of delinquency is concerned—they do not restore "good character." In this chapter, we will examine some of the methods used to minimize the effects of a conviction or adjudication of delinquency and will attempt to evaluate their effectiveness.

Methods Used

The methods used to remove the collateral consequences of a conviction or adjudication include [2] pardon, automatic restoration of rights, restoration of rights upon application, expungement and annulment, sealing, decisions of courts, opinions of the attorneys general, governors' executive orders, and acts of the legislature. Unfortunately, the methods in use, and many of those being suggested, neither seal, expunge, annul, nullify, nor restore, in any practical effective way.

The subject of pardon will be discussed in the following chapter. This chapter will examine other means and procedures by which the effects of conviction may be minimized.

The subject of pardon must be included in any comprehensive study of criminal justice release procedures. Operating as a distinct subsystem within the criminal justice process, pardon fulfills a needed and necessary function. Yet, despite its importance to a well-balanced system of justice, it has received little scholarly attention. Lack of penetrating study has led to misapplication and confusion as to its nature and function.

Even the courts have been misled into ambiguous dicta and insupportable holdings. Some jurisdictions, by dictum, have held that a pardon wipes out the crime as though it had never happened, yet others have held that for some purposes, a pardon does not wipe out the fact of a conviction and the recipient is regarded, not as a "new person," but as a convicted criminal. This is true, for example, when the pardoned criminal takes the stand as a witness in a trial.

In many cases, the effect that should be achieved by a pardon might well depend upon the ground for which it was granted. A pardon granted because later evidence showed the convicted person to have been innocent might be held to wipe out the crime for all purposes, whereas a pardon granted because a prisoner helped stop a prison riot might not.

---

2. These are listed by the American Bar Association National Clearinghouse on Offender Employment Restrictions, in a handbook entitled Removing Offender Employment Restrictions (1973), hereinafter referred to as the American Bar Association Handbook.

The authors of *The Collateral Consequences of a Criminal Conviction* classify the various procedures under the headings Pardon, Automatic Restoration, Expungement and Annulment, and Miscellaneous Procedures. Vand. L. Rev., *supra*, at 1143–54.

Model Annulment and Sealing Statute, Georgetown Law Institute. *See* Appendix.

Lawrence R. Booth, *The Expungement Myth*, 48 Los Angeles Bar Ass'n Bull. (1962–63) 161–66.

Loss and Restoration of Rights Incident to Conviction or Imprisonment. Model Penal Code, § 306.

Civil Rights, Their Loss and Restoration. Rubin, *supra*, at ch. 17.

Rudenstine, *The Rights of Ex-Offenders*, (New York: Avon Books, 1979), 140–153.

The Power to Pardon

The power to pardon has traditionally belonged to the king or sovereign. Since a crime was considered to be an offense against the king, he was deemed to have the power to forgive it. In early American law, however, the power to pardon was given to the legislature, or when granted to the executive, was severely restricted. By the time the Constitution was written, the older rule was again followed. The president was given the power of pardon except in cases of impeachment.[3] Today, in most states, the power to pardon is placed in the governor, either acting alone or in conjunction with some official or board.[4]

When granted to the governor, the power may be without limitation or it may be restricted. In a number of states, the power to pardon given the governor does not extend to treason and impeachment.[5] When the governor's power is restricted in this manner, these excepted crimes may usually be pardoned by the legislature. Normally, the power to pardon does not extend to violations of municipal ordinances—the power extends only to offenses against the state. In some states, the power to pardon permits a pardon at any time after charge or indictment; in others, the power can be exercised only after "conviction." California forbids the granting of any pardon or commutation of sentence to any prisoner twice convicted of a felony except upon the written recommendation of a majority of the judges of the supreme court.[6] Other states forbid pardon until the minimum sentence or a certain length of sentence has been served, or until after a stated number of years of successful parole. The pardoning power may also be limited by the character of the case. For example, disbarment of an attorney has been held to be a civil, not a criminal case, and

---

3. U.S. Const. art. II, § 2, cl. 1.   * * * and he (the president) shall have the power to grant reprieves and pardons for offenses against the United States except in cases of impeachment.

The president has no power to pardon a state offender. *In re* Bacchiaro, 49 F.Supp. 37 (W.D.N.Y. 1943).

4. In California, the general authority to grant reprieves, pardons, and commutations of sentence is with the governor, by virtue of its constitution. Calif. Const. art. V, § 8, Cal.Penal Code § 4800, *et seq.* The Board of Prison Terms has replaced the Advisory Pardon Board as the investigative/advising agency. Cal.Penal Code § 4801.

The governor cannot grant a pardon to any person twice convicted of a felony except upon written recommendation of a majority of the supreme court. The governor must report to the legislature at the beginning of every session all pardons and commutations of sentence granted by him or her. Cal.Penal Code §§ 4800–4852. California also has special procedures for restoration fo rights and application for pardon. *Id.* § 4852.01.

In New York, the power to pardon lies with the governor by constitutional provision. N.Y. Const. art. IV, § 4.

New York has a special procedure for granting relief from forfeiture and disabilities resulting from a conviction, N.Y. Correct. Law §§ 700–705 (McKinney), but the Certificate of Relief from Disabilities is not considered a pardon nor does it alter or modify the manner of applying for pardons to the governor. *Id.* § 706.

In Texas, the application for pardon is directed to the Board of Pardons and Paroles and the governor may not grant a pardon unless it has been recommended by the board. However, the governor may refuse to grant a recommended pardon. Tex.Const. Art. IV, § 11. Texas. Admin. Code, tit. 37, § 143.1.

5. California, New York, and Texas except treason and judgment on impeachment from the executive pardoning power.

6. Cal.Penal Code § 4852.16 (West).

hence not pardonable.[7] Where the state law so provides, both absolute and conditional pardons may be issued.

Objectives of Pardon

The pardoning power was originally seen as a method of righting legal wrongs and of freeing the innocent. Following this, a commutation of sentence or a pardon became an acceptable way to correct unduly severe sentences or to recognize mitigating circumstances that were not taken into consideration at the time of trial. The divergent views concerning the infliction of the death penalty have often been expressed in the use of the power of executive clemency to reduce the sentence to life imprisonment. Prisoners who are old, infirm, or have a fatal illness are pardoned for humanitarian reasons, and escaped prisoners who have rehabilitated themselves in the period after the escape may be pardoned in recognition of their exemplary lives during the period of freedom. The pardoning power is used to prevent deportation of an alien, and sometimes—in the form of amnesties or general pardons—to achieve political purposes.[8] The pardoning power is also used to remove some of the direct consequences of conviction for drunken driving or to remit fines or forfeitures. Either alone, or in connection with special statutory proceedings, the pardoning power is now frequently used to remove the civil disabilities that are a collateral consequence of a conviction. It is its use for this latter purpose—to restore civil rights—that we are chiefly concerned with in this chapter.

Kinds of Pardons

Pardons, generally, are either full (absolute) or conditional.[9] A pardon is full when it freely and unconditionally absolves an individual from the legal consequences of his or her crime and conviction. A pardon is conditional when it does not become operative until certain conditions are met or after the occurrence of a specified event.[10] A conditional pardon is generally held not to be effective to restore the full civil rights of the offender, unless there is express language to that effect in the proclamation of pardon.

Connecticut uses the pardon process—and the related clemency action of commutation—routinely to accelerate parole eligibility for certain inmates serving life sentences. The U.S. Supreme Court noted that as many as 75 percent of

---

7. Hankamer v. Templin, 143 Tex. 572, 187 S.W.2d 549 (1945).

8. Other forms of executive clemency that are utilized to carry out these purposes include commutation of sentence, reprieve of execution, emergency medical reprieve, and remissions of fines and forfeitures. Rudenstine, *supra,* at 141–2.

9. Virginia recognized four types of pardons—absolute pardon, simple pardon, pardon without conditions, and conditional pardon. William F. Stone, Jr., *Pardons in Virginia,* 26 Wash. & Lee L. Rev. 307–20 (1968).

10. For example, Texas grants an "Out-of-Country Conditional Pardon," which releases a prisoner to immigration officials for deportation. Texas used a conditional pardon in lieu of parole prior to September, 1956. Texas Board of Pardons and Paroles, *1978 Handbook on Parole, Mandatory Supervision, and Executive Clemency.*

all "lifers" benefited from such relief prior to parole release. However the Court did not require any due process in the denial of such relief.[11]

Revocation

A full pardon, once delivered, cannot be revoked. A conditional pardon may be revoked for violation of the conditions imposed. Some courts have attempted to restrict the right of the governor to revoke a conditional pardon by prohibiting revocation without some sort of determination that the person pardoned has violated the conditions.[12]

Procedure for Obtaining Pardon

The procedure for obtaining a pardon is fixed by statute or regulations of the pardoning authority. Generally, the convicted person must apply for a pardon, and some time must elapse after release from confinement or discharge on parole before an offender can apply for a pardon.[13] The offender must then make application and notify whatever persons are required to be notified—typically, the prosecuting attorney, the sheriff, and the court of conviction. Posting or publication of a public notice may be required. There may be limitations upon repeated applications for pardon, as for example, a time interval between applications. In most cases, investigations will be conducted by the pardoning authority. A hearing on the application may be held, and may also be open to the public, which is the case in some states.[14] Presence of attorneys at such hearings may be discouraged. In New York, the appearance of the district attorney is required in capital cases.[15] The purpose of the hearing is not to review the original criminal case, but to ascertain facts that have a bearing upon the propriety of granting clemency.

---

11. Conn. Board of Pardons v. Dumschat, 452 U.S. 458, 101 S.Ct. 2460, 69 L.Ed. 158 (1981). This much-litigated case ultimately held that no due process was mandated by the federal constitution in the clemency process. It is also reported at: 618 F.2d 216 (2d Cir.1980); 442 U.S. 926, 99 S.Ct. 2854, 61 L.Ed.2d 294 (U.S.S.C.1979); 593 F.2d 165 (2d Cir.1979); 432 F.Supp. 1310 (Ct.1977). The applicable statute is Conn.Gen.Stat. § 18–26 (1981).

12. In Texas, by administrative rule, a conditional pardon releasee is entitled to the same due process in revocation as a parolee or mandatory supervision releasee. Tex.Admin.Code, tit. 37, §§ 141.111, 143.21, 143.3, and 145.41–145.55.

13. *For example,* in Texas, an applicant must show a minimum of one year of good behavior after release from prison and completion of his or her sentence before an application can be made. A pardon will not be considered for an inmate still in prison unless his or her innocence has been established beyond a reasonable doubt, nor will a pardon be issued to a dead person.

An applicant must furnish letters of recommendation from three or more reputable citizens of the place where he or she is residing, and a letter of recommendation from a regular full-time peace officer, also of the place where the applicant is residing. If the applicant has other felony convictions in other states or in federal courts prior to the last Texas conviction, he or she must show a clearance by pardon from the previous convictions.

14. The hearings are open in New York, closed in California. No hearings are provided for in Texas.

15. In Minnesota, the trial judge may order the public defender to appear on the applicant's behalf in a pardon hearing. Minn. Stat. Ann. § 611.12.

Legal Effects of a Pardon

The most important question asked by the offender with respect to a pardon is: "What rights are restored by a full pardon?" The general answer to this question is: "A pardon restores certain civil rights that were lost upon conviction." To determine the precise legal effects of a pardon, resort must be had to both the statutory and case law in the jurisdiction where the pardon is granted. What civil rights are restored will depend upon: the civil rights lost; whether the offense was committed within or without the state; if it was committed outside the state, whether the state where the offense has been committed has granted a pardon; whether the ex-offender seeks to regain lost rights to property, office, or marital status, or merely seeks to establish these rights for the future; whether the ex-offender, was convicted in or is applying for pardon in a civil death state; and whether the offender seeks to claim his or her rights from a public entity or a private individual. The particular right sought to be restored or acted upon is always of prime importance in determining the effect of a pardon.[16] The general rules with respect to some of these questions are considered in this section.

There are two points of view as to whether or not a pardon wipes out guilt. The classic view, which today represents the minority position, was expressed by the U.S. Supreme Court over a century ago:

> A pardon reaches both the punishment prescribed for the offense and the guilt of the offender; and when the pardon is full, it releases the punishment and blots out the existence of the guilt, so that in the eyes of the law the offender is as innocent as if he had never committed the offense. If granted before conviction, it prevents any of the penalties and disabilities consequent upon conviction from attaching; if granted after conviction, it removes the penalties and disabilities and restores him to all his civil rights; it makes him, as it were, a new man, and gives him new credit and capacity.[17]

The opposite and majority view, stated in *Burdick v. United States,* is that a pardon is an implied expression of guilt and that the conviction is not obliterated.[18]

Depending upon which view prevails within a given state, as well as upon relevant statutory or constitutional provisions and the reasons for the granting of a pardon in a particular case, a number of consequences follow. For example, an offense for which the offender has been pardoned may or may not be "counted" for purposes of enhancing punishment or declaring the defendant to be an habitual offender. If the pardon is held to have wiped out the offender's guilt, or if it was issued on the basis of a finding or belief that the offender was in fact innocent of the offense, then it will probably not be used for enhancement.[19]

---

16. Rudenstine, *supra,* at 140–153.

17. *Ex parte* Garland, 71 U.S. 333, 18 L.Ed. 366 (1867). This rule is followed in Florida, Marsh v. Garwood, 65 So.2d 15 (Fla.1953), and in Louisiana, State v. Childers, 197 La. 715, 2 So.2d 189 (1941).

18. Burdick v. United States, 236 U.S. 79, 59 L.Ed. 476 (1915).
To same effect: Mason v. State, 39 Ala.App. 1, 103 So.2d 337 (1956), *affd.* 267 Ala. 507, 103 So.2d 341 (1958); Hozer v. State, 95 N.J.Super. 196, 230 A.2d 508 (1967).

19. In California, a "pardon" exempts the individual from punishment which the law inflicts for crime which he has committed, and generally, also removes any disqualification or disabilities which would ordinarily have followed from the conviction, but the individual remains a convicted criminal

However, the majority position is that, inasmuch as the pardon does not wipe out guilt for the underlying offense—but, indeed, implies guilt—the conviction remains and may serve to enhance punishment at the trial of a subsequent offense.[20]

Generally, a full pardon restores the ordinary rights of citizenship, such as the right to vote and hold public office. The effect of the pardon may be set out in the state constitution or statutes, or in the regulations of the pardoning authority. Pardon restores eligibility to public office, but does not restore a person to a public office that was held at the time of conviction.[21] A commutation or a conditional pardon, however, does not have the effect of restoring rights or removing disqualifications for office.[22] Generally, a conviction for which a witness has been conditionally, pardoned can also be used to impeach him or her. However, some states bar the showing of a conviction that has been pardoned; and even those that do not will allow the fact of the pardon to be offered in rebuttal.

Generally, where an occupational licensing law disqualifies persons convicted of crime, a pardon does not remove the disqualification, nor does it automatically restore a license that has been revoked on the ground of a criminal conviction. Disbarment of an attorney is not prevented by pardon, nor does a pardon restore the license or right to license.[23] Some decisions have indicated that although loss of a professional license is a "penalty," the proceedings to revoke a license are not penal.[24] The revocation may thus not be a conviction that is within the power of the executive to pardon. The California statute that provides generally that a pardon shall "operate to restore to the convicted person all the rights, privileges and franchises of which he has been deprived in consequence of said conviction or by reason of any matter involved therein," adds significantly that "nothing in this article shall affect any of the provisions of the Medical Practices

---

for purpose of increased punishment for those previously convicted of a crime. People v. Biggs, 9 Cal.2d 508, 71 P.2d 214 (1937).

But see West's Ann.Calif.Penal Code § 3045, which provides that parole eligibility shall not be delayed by virtue of a prior conviction which has been pardoned for innocence. Rudenstine, supra, at 146.

The New York enhancement statute specifically provides that a previous felony conviction can be counted provided that the defendant was not pardoned on the ground of innocence. McKinney Consol.Laws Penal Law § 70.10(b)(iii). But where the pardon was granted on the ground of innocence this should be taken into account. In re Kaufmann, 245 N.Y. 423, 157 N.E. 730 (1927).

State v. Luna, 319 N.W.2d 737 (Nebraska 1982).

20. *State v. Walker,* 432 So.2d 105 (La.Ct.App.1983).

Durham v. Wyrick, 665 F.2d 185 (8th Cir.1981).

In Texas, a prior conviction can be invoked as a basis for added penalty notwithstanding governor had granted full pardon after defendant has served part of sentence following prior conviction. Jones v. State, 141 Tex.Cr.R. 70, 147 S.W.2d 508 (1941), overruling a previous case to the contrary. See also, *Square v. State,* 167 S.W.2d 192 (1943, Tex.Crim.App.).

21. Rudenstine, *supra,* at 145.

22. *Ex parte* Lefors, 303 S.W.2d 394 (Tex.Crim.App.1957).

23. People *ex rel.* Deneen v. Gilmore, 214 Ill. 569, 73 N.E. 737 (1905).

24. Marlo v. State Board of Medical Examiners, 112 Cal. App. 2d 276, 246 P.2d 69 (1952). Murrill v. State Board of Accountancy, 97 Cal. App. 2d 709, 218 P.2d 569 (1950).

Act, or the power or authority conferred by law on the Board of Medical Examiners therein, or the power or authority conferred by law upon *any* board which permits any person or persons to apply his or their art or profession on the person of another."[25]   [Emphasis added.]

Upon Discharge

The American Bar Association Handbook Removing Offender Employment Restrictions lists thirteen states with statutes that provide for automatic restoration of rights upon discharge of the offender after completion of a sentence for a felony or after service under probation or parole.[26]   A number of these will be discussed briefly here.

The New Hampshire statute, which is given as an example of this type of legislation, simply provides that the certificate or other instrument of discharge shall state that the defendant's rights to vote and to hold any future public office, of which he or she was deprived, are restored and the defendant suffers no other disability by virtue of the conviction.   The act then goes on to provide for recognition of certificate of discharge issued by another state.   The governor of New Hampshire may, upon application, issue a certificate of restoration of rights—lost by reason of a conviction in a federal court or another state—in cases where the convicted person has received no restoration of rights from the federal authorities or those in the state of conviction.   The New Hampshire statute relating to the certificate of discharge reads in full as follows:

I. If the sentence was in this state, the order, certificate, or other instrument of discharge, given to a person sentenced for a felony upon his discharge after completion of service of his sentence or after service under probation or parole, shall state that the defendant's rights to vote and to hold any future public office, of which he was deprived by this chapter are thereby restored and that he suffers no other disability by virtue of his conviction and sentence except as otherwise provided by this chapter.   A copy of the order or other instrument of discharge shall be filed with the clerk of the court of conviction.

II. If the sentence was in another state or in a federal court and the convicted person has similarly been discharged by the appropriate authorities, the governor of this state, upon application and proof of the discharge in such form as the governor may require, shall issue a certificate stating that such rights have been restored to him under the laws of this state.

III. If another state having a similar act issues its certificate of discharge to a convicted person stating that the defendant's rights have been restored, the rights of

---

25. Cal.Penal Code § 4853 (West).

Where a prisoner has been adjudged an habitual criminal and sentenced under § 644, but has been granted an unconditional pardon by the governor, the application of the section (4853) was nevertheless proper, notwithstanding this section as to the effect of a pardon.   8 Op.Atty.Gen. 87.

Presentation of a full pardon granted to disbarred attorney does not, without more, satisfy burden resting on disbarred attorney to show that he possesses moral stamina essential to one qualified to practice law.   In re Lavine, 2 Cal.2d 324, 41 P.2d 161 (1935).

26. American Bar Association Handbook, *supra. See also,* Rudenstine, *supra,* at 147, 152.

The states listed are Colorado, Kansas, Minnesota, Missouri, Nebraska, New Hampshire, Ohio, Oregon, Pennsylvania, South Dakota, Washington, Wisconsin, and Wyoming.

Vand. L. Rev., *supra,* at 1147–48.

which he was deprived in this state under this chapter are restored to him in this state.[27]

The laws of the other twelve states granting automatic restoration of rights, although basically similar, have provisions peculiar to each state. Some of the states require the offender to complete his prison *or* parole term; in some states, restoration is awarded upon completion of the prison term; one state allows restoration only after the completion of a suspended sentence; and two states require the presentment of a certificate of good conduct obtained from the prison warden after imprisonment.

The Illinois Unified Code of Corrections contains the following language:

> On completion of sentence of imprisonment or on a petition of a person not sentenced to imprisonment, all license rights and privileges granted under the authority of this State which have been revoked or suspended because of conviction of an offense shall be restored unless the authority having jurisdiction of such license rights finds after investigation and hearing that restoration is not in the public interest.[28]

The Wisconsin statute was one of the earliest and most comprehensive of the statutes providing that every person who has been convicted of a crime obtains a restoration of his or her civil rights by serving out the term of imprisonment or otherwise satisfying the sentence. The statute reads:

> *Civil rights restored to convicted persons satisfying sentence.* Every person who is convicted of crime obtains a restoration of his civil rights by serving out his term of imprisonment or otherwise satisfying his sentence.

The certificate of the department or other responsible supervising agency that a convicted person has served his sentence or otherwise satisfied the judgment against him is evidence of that fact and that he is restored to his civil rights.[29]

Effect of Automatic Restoration

Most courts consider the effect of an automatic restoration of rights as equivalent to a pardon. In the usual situation, the conviction can be considered in any subsequent criminal action and under the enhancement statutes. The ex-offender is not restored to eligibility to receive an occupational or professional license and must report the conviction on job application forms.

EXPUNGEMENT AND ANNULMENT

Purpose of Expungement Statutes

The typical expungement statute does not amount to automatic restoration of rights because it requires affirmative action by the offender.[30] Expungement

---

27. N.H.Rev.Stat.Ann. § 607–A:5.

28. Illinois Unified Code of Corrections, § 1005–5–5(d).

29. Wis. Stat. Ann. § 57.078.

30. The American Bar Association Handbook lists the following states among those having expungement statutes: California, Idaho, Michigan, Minnesota, Nevada, New Jersey, North Dakota,

differs from the issuance of certificates of relief or good conduct, as in New York, in that the issuance of the certificates merely restores rights but does not attempt to wipe out the criminal record. The word "expungement" means to "erase." The purpose of expungement statutes is to erase a criminal record as if it never happened in the first place. Says one author:

> It is not simply a lifting of disabilities attendant upon conviction and a restoration of civil rights * * *. It is rather a redefinition of status, a process of erasing the legal event of a conviction or adjudication, and thereby restoring to the regenerate offender his status quo ante.[31]

One study of expungement statutes reported nine states with expungement procedures and three states with annulment procedures. In ten of the states, expungement or annulment is associated with probation and conditioned upon successful completion of probation. Expungement provisions sometimes apply where there has been a suspended sentence. In Michigan, an applicant must have been a first offender convicted before his or her twenty-first birthday, and the application cannot be submitted until at least five years after the conviction.[32]

After Successful Completion of Probation

Adult probation laws of many states contain procedures that permit the probationer, either after completion of probation or after a specified period on probation, to apply for an order terminating the probation and wiping out the conviction. One such statute provides that at any time after the defendant has satisfactorily completed one-third of the original probationary period or two years of probation, whichever is lesser, the court may, upon application, by order duly entered, amend or modify the original sentence imposed to conform to the probation period and discharge the defendant. In case the defendant has been convicted or has entered a plea of guilty or plea of *nolo contendere,* the court may set aside the verdict or permit the defendant to withdraw the plea, and shall dismiss the accusation, complaint, information, or indictment against such defendant "who shall thereafter be released from all penalties and disabilities resulting from the offense of which he has been convicted or to which he has pled guilty, except that proof of this said conviction or plea of guilty shall be made known to the court should the defendant again be convicted of any criminal offense."[33]

Texas, and Washington. The states of Delaware, Utah, and Wyoming have annulment statutes. California also has a sealing statute.

     Rudenstine, *supra,* adds New York and Washington to that list; although, as the text indicates, there may be some dispute as to whether the New York procedure should be called expungement.

     31. Gouth, *The Expungement of Adjudication Records of Juvenile and Adult Offenders: A Problem of Status.* Wash.L.Q. 149 (1966).

     But see Booth, *supra,* at 161–66.

     32. Vand. L. Rev., *supra,* at 1148–49.

     33. Tex.Code Crim.Proc.Ann. art. 42.12, § 7 (Vernon).

     The Texas Court of Criminal Appeals has held that it is improper to impeach a witness' testimony by proof of a felony conviction where probationary term had expired and conviction had

The Comprehensive Drug Abuse Prevention and Control Act of 1970 contains provisions that seek to protect the first offender from the collateral consequences of a conviction. A first offender is eligible for probation, and without entering a judgment of guilty and with consent of such person, the court may defer further proceedings and place the offender on probation upon such reasonable conditions as it may require for a period not to exceed one year. The court may dismiss the proceedings against the person and discharge him or her from probation before the expiration of the maximum period prescribed for such person's probation. If the person performs all the conditions of probation, then upon expiration of the period the court shall discharge that person and dismiss the proceedings against him or her. This form of discharge and dismissal shall be without court adjudication of guilt, but a nonpublic record thereof is retained by the Department of Justice solely for the purpose of use by the courts in subsequent proceedings, if any. This form of discharge or dismissal does not constitute a conviction for the purpose of disqualifications or disabilities imposed by law upon conviction of a crime. The record may be expunged on application of a first offender who is not over twenty one years of age at the time of the offense.[34]

The American Bar Association Standards Relating to Probation recommend that:

> Every jurisdiction should have a method by which the collateral effects of a criminal record can be avoided or mitigated following the successful completion of a term on probation and during its service.[35]

The advisory committee states that it "believes it to be of the utmost importance that at the very least the statutes authorizing a sentence to probation should address the problem of collateral disabilities, and should provide a method by which their effect can be individualized to the particular case."[36] Two approaches are taken by present statutes on the subject: (1) deferring the formal adjudication of guilt through the period of probation and discharging the defendant following successful service without ever declaring the defendant guilty, and (2) permitting the withdrawal of a guilty plea and a dismissal of the charges following the successful service of all or part of the probation term.[37] The advisory committee cites with approval the Maryland procedures that permit placing a consenting defendant on probation, after the determination of guilt but prior to the formal entry of judgment. The purpose of such a provision is to offer the possibility—upon successful completion of probation—of avoiding the disabilities that attach to a felony conviction.[38]

---

been set aside under provisions of art. 42.12. Good v. State, 464 S.W.2d 129 (Tex.Cr.App.1971); Martin v. State, 489 S.W.2d 282 (Tex.Crim.App.1973).

34. Pub.L. No. 91–513, § 404(b)(1)(2), 21 U.S.C.A. § 844(b).

35. American Bar Association Standards Relating to Probation, § 4.3.

36. *Id.* Commentary at 55.

37. The following states are listed: Cal.Penal Code § 1203.4 (West); Nev.Rev.Stat. § 176.225; N.D.Cent.Code § 12–53–18; Tex.Code Crim.Proc.Ann. art. 42.12(7) (Vernon); Utah Code Ann. § 77–35–17 (1953); Wash.Rev.Code Ann. § 9.95.240.

38. American Bar Association Standards Relating to Sentencing Alternative and Procedures, 68–69.

The North Dakota statute allows release from all disabilities of a conviction after the offender has successfully completed probation. Access to court records in such cases is limited to the clerk of the court, the judges, the juvenile commissioner, and the state's attorney; others may examine such records and papers only upon the written order of the district judge.[39]

The Washington statute, which is similar to the California statute discussed hereafter, has been interpreted to remove disabilities on holding public office. In one case the election of a county sheriff whose earlier conviction had been annulled was upheld.[40]

All of the statutes discussed in this section serve at least a limited purpose of mitigating the effects of a conviction but have the common characteristic of applying only to probationers. Some states, such as California, have enacted statutes that extend opportunities for expungement and annulment to offenders who have not been placed on probation as well. In other states, for example Pennsylvania, expungement provisions may be included in statutes relating only to particular crimes and may establish both general and probation-connected procedures.[41]

SEALING

Purpose of Sealing Statutes

Sealing statutes have the same objective as expungement statutes in that they seek to erase the record of a conviction. However, they go further in attempting to actually *conceal* the fact of conviction. Typically, sealing statutes relate to juveniles, or to persons who were under the age of twenty-one when the crime was committed. Sealing statutes are defended on the basis of public policy, which demands that certain documents and records—such as those kept on file in public institutions concerning condition, care, and treatment of inmates, and those in offices charged with the execution of laws relating to apprehension, prosecution, and punishment of crimes—be treated as confidential, and "there-

---

39. N.D.Cent.Code § 12–53–18.

40. Wash.Rev.Code Ann. § 9.95.240.
Matsen v. Kaiser, 74 Wash. 231, 443 P.2d 843 (1968).

41. The Pennsylvania Controlled Substance, Drug, Device and Cosmetic Act provides for probation without verdict and expunging the criminal record. The court may, without entering a judgment and with the consent of such person, defer further proceedings and place the defendant on probation for a specific time period not to exceed the maximum for the offense. Upon fulfillment of the terms and conditions of probation, the court shall discharge such person and dismiss the proceedings against him or her. Discharge and dismissal shall be without adjudication of guilt and shall not constitute a conviction for any purpose whatever.

Any records of arrest or prosecution for a criminal offense under the act, except for persons indicted for unlawful delivery or possession with intent to deliver controlled substances, shall be promptly expunged from all arrest and other criminal records and files when the charges are withdrawn or dismissed or the person is acquitted of the charges. Any expunged record of arrest or prosecution shall not at any time thereafter be regarded as an arrest or prosecution for any public or private purpose whatsoever.

Pa.Stat.Ann., tit. 35, §§ 780–101 *et seq.,* esp. §§ 780–117, 780–118, and 780–119.

fore not be open to indiscriminate inspection, even though they are in custody of a public officer or board and and are of a public nature."[42] Nevertheless, only a few states have sealing statutes, and the statutes that do exist tend to be limited in scope and the procedures for sealing cumbersome.

Provisions in Juvenile Court Statutes

Sealing provisions in juvenile court statutes must be read with reference to other provisions of such statutes that restrict access to juvenile records to persons with a legitimate interest in the protection, welfare, or treatment of the child,[43] and that provide for the destruction of fingerprints.[44] The provisions in such codes, which specifically state that neither an adjudication of delinquency or a commitment is a "conviction"[45] and statutes giving the juvenile court the authority to dismiss a petition and set aside findings are also related.[46] The sealing statutes operate to provide additional protection.

Under the terms of the Uniform Juvenile Court Act, application may be made by a person who has been adjudicated delinquent or unruly, on the person's or the court's own motion, for the sealing of files and records in the proceeding. The application may be made after two years have elapsed since the final discharge of the person if in the interval he or she has not been convicted of a felony or a misdemeanor involving moral turpitude, has not been newly adjudicated as a delinquent, and has been found by the court to have been rehabilitated. Notice must be given to the prosecuting attorney of the county, the institution, or the authority from which discharged or paroled, and to the law enforcement officers or department having custody of the records:

> Upon the entry of the order the proceeding shall be treated as if it never occurred. All index references shall be deleted and the person, the court, the law enforcement officers and departments shall properly reply that no record exists with respect to the person upon inquiry in any manner.[47]

The records are not destroyed and inspection of the sealed files and records may be permitted by order of the court upon the petition of the person who is the subject of the records and only by the persons named in the order.[48]

The Georgetown University Institute of Criminal Law and Procedure has proposed a Model Use of Juvenile Court Records Statute, first for sealing and then, after passage of time, for destruction of juvenile records. The statute includes in its protection records where adjudication of delinquency was not

---

42. Creamer v. Superior Court In and For Marin County, 265 Cal. App. 2d 216, 71 Cal.Rptr. 193 (1968).

43. Standard Juvenile Court Act, § 33.
Uniform Juvenile Court Act, § 55.

44. Standard Juvenile Court Act § 33.
Uniform Juvenile Court Act, § 56.

45. Standard Juvenile Court Act, § 25.

46. *See, for example,* Cal.Welf. & Inst.Code § 782 (West).

47. Uniform Juvenile Court Act, § 57.

48. *Id.*

entered, and also sealing of records where a delinquency adjudication was made. The sealed records may not be disclosed for purposes of employment, licensing, bonding, or any other civil right or privilege. Exceptions are made as to inquiries from courts, law enforcement agencies, and agencies involved with national security. Although most sealing statutes do not contemplate actual destruction of the records, the Georgetown Institute Model Act provides for destruction of records no later than two years after adjudication or termination of any juvenile proceeding, provided no subsequent adjudication or criminal conviction has occurred.

RESTORATION OF
RIGHTS UPON APPLICATION

Removal of Disabilities

Some states provide by statute for procedures to be initiated by the offender to remove the disabilities following a conviction. These procedures differ from expungement procedures in that they do not attempt to wipe out the conviction—they are a more or less straightforward attempt to remove the disabilities that are the collateral consequences of the conviction. Typically, the certificate or other document furnished upon completion of the proceedings specifies the rights restored.

New York has provided for two main ways of regaining some of the rights lost upon conviction. A first offender, or a former offender who has been convicted of more than one misdemeanor in addition to having been convicted of one felony, can apply for a Certificate of Relief from Disabilities.[49] The Certificate of Good Conduct, available to all offenders, is granted five years after release from custody, subject to certain conditions.[50] Possession of one or the other of these certificates is necessary to permit an ex-offender to apply for a job or license barred by virtue of a criminal conviction.

The Department of Labor has established a procedure to help a veteran to remove the stigma of a less than honorable discharge. The veteran who can display good conduct as a civilian for at least three years may apply to the Department of Labor for an Exemplary Rehabilitation Certificate. The certificate recites that the named person has, under the provisions of Public Law 80–690, established since separation from the Armed Forces of the United States a record of good character and exemplary conduct, activities, and habits for a period of not less than three years preceding the date on the certificate. The certificate can be presented to prospective employers. It also entitles the veteran to special job-counseling and job-placement services at the local state employment service office.

The act proposed by the Georgetown University Institute of Criminal Law and Procedures provides generally that application for an order of annulment and expungement may be made after termination of probation or parole supervi-

---

49. McKinney's Consol.Laws of N.Y., Correction Law §§ 701–03.

50. N.Y.Exec.Law § 242(3) (McKinney).

sion or after final discharge or release from imprisonment. If the order is not granted, the court must state in writing its reasons for refusing it; a denial can be appealed by the petitioner. The court is required to enter such an order on its own motion if within two years following termination of probation or parole and after final discharge from imprisonment or mandatory release, an order of annulment and expungement has not been granted and no subsequent criminal conviction has occurred.[51]

The act developed by the American Law Institute attacks the problem of collateral consequences of a conviction by limiting the definition of conviction, by stating that there must be a relationship between the crime or conviction and the deprivation, by providing procedures to keep the disabilities from attaching, and by providing additional procedures to remove disabilities that have attached. The Model Penal Code approach is thus a combination of expungement and restoration of rights.

In certain cases enumerated in section 306.6(1) of the Model Penal Code, the court may order that so long as the defendant is not convicted of another crime, the judgment shall not constitute a conviction for the purpose of any disqualification or disability imposed by law because of the conviction of the crime. This covers young adult offenders sentenced under special statutes or to conditions other than imprisonment; persons with suspended sentences or persons who have been placed on probation or parole and successfully completed the terms thereof; and a sentenced defendant who has led a law-abiding life for at least two years.[52] Under section 306.6(2), the court that sentenced the defendant may enter an order vacating the judgment of conviction when a young adult offender has been discharged from probation or parole before the expiration of the maximum term; or when a defendant has fully satisfied the sentence and has led a law-abiding life for at least five years.[53]

The provisions are made prospective and thus do not restore a person to employment or to a position forfeited or lost, do not preclude consideration of the conviction for purposes of sentence if the defendant is again convicted, and do not prevent use of conviction for impeachment purposes, although a defendant may show the order of the court as evidence of rehabilitation. The order does not justify a defendant in stating that he or she has not been convicted of a crime, unless the defendant also calls attention to the order.[54]

The Effect of Document
Evidencing Relief from Disabilities

While the Certificate of Relief from Disabilities, Certificate of Good Conduct, the Exemplary Rehabilitation Certificate, and Order of the Court usually serve

---

51. Model Annulment and Sealing Statute.

52. Model Penal Code, § 306.6(1).

53. *Id.* § 306.6(2).

54. Other sections of the code provide for forfeiture of public office (section 306.2); disqualification for voting so long as the offender is committed under sentence of imprisonment and from serving as a juror (section 306.3); and for appointment of a trustee to act upon the offender's behalf with respect to the offender's property or economic interests during the period of confinement (section 306.5).

to restore the ex-offender to such political rights as the right to vote and to provide the ex-offender with a document that is some evidence of his or her good conduct since release from custody, they do not prevent a prospective employer or a licensing agency from taking the fact of the conviction into account in deciding whether or not to admit the offender to a job or license. The Model Penal Code provisions that seek to prevent conviction may be of somewhat greater help to the offenders who can take advantage of such a statutory provision in the law of their jurisdiction.

National Advisory Commission Standards

The National Advisory Commission on Criminal Justice Standards and Goals makes proposals, which include legislative action to eliminate the loss of rights that follow upon conviction and which limit the restrictions imposed during confinement, the procedures for expungement, and restoration of rights upon application. The commission recommends repeal of statutes that impose civil disabilities upon the convicted offender, except provisions that impose restrictions on the right to hold public office, the right to serve on a jury during confinement, and the forfeiture of public office upon confinement. It would authorize a procedure for the denial of a license or governmental privilege to selected criminal offenders when there is a direct relationship between either the offense committed or the characteristics of the offender and the license or privilege sought. It recommends procedures for an ex-offender to have his or her conviction expunged from the record, and would require the restoration of civil rights upon the expiration of sentence.

The standard reads in full as follows:

Standard 16.17—Collateral Consequences of a Criminal Conviction

Each State should enact by 1975 legislation repealing all mandatory provisions depriving persons convicted of criminal offenses of civil rights or other attributes of citizenship. Such legislation should include:

1. Repeal of all existing provisions that a person convicted of any criminal offense suffers civil death, corruption of blood, loss of civil rights, or forfeiture of estate or property.

2. Repeal of all restrictions on the ability of a person convicted of a criminal offense to hold and transfer property, enter into contracts, sue and be sued, and hold offices of private trust.

3. Repeal of all mandatory provisions denying persons convicted of a criminal offense the right to engage in any occupation or obtain any license issued by government.

4. Repeal of all statutory provisions prohibiting the employment of ex-offenders by state and local governmental agencies.

Statutory provisions may be retained or enacted that:

1. Restrict or prohibit the right to hold public office during actual confinement.

2. Forfeit public office upon confinement.

3. Restrict the right to serve on juries during actual confinement.

4. Authorize a procedure for the denial of a license or governmental privileges to selected criminal offenders when there is a direct relationship between the offense committed or the characteristics of the offender and the license or privilege sought.

The legislation also should:

1. Authorize a procedure for an ex-offender to have his conviction expunged from the record.

2. Require the restoration of civil rights upon the expiration of sentence.

Because of the growing recognition of the handicaps imposed upon the ex-offender or the adjudicated delinquent in the matter of employment, increased attention is being paid to the matter of removing or reducing restrictions on employment, which are a collateral consequence of a conviction. The methods used take the form of: (1) court decisions that apply the broad definition of "conviction" or redefine "moral turpitude" and "infamous crime"; (2) statutes or executive orders announcing an official policy against discriminating against the ex-offender in public employment, and opinions of attorneys general establishing more liberal licensing policies and regulations; (3) offender rehabilitation acts and other special statutes removing or reducing licensing restrictions on the ex-offender; (4) statutes and court decisions imposing due process requirements in the denial or forfeiture of a license; and (5) statutes defining "good moral character."

Court Decisions

Elsewhere in this book we have discussed the broad and narrow definitions of conviction. It is clear that in many cases in which the broad definition was adopted (i.e., where sentence was required to constitute a conviction), the purpose, as well as the effect, of the decision was to protect the defendant's right to practice his or her profession or engage in other licensed occupation.[55] As one author has noted, the difference between two burglars, both on probation in California, can be dramatic. The sentenced burglar (broad definition) loses all civil rights; the unsentenced burglar (narrow definition) is a provisional or conditional felon and as such, retains his or her civil rights and is subject to no disabilities except those prescribed in the terms of probation.[56]

A similar purpose to minimize the effects of a conviction can be seen in cases that narrow the definition of moral turpitude or infamous crime.[57] Some of these cases are forerunners of the "reasonable relationship" statutes, which require a reasonable relationship between conviction and the exercise of the right or privilege of which the convicted person is deprived. In the *Otsuka* case,[58] where the issue was the right to vote, the court limited the meaning of "infamous crime" to those offenses where the elements of the crime are such

---

55. State Medical Board v. Rodgers, 190 Ark. 266, 79 S.W.2d 83 (1935).

56. *The Effect of Expungement on a Criminal Conviction.* 40 S.Calif.L.Rev. 127–47 (1967).

57. *In* Otsuka v. Hite, 51 Cal.Rptr. 284, 414 P.2d 412 (1966), the court held that a burglar no longer would be considered as convicted of an "infamous crime" for purposes of disfranchisement.

58. Otsuka v. Hite, 51 Cal.Rptr. 284, 414 P.2d 412 (1966).

that the person who committed it may reasonably be deemed to pose a threat to the integrity of the elective process.

Several courts have struck down regulations concerning licensing, holding that a state cannot, under the guise of protecting the public, arbitrarily deny access to lawful occupations by imposing unreasonable restrictions.[59]   Thus, licensing of photographers was held unreasonable in one case,[60] and licensing of watch repairmen held unnecessary in another.[61] The effect of decisions of this kind is, of course, to reduce the barriers to employment of the ex-offender by reducing the number of licensed occupations.

An important Supreme Court decision reached the issue of whether an ex-convict can possess "good moral character" as generally required in licensing statutes. In the case of *Schware v. Board of Bar Examiners,*[62] the evidence showed that the applicant to take the bar examination in New Mexico had used certain aliases some twenty years prior to his application, had been arrested but never tried or convicted, and had been a member of the Communist party seventeen years before. The State Board of Bar Examiners refused to permit him to take the bar examination on the ground that he had not shown "good moral character." The decision of the board was reversed by the Court, stating that a state cannot exclude a person from the practice of law or from any other occupation in a manner or for reasons that contravene the due process or equal protection clause of the fourteenth amendment. The court emphasized that the applicant had done nothing during the last fifteen years before the application to reflect adversely upon his character.[63]

A significant decision was handed down by the District of Columbia Court of Appeals in the case of *Miller v. District of Columbia.*[64] The agency involved had denied a vendor's license to an applicant, a former offender, because it found that he was not rehabilitated. Reversing the agency and finding that the applicant was rehabilitated, the court not only ordered the agency to grant the applicant a license, but also went on to express "serious concern" about the agency's lack of standards. The court said, in part:

> Unless there are some standards relating the prior conduct of an applicant to the *particular* business activity for which he seeks a license, the power to deny a license inevitably becomes an arbitrary, and therefore, unlawful, exercise of judgment by one official, a graphic example of which is so clearly revealed by the record in this case.
> * * *
> We commend to the specific attention of the council the need to clarify the requirements for business licenses by adopting appropriate regulations, which, among other things, will define the public health and safety dangers posed by the past histories of the license applicants with respect to each particular type of license, so that the danger of arbitrary administrative action based upon unarticulated and

---

59. Dent v. West Virginia, 129 U.S. 114, 9 S.Ct. 231, 32 L.Ed. 623 (1889).

60. State v. Ballance, 229 N.C. 764, 51 S.E.2d 731 (1949).

61. Livesay v. Tennessee Board of Examiners, 204 Tenn. 500, 322 S.W.2d 209 (1959).

62. Schware v. Board of Bar Examiners, 353 U.S. 232, 77 S.Ct. 752, 1 L.Ed.2d 796 (1957).

63. *Id. See also,* Mindel v. United States Civil Service Commission, 312 F.Supp. 485 (N.D.Cal. 1970); Morrison v. State Board of Education, 82 Cal.Rptr. 175, 461 P.2d 375 (1969).

64. Miller v. District of Columbia, 294 A.2d 365 (D.C.App.1972).

unannounced standards is removed and the possibility of constitutional assault upon the general licensing statute is blunted.

In some cases, however, a liberal reading of expungement statutes by a court has been followed by legislative action, which in effect overrules the court decisions. For example, the court in *People v. Taylor*[65] reasoned that since the prohibition against possessing concealable firearms applied only to convicted felons, it was clearly punitive and thus released under California Penal Code section 1203.4, which "seeks to effect the complete rehabilitation of those convicted of crime." The legislature then amended the section to specifically exclude the right to possess a concealable firearm from the penalties released.

Statutes or Executive Orders Authorizing Hiring of Persons with Criminal Records

A few statutes have announced a statutory policy of not automatically excluding applicants with criminal records. In Maryland, the statute declares that if otherwise qualified, applicants with criminal records shall not be rendered ineligible solely by reason of the conviction, although the hiring authority may consider the conviction.[66]

In Massachusetts, no person convicted of other than listed minor crimes (such as parking offenses) may be appointed or employed in public service within one year after conviction. However, the personnel director may appoint persons within a year of conviction if their offenses were minor. Applicants for public office in Massachusetts do not have to report in employment forms any adjudications prior to their seventeenth birthday.[67]

In New Jersey an individual guilty of a crime may be employed it if appears that the individual "has achieved a degree of rehabilitation that indicates that his or her employment would not be incompatible with the welfare of society and the aims and objectives to be accomplished by the agency."[68]

In 1972, the governor of Maine announced the official policy of the state to be that ex-offenders and ex-patients of state institutions should be given the opportunity to compete for state jobs on an equal footing with all other applicants. The executive order reads as follows:

WHEREAS, it is the desire and duty of his office and every department of State government to always enhance, promote, and insure the well-being of our citizens.

AND WHEREAS, it is appropriate that we take exemplary action to indicate by our actions, as well as our words, our commitment to the promotion of a successful transition and return to normalcy in society of ex-offenders and ex-patients of State institutions.

AND WHEREAS, it is essential in the attainment of that objective to reduce or eliminate the traditional stigma and discrimination attached to State incarceration and hospitalization.

---

65. People v. Taylor, 178 Cal.App.2d 472, 3 Cal.Rptr. 186 (1960).

66. Md.Ann.Code 1957, art. 64A, § 19.

67. Mass.Gen.Laws Ann. ch. 31, §§ 13, 17.

68. N.J.Stat.Ann. § 11–10–6.

AND WHEREAS, gainful employment has been proven to be a most important condition of successful transition into the community and society.

AND THEREFORE, it is declared to be the policy of the State of Maine in all the various departments and agencies to provide equal employment opportunities to former inmates and patients.

Only by support of this policy in spirit, as well as letter, can we expect to achieve the much needed end; equal employment opportunity for all and a speedy return to normalcy for ex-offenders and ex-patients.

In the implementation of this policy no department nor other agency shall discriminate in its hiring practices against an applicant who has been a former hospital patient or inmate, either in Maine systems or elsewhere;

Such applicant for employment shall be regarded the same as any other candidate with respect to suitability for employment;

They shall have the same opportunity to compete for positions within State agencies as any other citizen qualified for said positions;

In no case shall any unit of any department deny employment to an applicant simply because he or she has been a former patient or inmate.

Each department is hereby directed to advise all hiring authorities of this policy, which becomes effective immediately, and to adopt whatever internal procedures are necessary to implement said policy.[69]

The Commission on Human Rights of the city of New York has ordered the discontinuance of the practice of using arrest records by employers or labor organizations controlling hiring or apprentice training. The commission also declared it to be an unlawful discriminatory practice to discharge or to refuse to hire, promote, or refer to for employment, or to admit to union membership or to participation in apprentice training programs, any individual because of a conviction record unless it can be shown that a person with that particular conviction record could not satisfactorily perform the job in question, or that the prohibition is necessary to the safe and efficient operation of a business, or that a state or local licensing law or regulation prohibits the employment of such individuals.[70]

RESTORING GOOD MORAL CHARACTER

All of the methods and procedures that we have presented in this chapter, which have as their objective to remove or reduce the collateral consequences of a criminal conviction, suffer from one overriding deficiency—they do not restore "good moral character" to the ex-offender.

Since licensing statutes almost universally require that the holders of a professional or occupational license be of "good character," and private employ-

---

69. Maine Executive Order No. 8—Prohibiting Discrimination in the Hiring and Employment of Ex-Offenders and Ex-Patients of the State Correction and Mental Health Institutions.

70. Guidelines on the Use of Arrest and Conviction Records as Job Selection Criteria issued by the Commission on Human Rights of the City of New York, January, 1973.

See 2 Prison L.Rptr. (Feb. 1973), 178.

ers in nonlicensed occupations frequently impose the same requirement, the effect is, to quote one author, "to close the door of hope to a person once sentenced for a crime, frustrating his chances for rehabilitation in a useful occupation for which he is trained."[71]

One of the problems in applying the standard of good moral character is, of course, the vagueness of the term. The Supreme Court in *Konigsberg v. State Bar* noted:

> [T]he term, [good moral character] by itself is unusually ambiguous. It can be defined in an almost unlimited number of ways, for any definition will necessarily reflect the attitudes, experiences, and prejudices of the definer. Such a vague qualification, which is easily adapted to fit personal views and predelictions, can be a dangerous instrument for arbitrary and discriminatory denial of the right to practice law.[72]

Yet the rule remains as it was when announced by the Supreme Court more than eighty-five years ago:

> [The state] may require both qualifications of learning and of good character, and if it deems that one who has violated the criminal laws of the state is not possessed of sufficient good character, it can deny to such a one a right to practice medicine, and further, it may make the record of a conviction conclusive evidence of the fact of the violation of the criminal law and of the absence of the requisite good character.[73]

This rule has been generally observed in subsequent legislation and court decisions[74] in spite of the observation of a Michigan court in 1888 that "disabilities to transact business are almost or quite unheard of in this country," and on this basis struck a provision that prevented a convicted druggist from selling liquor for five years.[75]

Bad Character

The early law on restoring good moral character developed in the law of pardons. The general rule there seemed to be that all disqualifications that are imposed solely because of bad character—although this may be incidentally evidenced by a conviction for a crime—are unaffected by a pardon. According to this theory, a pardoned felon was restored the rights to vote, serve on a jury, receive a pension, and testify in courts, since these are rights of which the individual is not deprived simply because of bad moral character. But when the exercise of a right is associated with a character requirement, the result is different. In that case, the conviction may be evidence, even conclusive

---

71. *Entrance and Disciplinary Requirements for Occupational Licenses in California,* 18 Stan.L.Rev. 533–50 (1962).

72. Konigsberg v. State Bar, 353 U.S. 252, 77 S.Ct. 722, 1 L.Ed.2d 810 (1957).

73. Hawker v. New York, 170 U.S. 189, 18 S.Ct. 573, 42 L.Ed. 1002 (1898).

74. In 1960, the Supreme Court itself refused to overturn a civil disability law. De Veau v. Braisted, 363 U.S. 144, 80 S.Ct. 1146, 4 L.Ed.2d 1109 (1960).

75. *In* People *ex rel.* Robinson v. Haug, 58 Mich. 549, 37 N.W. 21 (1888), the Michigan court found that a prohibition that prevented a druggist, convicted of failing to keep record of liquor sales, from selling liquor for five years was a "cruel and unusual" punishment.

evidence, of bad character, unaffected by the pardon, and by extension of the same reasoning, unaffected by certificates of rehabilitation and similar procedures.[76]

Thus, when a qualification of good moral character is written into a licensing statute, or into a statute prescribing qualifications for public office, it has been held to be within the power of the legislature to require that weight be given to the fact of conviction of a crime as proving bad character. An Ohio court stated:

> Whatever the theory of the law may be with regard to a pardon, it cannot work such moral changes as to warrant the assertion that a pardoned convict is just as reliable as one who has constantly maintained the character of a good citizen.[77]

The Direct Relationship Test

While the authority of the legislature to impose civil disabilities upon offenders and of the licensing authorities to take the conviction into consideration in determination of good character has not been seriously eroded, the trend is to impose what is becoming known as the "direct relationship test." In a case in which the California Supreme Court declared that several convictions for participation in civil rights demonstrations did not determine the unfitness of an applicant to admission to the bar, the court states the fundamentals of this "test":

> The nature of these acts, moreover, does not bear a *direct relationship* to petitioner's fitness to practice law. Virtually all of the admission and disciplinary cases in which we have upheld decisions of the State Bar to refuse to admit applicants or to disbar, suspend or otherwise censure members of the bar, have involved acts which bear upon the individual's manifest dishonesty and thereby provide a *reasonable basis* for the conclusion that the applicant or attorney cannot be relied upon to fulfill the moral obligations incumbent upon members of the legal profession.[78]

Statutory Definitions
of Good Moral Character

The California statute defining good moral character is one of the first to establish specific criteria for determining lack of good moral character.[79] A person is deemed to possess good moral character for licensing purposes unless that person has done an act, which, if done by a licentiate of the business or profession in question, would be grounds for suspension or revocation of his or her license, or unless the person has done any act involving dishonesty, fraud, or deceit with the intent to substantially benefit the person or another, or substantially injure another. The statute includes the relationship test in these words: "No act shall be grounds for denial, however, which does not have a substantial

---

76. *See generally*, Note, *Constitutional Law—Power of Legislature to Exclude a Pardoned Felon from a Civil Service Position* 27 Iowa L.Rev. 305–09 (1942).

77. State *ex rel.* Attorney General v. Hawkins, 44 Ohio St. 98, 5 N.E. 228 (1886).

78. Hallinan v. Committee of Bar Examiners, 65 Cal.Rptr.2d 447, 421 P.2d 76 (1966).

79. Cal.Bus. & Prof.Code § 481; gen. §§ 480–488 (West).

relationship to the functions and responsibilities of the licensed business and profession." The board is admonished, when considering the denial of a license, to take into account all competent evidence of rehabilitation furnished by the applicant.

The California statute also imposes requirements of due process, which includes filing and serving of a statement of issues, notifying the applicant of the reason for denial, and permitting the applicant to have a hearing.

The California statute is one of the first to directly restrict the arbitrary application of the requirement of good moral character by licensing boards. It is of little benefit to the forger, the embezzler, or the seller of fraudulent securities, since under the act the board has no obligation to assume that persons who have "done any act involving dishonesty, fraud, or deceit with the intent to substantially benefit himself or another, or substantially injure another," possess good character. But the statute may help to open the doors to licensed occupations to persons convicted of other types of crimes.[80]

THE STATUS OF CIVIL DISABILITY STATUTES TODAY

The Criticisms

Civil disability statutes in general, and licensing statutes in particular, are being attacked in the courts on several grounds. The authors and researchers responsible for the definitive study of The Collateral Consequences of A Criminal Conviction[81] make the following points, among others: (1) Civil disability laws are overbroad, in that the laws of most jurisdictions provide for the blanket imposition of disabilities upon a criminal conviction. (2) The laws are inconsistent. (3) Although most jurisdictions provide for the eventual restoration of convicted criminals' rights, these procedures are of limited effectiveness and, as a result, many ex-convicts suffer disabilities long after deprivation is justifiable. (4) Among the disabilities suffered, the loss of employment opportunity is one of the most onerous. This is increasingly true as the number of licensed occupations continues to increase. Under existing laws, discrimination against convicted criminals by private employers is perfectly legal. (5) Although regulations of many public and licensed occupations are necessary, many of the regulations are unreasonable, and procedures with respect to denial and revocation of licenses are not fair.

The Constitutional Issues

The authors note that attacks on the constitutionality of civil disability laws are being made on the following grounds: (1) Civil disability laws are bills of attainder; (2) imposition of civil disabilities is cruel and unusual punishment;

---

80. *Id.*

81. *See* Vand. L. Rev., *supra.*
  Rudenstine, *supra,* at 150–51, 154–57.

(3) procedures with reference to the imposition and application of civil disability laws violate due process; (4) civil disability laws deny equal protection.

In addition, say the authors, these laws achieve none of the objectives of modern correctional theory and actually impede the rehabilitation of the offender, both within and without the correctional institution. Their recommendations are for: (1) the elimination of unnecessary restrictions, (2) the reasonable application of necessary restrictions, (3) the adoption of the direct relationship test, (4) greater participation by the sentencing court in the determination of the civil disabilities to be imposed on the individual defendant, and (5) automatic restoration of rights and privileges five years after the convict's release into the community.

The Effect of a Presidential Pardon*

Upon conviction of a felony a criminal defendant generally suffers the imposition of certain civil disabilities in addition to whatever specific penalty may be assessed by way of imprisonment or fine. Often this is termed a loss of civil rights. This article will be concerned with the effect of a Federal felony conviction, its attendant imposition of civil disabilities, and the effect of a Presidential pardon on removal of those disabilities. Guilt is presumed and the following discussion is not intended to describe the effects of a pardon based on innocence, which should have the same effect as a judgment of acquittal.[1] Before going further, a description of the Presidential pardoning process seems appropriate.

FUNCTION OF THE DEPARTMENT OF JUSTICE IN PARDON MATTERS

Under the Constitution, the President has the power to grant reprieves and pardons for Federal offenses and he looks to the Attorney General for advice on all matters concerning Executive clemency. Prior to 1850 the preliminary and advisory duties in pardon cases were performed by the Attorney General and the Secretary of State, jointly. About 1850 all the preliminary and advisory work was transferred to the Attorney General. However, warrants of pardon continued to be issued through the Department of State until 1893 when President Cleveland by Executive Order transferred that responsibility also to the Attorney General.[2]

The function of the Attorney General in pardon matters is based solely on the request or direction of the President and is not, in any sense, statutory.[3]

The Act of March 3, 1865[4] created the Office of Pardon Clerk in the Office of the Attorney General. By the Act of March 3, 1891[5] an Attorney in charge of pardons was

---

* From John R. Stanish, *Federal Probation,* Sept. 1978.

1. Weihofen, "The Effect of a Pardon," 88 *University of Pennsylvania Law Review* 177 at 179 (1939); *The Attorney General's Survey of Release Procedures* (1939). Vol. 3 (Pardon), p. 293.

2. *Preliminary Inventories Number 37, Records of The Pardon Attorney,* The National Archives (1955), pp. 1 and 2.

3. Id. at 1.

4. 13 Stat. 516.

5. 26 Stat. 946.

substituted for the Pardon Clerk. Thus the Office of the Pardon Attorney originated prior to the creation of the Department of Justice in 1870.[6]

The Pardon Attorney receives and reviews all petitions for Executive clemency, initiates the necessary investigations and prepares the Attorney General's recommendations to the President. It is the responsibility of the Pardon Attorney to provide the President with the best information available on which to base a fair and just decision.

The Pardoning power as set forth in the Constitution[7] is unlimited and unqualified.[8] It gives the President discretionary authority to grant a pardon or deny a pardon. His authority extends to all offenses against the United States excepting only impeachment cases. He has no authority to act in state cases.[9] The exercise of the authority is not subject to review by the courts, nor may it be circumscribed by Congress.[10] There is no appeal from a clemency decision.

The President has not delegated the power to any other official or agency though, as a matter of practice, he relies on the written advice of the Attorney General. The single exception is the modification of prison sentences in military cases. In such cases clemency (i.e., commutation of sentence) is exercised by Clemency Boards within the military departments.[11]

Clemency may take several forms such as amnesty, pardon, commutation of sentence, remission of fine and reprieve. "A pardon is an act of grace . . . which exempts the individual on whom it is bestowed from the punishment the law inflicts for the crime he has committed."[12] Amnesty generally has the same effect as a pardon but usually is extended to a class of individuals and obliterates the criminality of their acts.[13] Commutation or shortening of sentence is a form of restricted pardon. A commutation of sentence may reduce the number of years of a sentence to permit a prisoner to be released at some future time or to accelerate his eligibility for parole. It frequently reduces a sentence to time already served. Of lesser importance are remissions of fine and reprieves.

PROCEDURE TO OBTAIN A PARDON

The most common form of pardon is the pardon after completion of sentence and this is with what we are here concerned. Submission of a petition is the only formality required of an applicant for pardon. There is no hearing. A petitioner need not

6. See note 2, *supra*.

7. Article II, section 2, *United States Constitution*, reads as follows: "The President . . . shall have power to grant reprieves and pardons for offenses against the United States, except in cases of impeachment."

8. *Schick v. Reed, et al.*, 419 U.S. 256 at 263 & 267, reh. denied, 420 U.S. 939 (1974); *Hoffa v. Saxbe*, 378 F.Supp. 1221 at 1231 (D.C.1974); 6 *Fordham Law Review* 255 at 258 (1937).

9. See note 7, *supra*.

10. See note 8, *supra*; *Yelvington v. Presidential Pardon and Parole Attorneys*, 211 F.2d 642 at 643 and 644 (D.C.Cir.1954); Humbert, *The Pardoning Power of the President* (1941), p. 63.

11. Under the "Code of Military Justice" at 10 USC § 874 the Secretaries of the military departments and various officials under them are authorized to remit or suspend sentences not approved by the President. This function is not an intrusion into the Presidential pardon process.

12. *United States v. Wilson*, 32 U.S. 150 at 160 (1833).

13. *Knote v. United States*, 95 U.S. 149 at 152 and 153 (1877); *Bardick v. United States*, 236 U.S. 79 at 94 and 95 (1914); Humbert, *The Pardoning Power of the President* (1941), pp. 24–26.

be represented by an attorney but may if he desires.

All applicants for pardon must wait a minimum of three years after release from prison (or in the event no term of imprisonment was served, from their date of conviction) and they must have completed service of their sentence before applying for a pardon. For those convicted of more serious crimes such as a violation of narcotic laws, income tax laws, perjury or violation of public trust, a waiting period of five years is required.[14]

Upon receipt of an application from an eligible petitioner, the Pardon Attorney directs the F.B.I. to conduct an applicant-type background investigation into the petitioner's post-conviction activities.[15] The applicant, references, associates, neighbors and past and present employers are interviewed. Recommendations are sought from the United States Attorney, the sentencing judge, and other relevant agencies such as the Bureau of Alcohol, Tobacco and Firearms in weapons cases, the Internal Revenue Service in tax matters, the Drug Enforcement Administration in narcotics cases, etc. After the necessary reports and recommendations have been gathered, the Pardon Attorney determines whether the applicant has become and is likely to continue to be a good, responsible, law abiding person worthy of the President's forgiveness. Among the factors considered are the arrest record, financial responsibility, family responsibility, employment record, reputation in the community, effect on other persons and the nature of the offense for which the pardon

is sought. If favorable action is indicated, a recommendation is prepared for the signature of the Attorney General[16] recommending the granting of a pardon. The recommendation is received on behalf of the President by the White House Counsel, who generally adopts the views of the Department of Justice. Periodically, the President grants Executive clemency to groups of individuals usually numbering from twenty-five to seventy-five and their names are listed in a master warrant prepared for his signature. In it he also directs the Attorney General to issue an individual warrant signifying the grant of Executive clemency.

EFFECT OF A PARDON

What effect, then, does a Presidential pardon have on its recipient? In *Ex Parte Garland*[17] the court stated:

> A pardon reaches both the punishment prescribed for the offense and the guilt of the offender; and when the pardon is full, it releases the punishment and blots out of existence guilt, so that in the eye of the law the offender is as innocent as if he had never committed the offense . . . it removes the penalties and disabilities, and restores him to all his civil rights; it makes him, as it were, a new man, and gives him a new credit and capacity.[18]

A literal interpretation of this language would lead one to believe that every consequence of conviction is obliterated upon the issuance of a pardon.[19] This, however, is

---

14. 28 CFR § 1.3.

15. 28 CFR § 1.7.

16. Under Attorney General Bell this responsibility generally has been delegated to the Deputy Attorney General.

17. 71 U.S. 333 (1866).

18. 71 U.S. 333 at 380 and 381; Cf. see *Ex parte Hunter,* 2 W.Va. 122 (1867).

19. In *Thrall v. Wolfe,* 503 F.2d 313 at 315 (7th Cir.1974), the Court questioned the import of the above-quoted broad language citing *Richards v. United States,* 192 F.2d 602 at 607 (D.C.Cir.1951), cert. denied, 342 U.S. 946, reh. denied, 343 U.S. 921; Williston, "Does a Pardon Blot Out Guilt?", 28 *Harvard Law Review* 617 (1915).

not the case. The word "pardon" connotes guilt [20] and the very acceptance of the pardon acknowledges one's guilt. A pardon, therefore, never erases the basic fact of conviction.[21] Neither does it remove the social stigma attaching to a criminal conviction. It involves forgiveness, not forgetfulness.[22] Professor Williston, writing in "Does a Pardon Blot Out Guilt," [23] describes the effect of a pardon as follows:

> The true line of distinction seems to be this: the pardon removes all legal punishment for the offense. Therefore if the mere conviction involves certain disqualifications which would not follow from the commission of the crime without conviction, the pardon removes such disqualifications. On the other hand, if character is a necessary qualification and the commission of a crime would disqualify even though there had been no criminal prosecution for the crime, the fact that the criminal has been convicted and pardoned does not make him any more eligible.[24]

There is general agreement that a pardon removes any remaining legal punishment for the offense [25] so that any remaining term of imprisonment, parole or probation or any unpaid fine would be remitted by the issuance of a pardon. Unlike the court in *Garland*,[26] which seems to speak of a complete and total rehabilitation upon the issuance of a pardon, Professor Williston suggests that we need to draw a distinction in the disabilities sought to be removed by the pardon. We should ask whether the conviction alone caused disability, or whether it would have (or could have) arisen, independent of the conviction, but upon the commission of those acts which serve as the factual predicate for the conviction. Professor Williston also suggests that a pardon should not remove those disabilities if character or lack of moral turpitude is a necessary element in the exercise of a particular civil right, profession, etc.[27] Williston, however, does not address the question of whether a Federal pardon affects disabilities imposed under state law.

Civil rights may arise under both Federal and state law. Federal civil rights include the right to hold Federal office, the right to the care and protection of the Federal government when on the high seas or within the jurisdiction of a foreign government, the right to transact any business with the government, the right to come to the seat of government, the right to have access to the courts of justice and government institutions, the right to free access to seaports, the right to use navigable waters of the United States and the right to travel from state to state.[28] As a result of a felony conviction none of the foregoing Federal civil rights are lost. However, the right to hold Federal

20. Humbert, *The Pardoning Power of the President* (1941) p. 77. This article is concerned with the effect of a Presidential pardon on the removal of disabilities where guilt is presumed as opposed to a pardon for innocence. The latter form of pardon is rarely granted, the last instance occurring in 1965.

21. *Richards v. United States*, 192 F.2d 602 at 605 (D.C.Cir.1951).

22. *United States v. Swift*, 186 F. 1002 at 1017 (N.D.Ill.1911).

23. 28 *Harvard Law Rev.* 647 (1915).

24. Id. at 653.

25. Id.; *United States v. Wilson*, 32 U.S. 150 (1833); *Cummings v. Missouri*, 71 U.S. 277 (1866); *Ex parte Garland*, 71 U.S. 333 (1866); *United States v. Klein*, 80 U.S. 128 (1871); *Carlisle v. United States*, 83 U.S. 147 (1872); *Osborn v. United States*, 91 U.S. 474 (1875); *Knote v. United States*, 95 U.S. 149 (1877); *Carlem v. People*, 233 U.S. 51 (1913); *Bjerkan v. United States*, 529 F.2d 125 (7th Cir.1975); 6 *Fordham Law Rev.* 255 (1937).

26. 71 U.S. 333.

27. 28 *Harvard Law Rev.* 647 at 653.

28. "Loss of Civil Rights by Conviction of Crime" by Alexander Holtzolf, 6 Federal Probation 18, (1942), citing *Crandall v. Nevada*, 73 U.S. 35 at 13 and 44 (1867); *Slaughter-House Cases*, 83 U.S. 36 at 79 (1872); *Edwards v. California*, 314 U.S. 160 (1914).

public office may be lost upon conviction of treason,[29] advocating the overthrow of the Government,[30] inciting rebellion or insurrection against the United States,[31] interference with the activities of the armed forces,[32] bribery,[33] receipt of compensation by a Government officer or employee for services rendered to any person in relation to a matter in which the United States is interested before any Government department,[34] and mutilation, falsification or destruction of public records.[35] Following conviction for certain offenses, the right of citizenship or the right to remain in or enter the United States under the Immigration Laws [36] or the right to serve in a labor organization [37] may be lost. Also, felons lose the right to serve on Federal juries.[38]

By and large most civil rights arise by operation of state law. Depending on the state of residency all or some of the following common civil rights may be lost upon conviction: voting, the right to serve on a jury, the right to be a witness, the right to contract, the right to serve in a fiduciary capacity such as executor or guardian, the right to hold state public office, the right to pursue certain professions, businesses or employments, the right to marry (or a correspondent ground for divorce may arise upon felony conviction), the right to have custody

of children, the right to possess a driver's license, the right to own property, the right to sue, etc. (The foregoing list of civil rights which may be lost upon a felony conviction is not to be construed as exhaustive.) [39]

Additionally, a felony conviction may cause the loss of the right to bear firearms. In view of the Gun Control Act of 1968 [40] and its system of disabilities and procedures for removal thereof, and the various state and local laws proscribing the bearing of firearms by a convicted felon, a firearms disability may arise under Federal, state and/or municipal law.[41]

In a thoughtful decision the Seventh Circuit dealt with the effect of a Presidential pardon in *Bjerkan v. United States*.[42] This was an appeal from a district court decision denying a petition for *habeas corpus*.[43] *Bjerkan* was convicted of refusing to report for induction and sentenced to three years' imprisonment later reduced to eighteen months'. He filed his *habeas corpus* petition while incarcerated. He appealed the denial of his petition to the Seventh Circuit. Before that court rendered a decision, President Ford granted Bjerkan a full and unconditional pardon. The Seventh Circuit therefore had to decide whether the case had become moot due to the pardon or whether

---

29. 18 USC § 2381.

30. 18 USC § 2385.

31. 18 USC § 2383.

32. 18 USC § 2387.

33. 18 USC § 201.

34. 18 USC § 203.

35. 18 USC § 2071.

36. 8 USC §§ 1101, 1182 and 1251.

37. 29 USC § 504.

38. 28 USC § 1861.

39. *The Attorney General's Survey of Release Procedures* (1939). Vol. 3 (Pardon), pp. 267–294; 53 *Virginia Law Rev.* 403–405 (1967).

40. 18 USC § 921 et seq.

41. Eg. *Indiana Code* § 35–23–4.1–6; *Smith-Hurd Illinois Annotated Statutes,* Ch. 33, sec. 21–3.1.

42. 529 F.2d 125 (7th Cir.1975).

43. 28 USC § 2255.

"collateral consequences" remained notwithstanding the Presidential pardon.[44]

The court held:

> [A] pardon cannot erase the basic fact of conviction, nor can it wipe away the social stigma that a conviction inflicts . . .[45]

> [A] state may not take cognizance of the offense pardoned in any way which would constitute a "punishment" . . . [and] common sense would seem to indicate that the deprivation of certain basic civil rights resulting from a felony conviction constitutes a "punishment."[46]

Bjerkan went on to hold:

> [A] deprivation of a person's basic civil rights, including the right to vote, the right to serve on juries and the right to work in certain professions, by a state on account of a Federal conviction would constitute a punishment. If the conviction were pardoned . . . such attempted punishment would constitute a restriction on the legitimate, constitutional power of the President to pardon an offense and would be void as circumscribing and nullifying that power.[47]

Relying on the supremacy clause[48] and *McCulloch v. Maryland*,[49] *Bjerkan* held that the Presidential pardon power is supreme and that no state may hinder the intended effect of a pardon in reinstating its recipient to his full rights of citizenship.[50]

Bjerkan suggests a return to the broad effect of a pardon as found in *Garland*. *Bjerkan* quoted and at least implicitly approved of the statement of the Presidential Clemency Board regarding the effect of a pardon: "The pardon will restore *all* (emphasis added) Federal Civil rights . . ."[51] As to state imposed disabilities *Bjerkan* says a pardon restores only "basic" civil rights,[52] but the court did not distinguish between basic and non-basic civil rights. One might speculate that in the area of Federal civil rights Congress cannot place any penalty or consequence beyond the reach of the President's pardoning power and any such legislative attempt would be unconstitutional and could not be attributed to Congress.[53] Therefore, in accordance with the doctrine of separation of powers the Presidential pardon would be pervasive so that all Federal disabilities are removed, while the reservation of states' powers by the Tenth Amendment[54] limits the broad effect of a Presidential pardon to the restoration of only basic state civil rights. To put it another way would the Presidential pardon be all encompassing in the removal of Federal disabili-

---

44. 529 F.2d at 126.

45. Id.

46. 529 F.2d at 127 and 128.

47. 529 F.2d at 128.

48. Article VI, clause 2, *United States Constitution,* states in part: "This Constitution, and the laws of the United States which shall be made in pursuance thereof . . . shall be the supreme law of the land; and the judges in every state shall be bound thereby, anything in the constitution or laws of any state to the contrary notwithstanding."

49. 17 U.S. 316 at 427 (1819).

50. 529 F.2d at 129; *A.D. Jones v. Board of Registrars of Alcorn County,* 56 Miss. 766 (1879); Humbert, *The Pardoning Power of the President* (1941), p. 80.

51. 529 F.2d at 127.

52. 529 F.2d at 127–129.

53. *Thompson v. Duchay,* 217 F. 484 at 487 (W.D.Wash.1914); Corwin, *The President: Office and Powers* (1957) pp. 167–168.

54. 10th Amendment, *United States Constitution,* reads as follows: "The powers not delegated to the United States by the Constitution nor prohibited by it to the states, are reserved to the states respectively, or to the people."

ties, but because states can exercise necessary police powers,[55] would the effect of the same pardon be limited in its removal of state imposed disabilities? I think *Bjerkan* supports these differing effects of a pardon on federally and state imposed disabilities.[56]

I favor Williston's approach [57] and would give a Presidential pardon this effect. After pardon the fact of conviction should not be taken into account, but the fact of the commission of the offense, or to say it another way, the acts constituting the factual basis for the conviction, may be taken into account.[58] Therefore, if a disability is imposed simply, and only, as a result of the conviction, the disability should be removed. If a disability is imposed independent of (or jointly with) the conviction but because of the commission of those acts serving as the basis of the conviction, then the disability should not necessarily be removed by the Presidential pardon. This latter situation will necessarily involve those disabilities imposed because of the requirements of good character or moral turpitude,[59] such as might be found in licensing statutes for the professions. I would give a Presidential pardon this effect regardless of whether the disability sought to be removed arose under Federal or state law.

Another important aspect of a Presidential pardon is its great persuasive effect. The pardon does and should be recognized as an instrument which lessens the social stigma attached to a conviction. It is a very great gesture on the part of the Chief Executive and in that sense should carry much weight in the rehabilitative process.[60] Although a pardon recipient may not claim as a matter of right the reinstatement of professional licenses or the removal of other disabilities which may be grounded in the good character requirement, he should be allowed to claim an inference, if not presumption, that he has regained the stature of a person of good character. No one should doubt that a Presidential pardon does and should carry very great persuasive value in the community and before licensing authorities.[61] Maybe its greatest value, though, is in the personal satisfaction which its recipient experiences.

---

55. In *Carlesi v. People of the State of New York,* 233 U.S. 49 (1914), the Court held that a pardon recipient could be punished more severely for a subsequent offense. The state could take into account his past conduct and this would not constitute in any sense a punishment for his pardoned offense; *Thrall v. Wolfe,* 503 F.2d 313 (7th Cir.1974).

56. An excellent analysis of the *Bjerkan* decision can be found at 61 *Iowa Law Review* 1427 (1976). The commentator feels *Bjerkan* holds that in addition to basic state civil rights, only basic (not all) Federal civil rights are restored.

57. Williston, "Does a Pardon Blot Out Guilt?", 28 *Harvard Law Review* at 653.

58. *Bjerkan,* 529 F.2d at 128 (note 2); *Grosspold v. Supreme Court of Illinois,* 557 F.2d 122 at 125 (7th Cir.1977); *Bowles v. Laws,* 45 F.2d 669 at 671 (D.C.1930); *United States v. Swift,* 186 F. 1002 at 1017 (N.D.Ill.1911); 22 Op.A.G. 36; 61 *Iowa Law Review* at 1438 (1976).

59. See Williston, "Does a Pardon Blot Out Guilt?", 28 *Harvard Law Review* at 653; *Grossgold v. Supreme Court of Illinois,* 557 F.2d 122 at 125 (7th Cir.1977).

60. *Grossgold v. Supreme Court of Illinois,* 557 F.2d 122 at 126 (7th Cir.1977).

61. Id.

APPENDIX **A**

APPENDIX **A**

Model Presentence Report*

OFFENSE:

Official Version

Herman Hesse is the subject of two separate indictments, one in the District of Massachusetts and one in the Western District of Texas. On August 20, 1977, the Massachusetts Grand Jury returned an indictment against Hesse and Nancy Rooney, charging that they conspired between May 28, 1977, and July 30, 1977, to distribute a quantity of heroin, and that they distributed that heroin on June 23, 1977.

On August 26, 1977, a grand jury in El Paso, Texas, returned an indictment against Hesse and Rooney charging that they imported 101.7 grams of heroin into the United States on or about July 30, 1977, and that they distributed that heroin on the same date at El Paso, Texas. Hesse appeared on September 29, 1977, and pleaded guilty to the Massachusetts indictment. He has indicated his intention to plead guilty to the Texas indictment under Rule 20.

This investigation began in May 1977 when the Drug Enforcement Agency received information that Hesse was looking for a buyer for a large quantity of heroin. On May 28, 1977, an undercover agent was introduced to Hesse at a bar in Springfield, and Hesse acknowledged that he was looking for a buyer for a kilo of heroin. He was initially reluctant to deal with a stranger, but after four meetings he offered to make the agent a partner if the agent agreed to purchase the heroin as soon as it came across the border into Texas. The agent accepted the offer but insisted on first receiving a sample of the heroin.

On June 23, 1977, the agent and Hesse met in Springfield and drove to a shopping mall where they met Hesse's girl friend, Nancy Rooney. After receiving instructions from Hesse, Rooney went to her car and returned with a

---

* Reprinted from *The Presentence Investigation Report* published by the Administrative Office of the U.S. Courts, monograph no. 105 (1978).

333

PROB 2

UNITED STATES DISTRICT COURT

PRESENTENCE REPORT

NAME (Last, First, Middle)				DICTATION DATE	
Hesse, Herman P.				October 14, 1977	

ADDRESS			LEGAL RESIDENCE		SCHEDULED SENT. DATE	
Hampden County House of Correction			71 Lee Avenue Holyoke, Mass.			

DOCKET NO.
77-00124-01

CITIZENSHIP
U.S.

AGE	RACE	DATE OF BIRTH	PLACE OF BIRTH	SEX	EDUCATION
28	Caucasian	11-15-48	Boston, Mass.	Male	10th Grade

MARITAL STATUS	DEPENDENTS	SOC. SEC. NO.
Divorced	One, in custody of former wife	987-65-4321

FBI NO.	U.S. MARSHAL NO.	OTHER IDENTIFYING NO.
999-888 H		

OFFENSE

D/Mass.--Consp. & Dist. heroin, 21:USC, 841(a)(1) & 846

PENALTY

0-15 yrs. and/or $25,000 and SPT of at least 3 yrs. on each count

CUSTODIAL STATUS	DATE OF ARREST
In custody in lieu of 100,000 surety bond since 8-15-77	

PLEA

Guilty to Mass. Ind. 9-29-77; will plead under Rule 20 to W/D Tx. Ind.

VERDICT

DETAINERS OR CHARGES PENDING

Rule 20, W/D Tx, Doc. #77-00135-01, Violation of 21:USC, 952(a) & 960 (a)(1) & 841(a)(1), same penalty.

OTHER DEFENDANTS

Nancy Rooney, in local custody in Mexico

ASSISTANT U.S. ATTORNEY	DEFENSE COUNSEL
David Crawford, Esq.	Philip Pratt, Esq. 981 Main Street Springfield, Mass. (413) 555-4321 (Retained)

DISPOSITION

SENTENCING JUDGE	DATE	PROBATION OFFICER

sample of 2.70 grams of heroin, which she gave to the agent. The latter paid Hesse $300. The substance was tested and found to contain 31.7 percent heroin.

On July 21, 1977, the agent informed Hesse that the sample was of acceptable quality. On July 24, Hesse instructed the agent to meet him on July 29 in El Paso, Texas. The agent flew to El Paso where he met with Hesse and Nancy Rooney at the Yellow Rose Hotel. At 8:15 A.M., on July 30, Hesse and Rooney crossed the border into Juarez. They returned two hours later and Hesse told the agent that he was able to obtain only a quarter kilogram of heroin. The agent expressed disappointment, but Hesse said that the heroin was of very high quality and could be cut many times. Hesse then sold the agent the first installment of 101.7 grams for $4,000. Tests determined that this substance contained 44.6 percent heroin. Hesse explained that Rooney and he would return to Mexico that afternoon to obtain the balance.

Hesse and Rooney crossed into Juarez and were arrested by Mexican police later in the day. Nancy Rooney had 147.3 grams of heroin in her possession. No heroin was found on Hesse, who was released after two days in custody. Rooney was held for trial. Hesse returned to Massachusetts where he was arrested on August 15, 1977.

Defendant's Version

"I was going to Mexico on a vacation and Nancy decided to come with me. This guy she met in Springfield was pestering her to get him some heroin. I had seen him a couple of times in June. All of a sudden he shows up in El Paso and demands to know where the stuff is. She finally agreed to get him some and she asked me to come in case anything happened. I was there so I guess I'm guilty. All of a sudden I was arrested by the Mexican cops, but they let me go because they didn't have anything on me. Then, all of a sudden I'm arrested up here. My lawyer says entrapment is hard to prove so I guess I'm guilty. But I didn't say all those things the narc claims. I don't deserve to go to jail."

PERSONAL AND FAMILY DATA

Defendant

Herman Hesse was born on October 15, 1948, in Boston, Massachusetts. His parents, natives of Austria, came to the United States as displaced persons after World War II. The family has lived for the last fifteen years at their present residence in Holyoke. The defendant's early years were turbulent because of many violent arguments between his parents. These were caused by Mrs. Hesse's belief that her husband was an excessive drinker. She summoned police assistance on several occasions, although no arrests were made. In 1955, Mrs. Hesse contracted tuberculosis. She was hospitalized for almost one year and the father was unable to keep the family together. The defendant and his siblings were placed in the Western Massachusetts Home for Children but the family was reunited when Mrs. Hesse recovered. The defendant remained with his family until he married at the age of twenty. He returned to the family home after his divorce three years later.

Prior Record

Juvenile Adjudications

| 11–05–62 | Using motor vehicle | Springfield, Mass. | 1 year |
| Age 14 | without authority | Juvenile Court | probation |

Mr. Hesse was represented by counsel. He and two other juveniles stole a car and went on a "joy ride." Mr. Hesse made a good adjustment on probation during the initial months, but became increasingly uncooperative thereafter.

| 10–28–63 | Breaking & Entering | Holyoke | Committed, Youth |
| Age 15 | | District Ct. | Service Board |

Mr. Hesse was represented by counsel. He and one other juvenile broke into a home in Holyoke. The Youth Service Board sent him to the Industrial School at Shirley, Massachusetts, where he remained until June 1964 when he was paroled. He was discharged one year later. His institutional performance was routine. He participated in a woodworking course and was placed on report on one occasion for fighting in the dining hall.

Adult Record

| 12–23–68 | Shoplifting | Springfield P.D. | Dismissed, Lack |
| Age 20 | | | of Prosecution |

Hesse was arrested after he allegedly attempted to steal several jewelry items from a department store. The store manager declined to press charges.

| 5–11–69 | Receiving | Holyoke | 4 mos. County Jail |
| Age 20 | Stolen Property | District Ct. | ss; prob. 2 years |

Mr. Hesse was represented by counsel. He was arrested after he sold a stolen television set to a pawn shop. The probation officer reports that he had little success with Mr. Hesse, who was constantly on the borderline of violation.

| 9–15–70 | Burglary & Entering | Northampton | 6 mos. County Jail |
| Age 21 | in the nighttime | District Ct. | |

Mr. Hesse was represented by counsel. He was apprehended at 2:15 A.M., inside a drug store. He had activated a silent alarm when he entered the building. Jail officials recall that Mr. Hesse attempted to be reclusive while incarcerated. He voluntarily spent several months in segregation because of his fear of attack by other inmates.

| 6–27–75 | Larceny over $100 | Hampden Cty. | 2 yrs. prison ss; 18 mos. |
| Age 25 | and Forgery | Superior Ct. | prob. w/ restitution |

Mr. Hesse was represented by counsel. He withdrew $500 from a bank account using a stolen passbook and forged withdrawal slips. He was identified through bank photographs. Mr. Hesse paid $310 in restitution and the balance was remitted. He performed well under probation supervision.

Mr. and Mrs. Hesse picture their son as a well-intentioned individual whose difficulties with the law were caused by his unwise selection of associates. They are bitter towards codefendant Nancy Rooney, whom they believe was responsible for this offense. They view his previous juvenile and adult transgressions as minor matters that were treated with undue harshness by police and the courts. His parents describe the defendant as an intelligent and ambitious individual who values financial success above all else. They are proud of the fact that, in recent years, the defendant has acquired such material possessions as an expensive automobile and a boat. They also note that he has been especially generous with his younger brother and sister.

Parents and Siblings

The father, Henry Hesse, age 59, resides with his family and for the last seventeen years has been employed as a machine operator earning a moderate salary. The home atmosphere improved considerably when Mr. Hesse stopped drinking approximately five years ago. The mother, Geraldine Ericksen Hesse, age 58, resides with her husband and is a housewife. Her health is poor due to respiratory ailments.

There are two siblings. Stanley Hesse, age 24, resides with his parents and is unemployed. Stanley believes that his brother is the victim of harassment by law enforcement authorities. Audrey Hesse, age 19, resides with her parents and is a community college student.

Marital

Herman Hesse married Barbara Raymond in a civil ceremony in Hartford, Connecticut on November 22, 1968. Both parties were twenty years old at the time and she was pregnant. The couple had one child, Herman, Jr., who was born on April 29, 1969. Mrs. Hesse reports that the marriage was troubled from the start by financial problems since the defendant was unemployed. He turned to illegal means of supporting the family and his subsequent arrests caused even more strain on the couple's relationship. There were several brief separations during 1969 and 1970, and a longer separation when the defendant was sentenced to serve six months in September of 1970. When he was released, Mrs. Hesse found him a "different man" and that it was impossible to reconstitute their relationship. The Hampden County Probate Court granted a divorce on December 28, 1971, on grounds of incompatibility and awarded her custody of the child. The defendant was required to pay $20 a week child support. Mrs. Hesse is employed as a telephone operator. She reports that her ex-husband's support payments have been sporadic. He often goes for months without visiting the child or making any payments, but he will then arrive with lavish gifts for his son and lump sum support payments. Mrs. Hesse says that her relationship with the defendant is now amicable, but they see each other infrequently.

Mr. Hesse asserts that he has no plans to marry again. He stated that Nancy Rooney was merely a friend.

Education

Mr. Hesse was educated in local public schools. He left junior high school in October 1963 when he was committed to the Youth Service Board. He returned to Baran High School in Holyoke in the fall of 1964 and dropped out of the eleventh grade in November 1965.

School officials describe Mr. Hesse as an intelligent individual who never worked up to his capabilities. His grades were generally C's and D's. Mr. Hesse left school because he was older than most of his classmates and wanted to get a job.

Employment

Between November 1976 and the time of his arrest, Mr. Hesse was unemployed and collected unemployment compensation of $72 a week. From August 1974 to November 1976, he was a forklift operator at the Smith Chemical Company in Northampton. He earned $4.10 an hour, but he was subject to frequent layoffs. Company officials described him as an uncooperative employee with a high degree of tardiness. He would not be considered for reemployment.

Between March 1972 and December 1973, Mr. Hesse worked in the warehouse of the United Rug Company in Easthampton, Massachusetts. He earned $2.75 an hour and he quit after a disagreement over hours. Between 1968 and 1971, Mr. Hesse was sporadically employed in the roofing business. This work paid well but he seldom was able to get more than three or four months work in any year.

After he left high school, Mr. Hesse worked on a delivery truck for Central Bakery, Inc., of Holyoke. He held this job between April 1966 and October 1968 and earned the minimum wage. He lost this job when the company went out of business.

Mr. Hesse said that he would like some day to open his own business. He had no clear ideas about the nature of this business, but stressed that he saw himself in a managerial capacity and would hire others to the menial labor.

HEALTH:

Physical

Mr. Hesse is in good physical condition. He denies having used drugs of any kind, and he specifically disclaims the use of heroin. Discussion with family members as well as with law enforcement sources revealed no information that would contradict Mr. Hesse's assertions in this respect. A physical examination and urinalysis test performed at the jail were negative for heroin use.

Mental and Emotional

On two occasions Mr. Hesse was tested in public schools and received I.Q. scores of 102 and 113.

Mr. Hesse has been examined by mental health professionals on two occasions. The first occurred shortly after Mr. Hesse was committed to the

Youth Service Board in 1963. A psychologist diagnosed him as, "a person whose anxiety is stimulated by a frustrated need for affection. Herman has developed no healthy conscience. His response to social demands is not based on any close commitment to moral principles."

Mr. Hesse was examined once again as a result of this court's pretrial order. Dr. Robert Land administered a battery of psychological tests, the results of which suggested, "that he seems to be unusually fearful of being overpowered and destroyed. It is obvious that he has been unable to resolve childhood problems and continues to feel quite rejected. He tends to view threatening environmental forces as coming outside his control."

FINANCIAL CONDITION:

Assets
Mr. Hesse lists two main assets: one is a 1977 Cadillac purchased in January of this year for $10,640. This automobile was confiscated by the Drug Enforcement Administration. The other asset is a 19-foot fiberglass speedboat with a 115 horsepower Mercury outboard engine worth approximately $4,000.

Mr. Hesse's parents displayed to the probation officer a savings account passbook with a present balance of $7,146.23. The account was listed to Mr. Hesse and his mother, but the parents made it clear that the defendant had made the deposits. When questioned about this, Mr. Hesse asserted that the account in fact belonged to his mother and that his name was on it only as a matter of convenience. His mother subsequently contacted the probation officer and retracted her earlier statement. She said that she made a mistake and that the money in the account belonged to her.

Liabilities
The only debt Mr. Hesse lists is a loan from GMAC to finance the purchase of his 1977 Cadillac. The loan balance is presently $4,200 and Mr. Hesse plans to make no further payments until such time as his car is returned to him by the government.

EVALUATION:

Although he attempts to shift responsibility to his codefendant, Mr. Hesse was the principal figure in the importation and sale of over 100 grams of high quality heroin. Were it not for the intervention of the Mexican authorities, he would have completed the sale of a quarter kilogram to an undercover agent. Mr. Hesse is not a user of the drug. He apparently values financial success to the point that he made a calculated decision that heroin trafficking was profitable. His lack of concern about the moral aspects of his decision confirms the observation of mental health professionals that his personality lacks some of the constraints under which most people operate. For Mr. Hesse, participation in this offense, as well as in earlier offenses, was a logical means of satisfying his economic motives.

The members of Mr. Hesse's family are intensely loyal to him and they have an unrealistic view of his participation in criminal activities. They do not question the sources of his assets, which are surprisingly large for a person with his employment history. The family cannot be counted upon to exert the pressure that might convince Mr. Hesse to conform to law-abiding behavior. Mr. Hesse himself is unrealistic in his personal goals. Without much education or skill, he expects a high degree of financial compensation, but he has not thus far shown a willingness to work towards that goal. It is unlikely that Mr. Hesse will attempt conventional paths to economic success until he is convinced that illegal means are too hazardous.

Alternative Plans

Adult sentencing provisions apply in this case and a special parole term of at least three years is required. Under any sentence imposed, Mr. Hesse will eventually come under the supervision of the probation office. An appropriate supervision plan would require immediate attention to Mr. Hesse's lack of marketable skills. The first step would be participation in a GED program, either in an institution or in the community. This would prepare him to accept more specialized training under the auspices of the Massachusetts Rehabilitation Commission. At least during the first six months of supervision, he would require maximum supervision with weekly reporting. The probation office suggests a requirement that he reside in Northrop House where a highly structured environment is available. Northrop House has a contract with the Division of Legal Medicine and could provide Mr. Hesse with professional mental attention. Over the long term, the probation officer would pay particular attention to Mr. Hesse's financial dealings. He would also be encouraged to live independently of his family.

RECOMMENDATION

The probation office recommends commitment to the custody of the Attorney General and a mandatory special parole term of three years. This recommendation considers the quantity and quality of the heroin involved, and the defendant's prior record.

The court may wish to consider imposing sentence under 18 U.S.C. 4205(b)(2) so that the Parole Commission can release him in the event that institutional conditions present a critical hazard to his mental health. The court might also consider recommending commitment to a minimum security institution where Mr. Hesse would feel less threatened.

Respectfully submitted,

Matilda Gormally
U.S. Probation Officer

INFORMATION EXCLUDED FROM THE PRESENTENCE REPORT AS POTENTIALLY EXEMPT FROM DISCLOSURE: RULE 32(c)(3)(A)

Marital

The defendant's ex-wife reported that when he was released from jail in early 1971 he showed no interest in resuming sexual relations with her. His behavior was also unusual in other respects, and he exhibited great tension and insomnia. Mrs. Hesse began to suspect that he had some experience in jail that had affected his sexual function. She questioned him about this on several occasions and he responded with bitter denials. Mrs. Hesse became convinced that it was impossible to save the marriage and she filed for divorce. Mrs. Hesse was adamant that her husband not learn that she provided this information.

Officials of the Hampshire County Jail confirmed that Mr. Hesse was the victim of a homosexual assault in the jail. He refused to identify his attackers, but he asked to be moved to an isolated cell. This request was granted.

Officials of the Hampden County Jail, where Mr. Hesse is now lodged, report that he has displayed acute anxiety during his confinement. They are not aware of the reasons for this but they note that Mr. Hesse has requested a transfer to the administrative segregation section. The jail has not complied with this request because of overcrowding.

Mental and Emotional

The latest psychological report suggests that Mr. Hesse will continue to experience acute anxiety whenever he is placed in a situation that threatens recurrence of the homosexual assault. The psychologist believes that Mr. Hesse is not overtly homosexual, but that his sexual orientation is ambiguous. Since the attack, Mr. Hesse has reportedly experienced complete sexual dysfunction.

SUMMARY OF WITHHELD FACTUAL INFORMATION

If the court is of the view that the above information is excludable under Rule 32(c)(3)(A), and if the court intends to rely on that information in determining sentence, a summary of the withheld factual information is provided for disclosure to the defendant or his counsel.

The court has received information about experiences of the defendant while previously incarcerated, which caused him to have serious emotional problems. Subsequent psychological examination confirmed this existence.

Rule 32: Federal Rules of Criminal Procedure*

Sentence and Judgment

(a) Sentence.

(1) Imposition of Sentence. Sentence shall be imposed without unreasonable delay. Before imposing sentence the court shall afford counsel an opportunity to speak on behalf of the defendant and shall address the defendant personally and ask him if he wishes to make a statement in his own behalf and to present any information in mitigation of punishment. The attorney for the government shall have an equivalent opportunity to speak to the court.

(2) Notification of Right to Appeal. After imposing sentence in a case which has gone to trial on a plea of not guilty, the court shall advise the defendant of his right to appeal and of the right of a person who is unable to pay the cost of an appeal to apply for leave to appeal in forma pauperis. There shall be no duty on the court to advise the defendant of any right of appeal after sentence is imposed following a plea of guilty or nolo contendere. If the defendant so requests, the clerk of the court shall prepare and file forthwith a notice of appeal on behalf of the defendant.

(b) Judgment.

(1) In General. A judgment of conviction shall set forth the plea, the verdict or findings, and the adjudication and sentence. If the defendant is found not guilty or for any other reason is entitled to be discharged, judgment shall be entered accordingly. The judgment shall be signed by the judge and entered by the clerk.

(2) Criminal Forfeiture. When a verdict contains a finding of property subject to a criminal forfeiture, the judgment of criminal forfeiture shall authorize the Attorney General to seize the interest or property subject to forfeiture, fixing such terms and conditions as the court shall deem proper.

(c) Presentence Investigation.

(1) When Made. The probation service of the court shall make a presentence investigation and report to the court before the imposition of sentence or the granting of probation unless, with the permission of the court, the defendant waives a presentence investigation and report, or the court finds that there is in the record information sufficient to enable the meaningful exercise of sentencing discretion, and the court explains this finding on the record.

The report shall not be submitted to the court or its contents disclosed to anyone unless the defendant has pleaded guilty or nolo contendere or has been found guilty, except that a judge may, with the written consent of the defendant, inspect a presentence report at any time.

(2) Report. The report of the presentence investigation shall contain any prior criminal record of the defendant and such information about his characteristics, his financial condition and the circumstances affecting his behavior as may be helpful in imposing sentence or in granting probation or in the correctional treatment of the defendant, and such other information as may be required by the court.

(3) Disclosure.

(A) Before imposing sentence the court shall upon request permit the defendant, or his counsel if he is so represented, to read the report of the presentence investigation exclusive of any recommendation as to sentence, but not to the extent that in the opinion of the court the report contains diagnostic opinion which might seriously disrupt a program of rehabilitation, sources of information obtained upon a promise of confidentiality, or any other information which, if disclosed, might result in harm, physical or otherwise, to the defendant or other persons; and the court shall afford the defendant or his counsel an opportunity to comment thereon and, at the discretion of the court, to introduce testimony or other information relating to any alleged factual inaccuracy contained in the presentence report.

(B) If the court is of the view that there is information in the presentence report which should not be disclosed under subdivision (c)(3)(A) of this rule, the court in lieu of making the report or part thereof available shall state orally or in writing a summary of the factual information contained therein to be relied on in determining sentence, and shall give the defendant or his counsel an opportunity to comment thereon. The statement may be made to the parties in camera.

(C) Any material disclosed to the defendant or his counsel shall also be disclosed to the attorney for the government.

(D) Any copies of the presentence investigation report made available to the defendant or his counsel and the attorney for the government shall be returned to the probation officer immediately following the imposition of sentence or the granting of probation, unless the court, in its discretion otherwise directs.

(E) The reports of studies and recommendations contained therein made by the Director of the Bureau of Prisons or the Youth Correction Division of the Board of Parole pursuant to 18 U.S.C. §§ 4208(b), 4252, 5010(e), or 5034 shall be considered a presentence investigation within the meaning of subdivision (c)(3) of this rule.

(d) Withdrawal of Plea of Guilty. A motion to withdraw a plea of guilty or *nolo contendere* may be made only before sentence is imposed or imposition of sentence is suspended; but to correct manifest injustice the court after sentence may set aside the judgment of conviction and permit the defendant to withdraw his plea.

(e) Probation. After conviction of an offense not punishable by death or by life imprisonment, the defendant may be placed on probation if permitted by law.

(f) Revocation of Probation. The court shall not revoke probation except after a hearing at which the defendant shall be present and apprised of the grounds on which such action is proposed. The defendant may be admitted to bail pending such hearing.

Amended Feb. 28, 1966, eff. July 1, 1966; April 24, 1972, eff. Oct. 1, 1972; April 22, 1974, eff. Dec. 1, 1975; July 31, 1975, Pub.L. 94–64, § 3(31)–(34), 89 Stat. 375.

U.S. Supreme Court
Decisions Regarding Sentencing*

In *Tucker v. United States,* 404 U.S. 443 (1972), the Supreme Court ruled that it was constitutional error for a court to consider, in making its sentencing decision, prior convictions of the defendant that were invalid because, in violation of the sixth amendment, counsel had not represented the defendant or no waiver of counsel had been made. Prior criminal record is a determinative factor in sentencing; however, constitutionally infirm convictions may not serve to enhance the sentence an offender receives. The rationale of *Tucker* is that consideration of invalid prior convictions in sentencing decisionmaking misinforms rather than informs the court's discretionary judgment.

Accordingly, since convictions obtained in violation of a defendant's sixth amendment rights are improperly relied on as prior record, it is incumbent on the probation officer preparing the presentence report to verify, during the course of his investigation, whether the defendant's previous convictions[1] were obtained when the defendant was represented by or waived counsel. Examination of the court records relating to such convictions ordinarily will provide the requisite information. The fact of the verification process and its results should be listed as to each prior conviction. It will be the court's responsibility to disclaim on the record reliance on invalid convictions at the time of imposing sentence.

---

* Reprinted from *The Presentence Investigation Report* published by the Administrative Office of the U.S. Courts, monograph no. 105 (1978).

1. Under present constitutional doctrine no criminal defendant may be deprived of his liberty as the result of any criminal conviction, whether felony or misdemeanor, unless he was afforded the right to counsel. *See Argersinger v. Hamlin,* 407 U.S. 25, 37 (1972). As a general rule, a defendant has a right to counsel in all felony cases and in all other offenses, for which incarceration is a potential penalty. In petty offense cases for which only a fine is imposed, representation by counsel need not be verified.

A second limitation which the Supreme Court has placed on sentencing information, is found in *Townsend v. Burke,* 334 U.S. 736 (1948). In *Townsend* the Court ruled invalid the sentencing of a defendant based on assumptions about his criminal record that were materially false. For example, the sentencing court in *Townsend* had treated as convictions previous criminal charges against the defendant that either had been dismissed or had resulted in acquittals. Therefore, a probation officer must be careful to note, on the face of the presentence report, with respect to the arrest or criminal record of an offender, the disposition of all such charges or arrests. This rule of accuracy applies to all data in a presentence report because it is a patent violation of due process to sentence on the basis of materially untrue information.

APPENDIX *D*

Freedom of Information and Privacy Act: The Presentence Report *

The Freedom of Information Act (FOIA) and the Privacy Act impose limitations on the availability, use, and disclosure of government records and documents. The Freedom of Information Act, 5 U.S.C. 522,[1] establishes a scheme for gaining access to government records. On the other hand, the Privacy Act, 5 U.S.C. 552(a),[2] provides a structure for safeguarding the privacy of individuals by restricting the dissemination to third parties or agencies of records or the information contained in government records relating to such individuals who are given access to the records pertaining to them.

The FOIA enjoins governmental agencies to make available to the public its publications, orders, policy decisions, and other records unless they fall within certain enumerated disclosure exceptions. The "agencies" bound by the requirements of the FOIA are all establishments in the executive branch of government and independent regulatory agencies. The "courts of the United States" are excluded explicitly from the definition of "agency" found in the FOIA. [5 U.S.C. 551(1)(B), 552(e).]

Thus, federal courts are not bound by the requirements of the FOIA. Furthermore, neither are federal probation offices. As officers of the courts, they perform several major functions, one of which is the preparation of presentence reports, [*Fed.R.Crim.P.* 32(c)]. Presentence reports are thus without

---

* Reprinted from *The Presentence Investigation Report* published by the Administrative Office of the U.S. Courts, monograph no. 105 (1978).

1. Pub.L. No. 89–554, 80 Stat. 383 (Sept. 6, 1966); Pub.L. No. 90–23, § 1, 81 Stat. 54 (June 5, 1967); Pub.L. No. 93–502, § 1–3, 88 Stat. 1561–64 (Nov. 21, 1974).

2. Pub.L. No. 93–579, § 3, 88 Stat. 1897 (Dec. 31, 1974).

the coverage of the FOIA. [5 U.S.C. 551(1)(B), 552(e) (1970), (Supp. IV, 1974).]
Consequently, even though a presentence report may later be retained in the
files of the Bureau of Prisons, it retains its status as a court document *not*
discoverable under the FOIA. [*See* Cook v. Willingham, 400 F.2d 885 (10th
Cir.1968).][3] It is advisable, when forwarding a presentence report to an institution, to stamp it confidential and indicate that it is not to be disclosed pursuant
to the FOIA. Similarly, offenders sentenced by federal courts have no right
under the FOIA to obtain a copy of their presentence report directly from the
responsible probation office. A sample routine reply to such a request is
attached (Appendix E).

With respect to the question of an individual's access to his or her presentence report or probation files, the response is the same under the Privacy Act as
it is under the FOIA. The courts and their probation offices are not within the
coverage of the Privacy Act. [5 U.S.C. 552a(a)(1); *see* 5 U.S.C. 551(1)(b), 552(e).]
The sample letter mentioned previously applies to requests made under both acts
(Appendix E).

Nonetheless, the probation system must abide by the Privacy Act in obtaining for its use and the use of the courts information contained in governmental
records or files that are subject to the strictures of the Privacy Act.

---

3. While it is true that probation officers perform various duties as requested by the United States
Parole Commission and thus are "agents" of the commission for some purposes, such as parole
supervision or postrelease planning [18 U.S.C. 3655, as amended by Pub.L. No. 94–233, § 14 (Mar. 15,
1976); 18 U.S.C. 4203(a)(4) (Mar. 15, 1976)], the preparation of presentence reports is not one of those
duties. Presentence reports are used by the Bureau of Prisons and Parole Commission because the
courts have permitted such use. The reports are not converted, however, by such use into documents
of "agencies" subject to the prescriptions of the FOIA. Access to such reports at the time of parole
release hearings, when available to the Parole Commission, has recently been given inmates by the Parole Commission and Reorganization Act [18 U.S.C. 4207, 4208 (Mar. 15, 1976)]. Nothing in that act,
however, alters the fact that the presentence report is a court document that is not within the purview
of the FOIA. It cannot be obtained under the FOIA by an inmate or parolee from the Parole
Commission.

Standards For Adult Probation and Parole Field Services (selected)*

Probation and parole field services continue to be a vital component of not only the corrections system but also the overall criminal justice system. As noninstitutional measures, probation and parole are generally recognized as alternatives that need to be given even larger and more dynamic roles in a comprehensive response to the national dilemma about crime. Certainly they are seen as part of the solution to the current overcrowding that adversely affects the institutional component of the system. However, the full extent of the use of probation and parole has yet to be determined.

As with any public service, particularly one that faces potential growth, probation and parole have not escaped criticism and controversy. The healthy aspect to the controversy is the resulting array of responses, which should lead to better field services based on increased knowledge and understanding. Probation and parole field services, as any component in the corrections continuum, should benefit from a refined definition of purpose.

Recent reappraisals of parole have been so extensive that a few states have made substantial changes in their parole laws, and the general literature has been enlivened with writings that suggest that parole might well have little or no place in future correctional systems.

The healthy quality of the controversy is seen in the reactions: the writings that have come forth to defend or reappraise and explore the values of both probation and parole. Such reactions should lead to the shaping of better services based upon more perceptive understandings. Particularly encouraging is the new appreciation of ways to conduct both probation and parole with a quality of fairness. There is a growing appreciation of the need for a civilized society to apply its standards with dedicated impartiality to all conditions of its

---

* From the American Correctional Association (1980). Reprinted with permission.

citizenry. A characteristic of a mature society is the acceptance of the principle that fairness, even to the least of its members, must be supported as a virtue. Accordingly, an important aspect of probation and parole standards is the enforcement of practices that support current concepts of basic fairness to offenders under supervision.

One effect of argument in behalf of abolishing parole has been to emphasize the sensitive interrelationships that exist within the criminal justice system. Even if an impressive case could be made for the abandonment of the practice of parole supervision, the weight of the argument shifts immediately when consideration is given to the extent of the imbalance this must cause in the total system. Probation and parole exist in a fragile balance with sentencing practices and institutional systems, and any restatement of purpose in scope of responsibility must consider the simultaneous compensating adjustments required for the others to maintain the balance.

Probation and parole remain vital elements in the larger system and, in fact, their importance seems lately to be emphasized by the crippling overload that has affected the institutional component in the system. Without probation and parole, the extent of overcrowding in our correctional institutions would be much worse. Furthermore, the potential capability of probation and parole to serve as effective and sufficient criminal justice sanctions has seldom been realized due to lack of support, resources, and sound professional working concepts. The increasing importance of probation and parole to the correctional system requires the determination of proper standards for their design and conduct. The standards will promote additional efforts to create more effective policy and procedures systems that will provide better public protection and improved supervision and guidance to offenders.

SUPERVISION—PROBATION AND PAROLE AGENCIES

2–3105 The agency's statement of purpose affirms that the supervision program is to provide necessary services to the offender with the goal of reducing the probability of continued criminal behavior on the part of the offender. (Essential)

> DISCUSSION: Supervision should be intended for the protection of the community and for the provision of services to the offender in order to reduce the probability of continued criminal behavior. Provision of adequate assistance and services to the offender is the best insurance against harm to the community.

2–3106 There is a written work load formula which is implemented in the allocation of work to field staff. (Essential)

> DISCUSSION: This formula should consider factors such as legal requirements, goals, character, and needs of offenders to be supervised, geographic area, administrative tasks required of the field staff, and types of personnel to be utilized. A work load rather than case load model is based on programs of differential supervision ranging

from intensive to minimal. Supervision tasks must be identified, measured against a time requirement, and then translated into specific total time and staff requirements.

2–3107 A full-time supervisor does not supervise more than ten field staff members. (Essential)

DISCUSSION: The span of control of a supervisor in the agency should be large enough to provide economical supervision, but not so large as to prevent effective management. Exceptions should be justified based on the experience of the field officers supervised. Ideally, all personnel supervised should be located in the same office as the supervisor and perform the same function. For a supervisory span of ten, all personnel supervised should be experienced in their specific functions; a smaller ratio of supervision should be used with a high proportion of inexperienced field staff. In small or remote field offices where the supervisor has other duties, the supervisory time should be allotted at the ratio of one tenth for every field staff position in the office.

2–3108 Field staff who have case loads report to a designated supervisor who is trained in the supervisory function. (Essential)

DISCUSSION: Regular case conferences between field staff and their supervisors can provide training and improve professional development. Such contacts can also help to ensure maximum effectiveness and efficiency in job performance. The span of control for a supervisor should not exceed six, and the job of supervising field staff should be full time. (See related standard 2–3107.)

2–3109 Field supervision is continually reviewed by the supervisor from both an administrative and case management perspective. (Essential)

DISCUSSION: Administrative review of the conduct of field supervision should be ongoing and should focus on how well the field services comply with policies and procedures regarding the degree and type of supervision and assistance provided offenders.

2–3110 Written policy and procedure govern classification and supervision of offenders in order to safeguard the community and meet the program needs of the offender. (Essential)

DISCUSSION: Offenders should be placed in the appropriate supervision category immediately following the initial interview. Classification should be consistent with individual dignity and basic concepts of fairness, should provide for maximum involvement of the offender, and should include the concept of diminishing field supervision. Agency procedures should require that the initial classification be recorded and justified in the records. Reclassification should occur at quarterly evaluation periods, and are recorded and justified in the chronological record. (See related standard 2–3119.)

2–3111 The conditions of probation/parole are furnished in writing to the offender and translated into those languages spoken by significant numbers of offenders. When a problem prevents an offender from understanding proba-tion/parole conditions, a field officer or other person assists the offender in understanding them. (Essential)

DISCUSSION: Conditions of probation/parole must be in writing so that there is no uncertainty as to the expected standards of behavior or requirements imposed. Adequate provision should be made for the needs of the handicapped. Because the conditions of probation/parole may serve as the basis for violation hearings, it is essential that they be stated clearly and recorded.

2-3112 The offender acknowledges, in writing, receipt and understanding of the conditions of probation/parole. (Essential)

DISCUSSION: Because offenders are required to comply with court/authority orders to meet stated conditions for their behavior, it is essential that they receive a copy of the conditions and sign the form containing them. The acknowledgment includes a statement that the conditions are understood, that there are no questions as to expected behavior, and that the offender will comply with the conditions.

2-3113 Supervision services are available twenty-four hours a day. (Essential)

DISCUSSION: The needs of offenders do not emerge only during business hours; it is necessary that services exist around-the-clock and on weekends. The twenty-four-hour availability of supervision services should be made known to offenders, and staff should be advised of these hours by publication of formal schedules. Use should be made of split shifts, duty officers, paging systems, and all-night and weekend telephone numbers.

2-3114 Consistent with court or parole authority requirements, the field officer and the offender jointly develop objectives and a supervision plan. This plan includes whichever of the following is most appropriate for the supervision of the individual offender: field contacts, office contacts, or collateral contacts. The offender receives a copy of the plan. (Important)

DISCUSSION: Planning that incorporates the needs, problems, capabilities, limitations, and the participation of the offender provides a positive framework for the period of supervision. It is important that the goals and plans remain within the offender's capacity. The plan should incorporate those provisions necessary for proper supervision, such as reporting and testing requirements, compliance with regular and special conditions of probation/parole, etc.

2-3115 When specific services ordered by the court or releasing authority are not available, the field staff should return the case to the court or releasing authority for further dispositional consideration. (Essential)

DISCUSSION: Offenders often are subject to discriminatory treatment by noncorrectional agencies and are prevented from participating in service programs available to citizens. If access to ordered services is not being provided to the offender, the field office should so inform the releasing authority.

2-3116 The field supervision plan is reviewed with the offender on an as-needed basis and adjusted in accordance with the offender's performance in the community. (Important)

DISCUSSION: The agency's supervision system should include provision for the field officer to review with the offender the adjustment and/or progress the offender is making, and to revise the supervision plan and level of supervision as appropriate.

This review should take place on an as-needed basis, but no less often than once every three months. Changes in the supervision plan are reviewed with the field officer's supervisor.

2–3117 The supervision plan requires that the field officer or other duly authorized persons maintain personal contact with the offender according to the supervision plan. (Essential)

DISCUSSION: Supervision of the offender should include scheduled and unscheduled visits by the field officer to the offender's home and, when possible, place of employment. A duly authorized person is any agency or qualified person who offers the necessary services on an accepted contractual basis. Office interviews are a useful supplement to the field supervision and, at times, provide the best setting to resolve administrative questions regarding the offender's case.

2–3118 The supervision plan requires that the field officer contact the offender in the community and contact persons and agencies in the community that are familiar with the offender; such contacts are made according to the supervision plan and have a specific purpose. (Essential)

DISCUSSION: The monitoring of the offender's progress in the community is essential for the field officers. Field officers should not depend solely upon their own insights, but should supplement them with information from others, so that a more accurate evaluation and assessment will emerge. These contacts (i.e., employment, residence, family, friends) should be according to a plan, have a specific purpose, and be adjusted as offender performance and behavior in the community change. The field officer should meet with the offender outside of the office in such places as the home, on the job, or during recreational pursuits.

2–3119 The community supervision plan specifies the minimum number of contacts with the offender per time period. (Essential)

DISCUSSION: A specified minimum number of contacts with the offender helps ensure that the state, through the field officer, stays informed about the offender's location and activities. This monitoring requirement also serves to remind offenders that they remain under legal jurisdiction and must meet certain obligations. Provision should be made for officers and their supervisors, in case conferences, to determine the case services to be provided and the number of case contacts included in this service. The range and nature of field and office contacts should be commensurate with the agency's classification program and supervision plan for each offender. Waiver of the minimum contacts should be permitted under circumstances such as extreme climatic conditions, unusual tension, or violence potential in a neighborhood.

2–3120 Written procedure governing community supervision provides for review of levels of supervision at least every six months, with prompt reclassification where warranted. (Important)

DISCUSSION: A minimum of six months should elapse between reviews of minimum supervision cases, with three-month reviews for cases requiring maximum supervision. Reclassification should occur promptly when offender adjustment warrants. Reviews are conducted by the field officer and the supervisor.

2–3121 For those agencies that require written reports from offenders under supervision, the interval between them is modified in relation to community adjustment; information in the reports is relevant to the supervision plan and/or agency administrative requirements. (Important)

> DISCUSSION: Written reports by offenders do not substitute for personal supervision by field officers. They should be required only when an advantage in public safety or offender adjustment is obtained.

2–3122 Written policy and procedure provide that the confidentiality of the offender's probation/parole status is maintained. (Essential)

> DISCUSSION: Policies and guidelines relating to disclosure should be developed collaboratively by the agency with its parent agency, and other criminal justice agencies. Unless public safety is threatened, and within statutorily defined limits, the agency should keep the offender's probation/parole status confidential. The use of unmarked automobiles, discreet visits to places of employment and residence, and plain mailing envelopes are simple techniques to ensure confidentiality.

2–3123 Written policy and procedure preclude offenders from being confronted with possible probation/parole violations for failure to meet financial obligations other than those which are conditions of probation/parole. (Essential)

> DISCUSSION: The agency should not be placed in the position of collection agency for the community. The agency and field officer should not enforce the collection of civil obligations by threats of probation/parole violation. Court-ordered debts, such as fines, restitution, and child support should be paid, and provision is made in the supervision plan for payment of such obligations.

2–3124 Written policy and procedure provide that probation/parole agency staff may request the court or the paroling authority to add, remove, or modify any or all of the special conditions of supervision. (Essential)

> DISCUSSION: One condition of probation/parole is applicable to all offenders—that they obey the law. Other conditions are added to this basic requirement to the extent that they add protection to the public and/or ensure the delivery of services to the offender. Conditions should be tailored to individual offenders, reviewed regularly, and amended if required. They should be realistic, few in number, and phrased in positive rather than negative terms. There should be provision as the individual's adjustment warrants, for the supervising officer to petition the court or the paroling authority for changes in special conditions.

2–3125 A closing report is prepared that summarizes the performance of the offender during the entire period of supervision. (Essential)

> DISCUSSION: At the conclusion of probation/parole supervision, a "summary of supervision" report should be prepared that indicates what occurred during supervision. The report should include unusual occurrences, the use or unavailability of community resources that affected the outcome of the supervision, and the field officer's assessment of the reasons for the success or failure of the outcome. These reports may provide guidance for the conduct of future cases.

2-3126 Written policy and procedure provide for at least annual reviews of offender progress with a recommendation of early termination of probation/parole where indicated; the results of such reviews are recorded in the case file. (Essential)

> DISCUSSION: The agency should have the prerogative to recommend early termination of probation/parole when it is clear that the delivery of services to the offender is no longer required to protect the community or to enhance the individual's overall performance. The agency should develop, in collaboration with the courts, criteria for early termination of probation. It is important that the agency advise the court of those individuals whom it believes meet the criteria for early termination. Procedure may include case review by peers, supervisors, and administrators or their representatives. Reduced intensity of supervision may be an appropriate step prior to early termination of probation/parole.

2-3127 The field agency identifies the collective service needs of its probationers/parolees at least biennially. (Essential)

> DISCUSSION: Although the service needs of individual offenders are important, the agency has a responsibility to assess periodically the collective needs of all its offenders to ensure that it is maximizing the delivery of services. The agency should concentrate on developing these community resources that will be of value to many offenders. Determination of collective needs will emerge from a careful screening of case files and discussions with staff, offenders, and community agencies.

2-3128 Male and female offenders under supervision have equal access to all agency programs and activities. (Essential)

> DISCUSSION: Male and female offenders should be encouraged to participate equally in all programs and activities available through the agency.

2-3129 The field agency supports efforts to develop community resources that can provide services to offenders, and field staff actively support community efforts on behalf of offenders. (Essential)

> DISCUSSION: Probation and parole are community oriented and community centered. The agency should be a mobilizing force in the community and assist in the development of community resources so that offenders can benefit from a wide variety of these resources. Field officers should serve as community organizers in addition to their more traditional roles.

2-3130 The field staff maintains a cooperative working relationship with public and private service agencies. (Essential)

> DISCUSSION: The agency should maintain a list of the services that are available from public and private service agencies, and should outline the procedures whereby offenders are referred for assistance. This document should be distributed to all field staff. Designated field staff should serve as liaison with the larger service agencies, such as departments of employment, vocational rehabilitation, or public assistance.

2-3131 A current inventory of functioning community agencies is maintained, which is readily available to the field staff. The effectiveness of these resources is evaluated periodically. (Important)

DISCUSSION: To ensure that parolees and probationers are receiving the help for which they are referred to community service agencies, the probation/parole agency should evaluate these resources periodically, and maintain and distribute to all field officers a current inventory of effective agencies. Community resources that are not proving effective should be informed in writing and offered whatever assistance possible in order to become fully functional.

2–3132 When the incidence of special needs offenders warrants, the field agency initiates and/or supports provision of special programs for these offenders. (Important)

DISCUSSION: Offenders who should be part of special programs—such as drug abusers, alcoholics, the mentally ill, retarded, or otherwise handicapped—should be provided special programs when a sufficient number are found in the offender population.

2–3133 The field agency devotes specific resources to assist employable offenders in finding suitable employment. (Essential)

DISCUSSION: The agency should maintain close liaison with the state department of employment, both at the headquarters and at local offices, in order to remain abreast of the changing labor market and to ensure that eligible offenders obtain job placement assistance. Field staff should solicit job placement assistance from labor unions, private sector businesses, and community action and self-help groups.

2–3134 The agency maintains a file of those agencies providing financial assistance to offenders; field officers are instructed and trained in methods to obtain financial assistance for offenders from available community resources. (Essential)

DISCUSSION: Adequate financial support is essential for individuals beginning probation or parole with no income. Such offenders should have enough funds or resources to maintain themselves for at least three weeks or until a first payday. Public assistance and welfare officers increasingly are extending financial help to offenders in need, and field officers should know where and how this help is available. Other public and private agencies extend financial assistance in selected cases, and field officers should know how to use these sources. Agencies should plan for some form of unemployment compensation for released offenders until they are gainfully employed.

2–3135 Written policy and procedure provide for enrollment and support of offenders in educational programs and vocational training. (Essential)

DISCUSSION: Long considered part of the aftercare program for juveniles, educational and training programs are becoming significant resources for adult offenders. In recent years, more federal funds have been made available to finance the academic education and vocational training of selected adult and juvenile offenders. Vocational rehabilitation agencies are also active in providing services for eligible offenders. The agency should identify and support programs featuring education and training. Staff should be designated to serve as liaison with major program offices, and the agency should maintain close, cooperative relationships with colleges and trade schools for purposes of developing suitable programs of learning for offenders.

2–3136 The agency provides guidance to offenders on leisure time programs and activities available in the community. (Important)

DISCUSSION: Constructive and acceptable leisure time activities contribute to a satisfactory community adjustment, therefore, the agency should provide the necessary guidance for those offenders who want to learn how to use leisure time activities.

2–3137 The agency, in accord with the courts or parole authority, defines specifically the types of minor violations that can be resolved by field staff. (Important)

DISCUSSION: Although all major probation/parole violations are reported and final resolution is determined by the courts or parole authority, many minor violations can be handled satisfactorily by field staff. Written policy and procedure should be provided to permit field staff to resolve minor probation/parole violations. Records of all minor violations and their resolution should be maintained and be available to the courts or parole authority whenever a change is being considered in the legal status of that case.

2–3138 All alleged probation or parole violations are reviewed by the field officer with the supervisor. (Essential)

DISCUSSION: Following investigation of the alleged violation, the field officer should confer with his/her supervisor to determine what action is required. A decision should be made at this time regarding the need for a formal violation proceeding or an informal administrative adjustment. Any action taken should be noted in the case record.

2–3139 The field officer's written report of an arrest or violation includes the officer's recommendation and justification as to final action or resolution of the situation. (Essential)

DISCUSSION: Because the field officer is often very familiar with the case, his/her views on how best to resolve the matter will assist the final decision-maker. The officer's recommendation should be in accordance with the organization's policies and guidelines.

2–3140 All arrests and probation/parole violations are investigated immediately; all serious arrests and major probation/parole violations are reported promptly in writing to the proper authority within time deadlines previously defined in writing by the agency. (Essential)

DISCUSSION: All arrests and alleged probation or parole violations that come to the attention of the field officer should be investigated promptly and thoroughly, reviewed with the field officer's supervisor, and documented in complete written reports for the case record. This procedure is in keeping with the evidentiary requirements mandated by the United States Supreme Court regarding parole revocation, and should be followed in probation cases also. The investigations should include law enforcement reports, statements from victims or witnesses, and a statement or explanation from the offender.

2–3141 When a probationer or parolee is arrested on a detention warrant, or when a detention warrant is lodged as a back-up to bail in conjunction with pending criminal charges, a preliminary hearing is held within 14 calendar days after the arrest and detention of the offender or the lodging of the detention warrant; however, when there has been a conviction or a finding of probable cause on new criminal charges, the preliminary hearing is not required. (Essential)

DISCUSSION: The United States Supreme Court case of *Morrissey v. Brewer*, 408 U.S. 471 (1972) requires, as a matter of due process, that a preliminary hearing be conducted as soon as possible after an offender is taken into custody, so that evidence and sources are readily available. The purpose of the hearing is to determine whether probable cause exists which indicates that probation or parole conditions have been violated. Later cases in various jurisdictions have held that a conviction or a finding of probable cause on new criminal charges takes the place, for due process purposes, of the preliminary hearing.

2-3142 The preliminary hearing is held in or near the community where the violation is alleged to have occurred or where the offender has been taken into custody. (Essential)

DISCUSSION: None. (See related standard 2-3141)

2-3143 The preliminary hearing may be delayed or postponed for good cause, and the probationer/parolee may waive the hearing if first informed of rights pertaining to the hearing and of the consequences of waiving the hearing. (Essential)

DISCUSSION: Due process requires that any waiver of rights by the probationer/parolee be done knowingly and voluntarily. Therefore, the revoking authority should assure that no form of coercion is used to induce a waiver of the preliminary hearing and that the parolee understands the nature and consequences of the hearing before waiving it.

2-3144 When requested by the revoking authority, a member of the administrative staff or a field officer conducts a preliminary hearing and makes findings as to probable cause for revocation. (Essential)

DISCUSSION: The *Morrissey* case provides that the hearing officer need not be a judicial officer, but may be a parole staff member, so long as that staff member is impartial.

2-3145 The preliminary hearing is conducted by an administrative staff member or an officer who has not previously been involved. (Essential)

DISCUSSION: In view of the requirement that the hearing officer be impartial, it is inappropriate for the officer who supervised the offender, or an individual who authorized the offender's detention, to conduct the preliminary hearing.

2-3146 At least three days prior to the preliminary hearing, the probationer/parolee is notified in writing of the time and place of the hearing and of the specific violation(s) charged.   The probationer/parolee is also advised in writing of the right to:

— Present evidence and favorable witnesses

— Disclosure of evidence

— Confront adverse witness(es) unless the witness(es) would be subjected thereby to a risk of harm

— Have counsel of choice present, or, in case of indigent persons who request assistance to adequately present their case, have counsel appointed

— Request postponement of the hearing for good cause.

(Essential)

DISCUSSION: Due process requires that the parolee receive notice of the hearing, of the specific acts alleged to have constituted a violation, and of all rights with respect to the hearing.   Consistent with the United States Supreme Court case of Gagnon v. Scarpelli, 411 U.S. 778 (1973), a revoking authority should decide, on a case-by-case basis, whether to appoint counsel for an indigent probationer/parolee who requests such assistance.   Among the factors to be considered in making this decision are: whether the offender denies committing the alleged violation(s); whether there are mitigating factors that are complex or otherwise difficult to develop or present; and whether the offender appears to be capable of speaking effectively in his/her behalf.

2–3147 The person who conducts the preliminary hearing determines whether there is probable cause to revoke probation or parole and hold the offender for a revocation hearing before the revoking authority.   The revoking authority may empower the hearing officer to make the provisional revocation decision, or merely to report his/her findings and recommendation to the authority for a decision as to revocation.   The hearing officer issues a verbal decision or a recommendation immediately after the hearing and provides a written decision to the offender within twenty-one calendar days of the hearing.   (Essential)

DISCUSSION: The hearing officer should make a summary of the documents presented and responses made at the preliminary hearing in order to make a determination as to probable cause for revocation.   Although the findings need not be formal, the officer should state the reasons for the determination and indicate the evidence relied upon.

2–3148 The probationer/parolee is sentenced to or returned to prison only when probable cause is found at the preliminary hearing and when it is determined, after considering the appropriateness of less severe sanctions, that the clear interest of the public requires incarceration. (Essential)

DISCUSSION: The preliminary hearing has a usefulness that goes beyond the narrow fact-finding process.   The hearing may provide an occasion to identify and reverse potentially harmful patterns of conduct, or to identify gaps in the program of supervision and recommended alternatives.   The authority should consider not only whether a violation has been committed, but also whether a less severe sanction is appropriate.

2–3149 When violations occur, alternatives to revocation and incarceration are considered to the extent that public safety is not endangered and the possibility of successful community adjustment exists. (Essential)

> DISCUSSION: Alternatives to incarceration include: the imposition of special conditions of future probation/parole; increasing the intensity of supervision or surveillance; placement in a halfway house; enrollment in a local detoxification facility; transfer of the case to another district or area; and involvement with a community or self-help organization.

2–3150 Written policy and procedure govern, in conformance with prevailing law, cooperation with law enforcement agencies in efforts to apprehend offenders known to be or suspected of being involved in criminal activities. (Essential)

> DISCUSSION: When police are trying to detect and apprehend offenders known to be or suspected of being involved in new crimes, field staff should cooperate by furnishing photographs, descriptions, and all other information requested by police officers. If field officers have definite information that might assist in effecting a proper disposition, they should submit such facts immediately to the appropriate authorities. Field officers should establish and maintain effective communications with local police units for the exchange of information relative to offenders' activities.

2–3151 Agency policy prohibits the use of probationers/parolees as police informers; written policy and procedure specify the conditions for exceptions. (Important)

> DISCUSSION: Probationers/parolees should not be subjected to the criminal contacts and influences that are involved in gathering information for police in collaboration with other offenders. Procedures should specify the conditions under which exceptions are made. When an offender can and is willing to help the police, and a review of the situation indicates this is warranted, there should be a written agreement between the law enforcement agency and the probation/parole organization that specifies the conditions under which the offender will be used, including a definite time period. Procedures should include securing the approval of probation/parole administrators and authorities. The field officer should always be informed of such activity within his/her case load.

2–3152 Written policy and procedure specify the types of action required to locate and recover absconders. (Essential)

> DISCUSSION: Field investigation should include inquiry at the last known residence and place of employment, and checks with family, friends, local jails, hospitals, welfare and service agencies, and other agencies with whom the offender may have had contact. Also, tracer letters should be mailed to all possible contacts, including those outside the immediate area. When appropriate, all law enforcement agencies should be notified and an arrest warrant issued.

2–3153 When statute permits, written policy and procedure provide that recovered absconders who commit no new crimes, who are not viewed as an undue risk to the public or who surrender themselves, may be continued on community supervision. (Important)

DISCUSSION: Many absconders only avoid supervision. When such individuals are located, an evaluation should be made of their activities and their present situation should be assessed. Consistent with public safety, those with no delinquent behavior other than absconding should be restored to active supervision.

2-3154 Written policy and procedure govern the authorization of probation/parole officers to arrest offenders. (Essential)

DISCUSSION: When the power to arrest is allowed, any action taken should be preceded by a conference between the officer and the supervisor. If it is concluded that an arrest is necessary, trained field officers should make the arrest, using law enforcement personnel when personal or public safety may be endangered. While most arrests require warrants, warrantless arrests may be made when the violation involves the commission of a crime and current legal standards for warrantless arrests are met. (See related standard 2-3072.)

2-3155 Warrants for the arrest and detention of offenders, pending a determination by the revoking authority as to whether probation/parole should be revoked or provisionally revoked, are issued only upon the affirmative approval of a revoking authority, or the statewide or regional director of supervision services. (Essential)

DISCUSSION: The arrest and detention of an offender on violation charges is a serious act with profound implications for the offender. In view of the loss of liberty that results from the issuance of a detention warrant, the need for such a warrant should be reviewed by the revoking authority or the statewide or regional director of supervision services. The power to issue detention warrants should be exercised by such administrative personnel, not by the officer involved directly in the supervision process.

2-3156 Warrants for the arrest and detention of offenders are issued only upon adequate evidence that indicates a probable serious or repeated pattern of violation of conditions and a compelling need for detention pending the revoking authority's initial revocation decision. (Essential)

DISCUSSION: The standard for the issuance of detention warrants may not rise to the standard of probable cause required for arrest on criminal charges. However, to justify issuance of a detention warrant, sufficient evidence should be produced to indicate that conditions have been seriously breached and that detention is required. Detention may be required in order to prevent injury to an individual or the public, to interrupt a serious continuing violation of conditions, or to assure the presence of the offender at a preliminary hearing when it is determined that he/she would not attend voluntarily.

2-3157 When violation charges are based on the alleged commission of a new crime, a detention warrant is only issued when the offender's presence in the community would present an unreasonable risk to public or individual safety. (Essential)

DISCUSSION: The issuance of a detention warrant often precludes an offender who is charged with committing a new crime from the possibility of bail or other forms of pretrial release. As a general rule, offenders should be able to seek the forms of pretrial release that are available to other criminal defendants. However, the presence of other serious probation/parole violation charges or a danger to public or individual safety may justify the issuance of a detention warrant when the offender is charged with committing a new crime.

2–3158 Written policy and procedure provide for the use of physical force only in instances of justifiable self-defense, protection of others, prevention of property damage, and prevention of escapes, and only in accordance with appropriate statutory authority. Only the minimum force necessary is employed. (Essential)

> DISCUSSION: Sometimes offenders lose control over their actions, becoming violent, and they must be brought under control. Assistance should be sought from fellow field officers or from local police.

2–3159 All incidents involving use of physical force are reported fully, promptly, and in writing to administrative staff for their information and review. All injuries are reported in writing and treated promptly. (Essential)

> DISCUSSION: Prompt and complete written reports of any use of force are essential as a means of administrative evaluation and control of field officer actions; such reports are also essential basic documents for protection of the agency and the affected personnel in case of subsequent complaints, accusations, or court suits.

2–3160 Written policy and procedure govern searches of offenders by field officers and ensure the proper disposition of all confiscated items. (Essential)

> DISCUSSION: When allowed, searches of offenders should comply with legal requirements. Written regulations should detail how such searches are to be conducted and under what circumstances, and should require a stated reason for the search. Whenever circumstances permit, field officers should seek concurrence from their supervisors on the possible need for a search. The supervisor should conduct a postsearch review to ensure that the search was conducted properly. To prevent accusations, the field officer who confiscates any property should, for his/her own protection, report the incident to his/her supervisor as soon as possible and should promptly deposit the property with the appropriate law enforcement office.

2–3161 Special supervision reports are prepared whenever an unusual situation involving the offender occurs. (Essential)

> DISCUSSION: An unusual situation during the period of supervision is any occurrence or event that would impact significantly on public safety or probation adjustment. (See related standard 2–3087.)

2–3162 Probation/parole officers do not routinely carry weapons in the performance of their duties. Written policy and procedure specify those situations in which agency personnel may carry weapons. (Essential)

> DISCUSSION: Agency policy should authorize the use of weapons only in carefully defined and reviewed situations. The agency should train those probation and parole personnel who are authorized to carry weapons in the proper use of those weapons. (See related standard 2–3069.)

2–3163 Written policy and procedure require that all probationers/parolees are informed of the grievance program available to them at the time of the initial interview. (Essential)

DISCUSSION: Specific procedures should be defined so that all offenders who believe their rights have been or are about to be violated by administrative actions and conditions of correctional control, treatment, and other services can file complaints. Grievance procedures should include: a time limit for written responses and action, evaluation by someone not directly connected with the case under investigation, special provisions for emergencies, right to appeal, and a monitoring system. (See related standard 2–3023.)

2–3164 Written policy and procedure govern the transfer of supervision of offenders to and from other jurisdictions. Transfer policies are in accordance with the Interstate Compact on Probation and Parole and other interstate agreements. (Essential)

DISCUSSION: Supervision of offenders is transferred when offenders move into other jurisdictions. The new probation/parole agency is notified so as to permit continuing supervision and to preclude uncontrolled and unauthorized relocation of offenders outside the area of their original jurisdiction. Procedures should exist for the return of foreign nationals to their home countries under circumstances that are in concert with authorities in the home countries and in the best interests of all concerned. The interstate transfer of supervision of offenders is regulated by two compacts. Compliance with these compacts ensures the public the protection that probation/parole provides and provides offenders the services they need. Although the interstate compacts provide considerable detail on the transfer process, it is important that these policies be localized and supplemented as necessary.

2–3165 A staff member is designated to act as liaison for the transfer of offenders. (Important)

DISCUSSION: Effective administration of the compacts requires the clear assignment of responsibility to a designated staff member who should be thoroughly familiar with the rules and procedures for implementing transfers. The designated staff member also may provide training to field personnel and promulgate local guidelines. Regardless of the amount of interstate transfer activity, at least one staff member should be charged with and have expertise in this function.

SUPERVISION—PROBATION AGENCIES ONLY

2–3179 The administrator of the probation field agency organizes and manages the investigation function to maintain both presentence and supervision services. (Essential)

DISCUSSION: Investigations and reports constitute a significant amount of probation activity. Where demands for investigations are great, it may be more efficient and effective to provide for a substructure within the organization to carry out this function. Where investigation requirements are minimal, consolidation of the investigation and supervision functions may be practical. There should be a logical, orderly, and expeditious work flow from receipt of the request for an investigation to delivery of the report to the court.

2–3180 The priority assigned to the supervision function is equal to that assigned to the presentence investigation function. (Essential)

DISCUSSION: Supervision of the offender in the community is integral to effective probation. The probation administration should ensure that competing demands (e.g., presentence investigations and report deadlines) do not cause the relegation of supervision to a secondary function.

2–3181 The supervision of misdemeanant offenders is governed by standards, policies and practices comparable to those available to felony offenders. (Important)

DISCUSSION: Misdemeanants placed on probation should receive the same priority and quality of service as those accorded felony probationers. The agencies responsible for felony probation also should have responsibility for misdemeanant probation.

2–3182 The field agency has a written policy governing methods to be used in collecting the information essential in making recommendations of fines, restitution, family support, and their amount(s) to the court. (Essential)

DISCUSSION: While the offender should not have to pay more than a reasonable cost, it is important that the victim be given the opportunity to present information relative to the value of the loss. Value should be verified and the victim should be told the method to be used. The victim should be informed about the offender's ability to pay and whether or not the money will be paid in small amounts over a long period of time or at a specific time.

2–3183 Unless prohibited by statute, written policy and procedure preclude the requirement that probationers pay the cost of probation, but do not preclude the payment of court-ordered restitution or court costs. (Important)

DISCUSSION: The costs of probation should be borne by the jurisdiction that established the probation agency.

2–3184 A probation officer conducts an initial supervision interview with the probationer immediately after the individual is placed on probation. (Essential)

SUPERVISION—
PAROLE AGENCIES ONLY

2–3166 Unless precluded by statute or court order, parole agency policy specifies that no inmate is released on parole until the parole program is verified by a designated parole officer. (Essential)

DISCUSSION: To ensure that the inmate is being released to a legitimate parole program, policy should provide for authorizing release on parole only when the release program has been investigated and verified by a parole officer. The verification process should include field visits by the parole officer to the parolee's prospective employer and to family or friends with whom the parolee plans to reside. This investigative procedure should include the option to reject or modify the release program if circumstances warrant.

2–3167 Unless precluded by statute or court order, written policy and procedure provide that the parole agency receives pertinent information about a prospective parolee in advance of the parole date to allow for parole program development and/or verification. (Essential)

DISCUSSION: Adequate time is needed to develop a sound program for the individual about to be paroled. In cases where the parole officer must develop a parole program, particularly where a number of community resources and relatives may be involved, early receipt of referral material is essential. Even in cases where only verification of a job and residence is needed, early receipt and completion of this task by the parole staff eases the anxiety of the inmate. The options of placing the parolee in transitional release programs, such as work release and halfway houses, and the possible need to advance or modify the release date to accommodate a particular release program, require that the parole officer receive the referral material three months in advance of the parole date.

2–3168 The parole agency supports release policies that require employable inmates to have a visible means of support or a reasonable assurance of employment, rather than a promise of a specific job, before release on parole. (Essential)

DISCUSSION: Often inmates cannot be released on parole until there is a specific and verified job waiting for them. This results in many inmates being "overdue" or retained past their parole date in the institution. This is an expensive policy, both in terms of institutional costs and inmate anxiety and motivation. Family help, public assistance, halfway house placement, and direct financial assistance can maintain parolees adequately until they are self-supporting. A number of studies have shown that releasing parolees with "reasonable assurance" of employment does not adversely affect recidivism rates, and that offenders do as well or better if they can find their own jobs.

2–3169 The parole agency participates in programs that include provisions for graduated or partial release. (Important)

DISCUSSION: Sudden and direct release to the community after many years in a closed or maximum security institution can produce psychological shock in a releasee and may be a factor in a releasee's inability to adjust on parole. A few months in a minimum or open institution can help ease the transition to parole.

PRESENTENCE
INVESTIGATION AND REPORT

2–3185 Written policy specifies that the primary purpose of the presentence report is to provide the sentencing court with timely, relevant, and accurate data so that it may select the most appropriate sentencing alternative and correctional disposition; subject to this primary purpose, the report is prepared in a manner to serve the needs of any correctional institution or field agency that may receive the offender. (Essential)

> DISCUSSION: The needs of the sentencing court must have first priority in preparing the format and content of the presentence report. But if and when the offender goes to an institution, the staff there, and later the parole authority, may have little or no background information on the offender except as found in the presentence report. Accordingly, it is vital to the interest of both the institution and the sentencing court for the presentence report to serve the institution and the parole authority if they, in turn, are to handle the offender appropriately and with due respect to the intent of the court.

2-3186 The agency assigns the resources required to ensure the submission of investigation reports within three weeks for confined offenders and four weeks for offenders who are not confined. (Essential)

> DISCUSSION: Sufficient staff, time, space, and equipment should be assigned to all presentence functions. However, the resources assigned to the presentence investigation and report function should not adversely affect the delivery of other probation services. A presentence investigation and preparation of a report should not exceed four weeks in general, or three weeks for offenders in custody. These time frames, however, will vary depending on the nature of the offense, complexity of the offender's circumstances, possible dispositions, availability of prior reports, and necessity of delivering the report to the court in time for review and analysis.

2-3187 Written policy and procedure govern the conduct of presentence investigations, preparation of reports, and provision of sentencing alternatives for the court. (Essential)

> DISCUSSION: Written guidelines help ensure high quality investigations and reports, and minimal disparities in the provision of sentencing alternatives. The guidelines should be developed in collaboration with the court and reviewed regularly.

2-3188 Policy and procedure provide for interviewing the victim when appropriate or possible. The information obtained is contained in the presentence report. (Important)

> DISCUSSION: Interviewing the victim for the presentence investigation (victim impact statement) allows the victim to not only tell his story in his own words, but also offers an opportunity for him to express his feelings about the disposition. At the same time, the probation officer is given the opportunity to explain to the victim the offender's situation. For example, in some jurisdictions the victim and the offender are brought together in face-to-face confrontation, with the probation officer acting as a mediator. At that time the amount of payment is determined and agreed upon by both parties.

2-3189 The administrator of field services supervises and reviews, on a continuing basis, the conduct of presentence investigations, the preparation of reports, and the provision of sentencing alternatives for the court. (Essential)

> DISCUSSION: None

2-3190 Written policy specifies that a presentence investigation is not conducted and a presentence report not prepared until the defendant has been adjudicated guilty of an offense, unless the defendant, on advice of counsel, has consented to allow the investigation to proceed before adjudication, and adequate precautions are taken to ensure that information disclosed during the presentence investigation does not come to the attention of the prosecution, the court, or the jury prior to adjudication. (Essential)

DISCUSSION: While there are occasional and exceptional situations in which a short cut may be taken in the interest of both the court and the defendant, the basic rights of the defendant are ordinarily jeopardized if the investigative process is conducted before adjudication. Also, since a full account of the offense is an important element in a competent report, it is difficult for the probation officer to get the needed information in a case for which guilt has not been finally determined. If it does becomes necessary to conduct a preadjudication investigation, it is essential that the defendant's informed consent be given and that inadvertent premature disclosure of the report be conscientiously avoided.

2-3191 Written policy and procedure permit the use of staff other than probation officers to collect information during the presentence investigation. (Essential)

DISCUSSION: Some of the data required for an investigation and the presentence report may be collected by nonprofessional staff (i.e., paraprofessionals, volunteers, students, clerical), thus freeing probation officers to use their skills for interpreting the data and developing a probation plan.

2-3192 When probation is not prohibited by statute, a potential supervision plan is developed during the presentence investigation and included as part of the presentence report. (Essential)

DISCUSSION: It is necessary to ensure that, if probation is granted, a plan will be available on the first day of supervision. The plan should include such considerations as employment, residence, education, etc., and should be developed with the offender. To the degree possible, the probation officer who will supervise the probationer should participate in the development of this plan. The plan should be realistic in that both the goals set and the resources required are attainable.

2-3193 Written policy and procedure provide that probation officers are to consider innovative sentencing alternatives in all cases in which incarceration is not clearly imperative for reasons of immediate public safety. (Essential)

DISCUSSION: The traditional dispositions in adult courts are probation, confinement in a local facility, or confinement in a state correctional institution. It is important to seek other alternatives that may permit a better balance between the dual needs of protecting the community and providing for the welfare of the defendant. The appropriate time to search for alternatives is during the presentence investigation, and any feasible alternatives should be set forth in the presentence report. The use of alternatives such as halfway houses, detoxification centers, civil addict commitment programs, and self-help groups may be appropriate. Attention also should be given to finding resources that would permit use of individualized probation supervision programs if probation is ordered.

2–3194 The probation agency can document efforts to promote the resources necessary to process a presentence report in every case in which there is a potential sentencing disposition involving incarceration for one year or longer, and in every case involving first offenders and minors. (Important)

> DISCUSSION: As correctional institutions become more expensive and more crowded, it becomes especially important to ensure that incarceration is not resorted to in any case in which viable alternatives are available and appropriate. Minors and first offenders should be diverted from an institutional career whenever possible. The presentence report in such cases may have particular utility in outlining, when justified, feasible alternative plans.

2–3195 Written policy and procedure govern the use of different presentence report formats to meet the specific needs of the courts and correctional agencies. (Important)

> DISCUSSION: The establishment of standard formats to be used without deviation is an important contribution to quality control and efficiency in presentence report production. However, there may be proper reason to have more than one standard format to adapt efficiently to different types of cases while still avoiding uncontrolled variations from case to case. To this end, the agency should collaborate with the courts to design a standard report format to be used for particular types of cases. As a basic principle, enough data should be collected and analyzed so that the most appropriate sentencing alternative may be selected to protect the community and serve the needs of the offender.

2–3196 If probation is one of the sentencing alternatives, the probation officer identifies the need for special conditions of probation, if any, and recommends that these special conditions be appended to the general conditions of probation. (Essential)

> DISCUSSION: In addition to those general conditions of probation that are applicable to all probationers, possible special conditions should be identified during the presentence investigation, recommended to the court, and appended to the general conditions by the court if it appears that these additional conditions will enhance public safety or increase the probability of a successful community adjustment. Special conditions should be few in number, realistic, and phrased in positive rather than negative terms.

2–3197 When statutes permit, confinement, full or part-time, is part of a probation grant only in selected cases when circumstances clearly indicate the need for confinement as part of a prescribed program plan. (Important)

> DISCUSSION: Confinement disrupts many aspects of life. As a condition of probation, it should be discouraged unless it clearly will contribute to public safety or the likelihood of better community adjustment.

2-3198 The presentence report is submitted to the court for review and evalua-tion a minimum of two working days in advance of the date set for sentencing. (Essential)

DISCUSSION: The court requires sufficient time to read and assess the document and perhaps discuss it with probation staff. A minimum of two full days is seen as essential for the court's review, but this generalized time frame must be adjusted to judicial schedules and work loads.

2-3199 All presentence reports and recommendations are subject to review by a supervisor prior to submission to the court. (Essential)

DISCUSSION: Supervisory review of presentence reports and recommendations serves several purposes, including the following: ensures that functions are being properly implemented in accordance with policy, objectives, and procedures; helps to determine that the court will get the needed information in the correct format; ensures that each recommendation is reasonable and supported by the information provided; and contributes to the training of personnel and the development of skills and knowledge.

2-3200 Written policy and procedure protect the confidentiality of presentence reports and case records. (Essential)

DISCUSSION: The issue of confidentiality extends beyond the courtroom and should permeate the entire investigation-and-report process from receipt of the case for investigation through final destruction of documents. Information about cases should not be discussed openly, and files and records should not be left unattended or be given to persons who do not have a proper and legitimate interest in the case. This principle is not to interfere with the sharing of the report with the defendant and his counsel wherever "disclosure" is recognized in law or court policy.

2-3201 Written procedure provides for the prompt transmittal by the probation agency of presentence report data to institutional personnel when confinement of the adjudicated offender is ordered. (Essential)

DISCUSSION: In those instances in which the offender is ordered confined, presen-tence materials should be provided to the receiving institution to assist in its classification process. Written guidelines, developed in collaboration with agencies receiving committed offenders, should be available and cover such matters as method and timing of transmittal of documents. In consideration of vital institutional need, the agency should make every effort to deliver the presentence report to the institution at the same time that the offender is transferred there.

APPENDIX *F*

Standards for Adult Parole
Authorities (selected) *

Parole Authority Standards

These standards reflect this unfolding history of parole and contemporary
concern about it, without argument or speculation as to the future of parole in
the criminal justice system. Parole authorities require national standards to
guide them in protecting the public and in assisting the offender under circumstances that are understandable, fair, efficient, and effective. The standards
support Supreme Court decisions on the parole and revocation process as well as
those concerning due process in providing notice of hearings, written reasons for
decisions, and opportunities for appeal. The standards emphasize that parole
decision-making should occur under conditions of openness and should result in
the immediate availability to the inmates of the information on which decisions
are made.

Contemporary concerns are also reflected in the emphasis on predictability
and stability of parole decisions. Thus, parole dates are to be set as early as
possible, consistent with the appropriate sentencing system, and changes in
those dates are made only through a series of carefully articulated steps. The
use of general parole conditions is sharply limited. In the interest of both the
offender and the community, the parole authority must set conditions that are
tailored specifically to the individual. These conditions are linked clearly to the
potential for serious crime on the part of the parolee, rather than reflecting a
generalized concern for an acceptable lifestyle.

These standards call for long overdue substantial fiscal and organizational
support for parole. Failure to supply necessary resources has too often resulted
in parole programs that were basically ineffective and unfair, despite stated goals
and objectives. The standards also call for nonpolitical and well-administered

---

* From the American Correctional Association (1980). Reprinted with permission.

parole systems integrated with a variety of agencies and community organizations.

Perhaps as important as any other feature of these standards is the recognition of the need for increased knowledge in carrying out correctional responsibilities. In order to further develop information and knowledge called for by the standards, several standards relate specifically to the use of management information and research findings in parole decision making.

Goals for Corrections

These standards represent contemporary thought and judgment. They also set high levels of compliance for parole authorities pursuing accreditation. And they represent more than just a tool for accreditation. They are to be used by correctional administrators as guidelines for self-improvement and as a stimulus for change in the legislative, executive, and judicial branches of government. The standards in this appendix demonstrate that corrections professionals have the capacity to incorporate changing views of the parole process based on new experience, knowledge, and expertise. The capacity to change and evolve is vital to the continued acceptance and use of these standards in order to further the goal of the American Correctional Association and the Commission on Accreditation for Corrections. That goal is to help parole authorities throughout the country continue to upgrade and improve their operations.

ORGANIZATION
AND ADMINISTRATION

Organization and Legal Basis

2-1001 The jurisdiction has a single authority provided by statute that has parole decision-making power with respect to all offenders convicted of a felony who are sentenced to a term of imprisonment and are eligible for discretionary parole. (Important)

> DISCUSSION: Jurisdiction refers to a governmental level parole authority that handles convicted felony offenders. In order to ensure uniformity of procedures and to lessen the probability of disparate decisions, it is important that there exist a centralized source of parole decision making in a given jurisdiction. Decision making is defined here to mean release, revocation, and the establishment of the conditions of release. This does not exclude certain juveniles or misdemeanants under the authority's jurisdiction.

2-1002 When the parole authority is administratively part of a federal, state, or local overall correctional agency, it is independent from the control of any of the units in the agency in its decision-making functions. (Essential)

> DISCUSSION: A central principle of parole decision making is that a parole authority should base its decisions on an objective assessment of the needs of the offender and the community. Thus, while a parole authority needs to be sensitive to the views of many persons, particularly those who have responsibility for operating correctional

programs, the authority must retain its autonomy if it is to serve its purposes. A wide variety of factors may be properly weighed in reaching its conclusions. However, the authority must resist outside efforts to unduly attempt to influence its decisions, such as those of the affected institution. (See related standard 2–1007.)

2–1003 While parole investigation and supervisory staff may be administratively independent from the parole authority, they are responsive to the authority in all areas determined by statute, policy, or procedures. (Important)

DISCUSSION: There must be a cooperative effort between the parole authority and the parole investigation and supervisory staff in order to provide the offender with the best possible supervision. Feedback on the status of parolees is important to the parole authority's decision-making process. Likewise, changes in parole authority policy and procedure or conditions of parole can affect the work of parole supervisory staff.

2–1004 The parole authority has the power to require that general and specific conditions of parole be enforced during the supervision of parolees. (Essential)

DISCUSSION: Since a parole authority frequently bases its decisions on the assumption that certain specific procedures will be followed by parole supervisory staff, the authority should have the power to specify general and specific conditions regarding the supervision of parolees. This power should be indicated no matter where the administrative responsibility for field staff is located.

2–1005 All staff, including any hearing examiners employed by the parole authority, are directly responsible to the authority with respect to carrying out the policies of the authority. (Essential)

DISCUSSION: Hearing examiners should be considered staff of the parole authority and directly responsible to the authority both administratively and operationally. The decision to grant, deny, or revoke parole may be assigned to the hearing examiners. (See related standards 2–1047 and 2–1115.)

2–1006 The parole authority has the legal power to secure prompt and full information, which it deems necessary from courts, probation, institutions, parole, halfway houses, and other agencies or staff which would be applicable. (Essential)

DISCUSSION: A parole authority cannot operate without the kinds of information necessary for its task. It is crucial that timely and accurate information be made available from the required sources in a form useful to parole decision-makers. Though the parole authority has legal authority to require the submission of such information, it should collaborate with the agencies involved in developing the means through which it is to be delivered and the format in which it is to be presented.

2–1007 The parole authority has power to grant or deny parole and does not serve merely as an advisory body to another official or agency. (Essential)

DISCUSSION: In order to achieve competent and impartial parole decision making, with sound policies and their consistent application, the parole authority should have the power to act with finality. Serving simply as an advisory board to an elected or appointed state official does not meet this test. Such arrangements negate the required autonomous character of parole decision making. (See related standard 2–1002.)

2–1008 The parole authority has the statutory power to cause the arrest of parolees and the power to revoke parole. (Essential)

DISCUSSION: Basic to the functioning of the parole authority is the capacity to revoke as well as to grant parole. As with the power to grant parole, the authority's power to arrest and to revoke should be indicated by statute. Parole field staff may arrest parolees on the issuance of detention warrants.

2–1009 While the existence of a statutory limit may prevent discharge prior to two years of parole, the parole authority has the statutory power to discharge from parole in all cases subsequent to this limitation. (Essential)

DISCUSSION: It is sometimes costly to the resources of the jurisdiction, frequently an unnecessary impediment to a parolee, and always unfair to require a person to remain under parole supervision when it has been demonstrated that neither the jurisdiction nor he or she will benefit from continued parole supervision. The power to discharge from parole in some jurisdictions may apply only after statutory minimums of not more than two years have been met. Even if this is the case, the authority should have the ultimate power to discharge from parole. (See related ˌstandard 2–1124 and 2–1125.)

2–1010 When requested in matters of clemency, the authority conducts an investigation, provides necessary factual information, and when requested, makes a recommendation to the clemency authority. (Essential)

DISCUSSION: Forms of clemency include pardon, commutation of sentence, reprieve, and remission of fine. Statutes govern eligibility, specific requirements, and the method for obtaining clemency. Most often the parole authority is advisory to the governor in matters of clemency. When a request is made, the authority should complete a thorough investigation that covers all requirements of the law or the requesting body. When requested, the authority should make a recommendation regarding the granting of clemency.

2–1011 Written policy and procedure govern the handling of clemency requests when the authority is empowered to handle them. (Important)

DISCUSSION: Policy and procedure should be developed to encompass all aspects of clemency, although some types of pardons, such as those of "innocence," are handled through the courts. Pardons of "forgiveness" generally stipulate a time period between the completion of sentence and the time of petition for pardon. They require the individual to have shown respect for the law and obedience to it during that period. Parole authority policy and procedure should be developed with the governor's office or other appropriate body regarding the steps in the process. When a recommendation on clemency is requested, it should be made based on the unanimous vote of the full authority.

Administration and Staffing

2–1012 The parole authority has a current organizational chart that accurately reflects the structure of authority, responsibility, and accountability within the agency. The chart is reviewed annually and updated if needed. (Essential)

DISCUSSION: A current organizational chart is necessary for providing employees a clear administrative picture. The chart should reflect the grouping of similar functions, an effective span of control, lines of authority, and an orderly channel of communication. Names of units and duties should reflect precisely what is entailed.

2–1013 The chairperson of the parole authority initiates an annual review by all authority members of the authority's policies; revisions and updating of the policies are undertaken when necessary. (Essential)

DISCUSSION: Although the parole authority chairperson has specific executive responsibilities, it is crucial that all parole authority members be involved in the development and review of authority policy. The authority chairperson should operate within the policies fixed by the entire authority, moving beyond them only where expedient and with subsequent review. (See related standard 2–1017 and 2–1063.)

2–1014 The parole authority has a policy and procedure manual which is readily available to inmates, parolees, staff and the public and which is reviewed at least annually, and updated if needed. (Essential)

DISCUSSION: An administrative manual is important in order to assist staff in understanding the operating procedures of the agency. Important to an effective manual system is the capacity for periodic updating.

2–1015 The parole authority has sufficient staff to perform its responsibilities efficiently and without accumulating work backlog. (Essential)

DISCUSSION: In order to carry out the variety of administrative tasks which are required, the parole authority must be adequately staffed. There must be staff available to systematically prepare needed materials, answer correspondence properly, process legal and administrative documents, schedule and conduct interviews in the office, and prepare documents required by the legislature, executive, and the public. (See related standard 2–1029.)

2–1016 Administrative personnel are available to maintain supervision of the parole authority's staff, not to exceed a ratio of six to one, unless such a deviation can be shown to not impair effective staff supervision. (Important)

DISCUSSION: Although ideal ratios of supervisors to staff are difficult to specify, it is clear that sufficient supervisory personnel are needed to make certain that an organization functions well. Therefore, unless a deviation in the span of control can be justified, no more than six staff members should be supervised directly by an administrator.

2–1017 Written policy and procedure provide for a communications system within the authority that requires, at a minimum, that the authority chairperson meet at least monthly with all authority division heads and/or supervisors, and that all authority division heads and/or supervisors meet monthly with all employees. (Essential)

DISCUSSION: Regular staff meetings help ensure open communications among employees. The use of agendas and the preparation of minutes should be required at all staff meetings. (See related standard 2–1013.)

2–1018 Legal assistance is readily available to the parole authority to meet the authority's requirements in policy formulation, to advise in individual cases, and to represent the authority when required before courts and other appropriate bodies. (Essential)

> DISCUSSION: With present day demands on parole authorities, immediate availability of effective legal staff is required on a continuous basis.

2–1019 Parole authority headquarters are located in physical facilities that provide privacy for authority members and staff, and which have space and equipment necessary for the effective and efficient processing of business. (Important)

> DISCUSSION: Adequate facilities can increase the efficiency and quality of the work of the parole authority by providing sufficient space and privacy for hearings. Parole authority members must be able to provide each case the attention and thorough review necessary for a fair and impartial hearing. (See related standard 2–1029.)

2–1020 Offenders are furnished assistance in understanding the parole process, if needed, including written and/or oral translations; this includes the hearing process and the conditions of parole. (Essential)

> DISCUSSION: When physical or mental handicaps or language barriers prevent offenders under the control of the jurisdiction from fully understanding the parole process, parole conditions, parole procedures, or hearings and appeals, assistance is provided to the offender by personnel qualified in working within the offender's problem area. (See related standards 2–1084 and 2–1102.)

2–1034 Members of the parole authority are chosen through a system defined by statutes or administrative policy, and with explicitly defined criteria. (Essential)

> DISCUSSION: Partisan political considerations have too frequently entered into the selection of parole authority members. Though, from time to time, qualified persons are appointed under a system dominated by political considerations, often the result has been the appointment of unqualified persons as parole authority members. It is imperative that explicitly established criteria be employed in the appointment of parole authority members.

2–1035 At least two-thirds of the members of the parole authority have at least a baccalaureate degree. (Essential)

> DISCUSSION: A variety of educational backgrounds may qualify a person to sit on a parole authority, and individuals who do not have baccalaureate degrees may be uniquely qualified by other training or experience to serve on a parole authority. However, a parole authority must have a capacity for policy formation and articulation, an awareness of contemporary research findings and correctional techniques, and skills in system planning and management. These tasks require that an authority include in its membership some members with the minimum of a baccalaureate degree.

2–1036 At least two-thirds of the members of the parole authority have at least three years experience in a criminal justice or juvenile justice position, or equivalent experience in a relevant profession. (Essential)

DISCUSSION: While a variety of experience can be appropriate, it is expected that the parole authority membership will include persons who have had a substantial experience in professions, such as law and clinical practice, which are directly relevant to parole decision-making and policy development.

2–1037 Parole authority members represent a diversity of the significant population under the jurisdiction of the agency. (Essential)

DISCUSSION: It is vital for effective decision-making and public support that a parole authority be representative of the entire community, and that offenders are dealt with by persons who represent both sexes and the racial and ethnic groups in the jurisdiction.

2–1038 Members of the parole authority do not seek or hold public office which would represent a conflict of interest while a member of the authority. (Essential)

DISCUSSION: Members of the parole authority should not disenfranchise themselves during their term on the authority. During their term, however, political considerations should never enter the decision-making process. The avoidance of conflict of interest is essential to the objective role of the authority. (See related standard 2–1080.)

2–1039 Positions of members of the parole authority are full-time. In jurisdictions where the parole authority has a minimum of cases to be heard, the chairperson must be full-time but other members may be part-time. A full justification for such action is necessary. (Important)

DISCUSSION: The task and scope of the work of the parole authority is such that full-time members should be appointed. In small jurisdictions, or those where there are few cases to be heard by the authority, justification of an alternative to a full-time authority will be considered.

2–1040 Tenure on the parole authority is no less than five years. Legal provision allows for the removal of parole authority members for good and demonstrated cause only after a full and open hearing when one has been requested by the member. (Important)

DISCUSSION: While even longer terms are desirable, it is important that parole authority members have at least five-year terms on an authority to provide stability of membership and freedom from undue concern about reappointment. It should be understood that a term of five years does not mean that the expectation exists that a parole authority member will not be reappointed. Conversely, reappointment should not be considered automatic.

2–1041 If a fixed term of office is used in the appointment of parole authority members, the terms of the members are staggered. (Essential)

DISCUSSION: Continuity of policy is an important goal for a correctional system which seeks equity and efficiency. Static policy is not the general goal. Change will be an ongoing need; however, if it is to occur, it should be orderly with due regard for previous organizational history. Abrupt alterations of program which fail to consider prior efforts almost inevitably produce unwarranted disparities in decisions, and make stable program development very difficult. In a key correctional unit, such as the parole authority, continuity of policy is a necessity and staggered terms of appointment are one important means of achieving it.

2–1042 Salaries of parole authority members are within twenty percent of the salary paid to judges of courts having trial jurisdiction over felony cases. (Essential)

DISCUSSION: The decision-making responsibility of parole authority members is comparable to that of judges of courts having trial jurisdiction. This level of compensation can help attract persons with the required skills and experience to serve on parole boards.

2–1043 The parole authority consists of no less than three members. (Essential)

DISCUSSION: The breadth of skills and backgrounds required and the value of joint decision making in facilitating greater objectivity argue for a minimum of three parole authority members.

2–1044 One of the members of the parole authority is designated as chairperson. (Essential)

DISCUSSION: A single person on the authority must be designated as responsible for the authority's administrative management. The chairperson should have full authority for administrative detail, although on policies and case dispositions decision-making authority should be shared equally among all members.

2–1045 The authority chairperson has the responsibility to coordinate the work schedules of authority members, assign cases as provided by authority policy, and to chair meetings of the authority. (Essential)

DISCUSSION: The policies which govern their assignment should be developed by all authority members. However, it is essential that there exist within the authority efficient means of carrying out its work, including the coordination of activities and the assignment of cases. The chairperson is the appropriate person to carry out these executive tasks.

2–1046 The chairperson is the official spokesperson for the parole authority. When acting as the official spokesperson, the chairperson expresses views at all times which are consistent with approved policies of the authority. (Essential)

DISCUSSION: The orderly exercise of business requires that there exist a single person in the authority through which the flow of official business with outside agencies is controlled. Included here are such matters as press releases, budget presentations, and official communications. Of course, all authority members and staff will play important roles in dealing with persons external to the authority, but it is essential that such channels are governed by authority policy, and that the chairperson remains as the official source of communications for the authority. (See related standards 2-1126 and 2-1128.)

HEARING PROCESS

2-1080 Policy and procedure provide for the withdrawal of an authority member or hearing examiner in cases that represent a conflict of interest. (Essential)

DISCUSSION: In any case where a parole authority member or hearing examiner has personal knowledge of a case or could in any way benefit from the outcome of a case, that person should withdraw completely from the decision making process for that case. (See related standard 2-1038.)

2-1081 The person conducting the hearing is responsible for recording and preserving a summary of the major issues and findings in the hearing. (Essential)

DISCUSSION: The keeping of a record of the events of the hearing for the purpose of subsequent review is essential. It is particularly important for future hearings to be able to review the record of a hearing and have an awareness of the issues that had been raised previously. The use of dictating equipment is quite appropriate for this purpose. (See related standard 2-1067.)

2-1082 The criteria that are employed by the parole authority in its decision making are available in written form and are specific enough to permit consistent application to individual cases. Case decisions indicate that granting, denying, reviewing, and revocation decisions are in conformity with the written criteria. (Essential)

DISCUSSION: Various criteria should be developed that will assist the authority in making parole decisions. These criteria should go beyond statutory minimums to include the types of information that have a consistent relationship to parole success or failure.

2-1083 There is a process, available in written form, whereby the decisions of panels or hearing examiners can be reviewed by the full authority under rules fixed by it, and offenders are informed of the steps necessary to avail themselves of that process. (Essential)

DISCUSSION: The development of a decision review process is an important development in parole. In general, most parole decisions should be made by the hearing examiners or panels of parole authority members who interview the offender. However, a system of appeal, preferably to authority members not involved in the first hearing, should be established, and rules for the use of this process should be fixed. If there are only a few authority members, and all of them participate in initial decisions, some process of review or rehearing in a case should nonetheless be in effect. (See related standard 2-1009.)

2-1084 Offenders receive timely assistance—including translation for offenders with language difficulties—from qualified personnel on all parole procedures to help them in appearances before the parole authority, in appeals, and in dealing effectively with parole procedures. (Essential)

> DISCUSSION: For a number of offenders, parole procedures are complicated, and if they are without assistance, they are at a great disadvantage with respect to the parole system. The provision of representation can ease this problem, but it is crucial that qualified personnel assist offenders in all matters with respect to parole, including the development of resources that enhance the opportunities for an inmate to cope successfully with the requirements of release. Assistance includes interpretation of parole procedures to long-term offenders within one year of being received at an institution. (See related standards 2–1020, 2–1088, 2–1090, and 2–1114.)

2–1085 The offender is notified personally and orally by the parole authority members or hearing examiners who have heard the case as to the recommendation or decision immediately after the hearing. (Essential).

> DISCUSSION: The parole authority needs to clarify personally the meaning of its decision and to discuss the subsequent steps that might be taken by the offender. For all these reasons, it is essential that the parole authority meet personally with each offender after the interview to make the outcome of the case known and understandable to the offender.

PAROLE RELEASE HEARINGS

2–1086 At the first hearing of offenders eligible for parole, the parole authority sets a tentative release date. If circumstances prevent the setting of a tentative release date at the first hearing, a subsequent hearing is held within one year for the purpose of setting a tentative release date. In any event, the parole authority gives reasons in writing for any deferral of decision. (Essential)

> DISCUSSION: Uncertainty surrounding the time an offender must serve in an institution should be eliminated as soon as possible after commitment. Inmates need to establish goals based on tentative release dates and make plans for release. At the first parole hearing, a date of release may be considered but not fixed. Any date fixed at the first hearing or later hearings could be altered based on new information, institutional behavior, or the possibility of success based on the offender's ability to handle lesser levels of security. The reasons for deferral should be articulated and a definite review date established for a future hearing. (See related standards 2–1072 and 2–1123.)

2–1087 Offenders are held beyond tentative release dates only after a hearing by the authority, at which time the reasons for deferral of parole are articulated in writing. (Essential)

> DISCUSSION: In general, there is an expectation that a tentative parole date, once fixed, will be observed unless sound reasons to the contrary are evidenced. From time to time, sufficient information will come to an authority's attention to require it to defer a date. In such a case, the authority makes a record of the specific reasons for the deferral of parole and fixes a definite time for the next review of the case. The aim is to keep a clear release date, known to inmates and correctional officials, and to articulate the reasons for various actions taken by the parole authority.

2–1088 No offender is denied parole or given a deferment unless a personal hearing is held before the parole authority. (Essential)

DISCUSSION: Cases may be reviewed periodically through files and correspondence; however, each time that the denial of parole is possible, a personal hearing before a parole authority member or hearing examiner takes place. An important purpose of this hearing is to give the offender a chance to present his or her case directly to responsible decision making authorities, a basic and important element in a fair system. Further, no matter how carefully developed a record system may be, frequently during the course of a face-to-face interview, inaccuracies are discovered or relevant information that is not included in the official record is obtained. (See related standard 2–1084.)

2–1089 Policy and procedure exist for hearings in absentia. Hearings in absentia are limited to cases where the absence of the offender is unavoidable and where there is documentation of the reasons for this situation. (Essential)

DISCUSSION: In cases when the offender is in a mental institution or a facility in another jurisdiction, a hearing in absentia may be conducted. In no case should such a procedure be used where an offender simply refuses to attend a hearing. Hearings in absentia should observe the same safeguards as hearings where the offender is present, and should require that the offender knowingly and voluntarily absent him/herself from the hearing.

2–1090 Offenders are notified in writing at least fourteen calendar days in advance of their hearings and are specifically advised as to the purpose of the hearing. (Essential)

DISCUSSION: It is essential that offenders be well-advised as to the purpose of the parole hearing and have information about the kinds of issues that will be discussed. Too often, offenders are unclear as to precisely what is happening and are unable to take full advantage of the hearing that is given to them. In this respect, it is important that institution personnel work closely with offenders to help them prepare for the hearing and to assist in the development of material for presentation to the authority. (See related standard 2–1084.)

2–1091 Hearings are conducted in privacy. (Essential)

DISCUSSION: Parole hearings should be conducted in surroundings that are comfortable and appropriately furnished, which provide sufficient privacy for the offender and allow the authority to convey an atmosphere conducive to a dignified hearing. Where necessary, security should be provided.

2–1092 Parole hearings are conducted with careful attention to the inmate and with ample opportunity for the expression of his or her views. (Essential)

DISCUSSION: Fair parole hearings are an important part of the parole process. They should be conducted without extraneous interruptions and with very careful focus on the offender. A significant effort should be made to give the inmate a full opportunity to express his or her views, and to provide the inmate with an understanding of the requirements for release consideration.

2–1093 The parole authority has a written policy that determines who may be present at the parole hearing. (Essential)

DISCUSSION: The parole authority has a responsibility to see that parole hearings are carried out in an orderly and fair manner. This will limit the number of persons who may be in attendance. At the same time, the authority has a responsibility to the public and to the inmate to allow attendance at a hearing of those people who will be of assistance to the offender or to the authority.

2–1094 Materials on cases are reviewed before offenders are brought into a hearing room, and during the hearing, references are made to files by authority members, hearing examiners, and other staff, only to refresh their memories of the case and to determine questions of fact. (Important)

DISCUSSION: It is very distracting for files to be read while an offender is in the hearing room. This does not convey to the inmate a high level of awareness or concern for his or her case. Persons responsible for conducting parole hearings should review case material in advance of the hearing. (See related standards 2–1070 and 2–1074.)

2–1095 Offenders are provided with the information on which parole decisions are made, except that information that, in accordance with the authority's written policy, is specifically classified and so designated by an authority member or hearing examiner as confidential for good and sufficient reasons. Offenders are informed of the fact that information designated as confidential was used in making a decision. (Essential)

DISCUSSION: Parole, in a number of important respects, involves the delegation of sentencing power. Thus, the issues are very much the same as those involved in the defendant's right to disclosure of the presentence investigation, and similar rules should govern. In the absence of compelling reasons for nondisclosure, the inmate should be familiar with the information regarding his or her case. When information is not made available to an inmate because of its sensitive nature, it should be so identified in the file. Agency policy should spell out what information will be made available to the inmate, particularly when his or her mental and/or social adjustment might be affected, when a codefendant is involved, when a confidential juvenile record is included, or when informants are named in the record. Staff and authority members should have clear instructions on the release of official information. Records and documents must be handled in accordance with established procedures or upon other proper authorization. It is important for subsequent review that it be clear which material was not open to review by the offender.

2–1096 The reasons for a parole decision are written, signed by a person authorized by the authority, and made available to appropriate staff and to the offender within twenty-one calendar days of the offender's hearing. (Essential)

DISCUSSION: The writing out of the reasons for the decision is a crucial part of the parole decision-making process. Having this written document is essential for a number of reasons: it provides a basis of appeal, it is important for institutional officials and offenders in shaping their future programs, it is helpful for research purposes, and it provides for the continued development of criteria.

2-1097 The parole authority does not accept the presence of a detainer as an automatic bar to parole; it pursues the basis of any such detainer and it releases the offender to detainers where appropriate. (Important)

DISCUSSION: Detainers represent an outstanding charge that may or may not be adjudicated, and should not automatically constitute a bar to parole. Parole staff should, as a matter of practice, trace out detainers to determine their basis, and when appropriate, parole authorities should parole inmates to detainers.

2-1098 The status of the offender as a foreign national does not preclude access to parole consideration. (Essential)

DISCUSSION: Parole authorities should release foreign nationals for return to their home countries under whatever circumstances may be worked out with the home countries, and in the best interest of all concerned. At the present time, there are no formal agreements between the United States and other countries for completion of sentences. However, informal arrangements are sometimes possible and supervision when needed can be arranged on a courtesy basis with a governmental or nongovernmental organization in the offender's home country. Under the circumstances, and as a matter of principle, such arrangements should be undertaken only with the consent of the offender.

GLOSSARY OF TERMS

It is important in a book such as this to arrive at an agreement about the definition of terms. As many of the terms in this text have legal meanings, they may also have many different meanings, as courts and legislative bodies continue to define and refine the meanings. The definitions below are ours and may not be completely consistent with statutes and court decisions in every jurisdiction.

Adjudication of Delinquency An adjudication of delinquency is an adjudication of status or condition; a legal determination and judgment that the child belongs to the group of persons designated as "juvenile delinquents."

Commitment Commitment is a form of sentence or disposition under which a person convicted of a crime is ordered by a court to be confined in prison or other correctional or treatment institution.

Other definitions are: Commitment is a criminal sanction imposed by a court that requires the offender to be held in prison or other correctional institution. Persons not convicted of a crime may also be "committed" if the order of the court or magistrate is to keep them under restraint in a prison, jail, correctional institution, mental hospital, or the like.

"Commitment" and "committed" refer variously to the *warrant* or *order* by which a court directs an officer to take a person to prison or other correctional or treatment institution; to the *proceeding* for restraining and confining a person in a prison or other correctional or treatment institution; to the *act* of sending a person to prison or other institution by means of a court order or

legal proceeding; and the resulting *status* of the person so ordered confined.

Conditional Discharge A conditional discharge means a sentence of conditional and revocable release without probation supervision, but under such conditions as may be imposed by the court.

Conviction Narrow definition of conviction: a plea, finding, or verdict of guilt; *or* broad definition of conviction: a plea, finding, or verdict of guilt, followed by a final judgment of conviction and a sentence. Conviction means a judgment of conviction or sentence entered upon a plea of guilty or upon a verdict or finding of guilty of an offense, rendered by a legally constituted jury or by a court of competent jurisdiction authorized to try the case without a jury.

Other definitions are: The ordinary legal definition of conviction is a plea or verdict that ascertains and publishes the fact of guilt, while judgment or sentence is the appropriate word to denote action of court declaring consequences to the convict of the fact thus ascertained. In federal courts, a conviction from which disabilities flow refers to a conviction followed by imposition of sentence and which is a judgment in a criminal case. Where imposition of sentence is stayed, there is no "final judgment." An accused is termed a "convict" after the judgment of conviction has become final. In no event is [a defendant] a convict until sentence has been pronounced * *. It is the sentence and not the judgment that, under our code, concludes a prosecution in a trial court, and until it has been pronounced, it cannot be said that a conviction in the trial court is complete so as to work a forfeiture of civil rights.

Definite Sentence A definite sentence is a sentence where the commitment fixed by the court is for a term of years that may be less, but not more than, the maximum provided by statute for the particular offense.

In New Jersey, the term "definite sentence" is applied to the minimum-maximum type of sentence usually designated "indeterminate sentence," but called an "indefinite sentence" in Pennsylvania. The terms "fixed sentence" or "straight sentence" are sometimes used synonymously with "definite sentence."

Detainer A detainer is a legal or quasi-legal "hold order" under which a warden having a person in custody will not release the person when the person's sentence is completed, but will make the person available to the officers of another jurisdiction to answer to charges or accusations pending in that jurisdiction.

Other definitions are: A detainer is simply a request, grounded in notions of comity, that the detaining institution notify the law enforcement authorities in the demanding state when the inmate's release date is near. A detainer is a warrant filed against a person already in custody with the purpose of insuring that, after the prisoner has satisfied the terms of present custody, the prisoner will be available to the authority that placed the detainer.

Diversion Diversion refers to formally acknowledged and organized efforts to utilize alternatives to initial or continued processing into the justice system. To qualify as diversion, such efforts must be undertaken prior to adjudication and after a legally proscribed action has occurred. Diversion may be community-based, police-based, or court-based.

Felony Felony means an offense for which a sentence to death or to a term of imprisonment in a penitentiary for one year or more is provided.

Good-time Good-time is the time authorized by statute, which, as a reward for good behavior, may be deducted from or credited upon the sentence to be served by an offender confined in specified correctional institutions. Good-time is the time earned by an offender by good conduct and credited on his or her sentence at a rate and in the manner prescribed by statute.

Good-time is also referred to as "gain time," as "commutation for good conduct," or as "good conduct time."

Other definitions are: Good-time is one of several terms used to describe the "good behavior credits" or number of days deducted by statutory provision from the inmate's sentence as a reward for his good behavior. Good-time is diminution of sentence on account of good conduct or meritorious services of person committed to the Department [of Corrections].

Indeterminate Sentence An indeterminate sentence is a form of sentence to imprisonment that declares that imprisonment shall be for a period "not less than" so many years "nor more than" so many years, the exact length of term being afterwards fixed, within the limits assigned by the court, by action of an executive authority.

Other definitions are: An indeterminate sentence is a sentence imposed by a court upon an offender, which specifies a minimum and maximum period of years of imprisonment. An indeterminate sentence is a form of commitment in which a judge fixes a maximum within the limits specified by the statute and also a minimum within specified limits.

Some sentences indeterminate in form are fixed or definite sentences in practice, and the law may require that the judgment (as distinguished from the sentence) must fix a definite punishment. The matter of type of sentence can only be resolved by considering the operation of good parole laws upon the sentence and the authority of the executive agency (governor, parole board, etc.) to determine the exact length of time to be served.

Judgment A judgment in a criminal case is declaration of the results of the trial and must follow verdict as a matter of law and statutory procedures.

Other definitions are: Judgment means an adjudication by the court that the defendant is guilty or not guilty, and if the adjudication is that the defendant is guilty, it includes the sentence pronounced by the court.

A judgment in a criminal case is a declaration by the court of the results of a trial entered of record.

Judgment of Conviction A judgment of conviction consists of two parts: first, the facts judicially ascertained, together with the manner of ascertaining them, entered on record; and second, the recorded declaration of the court pronouncing the legal consequences of the facts thus judicially ascertained.

Mandatory Release Mandatory release is the release of a federal prisoner at the expiration of the maximum term less credit for good-time earned and not forfeited.

Other definitions are: Mandatory release is the release under supervision at the expiration of maximum term of imprisonment, less good-time credit allowed, or six months prior to the expiration of such maximum term of imprisonment, whichever is earlier.

Misdemeanor Misdemeanor means any offense for which a sentence to a term of imprisonment in other than a penitentiary for less than one year may be imposed.

Model Codes and Standards In our text, we frequently refer to model codes and standards developed by various groups and agencies such as the Model Penal Code, the Model Sentencing Act, the American Bar Association Standards Relating to the Administration of Justice, the National Advisory Commission on Criminal Justice, the National Advisory Commission on Criminal Justice Standards and Goals, and the like. The student should understand that these are just what they say—models and standards. They are not binding "rules" until they are adopted by the legislature of the state or are put into effect as rules of court and become the official policy of the operating agency, or until they are imposed in court decisions. Even when a state legislature adopts some of the procedures and other suggestions contained in the models and standards, it is highly unlikely that they will be adopted without modification to fit the particular conditions in that state or area. For example, the governor of the state of Texas sponsored an in-depth study of the National Commission on Goals and Standards that took several months before recommendations were made for their implementation in Texas. In this process, some of the standards were completely rejected by Texas, and others of the standards were significantly modified. Choices often have to be made between conflicting viewpoints set out in different sets of standards.

Nevertheless, the model codes and standards have an impact on the day-to-day operations of probation departments and the supervision of the probationer. They represent the best thinking of many knowledgeable people in the field who have been involved in their drafting, and point the way toward changes that will come about in the future. Courts frequently refer to such model codes and standards and make use of them in making judgments about whether certain practices and procedures at issue before them are in accord with the thinking of the experts in the field. Thus, a decision on due process may take into consideration recommendations about notice to the probationer contained in the models or standards.

The students who become familiar with the models and standards put themselves among the knowledgeable and contributing workers when they become practitioners in the field, and can thereby respond to the leadership demands made upon them.

Pardon A pardon is an act proceeding from the authority entrusted with the execution of the laws, which absolves an individual from the legal consequences of crime and conviction.

Other definitions are: Pardon is a form of executive clemency that absolves an individual from the legal consequences of crime and conviction. A pardon is an act of grace or a remission of guilt and is full when it freely and unconditionally absolves the party from the legal consequences of crime and conviction.

Conditional Pardon A conditional pardon is a form of executive clemency that does not become operative until the grantee has performed some specified act, or that becomes void after the occurrence of some specified event, or that remits only a portion of the penalties that are the legal consequences of a crime.

Parole Parole is the conditional release, by administrative act, of a convicted offender from a penal or correctional institution, under the continued custody of the state, to serve the remainder of his or her sentence in the community under supervision.

Other definitions are: Parole is the release of an offender from a penal or correctional institution, after the offender has served a portion of his or her sentence, under the continued custody of the state and under conditions that permit the offender's reincarceration in the event of misbehavior. Parole means the release of a prisoner from imprisonment, but not from the legal custody of the state, for rehabilitation outside of the prison walls under such conditions and provisions for disciplinary supervision as the paroling authority may determine. Parole means the conditional and revocable release under the supervision of the paroling authority of a person imprisoned in a state penal or reformatory institution or in the custody of the Department of Corrections. Parole is a treatment program in which an offender, after serving part of a term in a correctional institution, is conditionally released under supervision and treatment by a parole worker. Parole means the conditional and revocable release of a committed person under the supervision of the paroling authority.

The word parole can refer to a disposition, a status, a system or subsystem, a treatment program, or a process. As a *disposition,* it refers to an administrative act or expediency that releases the convicted offender from a penal or correctional institution to serve the remainder of his or her sentence in the community under supervision. As a *status,* parole reflects the position of an offender released from incarceration who is at liberty in the community under the conditions of parole. As a *system* or *subsystem,* parole is a subsystem of corrections, which is itself a subsystem of the criminal justice system. As a *treatment program,* the parole is seen as a form of treatment in the community, in the interest of society and the individual, under the supervision of a person trained to provide such treatment. The parole *process* refers to the set of functions, activities, and services that characterize the system's transactions with the administrative body, the executive, the offender, and the community.

The word is derived from a French word meaning "promise" or "word of honor." The choice of the word has been seen by some as unfortunate, inasmuch as most people distrust a "word of honor" given by a released convict. The French, from whom the word is borrowed, prefer the term "conditional liberation."

Plea of Guilty—Definition A plea of guilty is an act of the defendant and is a confession of guilt in open court.

Plea of Nolo Contendere—Definition A plea of nolo contendere (literally, no contest) is equivalent to a plea of guilty insofar as the criminal action is concerned, but does not bind the defendant in a civil suit for the same wrong.

Probation Probation is a form of criminal sanction imposed by a court upon an offender after verdict, finding, or plea of guilty, but before or in lieu of incarceration which allows the offender to serve his or her sanction under supervision in the community.

Other definitions are: Probation is the release of a convicted defendant by a court under conditions imposed by a court for a specified period during which imposition of sentence is suspended. Probation is a sentence not involving confinement, which imposes conditions and retains authority in the sentencing court to modify the conditions of the sentence or to resentence the offender. Probation means the conditional and revocable release before sentence, and under supervision of an officer of the trial court, of a person who has been found guilty of an offense. Probation is a disposition that al-

lows the convicted offender to remain free in the community while supervised by a person who attempts to help the offender lead a law-abiding life. Probation is the postponement of final judgment or sentence in a criminal case, giving the offender an opportunity to improve his or her conduct and to readjust to the community, often on conditions imposed by the court and under the guidance and supervision of an officer of the court. Probation is a treatment program in which final action in an adjudicated offender's case is suspended, so that he or she remains at liberty, subject to conditions imposed by a court, under the supervision and guidance of a probation worker. Probation means a sentence or adjudication of conditional and revocable release under the supervision of a probation officer.

The National Advisory Commission points out that the word "probation" is used in four ways. It can refer to a disposition, a status, a system or subsystem, and a process. As a court *disposition,* a convicted offender's freedom in a community is continued, subject to supervision and certain conditions established by the court. As a *status,* probation reflects the position of an offender sentenced to probation. Probation is a *subsystem* of corrections, itself a subsystem of the criminal and juvenile justice system. The probation *process* refers to the sets of functions, activities, and services that characterize the system's transactions with the courts, the offender, and the community. The process includes preparation of the reports for the court, supervision of probationers, and obtaining or providing services for them.

The word "probation" is derived from a Latin word meaning "the period of proving or trial."

Sentence A sentence is the order of the court made in the presence of the defendant, pronouncing the judgment and ordering the same to be carried into execution in the manner prescribed by law.

Other definitions are: The sentence is the final judgment in the case. A sentence is the order of the court in a felony or misdemeanor case made in the presence of the defendant, except in misdemeanor cases where the maximum possible punishment is by fine only, and entered of record, pronouncing the judgment, and ordering the same to be carried into execution in the manner prescribed by law. Sentence is the disposition imposed by the court on a convicted defendant.

Supervision Supervision is a process or relationship between a person in authority (probation or parole officer) and a person conditionally released (probationer or parolee) through which the conditions of release are interpreted and enforced, the activities of the released person are recognized and evaluated, and help in the form of counseling services, use of community resources, and friendly support for constructive effort is made available.

Suspended Sentence A suspended sentence is an order of court entered after verdict, finding, or plea of guilty, suspending or postponing during the good behavior of the offender the imposition or execution of sentence. In case of suspension of imposition of sentence, the sentence is not stated or pronounced; upon termination or revocation of the suspension, any legal sentence may be pronounced. In case of suspension of execution of sentence, the sentence is stated at the outset; upon termination or revocation of the suspension, a penalty greater than the original sentence cannot be imposed.

To "suspend" means to interrupt, to postpone, to cause to cease for a time. The word carries with it the expectation or purpose of resumption, particularly upon the happening of a certain contingency.

Verdict of Guilty A verdict of guilty is a written declaration by a jury of its decision that the defendant is guilty of one or more of the offenses charged in the indictment or information.

Table of Cases

Index